STUDIES IN ART,
ARCHITECTURE AND DESIGN
VOLUME TWO

STUDIES IN

NIKOLAUS PEVSNER

ART, ARCHITECTURE AND DESIGN

VOLUME TWO

VICTORIAN AND AFTER

with 519 black-and-white illustrations

THAMES AND HUDSON · LONDON

© NIKOLAUS PEVSNER, 1968
SECOND PRINTING 1969
500 2309 27
THIS COLLECTED EDITION FIRST PUBLISHED BY THAMES AND HUDSON, 1968
TEXT SET BY FILMTYPE SERVICES, SCARBOROUGH
PRINTED IN GREAT BRITAIN BY JARROLD AND SONS LTD, NORWICH

Contents

Preface

As an inveterate reader of the book reviews in the *Times Literary Supplement*, *The Listener* and now and then the *New York Review of Books* I know that books of essays collected years after they have been written get almost without exception a bad press. The reasons are not far to seek. Try as hard as he may, the author cannot perfectly blend into a whole what had been written over a period of many years and for a variety of purposes.

Yet it is my conviction that he should try and that books of essays should be published. For what had come out only in a learned journal, or in an ephemeral paper, and perhaps only in a foreign language, often fails to make its impact. And even if it had made an impact at the time when it was new, the record of the development of research tends to get blurred, if the research itself is no longer available.

I thought I ought to say this; for the papers represented in these two volumes stretch over a period of nearly forty years. To prepare them for re-publication allowed me, or forced me, to endeavour an objective assessment of their contents and also their significance for me and perhaps for others. They started in Germany and end in England; they started with lusty generalizations and end with humble specific facts; they started with scholarship and end in what strikes me often as superficiality. The substance, to put it in another way, tends to get thinner.

If readers agree with me in this I can plead mitigating circumstances. They will, I hope, appear convincing, if I try to show what fields I tilled in these forty years. My doctoral thesis dealt with German Baroque architecture and was complete by 1924. Between 1925 and 1935 I wrote only one book, and the papers here reprinted as Part One are a by-product of that book. They try to demonstrate that Mannerism is *the* style of the sixteenth century in Italy, in what ways it differs from the Baroque and in what way the Baroque ought to be divided into three phases. About 1930 I began to concentrate on nineteenth-century architecture, but all the notes I had made, including the preparation of a lecture course at Göttingen, were burnt in the war. Between 1935 and 1945 I brought out three books. The most scholarly of them was about the history of the artist's training (*Academies of Art, past and present*), sign of a change in interest to social problems of art history. The change to nineteenth century architecture was to a certain extent a reflection of this as well. The other two books were *Pioneers of the Modern Movement* and *An Outline of European Architecture*. The former is an attempt at distilling the history of one trend in the later nineteenth and the early twentieth century, the latter a summary, successful in the country where it was published, because the treatment of architecture primarily as space, a familiar treatment in Germany, was new for England.

These two books were an indication of a turn from writing for scholars to writing for laymen. The difference is not necessarily one of level, it can also be one of presentation. Positively speaking it may mean a shedding of abracadabra. Negatively I need not speak; for the dangers are patent. Readers who have the patience to go through the present two volumes must judge for themselves. To turn to papers, instead of books, was necessary as soon as I joined *The Architectural Review*. The influence of this event and especially the influence of the *spiritus rector* of the *Review*, H. de Cronin Hastings went deep, just as deep as in the German years and in the efforts to analyse Mannerism and Baroque the influence of Wilhelm Pinder had gone. *The Architectural Review*, in subject matter of research, directed me towards the history of the Picturesque and of visual planning and of course towards topical problems of architecture and design.

After 1945 finally my working life changed completely, owing to the willingness of Penguin Books, that is of that great patron Sir Allen Lane, to publish *The Buildings of England*. I had always felt the necessity of such an enterprise, i.e. of providing for England what Dehio had done in 1905–12 for Germany, but of providing it in much greater detail. That, and the editing of the *Pelican History of Art* and, alas, more and more committees and councils, cut down the possibilities of preparing and writing papers. Whether I was right in committing myself to *The Buildings of England* at the expense of all else is a moot point. There are pros and cons. The pro is that the layman and the scholar need such a comprehensive compilation, the con is that it is a compilation and that, in the absence of first-hand research and under the pressure of time, it is a faulty compilation.

The papers published in these two volumes then fall into three parts: Mannerism and Baroque; the Picturesque and the problems of Neo-Classicism; the Victorian Age and after.

There now remains only one more question. If essays qualify for re-publishing, how should they be re-published? Should they be left untouched, or should they be brought up to date? My rule has been this. Views must be kept. If my views had changed, i.e. if I thought no longer valid what I had written, I would have refrained from reprinting. But a foreword to a paper is occasionally provided to refer to more recent views contrary to mine. Factual errors on the other hand have been corrected and facts left out or only recently discovered by others or myself are incorporated. The paramount example of the unchanged view is the paper on Mannerism, the paramount examples of added facts are the two papers done in conjunction with Dr S. Lang (and added to by her as by myself) on the Doric and the Egyptian Revivals. Only one paper has been largely re-written, that on Voysey.

That the late Walter Neurath and Thames and Hudson should have wished to publish so bulky a collection of essays leaves me amazed and profoundly grateful. To his name I wish to add in gratitude those of Ian Sutton and Emily Lane who from inside Thames and Hudson helped in every possible way.

N.P.

References to notes, which will be found at the back of the book, are given by asterisks in the text and numbers preceded by 'n.' in the corresponding margin. References to illustrations are given by italic numbers in the margin.

Part One
Victorian Themes

I
Design and Industry through the Ages

W HAT is meant by industry, what by design for the purpose of this essay? Industry I want to be understood as meaning the production of identical objects in large numbers, and by the designer I mean a man who invents and draws objects for use. Hence dress-designer, aircraft-designer, and, up to a point, even stage-designer. As soon as the designer himself makes what he has invented and drawn, he ceases to be a designer. But he remains a designer, if he invents and draws something of which only one is to be made.

Let us then in the light of these definitions look for a moment at early industry and early designers. In the inventories of St Paul's Cathedral of 1295, we find 'vestimentum novum plenarium cum apparatus et parura de panno januen-

n.1 sis'—a vestment of Genoese cloth,* and in those of Canterbury Cathedral also
n.2 vestments 'de panno rubeo de Genue'.* These cloths may have been designed by those who made them. But in any case, we can assume that fairly large quantities of one design were carried out for the home market and for export. In the same way Paris ivories appear in the church treasures of Assisi and Trani, of Toledo

n.3 and Seville, of Cologne and Halberstadt, of Prague and Cracow,* and Notting-hamshire alabasters at S. Benedetto a Settimo near Florence, Rothenburg and
n.4 Danzig in Germany, Périgueux in France and Sitjes near Barcelona, in Spain.* Not many absolutely identical pieces have survived, but we hear of an action brought in 1491, where a Nottingham image-maker sues his salesman for the
n.5 value of fifty-eight heads of St John.*

So much for early art industry; now for designers. Antal in his book on
n.6 *Florentine Painting and its Social Background** says that Florentine artists of the fourteenth century designed for embroidery and horse-trappings among other things, and of the fifteenth century there are indeed in the Louvre sketch-book of
n.7 Jacopo Bellini,* several patterns for embroidered borders. But whether these are really meant as patterns, or whether they are sketches made from dresses to be used in the painted dresses in his pictures, is far from certain. Holbein's designs for silversmiths and jewellers on the other hand, and those of his German pre-decessors, such as the Master E.S. and Schongauer, were no doubt intended to be carried out. Those of the early engravers were probably made for the benefit of whoever wanted to buy them and make use of them, those of Holbein for particular jobs. In no case, however, has it so far been possible to connect him with any of the actual English craftsmen of his time. Yet there are masses of these drawings. The British Museum sketch-book alone contains close to two hund-red. They are for cups, goblets, tankards, dagger-hilts, sword-hilts, belts,
n.8 bucklers, book-covers and pendants.*

But in so far as Holbein designed emphatically for an individual craftsman's high skill, and never for repetition, he does not really belong to my present theme. Things are different, when we look to a type of book which came out first in Germany and then chiefly in Venice from 1525 onwards. It is of great import- ance to us, as it marks the beginning of designing proper, if not for industry, at least for repetition work. I am referring to pattern-books for embroidery, ribbon-making, and so on. One of the best of them is called *Opera Nuova che insegna alle donne a cucire, a raccamare e a disegnare a ciascuno*—a new work to teach ladies to sew and embroider and everybody to draw.* The author was Giovanni   n.9 Antonio Tagliente, a calligrapher by profession. The most famous German author of such a pattern-book is Hans Sibmacher, better known as one of the classics of heraldry. He was an alchymist as well, and altogether obviously, just as the other authors of the hundred such books issued before 1650, not primarily a designer.

And such remained the position for quite a long time to come, whether in manufacture conducted by private enterprise, or, with the coming of absolutism and mercantilism, also by State or rather Royal initiative. The designs needed came either from the makers themselves, *i.e.*, the craftsmen employed, or from artists not specialising entirely in design. Engravers were probably foremost among them, people who published series of patterns for metalwork or jewellery or ornamentation more generally, and sold them regardless of what use pur- chasers might care to make of them. As for designing procedure we can watch this most closely in the case of Louis XIV's national workshops, and especially the Manufacture des Meubles de la Couronne, which Colbert had created in 1667 out of the old Gobelins works.* For a while after that, they did not only tapes-   n.10 tries, but also silverwork, bronze-founding, cabinet-work, and so on. Charles Lebrun became the director,* Louis's Premier Peintre, and a man of great   n.11 ability, facility, versatility and industry. There are innumerable sketches of his at the Louvre, from tapestries to coaches, a gondola, wrought iron, etc. A whole staff of painters, engravers and *ornemanistes* worked under him. The factory (or rather the Savonnerie united by Colbert with the Gobelins) also comprised a school for sixty apprentices—the earliest example known of regulated teaching of the craftsman as against the usual practical training in the workshop. How large the Manufacture des Meubles de la Couronne was in its heyday under Colbert and Lebrun it is impossible to guess. Voltaire's figure of eight hundred must be an exaggeration based on numbers as he knew them from his own time.

For in the second half of the eighteenth century, it is true, factories already existed in France and other countries, of a surprising size, considering the fact that they did not yet use steam-driven machinery. Wedgwood's estimate their pay- roll in 1769 as about 120, and at the same time had cash sales for their London showrooms at a rate of about £100 a week.* When the chair maker Forget died in 1789, he left 400 chair frames.* Jacob-Desmalter & Co. in 1808 had a pay-   n.13 roll of nearly 350,* and it is known that they made fauteuils ranging in price   n.14 from 36 to 4,000 frs. and canapés at anything between 108 and 12,000,* the   n.15 Società Pensa Loria in Milan made textiles with between 350 and 450 workers, *   n.16 silk-weaving in Lyons kept about 18,000 people busy in 1732, and about 38,000 in 1788.* Réveillon, the wallpaper manufacturer, had a staff of 400 in 1786, and   n.17 his factory was called in 1788 by the ambassador of Tippoo Sahib (the Indian potentate who was defeated by Wellington) as large as a whole little province. *   n.18 In England, Seddon's furniture works also employed 400 at that time, or so we are told by Sophie von La Roche, German authoress, friend of Wieland and Goethe, follower of Richardson and of Rousseau. She visited London in 1786 and wrote:

'He employs 400 on any work connected with the making of household furniture—joiners, carvers, gilders, mirror-workers, upholsterers, girdlers— who mould the bronze into graceful patterns—and locksmiths. All these are housed in a building with six wings . . . Some departments contain nothing but chairs, sofas, and stools of every description . . . while others are occupied by writing tables, cupboards, chests of drawers, charmingly fashioned desks, chests, both large and small, work- and toilet-tables in all manners of wood and patterns'.

She also saw 'Chintz, silk and wool materials for curtains and bed-covers, hangings in every possible material, carpets and stair-carpets'.* So at Seddon's, we may note in passing, factory and showrooms were evidently combined and soft furnishings sold, although no doubt not made. n.19

And one more example amongst the leading European manufactures of the age: Oberkampf's factory at Jouy, near Paris.* He started his own linen-printing business in 1759. In 1805 he employed 1,322. The new building which he put up in 1791–93 was 350 feet long and three stories high. Oberkampf was an honest, likeable man, not an exploiter, it seems. Yet he did, of course, not hesitate to introduce machinery wherever possible. Copper-plates instead of, or side by side with, hardwood blocks came in in 1770, and in 1793 rollers. Roller-printing was a British invention, made about 1770 by a Scotsman, Bell. It enabled Oberkampf to produce by one machine over 5,000 yards a day, a tremendous improvement. n.20

That production on that scale could have its snags was only discovered much later. In the eighteenth and early nineteenth centuries machinery was still a thrill to all (except those who had to tend it), and inventiveness was prodigious. In the field of textile spinning and weaving the story is familiar. The fly-shuttle was followed by the spinning jenny, the spinning jenny by the mule, the mule by the Jacquard loom, and Boulton and Watt's steam engine joined in to increase speed and reliability of production. What else the steam engine made possible of industrial progress need not be repeated here either. Dr Giedion in his *Mechanization takes Command* * tells us that the first threshing machine dates from 1775, the first assembly line (to deal with grain inside the mill) from 1783, the first baking ovens with slow conveyor belts for the bread from 1810, the first reaping machine from 1811 and the first combine harvester from 1836. n.21

There is no point in continuing the list. But what is easily forgotten is the genuine enthusiasm with which improved machinery was greeted still by those with faith in human perfectibility and progress towards a better world. Sophie von La Roche after describing her visit to the Royal Society of Arts, founded for the explicit purpose of encouraging arts, manufactures and commerce by awarding prizes to inventors as well as artists, wrote: 'My heart was big with blessings, and tears of joy filled my eyes, at the list of the many names to whom rewards had been given for improved methods of cultivation and inventions of tools.'

But we are only marginally concerned with the inventors and the manufacturers. So far as the designers went, the Royal Society of Arts was curiously inactive at the beginning. In the oldest list of premiums to be awarded we do find indeed offers for designs for weavers, and calico-printers, cabinet-makers and coach-makers, iron, brass, china and earthenware manufacturers and 'any other Mechanic Trade that requires Taste'.* But they were to be by children under seventeen, and thus appear to have had so little success that after 1778 they were dropped, although very occasional awards occur later. n.22

Yet the designer in the eighteenth century was becoming a professional man of, here and there, quite some standing. The most telling examples are again French. Here are a few: Hugues Simon to whom the City of Lyons gave a gratuity of 6,000 l., calling him 'dessinateur pour les fabriquants en étoffe de soie, d'or et d'argent de cette ville',* Joubert de L'Hiberderie, who wrote a textbook called *Le Dessinateur pour les Fabriques d'étoffes d'or, d'argent et de soie,* and, most famous of all, Philippe de la Salle who was knighted by Louis XVI in 1776.* These designers, we are told, went once a year to Paris to see the new fashions and look at the museums,* just as Oberkampf went himself to London every year to see what was going on across the Channel.* n.23
n.24
n.25
n.26

Leading manufacturers paid their designers quite handsomely too. On that it is not easy to obtain information, but in the case of Réveillon, who has been mentioned before, we hear—from him though, and he was rather inclined to pull the long bow—that he paid his chief artist, a free-lance artist, 10,000 l. a year, his chief studio *dessinateur* 3,000 plus free lodgings, another 2,000 and three others 1,200 each.* Be that as it may—there is no question that by 1800 the designer as a specialist had come to stay.

n.27

That does not mean, of course, that all the designing henceforth was done by specialists. Far from it. In the majority of cases the methods of the seventeenth century continued unchanged. Take only a few of the best-known cases. Ober-kampf's best designer was Jean-Baptiste Huet, *Académicien* and celebrated still-life painter. Vernet, the landscape painter, and Prud'hon also occasionally worked for him. The great Jacques-Louis David, painter of the Revolution and of Napoleon's court, designed a few pieces of furniture in a severely antique style for Jacob.* Then there were the architects, and there I need only mention Robert Adam, and his splendid *Works of Architecture*, which he began to publish as a bit of a self-advertisement in 1773, and which contains so many pieces of furniture of all kinds. He also designed metalwork and carpets. Even so, he is not strictly part of the story of design for industry; for after all, his designs including the carpets, were never made for quantity production but exclusively for his own special jobs.

n.28

That was different in the case of a less familiar but very interesting French architect of about the same period: Jean-Démosthène Dugourc whose short autobiography is known.* Although he had the good and lucrative job of *Dessinateur de la Couronne et des Menus Plaisirs,* he mentions in the autobiography specially that 'tous les dessins exécutés à Lyon par Pernon [the leading manu-facturer] ont été inventés et dirigés par lui' (he speaks of himself in the third person). He was a firm believer in antiquity and proud to have been introduced, when he was in Rome as a boy, to 'le célèbre Winkelmann'.

n.29

But to return to Adam, who had come back from Rome six years before Dugourc arrived; the fact that we know of no work of his for production in quantity, does by no means imply that he was hostile to industry. On the con-trary, we find that he was one of the first to replace in his buildings tooled ashlar by an imitation finish—compo as they called it later. The material was Liar-det's Patent Cement Stucco,* and it was only one of many such compositions to imitate stone. The most successful of them was Coade's.* Keystone heads and figure reliefs, urns and funerary monuments moulded by Coade appear in many places. The door surrounds in Bedford Square are specially well known. The British Museum has Coade catalogues of 1777–79, 1784 and 1799.

n.30
n.31

Coade marks an eminently significant moment. Obviously the nineteenth century was now near. Imitation materials appear and imitation processes—and with them firms' catalogues. Wedgwood's had issued their first in 1773, and then there are, of course, those of the cabinet-makers. But there we have to be careful. Chippendale's *Director* is not a catalogue. It is much rather what Robert Adam's *Works in Architecture* are, self-advertisement. Chippendale did not publish his furniture to sell it from the book, but partly to show potential clients what excellent things he could make for them, and partly also to make profits out of the book itself simply by selling it to whoever might want to copy the designs himself or have them copied. The *Cabinet-Maker's Book of Prices* of 1778, it is true, has prices entered against the furniture shown and thus looks at first glance like a catalogue. But the prices are not selling but making prices, that is fair wages to workmen. The book was intended for the cabinet-maker, not for the public.

Now after the painters, the architects and the craftsmen as designers or authors of books of design, one word about the sculptors. John Bacon, from 1769, worked for Coade's. He was their chief designer for thirty years, although they also occasionally employed Rossi, Banks and Flaxman, and although Bacon also did two reliefs for Wedgwood's.* But Wedgwood's chief connexion with a sculptor was with Flaxman. He started work for Josiah Wedgwood in 1775, when he was only twenty years of age. Josiah Wedgwood is the best type

n.32

of eighteenth-century manufacturer, enlightened, keen on science, keen on technique, keen on art, and certainly also keen on sales. In a letter of 1779 he wrote up to Etruria from the London showrooms (for Wedgwood's had London showrooms at that time) that they urgently needed 350 Dolphin ewers, 450 Bedfordian goats' head vases, 445 'of the Sacrifice, with abundance of Sugardish vases'.*

n.33

So here we have quantity in full swing. But side by side with the manufacturer as promoter of a new style and of civilisation altogether, there also arrives now the commercially minded, advertisement-minded, *nouveau-riche* type of manufacturer, perhaps best exemplified by Réveillon, who in 1769 bought for himself one of the showiest and most fashionable houses close to Paris, the so-called Folie de Titon, and who there, in his gardens, arranged for the very first passenger balloon ascent ever undertaken. The balloon was called Réveillon. It reminds one of the procession sent round London in 1776 to advertise the *Morning Post*, men in yellow with blue waistcoats, distributing handbills.* Obviously the nineteenth century was on the doorstep.

n.34

And although Britain was leading in Europe in everything pertaining to the Industrial Revolution, including France whose leadership was now confined to taste, economic changes made themselves felt in France as well, and there they were the direct outcome of the Revolution. Henri Grégoire, member of the Public Education Committee of the National Convention and later Bishop of Blois, put the new attitude neatly in his report of 1794:* 'Il est temps que les arts utiles soient honorés'. So at once the Conservatoire des Arts et Métiers was founded, as a school and a museum, and in 1798 the first exhibition of the products of French industry was held. From here a line runs direct to South Kensington.

n.35

But the school part of Grégoire's scheme was not entirely new. Ever since the 1750s France had, first through Mme de Pompadour and her circle of friends, been interested in social, aesthetic and educational reform. In connection with this J. J. Bachelier could start his Ecole Royale Gratuite de Dessin in 1767, meant to teach drawing—still drawing only, of course—to those working in 'métiers relatifs aux arts'.* A drawing school for the silk industry at Lyons had already been opened in 1756.* But the French Revolution added a new impetus, and its emphasis on the importance of helping the useful arts by teaching and by providing examples spread to other countries on the Continent, notably Germany. Prussia is specially interesting, as it was then administered in the enlightened liberal spirit of Weimar, that is of Goethe, of Schiller and Humboldt. Here in 1821, a publication began to appear under the names of the President of the Board of Trade and of Schinkel, the greatest German architect then alive, which was meant as an *exemplar* for manufacturers and craftsmen.* In the foreword it is stated that 'only by adding perfection of form to technical perfection can products be imprinted with the marks of true civilisation', and only a perfect product can hope to achieve 'thriving sales'. An example to which explicit reference is made is Wedgwood's wares in England, designed in the true taste of antiquity, besides being of excellent make. But, Schinkel added, and in this now you hear the new note of the nineteenth century, one cannot alway apply antique forms direct to modern products. Some adapting will as a rule be necessary, and there 'it would be asking too much from the craftsman [the German *Handwerker* is ambiguous and should here probably be translated as worker rather than craftsman] who has been to a school of design to leave the adapting to him'. He should not be 'tempted to design himself'.

n.36
n.37

n.38

So the cleavage between maker and designer was now final. In England it was bound to be even more obvious than in other countries. And so, at last, in 1835, a Parliamentary Committee was appointed 'to inquire into the best means of extending the knowledge of the arts and of the 'principles of design among the people (especially the manufacturing population) of the country',* and the outcome of its meetings was the opening of the Normal School of Design at Somerset House in 1837. In 1838 the romantic pre-Pre-Raphaelite painter,

n.39

William Dyce, set up a loom in it but was not successful. Altogether the Normal School did abnormally badly. Nor did the provincial branch schools, of which there were soon more than a dozen, do better. Another committee was set up to look into the results of the new school system and reported 'an utter and complete failure'. That was in 1846.

But in 1843 the Prince Consort had accepted the presidency of the Royal Society of Arts and now for a while under his guidance and that of that model Victorian, Henry Cole, it assumed the leading role in the promotion of British industrial art. Both men were probably equally important, Prince Albert for his high ideals, his sense of duty, his seriousness of purpose and his position, Cole for his unbelievable energy and tenacity. Between them they made the 1851 Exhibition and got the first conscious reformatory movement in industrial design going.*   n.40

For, by the 1840s, some people at least had begun to realise that the aesthetic standard of English and, indeed, European, industrial products had gone down by leaps and bounds. The reasons which we can see quite clearly now, but which were yet obscure at the time, are manifold: pride in technical inventiveness regardless of whether it was applied to the construction of a comfortable invalid chair, or the imitation of the grain of wood by paint, or the moulding of Gothic ornament by machine; then ease of production which removed the healthy barrier between flights of fancy and execution by the human hand; cheapness of production which suddenly made so many products available to so many who were uneducated and aesthetically untrained, and, therefore, of necessity, more impressed by elaboration than by soundness; and finally, the lack of education and aesthetic training in the very manufacturers responsible for the making of the cheap things.*   n.41

Henry Cole started from the right end, the production end. He had a few designs of his own carried out by reputable makers and sold in the West End. His pseudonym—for he was a civil servant—was Felix Summerly, and his products were called Art Manufactures. The enterprise started in 1845. In 1846 the Society of Arts returned to its former practice of offering awards for designs of 'useful objects calculated to improve general taste'.*   Whose idea, we may ask   n.42 ourselves, was this resumption of forgotten duties? Prince Albert's, who had told the Council of the Society that 'the department most likely to prove immediately beneficial to the public would be that which encourages most efficiently the application of the Fine Arts to our Manufactures'?*   Or Cole's, who had joined   n.43 the Society in 1846 and at once become a member of the Fine Arts Committee? Anyway, a tea-set produced for his Art Manufactures by Minton's received a Silver Medal that year. The prizes of 1846 were followed by a first exhibition of British manufactures, and then by Cole, in 1849, coming out with a magazine, the *Journal of Design*, intended to preach better standards to industry and the public. The six volumes of the *Journal* are worth close study.

What is most important for us in them and in the activities of the Society of Arts altogether is that evidently industrial art between 1750 and 1850 had become a completely different matter. In 1750 nobody queried the good taste of its products, nor had anybody much reason to query it. If education was urged, it was education in draughtsmanship for the workman, education of skill not of taste. Now the Society was asking for objects 'to improve general taste', and Prince Albert also wanted the Society to do things 'beneficial to the public'.

These are the sources of the Great Exhibition of 1851, and of the creation of the South Kensington Museum a few years later. The museum was intended to be used by manufacturers to improve the taste of their products. Some did it, but that alone could not be enough to create a new style.

To have done that, is the immortal merit of William Morris. But, in spite of it, Morris is not really part of the history of industrial design, for the simple reason that he hated industrial design and industry altogether. Here is his most interesting comment on the designer in a reformed, liberal, nineteenth-century industrial world:

'A highly gifted and educated man shall . . . squint at a sheet of paper, and

... the results of that squint shall set a vast number of well-fed, contented operatives ... turning crank handles for ten hours a day ... Well, from this system are to come threefold blessings—food and clothing, poorish lodgings and a little leisure to the operatives, enormous riches to the capitalists that rent them, together with moderate riches to the squinter on the paper; and lastly, very decidedly lastly abundance of cheap art for the operatives or crank-turners to buy'.*

n.44

Now what we can learn from Morris's splendid vituperation is that the designer by then was an accepted member of the production process. Indeed, the catalogue of the Great Exhibition is full of designers' names, although factories still disliked disclosing the names of their fully-employed studio designers. That was still the same when the Arts and Crafts Exhibition Society started in 1888, one of the outcomes of Morris's teachings, and their insistence on showing the designer's name against every article cost them a good deal of support from some manufacturers.

Amongst other outcomes of Morris's doctrines was a new type of art school, first, I think, realised at Birmingham and then at the Central School of Arts and Crafts in London. They emphasised Arts and Crafts in their names, because they wanted to teach equally the Fine Arts and what Lewis F. Day, one of the leading designers of the late nineteenth century, has called the Arts Not-Fine.*

n.45

But the drawback of the Morris firm remained that neither their art nor their craft was in sympathy with industry. The new schools helped their students a lot by fostering a freer, more imaginative draughtsmanship and a truer understanding of materials and processes of making (by hand, of course), but they would not listen to the needs of the manufacturers. However, the story does not end there. For amongst those who had been impressed by Morris's noble style of designing, without being led astray by his medievalising and socialising theory, were some manufacturers and some artists, and they attempted to achieve a reform in industrial design proper. Among manufacturers I am chiefly thinking of Metford Warner of Jeffrey's, the wallpaper manufacturers, who got Walter Crane and Edward Godwin, and a little later, Charles Voysey to design for him.* Voysey

n.46

also designed textiles for Morton's, and carpets for Tomkinson's and for Ginzkey's of Maffersdorf. Concurrently Sir Ambrose Heal appeared with modern furniture. There were others as well, though admittedly not many as compared with the total of British industrial production.

After that the story leaves England and becomes familiar. The German Werkbund was founded in 1907 to join artists and architects with manufacturers and to work for higher standards of design. In England the DIA followed in 1915 (see p. 227), and a little later in America, a new type of free-lance appeared who concerned himself with things, such as refrigerators and sewing-machines, and not only with pattern in the flat. Not that this new type of designer was an unmixed blessing. He called himself a stylist and styling is far from a guarantee of aesthetic value. 'The most important curve is the sales curve' is not only a manufacturer's but also a stylist's saying—to this day. Industrially made greenery-yallery of 1900, industrially made modernistic of 1925 and 1930, streamlining where no speed matters, and now splayed and tapered chair and table legs which trip you up, all that is created or condoned by the designers as willingly as by the makers. But that is the critic's concern, not the historian's.

1 'Model Houses for Families' of 1849 in Streatham Street, Bloomsbury, by Henry Roberts

The Architectural Review, XCIII, 1943

II
Early Working Class Housing

This is a documentary of the first twenty years of tenement house building for the working classes of London. As plenty of original evidence on a topic so much discussed at the time is still in existence, and as most of this evidence is buried in old volumes of architectural magazines, I have confined myself almost entirely to quotations from contemporary sources.

The story which thus takes shape is one of equal historical and topical interest. Historically it introduces a number of buildings all but forgotten, yet by no means devoid of architectural merit, and certainly of an exceptionally high social significance. As for their topical importance, it lies in a development which over the twenty years here examined made of pleasant moderately-sized dwelling-houses the grim and grimy barracks of the poor which between the sixties and the eighties succeeded in destroying any chance for flats to become popular in England with the class for which they could be such a blessing.

(In the past few years important research has been done on the subject of this paper. Outstanding is J.N. Tarn's Housing in Urban Areas, 1840–1914, *Ph.D. thesis, Cambridge, 1962. Dr Tarn has also published papers on the Improved Industrial Dwellings Company, Peabody Trust housing, and housing at Liverpool and Glasgow, the latter in the* Town Planning Review. *In* Victorian Studies, *XI, 1967–8, is a long and fully annotated paper by H.J. Dyos on the Slums of Victorian London. In Henry-Russell Hitchcock's* Early Victorian Architecture in Britain, *New Haven and London, 1954, part of Chapter XIV deals with working class housing, including the model cottages.)*

THE SLUMS OF
A HUNDRED YEARS AGO

The first five quotations are taken from the Report to Her Majesty's Principal Secretary of State for the Home Department from the Poor Law Commissioners, on an Inquiry into the Sanitary Conditions of the Labouring Population of Great Britain. It was written in 1842 by the secretary to the investigating committee, the great Edwin Chadwick, and based on evidence given by Dr Neil Arnott, James Phillips Kay (later Sir J. Kay Shuttleworth), Dr Southwood Smith, and others. It is the foundation of all slum clearance and re-housing endeavours.

*2-5 Four storeys of a house near
Gray's Inn Road, London, in 1853*

THE SLUMS OF GLASGOW (DR ARNOTT)

'We entered a dirty low passage like a house door, which led from the street through the first house to a square court immediately behind, which court, with the exception of a narrow path around it leading to another long passage through a second house, was occupied entirely as a dung receptacle of the most disgusting kind. Beyond this court the second passage led to a second square court, occupied in the same way by its dunghill; and from this court there was yet a third passage leading to a third court, and third dung heap. There were no privies or drains there, and the dung heaps received all filth which the swarm of wretched inhabitants could give; and we learnt that a considerable part of the rent of the houses was paid by the produce of the dung heaps. Thus, worse off than wild animals, many of which withdraw to a distance and conceal their ordure, the dwellers in these courts had converted their shame into a kind of money by which their lodging was to be paid. The interior of these houses and their inmates corresponded with the exteriors. We saw half-dressed wretches crowding together to be warm; and in one bed, although in the middle of the day, several women were imprisoned under a blanket, because as many others who had on their backs all the articles of dress that belonged to the party were then out of doors in the streets. This picture is so shocking that, without ocular proof, one would be disposed to doubt the possibility of the facts; and yet there is perhaps no old town in Europe that does not furnish parallel examples.'

SEWERAGE AT LEEDS (MR BAKER)

'Numbers of streets have been formed and houses erected without pavement, and hence without surface drainage—without sewers—or if under drainage can be called sewers, then with such as, becoming choked in a few months, are even worse than if they were altogether without. The surface of these streets is considerably elevated by accumulated ashes and filth, untouched by any scavenger; they form nuclei of disease exhaled from a thousand sources. Here and there stagnant water, and channels so offensive that they have been declared unbearable, lie under the doorways of the uncomplaining poor; and privies so laden with ashes and excrementitious matter as to be unusable prevail, till the streets themselves become offensive from deposits of this description.'

SEWERAGE IN THE PARISH OF ST GILES (MR HOWELL)

'I would instance a recent case in my own parish, where I was called to survey two houses about to undergo extensive repairs. It was necessary that my survey should extend from the garrets to the cellars; upon visiting the latter, I found the whole area of the cellars of both houses were full of night-soil, to the depth of three feet, which had been permitted to accumulate from the overflow of the cesspools; upon being moved, the stench was intolerable, and no doubt the neighbourhood must have been more or less infected by it. I should mention that these houses are letting at from £30 to £40 a year each, and are situated in a considerable public thoroughfare.'

OVERCROWDING AT HULL, LIVERPOOL AND MANCHESTER (MR RIDDALL WOOD)

'In Hull I have met with cases somewhat similar. A mother, about fifty years of age, and her son, I should think twenty-five, at all events above twenty-one, sleeping in the same bed, and a lodger in the same room. I have two or three instances in Hull, in which a mother was sleeping with her grown-up son, and in most cases there were other persons sleeping in the same room, in another bed. In a cellar in Liverpool, I found a mother, and her grown-up daughters sleeping on a bed of chaff on the ground in one corner of the cellar, and in the same corner three sailors had their bed. I have met with upwards of forty people sleeping in the same room, married and single, including, of course, children and several young adult persons of either sex. In Manchester I could enumerate a variety of instances in which I found such promiscuous mixture of the sexes in sleeping-rooms. I may mention one; a man, his wife and child sleeping in one bed; in another bed, two grown-up females; and, in the same room, two young men, unmarried. I have met with instances of a man, his wife, and his wife's sister, sleeping in the same bed together. I have known at least half-a-dozen cases in Manchester, in which that has been regularly practised, the unmarried sister being an adult.'

A MANCHESTER LODGING HOUSE (DR HOWARD)

'In some of these houses as many as six or eight beds are contained in a single room; in others, where the rooms are smaller, the number is necessarily less; but it seems to be the invariable practice . . . to cram as many beds into each room as it can possibly be made to hold, and they are often placed so close to each other that there is scarcely room to pass between them. The scene which these places present at night is one of the most lamentable description; the crowded state of the beds, filled promiscuously with men, women and children; the floor covered over with the filthy and ragged clothes they have just put off; and with their various bundles and packages, containing all the property they possess, mark the depraved and blunted state of their feelings, and the moral and social order which exists. The suffocating stench and heat of the atmosphere are almost intolerable to a person coming from the open air, and plainly indicate its insalubrity. Even if the place be inspected during the day, the state of things is not much better. Several persons will very commonly be found in bed; one is probably sick, a second is perhaps sleeping away the effects of the previous night's debauch, while another is possibly dozing away his time because he has no employment, or is taking his rest now because he obtains his living by some night work. In consequence of this occupation of the room during the day, the windows are kept constantly closed, ventilation is entirely neglected, and the vitiated atmosphere is ever ready to communicate its poisonous influence to the first fresh comer whom habit has not yet rendered insensible to its effects.'

6 A court in Soho, 1853

THREE PLANNERS AHEAD OF THEIR TIME

J. C. LOUDON, 1818

'It is singular that so long ago as 1818, I contrived a college [for working men] . . . and made out a plan and elevation, which I showed at the time to the late Sir Joseph Banks. . . . I have now looked out the plan, and I send it you exactly as it was prepared. . . . The college was to have seven stories, exclusive of a sunk story and enclosed flat roof. Each story contains 8 dwellings, marked 1 to 8, with a gallery and inclined plane in the centre, marked 9 and 10. The side of the square containing the gallery and inclined plane, is 20 feet. All the walls and partitions are to be of brick, and all the floors of Arbroath pavement, resting on the walls, or on cast-iron rafters . . . 12, 12 are the two steam tubes for supplying heat to the air, and steam to the cooking and washing apparatus at 13. . . . In one of the light closets of each dwelling is a water-closet (15, dwelling 1), a sink-stone (16), and a supply-cistern over. 17, 17 in the inclined plane are tubes for the descent of heavy refuse. . . . 18, 18 steam tubes for heating the air of the central well, by which means . . . it may be used as a drying room; each family having two or three lines across the inclined plane allowed to them.'

From a letter to the editor of the Mechanics' Magazine, *vol. 16, 1831–32. The writer is J. C. Loudon, the famous author of many handbooks on building and gardening.*

JUNIUS REDIVIVUS, 1831

' . . . To erect small houses for the residence of the poor is bad, because there is so much multiplication of expenses. . . . The combination of a number of dwellings under one roof diminishes the total expense. . . . In a large city the want of room renders it necessary to pile as many stories as possible one on the

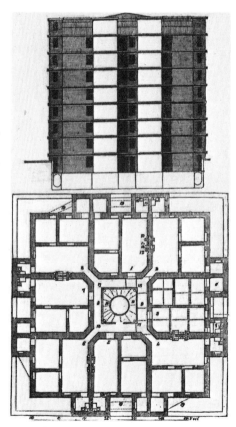

7 Loudon's college for working men, 1818: eight dwellings on each floor, with a central gallery and ramp

other; and if the erection be well constructed there is no objection to it . . . [Nor can it] be doubted that a capitalist, building for the poor on a large scale, could afford them every comfort at a . . . cheap rate, and secure himself seven and a-half per cent. without difficulty. . . . Nine feet would probably be ample height for rooms of 15 feet square. For, say, 400 families, 800 rooms would be required, giving a bedroom and a sitting-room for each. The best form of building would probably be a hollow square, . . . fireproof by means of . . . cast-iron. The bed-rooms should all be in the outer side of the building . . . the access to them being through the sitting-room, which should look into the interior of the square . . . The length of each side of the building would be about 350 feet. At each angle there should be a staircase; and the access to the rooms should be by galleries, 10 feet wide round each story, after the manner of the old-fashioned inns . . . two stories would contain the whole number of apartments.'

Letter from Junius Redivivus to the editor of the Mechanics' Magazine, *vol. 16, 1831–32, published a few months before Loudon's letter. Junius Redivivus was William Bridges Adams (1797–1872), a railway engineer and public writer of pamphlets. The inner courtyard of his building was to be 262 feet square. Each wing would have a kitchen to sell cooked provisions to the tenants, hot baths and laundries. In the centre of the square a three-storied building with school, nursery school, and library accommodation was planned—probably the first suggestion of an arrangement so decidedly twentieth century in character.*

ELEVATION OF THE ENTRANCE FRONT

8 *Smirke's public lodging-house, 1841 (with single rooms, not flats)*

SYDNEY SMIRKE, 1834

'Portions of unoccupied ground should be taken in the skirts of the town (such, for example, as the waste land beyond Vauxhall Road, the open fields west of the Edgware Road, those behind Euston Square, or other similar spots), and let a village, expressly dedicated to the working classes, be there erected. The avenues should be so laid out, as to be wide, clear and regular; and every means that ingenuity can devise for securing cleanliness and airiness should be adopted. The houses should be arranged and constructed on a plan totally differing in every respect from the small, close, inconvenient tenements usually let out into lodgings. . . . Except in the boarded floors, timber might be entirely discarded in the construction of the houses. . . . The roofs and floors should be supported by iron or brick, and even the window sashes and frames might be advantageously made of the same material. . . . A perfect system of drainage should be adopted throughout, and an abundance of water supplied to each floor. . . . Mr Brunel has suggested to the author the practicability of laying on heat to a long range of these dwellings from one common source. . . . Nor should we forget to provide for the inmates of these groups of dwellings some open place for recreation, where healthy exercises and the innocent pleasures of society might be enjoyed during the hours of leisure. . . . The ground should be purchased by the public money . . . and a commission or some such permanent Board . . . should assume the whole direction and superintendence of the works. If the requisite sum for the completion of this project be advanced by way of a loan, and entrusted to the management of the Board, there is every reason to hope that, even supposing these tenements to be let at the rate far lower than the usual rent, . . . an income would arise quite sufficient to pay a reasonable interest on the money expended . . .'

From Sydney Smirke's Suggestions for the Architectural Improvement of the Western Part of London, *1834. Sydney Smirke (1799–1877), Sir Robert Smirke's less known but more interesting brother, was the designer of the Carlton Club, the Inner Temple Hall, Burlington House, a part of Knowsley near Liverpool, and the Reading Room of the British Museum with its furniture. The elevation illustrated is from the Chadwick Report. It shows a model lodging-house, not tenement house, but it indicates the architectural character that Smirke wished to give to working-class buildings, and obviously influenced Henry Roberts.*

8

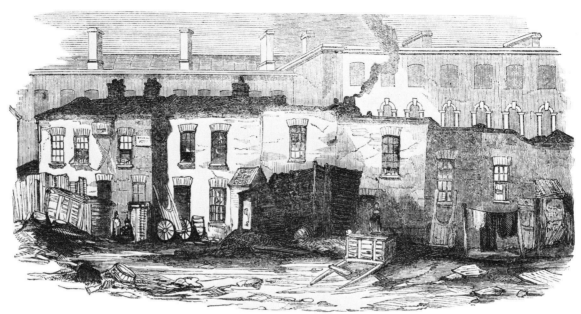

9 Paradise Row, Agar Town, London, in 1853

SOCIAL REFORMERS—COMMUNIST AND LIBERAL

Friedrich Engels, Karl Marx's friend and staunchest follower, made use of the Chadwick Report to proclaim a fervent indictment of contemporary society, but he knows of no immediately applicable remedies. Chadwick himself, on the other hand, more concerned with alleviating the miseries that surrounded him than with altering the state of society, appeals to the wealthy and cultured for charitable help. His course, not Engels's, was at first followed.

'The great towns are chiefly inhabited by working-people, since in the last case there is one bourgeois for two workers, often for three, here and there for four; these workers have no property whatsoever of their own, and live wholly upon wages, which usually go from hand to mouth. Society, composed wholly of atoms, does not trouble itself about them; leaves them to care for themselves and their families, yet supplies them no means of doing this in an efficient and permanent manner. Every working man, even the best, is therefore constantly exposed to loss of work and food, that is to death by starvation, and many finish in this way. The dwellings of the workers are everywhere badly planned, badly built, and kept in the worst condition, badly ventilated, damp, and unwhole-some. The inhabitants are confined to the smallest possible space, and at least one family usually sleeps in one room. The interior arrangement of the dwellings is poverty-stricken in various degrees, down to the utter absence of even the most necessary furniture. The clothing of the workers, too, is generally scanty, and that of great multitudes is in rags. . . . Thus the working-class of the great cities offers a graduated scale of conditions of life, in the best cases a temporarily en-durable existence for hard work and good wages, good or endurable, that is, from the worker's standpoint, in the worst cases, bitter want, reaching even homelessness and death by starvation. The average is much nearer the worst case than the best.'

From Friedrich Engels's The Condition of the Working Class in England in 1844.

'It would have been matter of sincere congratulations to have met with more extensive evidence of spontaneous improvement amongst the classes in receipt of high wages, but nearly all the beneficial changes found in progress throughout the country are changes that have arisen from the efforts of persons of the superior classes. . . . In the rural districts, the worst of the new cottages are those erected on the borders of commons by the labourers themselves. In the manufacturing districts, the tenements erected by building clubs and by speculating builders of the class of workmen, are frequently the subject of complaint as being the least substantial and the most destitute of proper accommodation. The only conspicuous instances of improved residences of the labouring classes found in the rural districts are those which have been erected by opulent and benevolent landlords for the accommodation of the labourers on their own estates; and in the manufacturing districts, those erected by wealthy manufacturers for the accommodation of their own work-people.'

'My belief is that, without ultimate pecuniary loss, and with the utmost direct and indirect benefit, buildings, placed under some public control, might be erected for the joint occupation of many families or individuals, and so arranged that each tenant might feel that he had the exclusive enjoyment of a home in the room or rooms which he occupied; and yet might partake, in common with his neighbours, of many important comforts and advantages now utterly unknown to him. I propose that there should be erected buildings, in various parts of the suburbs, consisting of perhaps fifty or sixty rooms, high, airy, dry, well ventilated, light and warm, comfortably filled up, fire-proof, abundantly supplied with water and thoroughly drained; such regulations might be laid down for the conduct of the inmates as may be necessary for the common good, without undue rigour or interference with natural and proper feelings of independence . . .'

From Edwin Chadwick's own remarks in the Report of 1842.

ENCOURAGEMENT FROM ON HIGH

The seventh Earl of Shaftesbury (1801–85) was the incarnation of the humane spirit of a group of enlightened English noblemen during Queen Victoria's reign. His name is connected with nearly all the endeavours to mitigate the evils of industrialization: the Factory Act of 1833, the Chimney Sweeps Act of 1834, the Mines Act, the Ragged School Movement, the Children's Employment Commission, the Ten Hours Bill, the Lunacy Acts, and all housing improvements, insisted upon by law or carried out by charitable private enterprise during his life-time. Prince Albert was greatly impressed by Shaftesbury's initiative. His own kind heart and sense of the orderly, well regulated and beautiful answered readily to appeals for encouragement from the societies for the promotion of improved housing.

'On the 22nd of May [1846] we find him at a meeting of the Society for Improving the Condition of the Working Classes, bringing the subject before an influential audience as vividly as it could be brought. 'I do not,' he said, 'speak merely from books; I do not speak merely from the accounts that have been given me; because I have, not only in past years, but during the present year devoted a very considerable number of hours to going over some of the worst localities in various parts of this great Metropolis.' He startled his audience by some of the revelations he made, of rooms 'so foul and so dark that they were exposed to every physical mischief that can beset the human frame'—so foul that when a physician visited them, he was obliged to write his prescription outside the door; of courts and alleys thronged with a dense and most immoral population of every caste and grade of character, but almost every one of them defiled by perpetual habits of intoxication, and living amid riot and blasphemy, noise, tumult and indecency.'

From Edwin Hodder: The Life and Work of the Seventh Earl of Shaftesbury, K.G., *1886, vol. 2, p. 160.*

'I feel convinced that the existence [of model houses] will, by degrees, cause a complete change in the domestic comforts of the labouring classes, as it

*10 The Fleet Ditch in Clerkenwell: by
1853 the river was an open sewer*

will exhibit to them that with real economy can be continued advantages with which few of them have hitherto been acquainted, whilst it will show to those who possess capital to invest, that they may do so with profit and advantage to themselves, at the same time that they are dispensing those comforts to which I have alluded, to their poorer brethren. . . . To show how man can help man, notwithstanding the complicated state of civilized society, ought to be the aim of every philanthropic person; but it is more peculiarly the duty of those who, under the blessing of Divine Providence, enjoy station, wealth and education . . .'

Prince Albert at the Annual Meeting of the Society for Improving the Conditions of the Labouring Classes, 18th May, 1848. More about the Society will be found below. The quotation is taken from The Principal Speeches and Addresses of His Royal Highness the Prince Consort, *1862.*

THE WRITERS JOIN IN

'They went along till they arrived in Berry Street. It was unpaved; and down the middle a gutter forced its way, every now and then forming pools in the holes with which the street abounded. . . . As they passed, women from their doors tossed household slops of every description into the gutter; they ran into the next pool, which overflowed and stagnated. Heaps of ashes were the stepping-stones. . . . Our friends were not dainty, but even they picked their way, till they got to some steps leading down into a small area, where a person standing would have his head about one foot below the level of the street, and might at the same time, without the least motion of his body, touch the window of the cellar and the damp muddy wall right opposite. You went down one step even from the foul area into the cellar in which a family of human beings lived. It was very dark inside. The window-panes were many of them broken and stuffed with rags, which was reason enough for the dusky light that pervaded the place even at mid-day. After the account I have given of the state of the street, no one can be surprised that on going into the cellar, the smell was so fetid as almost to knock the two men down. Quickly recovering themselves, as those inured to such things do, they began to penetrate the thick darkness of the place, and to see three or four little children rolling on the damp, nay wet, brick floor, through which the stagnant, filthy moisture of the street oozed up; the fireplace was empty and black; the wife sat on her husband's lair, and cried in the dark loneliness.'

From Mrs Gaskell's Mary Barton, *1848, Chapter 6.*

'And he dashed across the broad roaring thoroughfare of Bridge Street and hurrying almost at a run down Tooley Street, plunged into the wilderness of

Bermondsey. He stopped at the end of a miserable blind alley, where a dirty gas-lamp just served to make darkness visible, and show the patched windows and rickety doorways of the crazy houses, whose upper storeys were lost in a brooding cloud of fog; and the pools of stagnant water at our feet; and the huge heap of cinders which filled up the waste end of the alley—a dreary, black formless mound on which two or three spectral dogs prowled up and down after the offal. . . . The house at which we stopped was the last in a row. A group of slatternly people were in the entry. . . . But Downes pushed past unheeding, unlocked a door at the end of the passage, locked it again, and then rushed across the room in chase of two or three rats, who vanished into cracks and holes. And what a room! A low lean-to with wooden walls, without a single article of furniture; and through the broad chinks of the floor shone up as it were ugly glaring eyes, staring at us. They were the reflections of the rushlight in the sewer below. The stench was frightful, the air heavy with pestilence. The first breath I drew made my heart sick, and my stomach turn.'

Charles Kingsley: Alton Locke, tailor and poet, *1849, Chapter 35. Kingsley's part in the Christian Socialist Movement of the mid-nineteenth century will be familiar to readers of this compilation.*

'Jo lives—that is to say, Jo has not yet died—in a ruinous place, known to the like of him by the name of Tom-all-Alone's. It is a black, dilapidated street, avoided by all decent people; where the crazy houses were seized upon, when their decay was far advanced, by some bold vagrants who, after establishing their own possession, took to letting them out in lodgings. Now, these tumbling tenements contain by night a swarm of misery. As, on the ruined human wretch, vermin parasites appear, so these ruined shelters have bred a crowd of foul existence that crawls in and out of gaps in walls and boards; and coils itself to sleep, in maggot numbers, where the rain drips in; and comes and goes, fetching and carrying fever.

'Twice lately, there has been a crash and a cloud of dust, like the springing of a mine, in Tom-all-Alone's; and, each time, a house has fallen. These accidents have made a paragraph in the newspapers, and have filled a bed or two in the nearest hospital. The gaps remain, and there are not unpopular lodgings among the rubbish. As several more houses are nearly ready to go, the next crash in Tom-all-Alone's may be expected to be a good one.

'Much mighty speech-making there has been both in and out of Parliament, concerning Tom, and much wrathful disputation how Tom shall be got right. Whether he shall be put into the main road by constables, or by beadles, or by bell-ringing, or by force of figures, or by correct principles of taste, or by high church, or by low church, or by no church; whether he shall be set to slitting trusses of polemical straws with the crooked knife of his mind, or whether he shall be put to stone-breaking instead. In the midst of which dust and noise there is but one thing perfectly clear, to wit, that Tom only may and can, or shall and will, be reclaimed according to somebody's theory, but nobody's practice. And in the hopeful meantime, Tom goes to perdition head foremost in his old determined spirit.

'But he has his revenge. Even the winds are his messengers, and they serve him in these hours of darkness. There is not a drop of Tom's corrupted blood but propagates infection and contagion somewhere. It shall pollute, this very night, the choice stream of a Norman house, and his grace shall not be able to say Nay to the infamous alliance. There is not at atom of Tom's slime, not a cubic inch of any pestilential gas in which he lives, not one obscenity or degradation about him, not an ignorance, not a wickedness, not a brutality of his committing, but shall work its retribution, through every order of society, up to the proudest of the proud, and to the highest of the high.'

Charles Dickens: Bleak House, *1853, Chapters 16 and 46. Dickens' fight for better conditions for the poor was a direct outcome of his study of Chadwick's Report.*

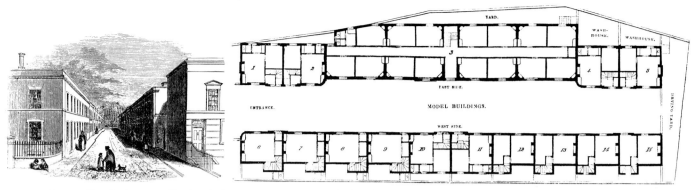

11, 12 Lower Road, Pentonville, by Roberts, 1844–5. One side had flats, the other rooms, with a washhouse at the end

THE FIRST BUILDINGS (1844–1847)

The Metropolitan Association for improving the Dwellings of the Industrious Classes was formed in 1843, the Society for Improving the Conditions of the Labouring Classes in 1844. Their first model buildings date from 1844. These are still modelled on the example of the traditional terrace-house. The first blocks of working-class flats were, it seems, put up at Birkenhead in 1845. We are here only concerned with the early development of flats. Experimental model cottages, however, ran parallel, and also model lodging-houses, and public baths and wash-houses.

On model cottages see Loudon's Encyclopaedia, *H. Roberts's book of 1850, mentioned in more detail below, and* The Builder, *III, p. 47, 485; V, p. 40; VI, p. 226, 466, etc. On baths and wash-houses,* The Builder, *III, p. 25; IV, p. 262; VI, p. 490; VII, p. 478. On model lodging-houses see H. Roberts's book of 1850. The example which he followed was the Asylum for Destitute Sailors, Dock Street, London Dock, of 1835.*

The first model-lodging-houses of the Society for Improving the Condition of the Labouring Classes were 76, Hatton Garden and George Street, Bloomsbury. The Metropolitan Association built one for 234 men in 1848 in connection with the Albert Family Dwellings (see below).

'[The Metropolitan Association] partakes quite of the commercial character, being a Joint Stock Company, having a capital of £100,000 in 4,000 shares of £25 each, though, at the same time, the interest of the class sought to be benefited is protected by the charter, limiting the dividends at any time to be paid to £5 per cent., any surplus being directed to be applied in extension of the object . . .'

The Builder, VIII, 1850, p. 589. Henry Roberts, on whose important role in the campaign for model houses more will be said presently, also believed this to be the only reasonable foundation for building enterprises. Municipal or public utility building was yet a far cry.

11, 12 LOWER ROAD, PENTONVILLE

'SOCIETY FOR IMPROVING THE DWELLINGS OF THE LABOURING CLASSES.—This society has lately put forth a statement accompanied by an engraved plan of the fifteen houses now in course of erection in the Lower Road, Pentonville. The following extract . . . explains the humane objects they have in view, and the means by which they propose to carry them out: "The committee, feeling that no description or reasoning, however accurate, is likely to make such an impression on the public as an actual experiment, have resolved to build a certain number of houses, as models of the different kinds of dwellings which they would recommend for the labouring classes in populous towns. The buildings are of three different classes and designed to accommodate in the whole twenty families and thirty single persons. Eight of the families are to occupy each an entire house, with a living-room on the ground floor, having an enclosed recess or closet large enough to receive beds for the youths of the family, and two bed-rooms on the upper floor. The remaining twelve families are to be distributed in six houses, each family occupying a floor of two rooms, with all requisite conveniences; and as the apartments on the upper floor are to be approached through an outer door distinct from that belonging to the lower floor, their respective occupants will thus be kept entirely separate, and each floor be virtually a distinct dwelling. The centre building on the east side is intended for the accommodation of thirty widows or females of advanced age, each to have a room, with the use of a wash-house common to all.'''

The Builder, II, 1844, p. 630. The street mentioned is now King's Cross Road; the houses have disappeared. They were designed by the Society's honorary architect, Henry Roberts. Roberts, the most important working-class architect of the mid-nineteenth century, was born about 1800 or a little earlier. He died in 1876. Before he began to take an interest in building for the poor, he had made a name as the designer of the Fishmongers' Hall by London Bridge (1831–33), and the Camberwell Collegiate School (1835–36). The Pentonville houses were his first experiment in working-class architecture. He had not then grasped the problems involved, as contemporary critics justly pointed out.

'MODEL (?) HOUSES FOR THE LABOURING CLASSES.—Anxious to examine the society's first work, . . . we hastened to the site of the new houses. . . . We regret to say . . . that our worst anticipations are confirmed. The arrangment is a disgrace to the society, and cannot surely have been seen by Lord Ashley, the chairman of the committee. . . . These houses, model houses remember, . . . are actually arranged to form a court open at one end only, and less than 23 feet in width at the widest part! The plot of ground, on which the fifteen buildings are crammed is so small, that, notwithstanding this proximity, the yard attached to each house, is literally what its name imparts in fact, or very little more. We call most urgently on the committee and the shareholders to prevent the consummation of this most dangerous mistake, or they will rear a hot-bed for infection, and throw a great impediment in the way of that improvement which they profess to seek.'

The Builder, III, 1845, p. 1. Lord Ashley is, of course, the Earl of Shaftesbury, before he inherited the title in 1851. The article is by the editor of The Builder, *George Godwin (1815–88), a man keenly interested in new materials—he submitted an essay on concrete to the Institute of British Architects at the age of twenty—and in new problems, such as* The Architecture of the Poor. *This is the title of a paper which he wrote in 1843. Recently Anthony King has brought out a paper on Godwin (*The Architectural Review, *CXXXVI, pp. 448 ff. In the same year in which he so severely criticized Roberts's cottages, he published the following account of what appears to be the earliest working-class flats ever erected:*

BIRKENHEAD

'The Birkenhead Dock Company have . . . found it better economy to build large houses rather than cottages; they have adopted a plan prepared by Mr Charles Evans Lang, of London; and the buildings are now in progress. The ground . . . lies between two of eight streets that meet in a circus, and may be described as a triangle; houses are erected in rows, with alleys in between; there is a school-house at the apex of the triangle, and in the centre of the circus a handsome church. Each row [is] a pile four stories high, comprising several distinct houses, each house having a public staircase communicating with the several 'flats' or stories; each flat divided into two separate dwelling-places. Each dwelling contains a living-room, two bedrooms, and a scullery.'

'The houses built at Birkenhead . . . are of red brick, with light sandstone window-cills and copings. Their external aspect would suggest to a Londoner the idea of a block of buildings constructed for professional persons, . . . and,

A *living room*
B *bedroom*
C *scullery with sink*

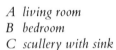
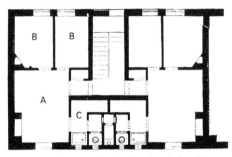

13 *Two flats in the Birkenhead dwellings of 1845: they were entered from a central staircase, and each had a living room, two bedrooms, a cupboard, a scullery with sink, and a WC*

with little addition and variation of ornament, they might match with the new Hall of Lincoln's Inn. . . . The staircases are of stone, with iron balustrades. The flat brick arches of which the floors are constructed, are tied together with iron ties, and the whole building is fireproof. . . . Each set of rooms is furnished . . . with sinks for washing, and a water-closet, and means of communication with a dust shaft, . . . by which all dust and ashes might be removed at once from the apartments. . . .'

'The rents charged were from 3s. 6d. to 5s. each set. . . . They included a constant supply of water, and the use of one gas burner in each set of rooms, and all rates and taxes, and moreover two iron bedsteads, and a grate with an oven. . . . Mr Chadwick, who was one of the party, whilst expressing his warm concurrence as to the advance made, stated his opinion that further improvements might yet be achieved, especially in the mode of warming and ventilation. . . . He considered that in such a range of buildings [ventilation] might be accomplished with air that was warm as well as fresh.'

The Builder, *III, 1845, p. 220, and IV, 1846, p. 537. The houses were for 324 families, an enormous advance in scale over Pentonville. Henry Roberts said about them:*

'. . . There is much to commend in this early effort . . . but in several important points, there appears to be such great room for amendment . . . that I venture to refer to a Report made on them, under date May 1, 1845, and addressed to Lord Ashley. . . . The width of the proposed avenues is only 18 feet, whilst the houses are designed to be nearly 40 feet in height. . . . The width of such avenues ought to be not less than the height of the buildings or . . . at least 30 feet. . . . The general arrangement of the houses appears to be good; [but] . . . all the rooms are small, particularly those for sleeping.'

H. Roberts: *The Dwellings of the Labouring Classes, 1850, p. 13. Contemporary with these blocks at Birkenhead, the first were put up at Liverpool (Kent Terrace, see* The Builder, *III, 1845, p. 220) and in Scotland. On the Pilrig Buildings, near Leith Walk, Edinburgh, see* The Builder, *III, 1845, p. 29, and XVIII, p. 682. On the earliest examples in Glasgow, see* The Builder, *V, p. 341, and VI, p. 505.*

A living room
B bedroom
C scullery with sink

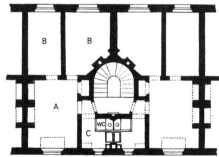

14, 15 Metropolitan Model Buildings in St Pancras, 1848, by Moffat. The plan of each pair of flats is similar to Birkenhead (Ill.13)

EIGHTEEN FORTY-EIGHT TO EIGHTEEN FIFTY

14, 15 OLD PANCRAS ROAD

'METROPOLITAN ASSOCIATION FOR IMPROVING THE DWELLINGS OF THE POOR.— At the first annual meeting of this association . . . [it was stated] that an agreement for a lease . . . had been entered into for a piece of ground opposite the church in the Old Pancras Road. . . . The building . . . which the association proposed to erect, would consist of twenty-one sets of two rooms, and ninety sets of three rooms of various sizes. . . . Each dwelling was to be supplied with water, . . . with a sink, with a means of carrying of refuse and ashes through a shaft . . .'

'The area occupied is large, and the dimensions of the building are 222 feet frontage to Platt Street, 108 feet to St. Pancras Road, and about the same to Goldington Street.'

'These buildings have the advantage of larger-sized apartments, and un-obstructed light and air. The internal staircase arrangement involves them in the heavy charge of window-tax.'

'The buildings . . . have more applicants than can be accommodated. . . . The rents vary from 3s. to 7s. a week.'

The first paragraph is from The Builder, *V, 1847, p. 16, the second from XIV, p. 397, the fourth from VI, 1848, p. 376. The third stands on p. 14 of H. Roberts's* The Dwellings of the Labouring Classes. *The architect of this first block of working-class flats in London (now demolished) is called Moffat, presumably W. B. Moffat (1812–97), the early partner of Gilbert Scott. The two built chiefly for the Poor Law Commissioners. The arrangement of the flats is similar to that at Birkenhead, but the staircase has no windows.*

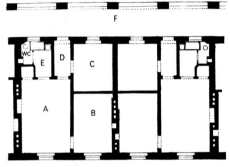

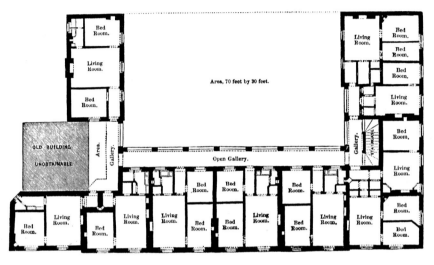

A *living room*
B, C *bedrooms*
D *lobby*
E *scullery with sink*
F *gallery*

16-19 Model Houses in Streatham Street by Henry Roberts, 1849: each flat opens off a gallery, and has, in addition to the standard two bedrooms, a bed cupboard off the living room

STREATHAM STREET, BLOOMSBURY

This block—the aesthetically most satisfactory example of early working-class archi-tecture—is still in existence, two minutes from the British Museum, yet utterly for-gotten. The photographs show its surprisingly dignified design, the work of Henry Roberts.   1, 16–1

'The Society for Improving the Condition of the Labouring Classes . . . have commenced a block of new Model Houses for 48 families in Streatham Street, Bloomsbury, . . . designed by Mr H. Roberts, the society's honorary architect. . . . In undertaking to provide in one pile of building for the accom-modation of a large number of families, amongst the most important considera-tions was that of preserving the domestic privacy . . . of each distinct family, and so disconnecting their apartments as effectually to prevent the communication of contagious diseases; this . . . is accomplished by dispensing altogether with separate staircases . . . and by adopting one common open staircase leading into   18
galleries or corridors, open on one side to a spatious quadrangle, and on the other side having the outer doors of the several tenements. . . . The slate floors of these   19
. . . galleries rest on iron beams. . . . The question of rendering the building fire-proof had much consideration. . . . The floors and roofs . . . are to be rendered fireproof by arching with hollow bricks . . . set in cement. . . . At the extremi-ties, . . . they will be tied in with iron rods. . . . The tenements being . . . separate dwellings, and having fewer than seven windows in each, it is hoped   17
that they will not be liable to the window duty.'

'The Model Houses in Streatham Street . . . are now nearly ready for occupation, and were opened to private view on Tuesday.'

The Builder, *VII, 1849, p. 325, and VIII, p. 250. The basement also contains flats. This brought the total up to fifty-four. They were let at 2s. to 4s. a week. In 1852 the house yielded a profit of 5·75 per cent. On the window tax see below. The outer gallery had been used a few years before in Kent Terrace, Liverpool (The Builder, III, 1845, p. 220). It had also been recommended by Junius Redivivus in 1831 (see page 22) and, in 1848, by an anonymous contributor to* The Builder *(VI, p. 124).*

20–21 Albert Family Dwellings in Deal Street, 1848

20, 21 DEAL STREET, SPITALFIELDS

'We are happy to find the "Metropolitan Association" pursuing their object energetically, as well as, we believe, with a sincere desire for the public good. The last step they have taken has been the purchase of a piece of ground in one of those localities in which their efforts may be particularly beneficial—the district of Spitalfields. A piece of freehold ground has been obtained . . . on which they are about to erect a dormitory, or lodging-house for 300 single men, and residences for forty families at the least; and they applied to six architects to send designs in competition. Five of these, only, answered the call. . . . They were Mr Beck, Mr Barnett, Mr Grellier, Mr Daukes and Mr Ricardo.'

The Builder, *VI, 1848, p. 376. Mr Ricardo is, of course, not Halsey Ricardo, but Mr Dawkes may be Samuel W. Dawkes, the architect of Colney Hatch Asylum, the gorgeous Italianate mansion of Witley Court, Worcestershire, and the church of St Andrew, Wells Street, London. Beck was in the end commissioned. The façades illustrated are at the corner of Underwood Street and Deal Street. There are now sixty flats in the 'Albert Family Dwellings.' Ten of them are in the basement. Each staircase serves fifteen flats. Within the next ten years after the Albert Dwellings the Metropolitan Association built several other blocks. They are enumerated in H. Roberts's* The Improvements of the Dwellings of the Labouring Classes, *1859, p. 15. Amongst them are Ingestre Buildings, off Golden Square, for sixty families (completed in 1856, cf.* The Builder, *XIV, p. 396) and Nelson Square, Bermondsey, for 108 families (completed in 1860,* The Builder, *XVIII, p. 409). The other early schemes of the Metropolitan Association were smaller. But in 1875 the society housed 5,300 people in 1,060 dwellings.*

22, 23 PORTPOOL LANE, GRAY'S INN ROAD

'Liberal contributions received in response to an appeal by the Bishop of London, have enabled the committee appointed for the purpose, to purchase a freehold site in Portpool Lane, Gray's Inn Road, on which is to be erected a model dwelling for 20 families and 128 single women. . . . The accommodation for 20 families will consist of two buildings four stories in height, one having three tenements with three rooms on each floor, and the other two tenements with two rooms on each floor; . . . to both houses there will be an open staircase, and to the larger one a gallery of communication.'

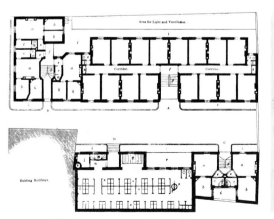

22–23 Thanksgiving Model Buildings, Portpool Lane, 1850–51. They included family dwellings (top left and bottom right in the plan), single rooms, and a lodging-house (bottom centre)

'The "Thanksgiving Model Buildings" in Portpool Lane, Gray's Inn Road [were] built in commemoration of the removal of the cholera. They were commenced in 1850, and occupied in 1851.'

The Builder, VIII, 1850, p. 297, and X, 1852, p. 705. The buildings no longer exist. In The Builder for 1850 (pp. 10 and 105), and for 1852 (p. 427) a few other model houses are mentioned. Now the movement began also to spread to the Continent. Henry Roberts's book was translated into French, and a Société des Cités Ouvrières founded in Paris.

A *living room*
B *bedroom*
C *scullery with sink and larder*
D *lobby*

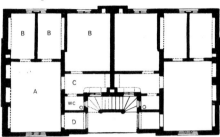

24, 25 Model houses by Henry Roberts for the Great Exhibition: there are now three bedrooms, but the WC still opens off the scullery. The recessed stair became standard

EIGHTEEN FIFTY-ONE

The year of the Great Exhibition, of the abolition—at long last—of the Window Tax, and of Shaftesbury's Labouring Classes Lodging House Act. The window tax had been a scandal ever since the industrial revolution. When it was introduced in 1687, it was a form to regulate in quite an innocuous way the size of houses. The placing of windows was virtually standardized. As soon as cheap housing on a large scale was needed early in the nineteenth century, the tax became a menace. It made blocks of tenement houses impossible, unless it could be proved that they were agglomerations of independent small houses. Hence the open galleries and open staircases—which were of course also useful for ventilation. The Lodging House Act enabled large parishes and boroughs to build better houses out of the poor rates. But few took advantage of the act. Prince Albert's object lesson in better housing at the Exhibition was badly needed.

'Model Houses for four families erected at the Cavalry Barracks, Hyde Park.—His Royal Highness Prince Albert, as President of the Society for Improving the Condition of the Labouring Classes, has had this building raised with a desire of conveying practical information calculated to promote the much needed improvement of the dwellings of the working classes, and also of stimulating visitors to the Great Exhibition whose position and circumstances may enable them, by the carrying out of similar undertakings, without pecuniary sacrifice, permanently to benefit those who are greatly dependent on others for their home and domestic comforts. In its general arrangement the building (designed by Mr Henry Roberts, F.S.A., the Society's honorary architect) is adapted for the occupation of four families, and . . . as the value of land . . .' in some cases, renders the addition of a third, and even of a fourth, story desirable, the plan has been suited to such an arrangement. . . . The most prominent peculiarity of the design is that of the receding and protected central open stair-

24, 25
p. 46,

case, with the connecting gallery on the first floor. . . . The peculiarities of the building in . . . respect [to construction] are the exclusive use of hollow bricks for the walls and partitions . . . and the entire absence of timber in the floors and roof, which are formed with flat arches of hollow brickwork . . . and tied in by wrought-iron rods connected with cast-iron springers.'

The Builder, IX, 1851, p. 311. Henry Roberts was a firm believer in hollow bricks. The ground plan is far in advance of later buildings. The position of lobby, lavatory and scullery should be noted and compared with the plans on pages 34 and 36.

STAGNANCY AND NEW IMPULSES

By 1851 the work of the early reformers was done. The Society for Improving the Conditions and the Metropolitan Association entered into a phase of sluggish progress. In 1853 Roberts left for abroad; in 1856 he resigned his job; in 1860 he wrote that the societies' financial position had 'lately become discouraging.'

Some new societies appeared, such as the Lambeth Association, founded as an outcome of the Labourers' Dwellings Act of 1855, an act to facilitate the formation of joint-stock house-building companies (c.f. The Builder, XII, p. 577, and XIII, p. 490). *Private humanitarian enterprise also was not absent (cf. H. Roberts:* The Progress of the Movement . . . , *1860).*

But nothing was done on a large scale. Prince Albert died in 1861. Then, immediately after his death a new phase began, characterized by the Peabody Trust, by Alderman Sydney Waterlow's building enterprise, and the earliest municipal working-class flats.

26–28 The first Peabody Building, in Commercial Street, 1864. The close-set top floor windows lit baths, drying rooms, and children's play areas, but the cramped plan with its long corridors was a step backward

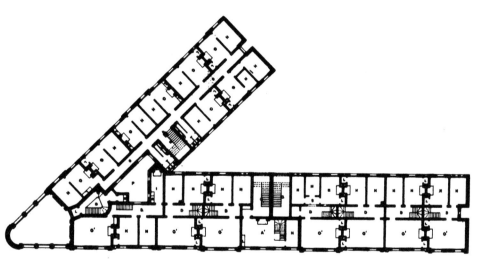

GEORGE PEABODY AND THE PEABODY TRUST

'Mr Geo. Peabody, the American banker, has given a formal shape to his intention, already mentioned by us, of conveying to trustees £150,000 to be applied "exclusively to such purposes as may be calculated directly to ameliorate the condition and augment the comforts of the poor . . . of London."'

George Peabody (1795–1869) was an American. His parents had been poor. He started independent life as a grocer's apprentice. At the age of nineteen he opened a wholesale dry goods warehouse. In 1815 he opened a branch at Baltimore, in 1822 at Philadelphia and New York. In 1837 he settled down in London, a very rich man. In 1843 he retired from his American business and started banking in London. The American section of the 1851 exhibition was paid for by Peabody privately.

'Mr Peabody points out the probable desirability of applying "the fund or a portion of it, in the construction of such improved dwellings for the poor, as may

29, 30 Peabody Trust Islington Estate, 1865: it originally consisted of four blocks of dwellings in an Italianate style, each with a decorated doorway

combine in the utmost possible degree the essentials of healthfulness, comfort, social enjoyment, and economy."'

'The Peabody Building [in Commercial Street, Whitechapel] on which is   26–28 being expended a part of Mr Peabody's gift, is rapidly approaching completion. This is satisfactory; but, after careful inspection we are forced, somewhat unwillingly, to say that this structure will not meet the demands of the poor. . . . We shall find there well-paid mechanics . . . [but] not the poor of Bethnal Green . . . who can only afford to pay a weekly rent of from 2s. to 3s. a week . . .'

The Builder, XX, 1862, p. 228, and XXII, 1864, p. 67. The Peabody Building situated at the corner of Commercial Street and White Lion (now Folgate) Street was opened in March, 1864. It is a four-storeyed block of stock brick, with frontages of 215 and 140 feet. The ground floor has shops towards Commercial Street. The rusticated bands on ground floor and first floor follow Roberts's example. The top floor was entirely given to baths, drying areas and playing areas for children in wet weather. There is a certain amount of Gothic decoration, gables with tall pointed windows, etc. The staircases face the court and are open. Rooms are on either side of long corridors, lavatories only by the staircases. The walls were originally without wallpaper or distempering. Rents ranged from 2s. 6d. to 5s. a week; 48 of the 57 dwellings were 4s. 6d. or 5s. The architect was H. A. Darbishire who had in 1860–61 built a group of working-class dwelling-houses for that lovable Victorian character, Baroness Burdett-Coutts, at Columbia Square, Bethnal Green (cf. The Builder, XIX, p. 530). He lectured on working-class houses in 1863 (The Building News, X, 1863, and The Builder, XXI, 1863). His design for the Peabody Trust was illustrated in the Civil Engineer, XXVII, 1864, p. 124. It was for the next block, in Greenman Street, Islington, replaced by a more austere Italianate design, which with a few additional   29, 30 modifications was applied identical, down to minute details, in the later buildings, erected when Mr Peabody had raised his gift to £500,000. Here is a list of them, down to 1875: Greenman Street, Islington (opened 1865; 244 tenements); Glamis Place, Shadwell (1867; 199); Horseferry Road, Westminster (1869; 146; now re-built); Lawrence Street, Chelsea (1870; 67); Blackfriars Road (1871; 367); Stamford Street (1875; 438); East Lane, Bermondsey (1875; 72). At the end of 1874, 3,815 people lived in Peabody tenements. The average rent was 3s. 11d. a week for two rooms.

ALDERMAN SYDNEY WATERLOW

'Mr Alderman Waterlow has built for £2,000 in Mark Street, Finsbury, for the industrial classes, a pile of "chambers" of middling quality and not agreeable   32, 33 forms, from which he expects to receive 9 per cent. for his money; and on

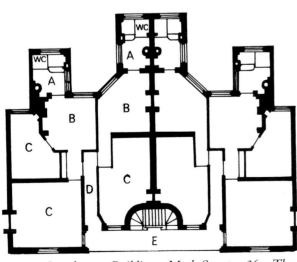

A scullery
   and wash-house
B living room
C bedroom
D passage
E landing

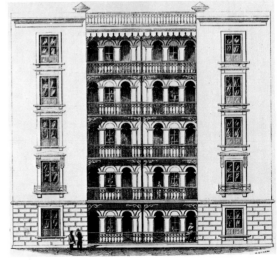

31, 32 Langbourne Buildings, Mark Street, 1863. The flats are long and narrow (four are shown), and open off a recessed stair

Saturday last, Lord Ebury, Lord Radstock, Mr Samuel Morley, Mr A. Kinnaird, M.P., Mr Gregson, M.P., Mr W. Hawes, Mr Roberts, Mr E. Chadwick and many more assembled on the roof of the building to express with somewhat overloud trumpets the debt the community owed to him. . . . The main cause of its cheapness is said to be the adoption of a concrete or artificial stone, composed of clinkers, culm, hard broken coke and similar rough porous calcined substances, . . . for lintels, arches, chimney-pieces, stairs, balconies, the floors of the wash-houses and passages, and the roof. . . . Another reason given for the cheapness, if we understand rightly, is the non-employment of an "architect." . . . The rents expected are . . . from 5s. to 7s. per week.'

31   *The Builder, XXI, 1863, p. 198. The block is called Langbourne Buildings. Its groundplan differs from all the earlier ones in the removal of scullery and lavatory to the back of each flat, and the absurd narrowness of the staircase. The architect was W. Allen. Sydney Waterlow was born in 1822 as the son of a small stationer. He was apprenticed in 1836 to Harrison's and added printing to his father's business in 1844. He was knighted in 1867, and Lord Mayor in 1872. Waterlow's are to-day one of the largest printing houses of Britain.*

Two important events were the outcome of this venture and must here be recorded: the foundation of the Improved Industrial Dwellings Company, and the erection of the first City of London municipal flats.

The Improved Industrial Dwellings Company

'On Saturday, a meeting of merchants, bankers, and others desirous of co-operating with a view to improve the homes of the working classes, was held at the Mansion House, Lord Stanley presiding. It is proposed to form an association of twenty or thirty gentlemen, protected by the Limited Liability Act, and having a capital of £25,000 to £50,000, to be invested in the erection of a series of blocks of improved dwellings . . . upon the experience which Mr Waterlow had obtained in erecting a block of buildings in a crowded part of Finsbury. Mr Waterlow said that for . . . £25,000 . . . they would be able to put up buildings for . . . 200 families [with] a net return of 6 per cent. . . . after the payment of all expenses . . .'

The Builder, XXI, 1863, p. 429. So Waterlow still regarded working-class housing as a profit-yielding proposition.

Waterlow was the first chairman of the Improved Industrial Dwellings Company. Its earliest buildings (near King's Cross) are mentioned in The Builder, *XXI, p. 736. In 1875 it housed 1,433 families in fifteen blocks, in 1906 6,000 with a population of nearly 30,000. Soon, on the example set by Waterlow, other large companies were founded to do as good business what the earlier societies had done in a humanitarian spirit. The Artizans', Labourers' and General Dwelling Company was founded in 1867. Its first estates (of small houses) were the Shaftesbury Park Estate between Lavender Hill and Eversleigh Street of 1872, etc., and the Queen's Park Estate, Harrow Road, of 1875, etc. These and many other similar firms paid; but they did not cater for the really poor. To them—this had already been recognized in 1865—no help could be brought by the capitalist.*

33 Langbourne Buildings today

Working-Class Flats are no Lucrative Investment

'The committee appointed by the Society of Arts with the view of ascertaining if anything can be done to remedy or mitigate the evils arising from the want of proper dwellings for the labouring classes . . . includes the names of Mr Akroyd . . , Mr Chadwick . . . , Mr Cole . . . , Mr G. Godwin . . . , Mr J. Stuart Mill . . . , Earl of Shaftesbury, Sir J. Kay Shuttleworth, Lord Stanley . . . , Alderman Waterlow. . . . The committee have made a report in which . . . it was shown that . . . at present the dwellings provided . . . by societies and benevolent individuals . . . in the metropolis only accommodate about 7,000 persons, and the commercial results are not so as to encourage builders and capitalists to undertake the building of dwellings for labourers as an ordinary matter of business. It appears . . . that it rarely happens that such undertakings produce a higher dividend than five per cent. . . . and . . . it can hardly be expected that dwellings will be provided in anything like sufficient numbers, until they can be made to produce such a return as will compensate a builder for investing his capital in this kind of property, attended as it is with so much more risk and trouble than houses of a superior kind.'

The Builder, XXIII, 1865, pp. 88 and 251. Mr Akroyd is the Yorkshire manufacturer who built the working-class suburb of Akroydon at Halifax. The other names have already been mentioned.

THE FIRST MUNICIPAL WORKING-CLASS FLATS

If therefore better dwellings for the poor were needed—and it was well enough known that they were—they had to be supplied by public authorities out of public funds. This, however, nobody recognized. Yet, as a pointer in the right direction, and a decidedly promising last item in this anthology, the second outcome of Waterlow's enterprise must be quoted:

'CORPORATION BUILDINGS, FARRINGDON ROAD. The necessity for providing accommodation for the large number of the poorer classes displaced by street improvements and other great public works in the City, has for some time past occupied the attention of the Corporation; but it was not until 1862 that any positive steps were taken to erect improved dwellings. At the close of that year Mr Alderman Waterlow drew the attention of the Common Council to the subject, . . . the Corporation realized its obligations, and has discharged them. A piece of freehold land in the Farringdon Road was at once appropriated, and a pile of buildings . . . containing accommodation for 168 families . . . erected

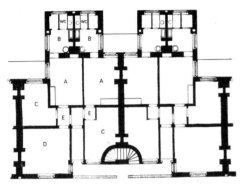

A *living room*
B *scullery with sink and boiler*
C *bedroom*
D *parlour*
E *lobby*

34, 35 Corporation Buildings, 1865: plan of four flats (compare Mark Street, Ill. 31), and frontage with shops

34–36

36 Corporation Buildings: on the top floor, crests of the City of London

31–33 at a further cost of £37,000. The buildings are similar in design to those erected in 1863 by Mr. Alderman Waterlow, in Finsbury. . . . The rents range from 4s. 6d. to 7s. 6d. per week. . . . These buildings were built from the designs, and under the superintendence, of the City Architect, Mr Horace Jones.'

The Builder, *XXIII, 1865, p. 484. Horace, later Sir Horace, Jones (1819–1887) is the architect of the Smithfield Markets and Tower Bridge.*

So here the Corporation of the City of London appeared for the first time as a house building authority. The venture was possible under the Lodging Houses Act of 1851. But such ventures remained exceptional until much later. The Metropolitan Board of Works did not start on slum clearance until 1875. And these cleared areas were handed over to the Peabody Trust, the Artizans', Labourers' and General, or similar companies for erecting new houses. The London County Council was founded in 1889. The Housing of the Working Class Act became law in 1890. This at last altered things fundamentally. The L.C.C. had fresh social ideas and fresh ideas on architectural style and domestic comfort too. It realized that nothing adequate could be achieved, unless the notion of private profit was abandoned and housing recognized as a public duty. And it also realized that flats would never be really welcome to the London workmen unless they were made much more cheerful. So the Neo-Georgian of the L.C.C.—an outcome of the style of the Shaw school—replaced the grim austerity of the earlier blocks. These had been—there is no question about that—a great improvement on the slums of Chadwick, Alton Locke and Tom-all-Alone's. But they are—this is equally undeniable— the slums of today, a little more hygienic perhaps than Bethnal Green cottages (I say perhaps, because a tenant stopped me, while I was making notes in the court of one block of c. 1860 not here illustrated, and—probably taking me for a surveyor—confided to me that she never 'got a rest from them bugs'), but far more harsh and depressing. Their blackness has made it extremely difficult for architects to this day to enlist amongst the working class any sympathy with rehousing in flats. Nor has the necessary campaign for flats been made easier by these very architects of today building blocks of ten and twenty storeys, thereby creating a new aversion among those to be re-housed, over and above the old one.

1 *'Waiting for the Queen, May 1851': the transept of the Crystal Palace, looking past the great Coalbrookdale gates*

Architectural Press, London, 1951

III
High Victorian Design

IN the most intelligent and knowledgeable description of the Crystal Palace
n.1   which we possess, Mr Morton Shand* writes: '[The building is] a precept in-
spiring as the Parthenon, an exemplar vital as the Pont du Gard, . . . as important
as Stonehenge or Ely Cathedral'. The exhibits shown inside the building on the
other hand, Miss Yvonne ffrench in her competent monograph on the Great
n.2   Exhibition* calls 'examples of the hideous and the debased . . . , of a bastardization of taste without parallel in the whole recorded history of aesthetics'. Are
these two statements true? And do they correspond to the reactions of distinguished visitors to the building and the exhibition?
n.3   If for the building we choose Ruskin as our guide, we hear this:*

'The quantity of bodily industry which the Crystal Palace expresses, is very
great. So far it is good. The quantity of thought it expresses is, I suppose, a single
and admirable thought . . . probably not a bit brighter than thousands of
thoughts which pass through [its designer's] active and intelligent brain every
hour—that it might be possible to build a greenhouse larger than ever greenhouse
was built before. This thought and some very ordinary algebra are as much as all
that glass can represent of human intellect.'

Now after Ruskin on the building, Tennyson on its contents:

> . . . lo! the giant aisles
> Rich in model and design;
> Harvest-tool and husbandry,
> Loom and wheel and enginery,
> Secrets of the sullen mine,
> Steel and gold, and coal and wine,
> Fabric rough or fairy-fine . . .
> And shapes and hues of Art divine!
> All of beauty, all of use,
n.4   > That one fair planet can produce.*

There are obviously problems in these four quotations which need some thought.
The contrast in the reaction to the architecture and the design of 1851 amongst
critics of a hundred years ago is as puzzling as that amongst critics of today.
    To understand a spirit which can express itself in the Crystal Palace as well
as in the style of the objects shown in it, it may be useful to look for a moment at
the pre-history of the Great Exhibition. Its originators were Henry Cole and
Prince Albert. Henry Cole was born in 1808, Prince Albert in 1819. At the time
of Albert's wedding with Queen Victoria, Cole was a promising young civil
servant. He worked first on the preservation and storing of public records, then

on the introduction of penny postage, then on the propaganda for unified railway gauges. He was instrumental in bringing about the establishment of docks at Grimsby, and he edited illustrated railway charts with geological and antiquarian notes. These he followed by a series of children's books illustrated by such well-chosen painters as Mulready, Horsley, Richard Redgrave and Linnell, and another series, also for children, with pictures from Holbein, Dürer, Raphael and even Giotto. He thought out a box of terracotta bricks for children and had it made by Minton's, published the first Christmas Card ever issued (designed by Maclise), and finally entered the market of art applied to industry by designing a tea-set which Minton's made and which was exhibited at the Society of Arts in 1846. Of this society he was a member and Prince Albert was the president. The set was given a prize and proved commercially successful over a long period. It was followed by a beer-mug (designed by H. J. Townshend) and other objects for everyday use. On their quality of design more will be said later. Cole produced them under the pseudonym Felix Summerly and called them Art Manufactures. Prince Albert in his presidential address to the Society of Arts in 1846 spoke of the urgent necessity to encourage 'most efficiently the application of the Fine Arts to our manufactures' in order 'to wed high art with mechanical skill'.*   n.5

Out of these ideas shared by the Prince Consort and Cole and out of an energy and tenacity also shared by the two men, the Great Exhibition was born, the first international exhibition ever held. A Royal Commission was appointed, and in due course a building committee, consisting of the architects Sir Charles Barry of the Reform Club and Bridgewater House, C. R. Cockerell of the Ashmolean Museum and the Monument on Calton Hill at Edinburgh, and Professor C. L. Donaldson, and the engineers Robert Stephenson, designer of the Conway Tubular Bridge and son of George Stephenson of The Rocket, Isambard Kingdom Brunel, designer of the Clifton and Saltash Bridges and the *Great Eastern,* and engineer to the Great Western Railway, and William Cubitt. For a long time they could not agree. Finally a compromise was accepted—a long building of brick with a central glass dome somewhat wider in diameter than that of St Peter's in Rome. It would have been costlier than had been budgeted for and would have taken a long time to erect.

This is when Joseph Paxton (1801–65) appeared on the stage. He was superintendent of the gardens of the Duke of Devonshire at Chatsworth, and by 1850 a celebrated horticultural expert and an ingenious designer of glasshouses. He challenged, first in private conversation, the soundness of the building committee's design and took it on himself to produce something better, cheaper and more practical. The fundamental idea for the Crystal Palace was first scribbled on a piece of blotting paper during a tribunal of the Midland Railway at Derby which Paxton had to attend. The scribble is now preserved at the Victoria and Albert Museum. It was converted into proper drawings in the course of a week by Paxton's Chatsworth staff and then presented. The building committee was of course unwilling to scrap its own solution in favour of that of an outsider, but Paxton forced its hand by allowing the publication of his project in the *Illustrated London News.* It appeared on July 6, 1850, and its boldness and novelty captured popular opinion at once. *Punch* christened it the Crystal Palace, and it was accepted on July 15.

It was a triumph of logical construction, wholly independent of any architectural traditions. The two governing problems were fearlessly faced and solved without compromise. How can the best lighting be obtained for an exhibition building? And how can a building, 1,848 feet long by 408 feet wide, be constructed most speedily? The answer was complete reliance on iron and glass as building materials, and on standardization of parts. The whole plan of the building was worked out on a twenty-four-foot grid. The parts, according to a lecture which Paxton himself delivered at Bakewell near Chatsworth in the winter of 1850–51, were to be 6,024 columns all 15 feet long, 3,000 gallery bearers, 1,245 wrought-iron girders, 45 miles of standard length sash-bars and 1,073,760 square feet of glass. With these parts the putting together should work as with 'a perfect

2 Lithograph of the Crystal Palace in Hyde Park, in 1851

n.6 piece of machinery'.* Only by means of this completely new principle of pre-fabrication was the erection of the building possible, and its aesthetic effect was consequently one of uniformity, but of a uniformity on a scale raising it to monumentality. Moreover, Paxton—being a gardener—had provided light relief of the most imaginative kind. Two full-grown elm trees of Hyde Park were left standing inside the building, and the contrast between their foliage and the rigid grid of Paxton's iron framework greatly helped the visual success of the interior. The building was indeed, as Thackeray said in his Ode on the Opening:

> A palace as for fairy prince,
> A rare pavilion, such as man
> Saw never since mankind began,
> And built and glazed.

And it must be remembered while inspecting the exhibits that England in 1851 possessed the ingenuity of such a novel design and the courage to vote for its execution.

1   The opening took place on May 1. Queen Victoria who, no one can deny, was a pious as well as a conscientious young woman, wrote of it that, standing in the middle of the building, she was 'filled with devotion, more so than by any
n.7 service I have ever heard'.* This is a remarkable reaction, and equally remarkable are the words used by Prince Albert in his speech at the Lord Mayor's Banquet given in 1850 to win the City over to the idea of the exhibition. They have been quoted more than once before, but they are indeed a master key to the state of mind of progressive man in mid-nineteenth century England.

    'Nobody who has paid any attention to the peculiar features of the present era, will doubt for a moment that we are living at a period of most wonderful

3 A contemporary photograph of the west end of the Crystal Palace

transition, which tends rapidly to accomplish that great end, to which, indeed, all history points—the realization of the unity of mankind . . . The distances which separate the different nations and parts of the globe are rapidly vanishing before the achievements of modern invention, and we can traverse them with incredible ease . . . Thought is communicated with the rapidity and even the power of lightning. On the other hand, the great principle of division of labour, which may be called the moving power of civilization, is being extended to all branches of science, industry, and art. Whilst formerly the greatest mental energies strove at universal knowledge, and that knowledge was confined to the few, now they are directed on specialities . . . but the knowledge acquired becomes at once the property of the community at large. The products of all quarters of the globe are placed at our disposal, and we have only to choose which is the best and the cheapest for our purposes, and the powers of production are intrusted to the stimulus of competition and capital. So man is approaching a more complete fulfilment of what great and sacred mission he has to perform in this world . . . I confidently hope that the first impression which the view of this vast collection will produce upon the spectator will be that of deep thankfulness to the Almighty for the blessings He has bestowed upon us already here below.'*   n.8

Competition and capital; man's sacred mission; sub-division of labour as the moving power of civilization; the Almighty; what is best and cheapest—it is a curious assembly of conceptions, utterly impossible in such a form a hundred or indeed only twenty-five years later. That unquestioning optimism, that yet unarrested drive, that naïvety in overlooking bleak problems, belong wholly to 1850. Macaulay wrote of 1851 that it would be 'long remembered as a singularly happy year of peace, plenty, good feeling, innocent pleasure, and national glory',* and Cole began his Introduction to the Official Catalogue by saying that   n.9
the exhibition was only made possible by 'the perfect security for property, the commercial freedom, and the facility of transport which England pre-eminently

n.10 possesses', and ended, like Albert, with his 'deep thankfulness to the Almighty for the blessings which He has bestowed upon us already here below'.* G. M. Young in his *Victorian England* quotes Newman in his *Apologia* writing: 'Virtue is the child of knowledge, vice of ignorance: therefore education, periodical literature, railroad travelling, sanitation and the arts of life . . . serve to make a population moral and happy'. Mr Young also quotes the prospectus of the *Rochdale Pioneers* (1844): 'The objects of this society are the moral and intellectual advancement of its members. It provides them with groceries, butcher's meat, drapery goods, clothes and clogs'.

Such was the spirit that conceived the Exhibition and carried it through triumphantly. Its success was enormous. More than six million visitors came, £186,000 remained as net profit at the end. Victoria herself after the opening attended on May 3, 7, 12, 14, 16, 17, 19, 20, 21, 22, 27, 29, 30; June 2, 7, 16, 20, 21, 24, 26, 28; July 2, 5, 9, 11, 15, 16, 17, 18 (after which the Royal Family went to Balmoral), and the Duke of Wellington speaks of his daily visit.

The explanation of these remarkable attendances is a universal eagerness to learn, and especially to learn factual things, the intensity of which one can hardly conceive any longer today. Here is one example of it. When Prince Albert went to open the new Grimsby Docks, Cole arranged some entertainment for him in his special train. This is what it was: John Britton's *Lincoln Cathedral,* John Britton's *Peterborough Cathedral,* a plan of Lincoln, a plan of Roman Lincoln, Sidney on Agriculture and Railways, a portfolio of Dürer woodcuts and a case of geological specimens and fossils. With all due respect to the present Royal family one cannot but assume that the choice in 1951 would have been different.

Thirst for information, faith in commerce and industry, inventiveness and technical daring, energy and tenacity, and a tendency to mix up religion with visible success—all these qualities have to be remembered as one embarks on a conducted tour of some of the exhibits of 1851.

4 A statuette of Prince Albert crowns a vase exhibited by Elkington's. The vase is four feet tall and not of silver as it would at first appear, but electro-plated. It has a name: *The Triumph of Science,* and was designed and modelled by William Beattie. The statuettes against the sides are Newton standing for Astronomy, Bacon standing for Philosophy, Shakespeare standing for Poetry and—this is where the nineteenth century speaks—James Watt standing for Mechanics. The reliefs between the statuettes display 'practical operations of Science and Art'. The style is to our surprise called by the catalogue Elizabethan. To us it looks rather Dixhuitième if anything. This bastardization of period styles is, as we shall see, as characteristic of 1851 as the replacement of silver by electro-plating, a process discovered only in 1836 and commercialized by Elkington's in 1840, and as the elevation of mechanics and applied science to the level of philosophy and the fine arts.

4 'The Triumph of Science and the Industrial Arts', a vase by Elkington's

The Machinery Court was indeed the grandest spectacle inside the Crystal   7
Palace. Machines of many kinds could here be seen and noisily heard in motion.
Of some of them people nowadays do not usually realize that they existed as
early as 1851. McCormick's reaping machine for instance was shown in the   5
section of the United States, an invention of 1831 which the *Journal of the Royal
Agricultural Society* called 'the most important addition to farming machinery
since the threshing machine took the place of the flail'. Several gas cookers were
amongst British inventions, the Phoenix Foundry at Wakefield showed 'An
apparatus for supplying rooms and buildings with pure warm air', and electric
clocks were displayed prominently at the main entrances to the buildings.*   n.11

As for the appearance of some of the machines, the illustrations in the Cata-

5   *McCormick's reaping machine*

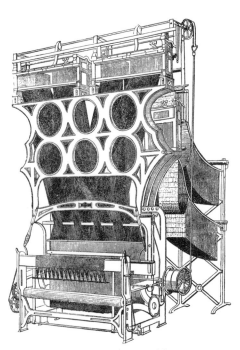

6   *Taylor and Son's jacquard loom*

logue and the *Illustrated London News* show us that a steam engine could still in
1851 masquerade in an early nineteenth-century Empire style. At that time
Greek Doric columns and a frieze with triglyphs and metopes were favoured.*   n.12
At the exhibition B. Hick & Son of Bolton showed an engine driving cotton
machinery which was in the Egyptian style, complete with scarab. This was, as   9
far as taste goes, a conservative design. More up-to-date was Pope's oscillating
engine, clothed in iron Gothic tracery. But Taylor & Son's jacquard loom is   8, 6
neither antique nor Gothic but of an undisguised Victorian appearance, fat and
bulging. The effect is powerful and more truly illustrative of the spirit of mid-
nineteenth century industry than prettier pieces. De la Rue's much admired
envelope machine which in its various motions (as the *Illustrated London News*   10
said) 'closely followed several actual movements of the human form divine' and
thereby folded and gummed sixty envelopes a minute looks at first in the en-
graving specially pretty. But the attendants are children, and this grim aspect of
the Early Victorian factory should not be forgotten over Prince Albert's en-
thusiastic prophecies of the approaching fulfilment of man's sacred mission. It
evidently did not occur to him, charitable and conscientious as he was, that the
reduction of child labour in textile factories to ten hours a day as obtained by the
Fielden Act of 1847 and the abolition of the employment of children under ten
in the mines by the Shaftesbury Act of 1842 were perhaps not quite enough. Boy
chimney-sweeps indeed were still tolerated as late as the 1870s.

While this sinister side of the age appears only as a dark shadow behind the
exhibits, another had been squarely faced by Prince Albert, and the result of his
reforming efforts were shown. Slum conditions of the forties, as described in
Chadwick's *Report on the Sanitary Conditions of the Labouring Classes,* make just as
gruesome reading as reports on child labour.

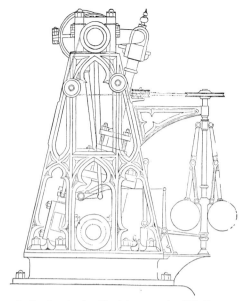

8 *Engine in the Gothic taste, by W. Pope and Son*

9 *Engine in the Egyptian taste, by B. Hick and Son*

7 *The Machinery Court*

10 *De la Rue's envelope machine*

Significant quotations have been collected in one of the preceding essays. By 1851 some of the new cottages and blocks of tenements had been completed. Prince Albert, as we have seen, commissioned Henry Roberts to build a model house for the exhibition. It looked a cottage, but it could be multiplied horizontally as well as vertically into a block of flats of substantial dimensions. It heralded the later estates of the Improved Industrial Dwellings Company and the Peabody Trust, and they all·strike us today as exceedingly grim, the reason being that in 1851 the dwelling of the operative was not yet seen in conjunction with his life nor his life in conjunction with the conditions under which he worked. It is true that Carlyle had preached in 1843 that 'we have profoundly forgotten everywhere that cash-payment is not the sole relation of human beings' and that 'all work, even cotton spinning is noble',* but he had not told his listeners how a boy behind an envelope machine at sixty a minute can be made to feel that nobility. And it is also true that Ruskin two years before the exhibition had gone further and declared that 'the right question to ask regarding all ornament is simply this: was it done with enjoyment, was the carver happy while he did it'.* Evidently the man behind a carving machine is less happy than the craftsman, and so Ruskin condemns all machine-made ornament as Pugin had done before him. Pugin was not concerned however with the social faults of the machine replacing handwork, but with the untruth of the results, and Ruskin agreed in this. He calls it 'operative deceit.*

Now these views of Pugin and Ruskin were in complete opposition to those represented by innumerable examples shown in the Crystal Palace, and the arguments of the exhibitor of such a work of machine art as for instance the church screen machine-carved by Jordan's Patent Mechanism are worth some consideration. Our accepted argument today is, and has been ever since Ruskin and Morris: ornament is valuable only in so far as it represents the imagination of the human mind and the skill of the human hand. To imitate it mechanically is too easy a substitute. 'A surfeit of means' is a danger to design. This last passage comes from a pamphlet commenting on the exhibition from which more will be

p.32,2

11

n.13

n.14

n.15

12

11 Prince Albert's model house, designed by Henry Roberts

12 *Church screen machine-carved by the Patent Wood Carving Company*

quoted later. Its author was Gottfried Semper (1803–79) the best German architect of the mid-nineteenth century, a believer in the nobility of the Italian Renaissance and an eminently intelligent theorist of design. His book *Der Stil* in two volumes dealing with basic principles of decorative art is a classic. He was at the time of the Exhibition in London, as a refugee of the 1848 revolution, and was evidently a man in the confidence of Prince Albert. His *Wissenschaft, Industrie und Kunst* * from which the quotation above is taken was written in November 1851 'in consequence of a private request'. It may well be that this request was Albert's. Semper was fully aware of the difficulties in keeping up standards of design at a time when the accepted relations between materials, processes of production and design were no longer valid. Capitalism, he wrote (he calls it Speculation), 'thanks to means borrowed from science, achieves without effort the most difficult and laborious; the hardest porphyry and granite can be cut like chalk, and polished like wax, ivory can be softened and pressed into moulds, metal is no longer cast or chased but by natural forces unknown until recently deposited galvanoplastically, . . . the machine sews, knits, embroiders, carves, paints and . . . puts to shame all human skill'. Semper is ready to admit that these achievements will at some future date be used 'to the benefit and honour of society', but for the time being they have only led to 'confusions'. *

But the many admirers of the machine-carved screen would not have admitted that. They would have argued something like this: It may be very difficult to carve a screen by hand and it might take three years to do. What a triumph of the human mind is it then to invent machinery which can do the same work in one hundredth of the time and in addition do it more exactly. *

This pride in ingeniousness which took the place of aesthetic appreciation appeared in many of the exhibits of 1851. There are first of all the cases of imitation of one material in another. 'Specimens of grained woods, and veined marble, porphyry, agate, and madrepores, figured on the back of plate, crown

n.16

n.17

n.18

or steel glass' (Class 24, No. 24), 'Slabs of glass to imitate various kinds of marble' (Class 26, No. 2), 'Slab of artificial marble of baked and polished clay' (Class 26, No. 9), 'Specimens of wood painted in imitation of mahogany, maple and oak' (Class 26, No. 109), 'Plain deal lobby-table, painted in imitation of various marbles' (Class 26, No. 120), and so on. Ruskin of course branded this also amongst his deceits: 'the painting of surfaces to represent some other material than that of which they actually consist (as in the marbling of wood)'.*   n.19

Similar but more interesting is the reproduction of things familiar in one material by means of another newly developed or unusual one. Of iron bed-steads for instance the special volume on the Exhibition published by the *Art Journal* says that they have become general only 'within the last five years', owing to their 'lightness and elegance'. The two specimens illustrated here seem   13, 14 to fall neatly into these two categories, elegance being represented by the unmis-takable bulginess of 1851. The period style behind it is this time the French Rococo. Brass was also used for bedsteads such as the one shown by the re-   16 nowned firm of R. W. Winfield at Birmingham, of which the *Art Journal* said that its style is Renaissance and that 'it is one of the best objects of its kind ever brought before our notice'. There was even brass drawing-room furniture. Winfields exhibited for instance a brass rocking-chair, a brass armchair and brass tables (Class 22, No. 373).

It may be of special interest to our time to be reminded that tubular metal furniture existed already a hundred years ago. Messrs Kitschelt of Vienna for instance showed a table and some fauteuils 'of hollow wrought-iron tubes'. The   15 pieces are rightly called in the caption 'ornamental furniture', and their style can once again serve as an example of what the mid-nineteenth century demanded from its furnishings. All curves are eminently generous, all outlines broken or blurred, and a general tendency to top-heaviness is essential to the authentic effect. We shall find all these qualities frequently in the following pages and have to try and interpret them at a later stage.

Meanwhile there was also zinc. Kitschelt's had a table on show 'cast in zinc', and Professor Kiss's celebrated Amazon was exhibited cast in this novel material. A zinc industry had, it is true, existed in England since before the middle of the eighteenth century, but the discovery of hollow casting in zinc had only been made in 1833.

13, 14 (above) Cowley and James's patent iron bedstead; (below) Tomkin's ornamental iron bedstead

15 Furniture of hollow iron tubing, by Kitschelt of Vienna

16 R.W. Winfield's brass fourposter bed, in the Renaissance style

Papier mâché was another material not new in itself to the nineteenth century, but owing to recent new patents suddenly made available to the furnishing trades. Papier mâché is pressed and moulded paper pulp. It had been used for trays, trinket boxes and so on in Europe since the middle of the eighteenth century, but it was through C. F. Bielefeld's and others' application to interior decoration that the exhibitors at the Crystal Palace could make such proud uses of it. Not only does it appear in such small things as a curtain rod or a
18 bracket—the material here is called *carton pierre,* and the maker was Paul Gropius
n.20 of Berlin, first cousin of Walter Gropius's grandfather*—but there were even

complete chairs of papier mâché.* We should be careful not to make the applica- n.21
tion of this particular material to this particular use a source of merriment. It is
exactly on the same plane as our use for furniture of plastics. The chair illustrated 17
is a keypiece for the understanding of the spirit of 1851, in its appearance as well
as in the generous admittance of figure sculpture and especially its name. It is
called in the catalogue *The Daydreamer*, and its success was no doubt largely
determined by this title—a title good enough for a Royal Academy picture.
More about this will be said later.

An even larger piece of furniture, a whole sideboard in a wild mixture of 19
Elizabethan and naturalistic ingredients, consisted entirely of gutta-percha, a
material extracted from the sap of a Malayan tree and for the first time presented
to the learned societies of Paris and London in 1842 and 1843. So here again,
although the manufacturers' optimism regarding the range of its application has
proved wrong, the exhibition showed enterprise and daring. A Sou'wester of
gutta-percha could also be seen, a sculptural group called *Deer and Hounds,* printing type, a brass chaiselongue with elastic gutta-percha backing, a gutta-percha
lifeboat and so on. The *Illustrated London News* however said it could discover
cracks and discoloration in the sideboard.* n. 22

It is probable that the Gutta Percha Company itself did not believe in the
prospects of its material for such furniture as sideboards, but any manufacturer in
1851 could be sure of attention and enthusiasm if his exhibits had novelty and
displayed cuteness. In this respect the range of the articles on show reached from
the most intelligent and functionally sound to the most futile. In the American
section (No. 229) was an 'Air exhausted Coffin, intended to preserve the dead
from putrefaction'—a remarkably early piece of care for the loved ones. R. W.
Laurie of Glasgow showed a life-preserving portmanteau to reduce the hazards 20
of the sea. A much more elaborate contraption for the same purpose came from
Taylor & Sons of Great Dover Street, in South London: 'Furniture for a steamship on a new and condensed form consisting of a self-acting washstand' on the 21
right, a water closet on the left, and in the middle a 'walnut-wood couch, forming a bed when required, stuffed with the exhibitors' patent cork fibre, to make
it buoyant when placed in the water. Each part, being made portable, is immediately convertible into a floating life preserver; and the whole forms a floating
surface of 50 feet, or life-raft, in the case of danger at sea.' Even more manifold

17 'The Daydreamer', easy chair of
papier mâché

18 Articles of 'carton pierre'
by Paul Gropius of Berlin

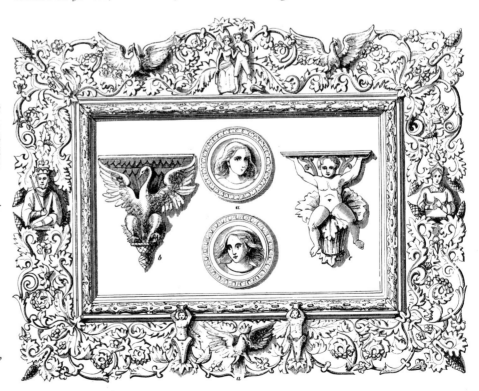

19 *Sideboard by the Gutta Percha Company*

20 *Life-preserving portmanteau*

21 *Steamship furniture convertible into a raft*

are the components of Messrs. Isaacs & Campbell's 'Patent portable barrack, college, camp and cabin furniture containing a chest of drawers, a wash-hand-stand, dressing-table and glass, iron bedstead, with curtains and bedding, reclining chair, towel-horse, writing and dressing-case, and having sufficient room in the drawers to contain a complete military outfit—the cases at the same time forming a wardrobe' (Class 26, No. 241). Here clearly is the anticipation of such modern things as packable furniture, and clearly also the progeny of English furnishing gadgets worked out in the early years of the Industrial Revolution.

Professor Giedion* has illustrated a Gentleman's Dressing Stand from Sheraton's *Cabinet-Maker's Book of Prices* of 1788 containing the most ingenious flaps and drawers. Ingeniousness and unconcern with conventions and traditions had indeed been typical of British industry during the whole century preceding the exhibition, ingeniousness in the invention of the steam engine, the locomotive, the various spinning and weaving machines and so on, unconcern with the accepted in such facts as Wilkinson, the great Staffordshire iron-master, making a pulpit of cast iron for a church and an iron coffin for himself, Coade & Sealy's using their patent artificial cast stone for decorative reliefs, keystone heads and even rusticated blocks for door and window surrounds, or Wedgwood's casting fireplaces of earthenware and so on. *n.23*

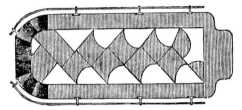

22 J.A. Franklinski's patent omnibus

The exhibition in this respect only continued a line of undaunted progressiveness for which Britain at the time was still famous, but which has since become connected chiefly with the United States and Germany. Today indeed Britain is regarded as a bulwark of conservatism and solid tradition, a complete *volte face* of distressing effect on industrial prosperity. The change began as early as the seventies, when German and American competition was first felt as a nuisance.

The buoyancy and showiness of so much at the Crystal Palace thus marks the final flourish of a century of greatest commercial expansion. Hence the amplitude and lavishness of the style, and hence the indiscriminate faith in novelty and tricky gadgets. One could for instance admire Rogers & Dean's 'Ottoman Coal Sarcophagus, answering the purpose of an ottoman and coal receptacle' (Class 26, No. 264), 'an omnibus divided into compartments, by which the annoyances so frequently complained of in the common vehicles will be prevented' (Class 5, No. 816)—Monsieur J. A. Franklinski's idea was to avoid the sight by any one passenger of any other—'a patent double grand piano, upon which four performers at a time can execute compositions arranged for eight hands and two pianos' (U.S. No. 90), 'Lady's parasol driving whip' (Class 29, No. 135), an 'Alarm bedstead, causing a person to arise at any given hour' (Class 22, No. 56), and a 'Cricket catapulta, for propelling the ball in the absence of a first-rate bowler' (Class 29, No. 199). *22* *24*

23 F.W. Harvey's collapsible easel

But the same mechanical cunning which succeeded in producing such absurdities appeared in many more sensible ways. The collapsible easel for instance which Mr Frederick Harvey of 1, Oriel Street, Oxford, exhibited is strong and light, the *Art Journal* tells us, slides into a mackintosh case and contains 'every requisite, on no limited scale, for both oil and water-colour painting'. Jackson's Annunciator, or bell-telegraph, an American exhibit, 'does away with the array of bells now in use' (and who has not seen them in Victorian basements?) 'substituting in their place a compact piece of furniture, that can be fixed to the wall. Its chief excellence consists in its continuing to indicate the number of the room whence the call was made, until the servant has answered it'. (U.S. No. 222). *23*

Then there was quite a range of intelligently devised furniture for invalids, a bedstead 'capable of being converted into an arm-chair, with wash-stand, table and reading-desk' (Class 26, No. 2A), a couch on which the patient 'can be raised from a horizontal to a sitting position without being disturbed' (Class 26, No. 211) and numerous chairs designed on the principle re-invented for the able-bodied of a more informal age by Marcel Breuer (Isokon chair) and Le Corbusier. Examples are J. M. & F. Brown's 'Patented suspensory chair, forming a couch or camp-bed and adapting itself to every movement of the body; fitting closely to *25*

24 Double-ended grand piano for four performers, by J. Pirsson of New York

the back and loins, and giving great support and rest to invalids' (Class 26, No. 15), William Ryan's 'Reclining Chairs . . . constructed so that the degree of inclination is regulated with facility by the weight of the body' (U.S. No. 193), and Tunstall & William's 'Self-acting invalid chair enabling the invalid to alter the recumbent position with facility' (Class 5, No. 1000). Some of these chairs and couches—as the collapsible easel—are frankly utilitarian, others tried to apply ornaments, and even in a case such as Jackson's Annunciator we are told that 'it is ornamental', although no illustration tells us how. The exhibits of the American Chair Company are a specially enlightening case of how the technically adventurous was expressed in artistic terms. The bloated shape and the exuberant and useless excrescence at the top are familiar from previous illustrations. They are here however applied to a chair 'with patent centripetal springs and railroad-car seats . . . capable of almost universal movement'.* The frame of the chair, needless to say, is of iron. It curves freely wherever possible.

26

n.24

26 Swivelling iron chair by the American Chair Co.

25 Minter's invalid couch

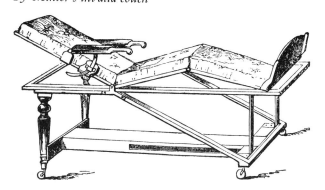

A universal replacement of the straight line by the curve is one of the chief characteristics of mid-Victorian design. As against other styles favouring curves, the Victorian curve is generous, full or, as has been said more than once before, bulgy. It represents, and appealed to, a prospering, well-fed, self-confident class. A peculiar top-heaviness often to be met is only a special case of this delight in abundant protuberances. Another hallmark of 1850 is equally telling. There must be decoration in the flat or in thick relief all over all available surfaces. This obviously enhances the effect of wealth. Critics of Victorian design have not always recognized these basic qualities, deceived sometimes by dislike, sometimes more recently by a nostalgia in revolt against the austerity of twentieth-century shapes and surfaces, and sometimes by the fact that the mid-Victorian style rarely appears without a historical costume. One is so used to defining Victorian architecture and design in terms of what style of the past it imitated that not enough attention is generally given to the fact how very rarely the real date of a piece of 1850 is not written all over its period disguise. It is known that the sources of inspiration used by Victorian designers grew in a certain order. First, still in the eighteenth century, the Gothic and Greek were added to the Roman style, then some occasional Egyptian, Hindoo and so on. By 1830 the Italian Renaissance and the Elizabethan and Jacobean styles re-appeared, and occasionally even a Neo-Louis Quinze for specially festive occasions. At the time of the Great Exhibition the styles available had become unlimited. Richard Brown's *Domestic Architecture* of 1841* lists and illustrates everything from Cottage Orné and Swiss Cottage to Norman, Lancastrian, Tudor, Stuart, Anglo-Grecian, Grecian, Pompeiian, Florentine, Venetian, Anglo-Italian, French, Persian, Moorish-Spanish and Chinese. Only Gothic is left out, because it 'exclusively belongs to sacred architecture and not to domestic'. n.25

This limitation was accepted by men more competent and intelligent than Mr Brown. It involved condemnation of much in the Mediaeval Court at the Exhibition which had been arranged by Pugin and was filled largely with objects designed by him and made by his friends John Hardman of Birmingham (for metalwork), George Myers of Lambeth (for stone and wood carving), Herbert Minton (for tiles) and John G. Crace, the distinguished interior decorator of 14 Wigmore Street, for furniture.* It was the only part of the Exhibition which appeared aesthetically as a unity. None of the wild mixture of styles was admitted here which crowded the Crystal Palace everywhere else. According to Pugin there could be only one style, as there could be only one faith. We have so far met Pugin only as a theorist condemning shams, we shall meet him again later because of the remarkable functionalist aspects of his theory. But this theory was firmly if oddly rooted in his conviction that Christian architecture could only be 29

30, 31

27, 28
n.26

27, 28 Cabinet and bookcase designed by A.W.N. Pugin and made by J.G. Crace

29 The Mediaeval Court

Pointed Architecture and that all other styles were pagan and therefore bad, morally as well as aesthetically.

The religious foundation of Pugin's work estranged many from him, even if few were so raving-mad in their detestation as Ruskin. Just as Pugin himself was unable to separate religion from art, so was Ruskin, and one feels that in the objections of Ralph Nicholas Wornum for instance, a friend of Ruskin, Lecturer on Art at the Government School of Design and Keeper of the National Gallery (1812–77),* whose paper on *The Exhibition as a Lesson in Taste* we shall come across more often,* there are the same protestant undertones as in Ruskin. Wornum called the Gothic style 'fatiguing', 'dead and bygone' and 'only a cowl to smother all independent thought'. *

Semper on the other hand said: 'Amongst genuinely English products of industrial art the first place is due to the achievements of Mr Pugin, well-known also abroad, and some artists belonging to the same trend'. Semper was here in agreement with two others among the most intelligent commentators on the Exhibition, Richard Redgrave (1804–88) and Matthew Digby Wyatt (1820–77).

n.27
n.28
n.29

Redgrave later became Superintendent of the Government School of Design and Keeper of the King's Pictures, Wyatt the first Slade Professor at Cambridge.* n.30 Wyatt in his lavish folio publication of selected exhibits called *The Industrial Arts of the Nineteenth Century** said that 'great praise is due' to a tile and iron stove by n.31 Pugin and Hardman, and that a carpet by Pugin and Crace displays 'in a remarkable degree the admirable taste and feeling of the highly-gifted artist', and Redgrave, in his *Supplementary Report on Design* prepared officially, characterizes a candlestick by Pugin and Hardman as 'honest, useful, characteristic' and sums up the whole achievement of the Mediaeval Court as follows: 'Some may object to the exclusiveness of the style . . . but for just principles of decoration, for beautiful details, for correct use of materials, and for excellent workmanship, the general collection is unique'.* n.32

Perhaps all these qualities could only be achieved in the mid-nineteenth century, if a designer renounced the temptations of variety and originality and self-effacingly concentrated on one style and its imitation. Pugin said in 1841: 'If we view pointed architecture in its true light as Christian art, as the faith is perfect, so are the principles on which it is founded. We may indeed improve in mechanical contrivances to expedite its execution, . . . but we can never successfully deviate one tittle from the spirit and principles of pointed architecture. We must rest content to follow, not to lead'.* n.33

30 *Church plate designed by Pugin and made by Hardman's*

31 *Chalice designed by Pugin (visible at the left in Ill.30, above)*

32 Gothic clock by G.G. Adams

In this also Ruskin only continued what had been established by Pugin, though he gave it a personal twist. In the *Seven Lamps of Architecture,* that is in 1849, he pleaded for the universal acceptance of one style as the only remedy against the chaotic condition of contemporary architecture, and added that this universally accepted style should not be new. 'The forms of architecture already known to us are good enough for us', he said in his irritable way. What is necessary is that the accepted style should be 'Augustan' in its authority. And as the vulgarization of Greek architecture is excluded as insane, Tudor as 'a degradation', early styles as 'infantile or barbarous', in the end the choice according to Ruskin lies between Pisan Romanesque, the Early Gothic of the Western Italian Republics, the Venetian Gothic in its purest development, and the English earliest Decorated.* Ruskin's teaching began to have its effect a few years after the n.34 exhibition. Deane & Woodward built in Venetian Gothic the Library of Trinity College, Dublin, and then the Oxford Museum, and in London the Crown Life Assurance in New Bridge Street and a private house in Upper Phillimore Gardens, Kensington; and George Gilbert Scott in his *Remarks on Domestic Architecture* of 1858 quotes Ruskin as well as Pugin.

But in 1851 correct Gothic was still reserved for sacred purposes and a wilder, more ignorant brand pervaded the domestic market. The Gothic Timepiece in imitation oak designed and modelled by G. G. Adams shows clearly in 32 its restless outline, its topheaviness and its outward-bulging corners what date it really belongs to, and the Gothic fireplace designed by H. Duesbury, the 35 architect of the Italianate Corn Exchange at Newark, is essentially the same as the Rococo fireplace exhibited by the same Sheffield firm—the same broad semi- 36 circular opening, the same lapping forward into the room with scrolls or lambrequins, and the same undulations, whether in tracery or foliage and rocaille.

Fireplaces altogether are specially eloquent in their blown-up curves. To give the whole centre—coal receptacle and fireback—a circular outline appealed 33 to the mid-Victorians for novelty as well as rotundity. In other fireplaces large

33 Fireplace by the Coalbrookdale Company, with a circular reflecting back

34 Renaissance fireplace by Alfred Stevens, for Hoole's of Sheffield

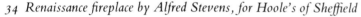

figure-sculpture provides the desired thick relief. Thus John Thomas (1813–62),
an architect-sculptor much favoured by the Royal Family—he began as a stone-
carver under Barry at King Edward's School, Birmingham, was later in charge
of the sculptural decorations of the Houses of Parliament, designed two important mansions,* took to 'ideal sculpture' only in 1844 and towards the end of his
life built and decorated the Dairy at Frogmore (with an interior all of Minton
tiles)*—John Thomas gave two semi-reclining figures from Chaucer and
Chaucer's head in a medallion to his fireplace, and the *Illustrated London News*
called the result 'very classical'. No wonder that Alfred Stevens's much more
truly classical, that is much more purely Renaissance, designs for fireplaces and
stoves for Hoole's of Sheffield were not much noticed, except by the most
discriminating critics.*

The case of Stevens is of special interest. He was one of the rare representatives of the fine arts who were tempted by the social and aesthetic implications of
design. He left London and lived at Sheffield from 1850 to 1852. Mr Hoole paid
him at a rate of £20 a month and allowed him in addition to work for firms in
other trades.* His name does not appear in the catalogue nor in the special volume of the *Art Journal*. Altogether few names turn up; manufacturers evidently
were not keener to disclose names of designers to the general public than they are
now.* The most widely employed and successful artist working for industry
was, it seems, the sculptor John Bell, ('Mr Bell has contributed more to ornamental manufacture in the plastic line, than perhaps any other artist of the day',
wrote the *Illustrated London News*), but his work was more sculpture on a small
scale than design proper. Maclise and Richard Redgrave appear occasionally.*
Art students from the Government Schools of Design were asked for designs by
some textile manufacturers.* Architects apart from Pugin, Matthew Digby
Wyatt and also Owen Jones (to whom we shall have to return later) did hardly
anything, and full-time free-lance designers seem only very infrequently to have

n.35
n.36
37
34
n.37
n.38
n.39
n.40
n.41

35, 36 Rococo and Gothic fire-grates by Stuart & Smith of Sheffield

37 Chaucer fireplace by John Thomas

38 Fire-grate by Owen Jones

*39-41 Caddy-spoons by W. Harry
Rogers, 'in the style of the 16th
century'*

achieved some fame. Two of these are Ludwig Grüner who worked for instance
for Elkington's, but also designed a carpet for Windsor Castle and the chandelier
for Prince Albert's Casino in the garden of Buckingham Palace on which more
will be said later,* and W. Harry Rogers, son of the woodcarver W. G. Rogers,   n.42
who designed a cradle in a surprisingly pure Italian Renaissance style which Her   42
Majesty the Queen exhibited, a State Pony Bridle belonging to Prince Albert,
the binding of Nisbet's Ornamental Bible, a chatelaine, embroidery, pipes, keys,
encaustic tiles, book clasps and also the head and tail-pieces for the *Art Journal*   *131*
volume on the exhibition.* One would like to know more about him.* The   n.43,
spoons by him illustrated in the *Art Journal* volume are uncommonly revolting.   *39–41*
They exhibit the swollen corpulence of the mid-century at its most self-satisfied.
Yet they were praised for 'the intimate knowledge of the Italian style of the
sixteenth century' which they are supposed to display, and if that is possible, one
need not be surprised to find Cornelius's chandelier described as combining 'the   *43*
Louis Quatorze and the Renaissance'.

This whole terminology seems to us so vague and arbitrary that it calls for
some explanation. Was the age still so ignorant of the accurate forms going with
particular styles? Or what are we to understand for instance by Renaissance as
mentioned in the catalogue? In this confusion the prize essay, which was written
for the hundred guineas competition of the *Art Journal* and published as an
appendix to its volume on the exhibition, proves of great help. It is the essay by
Ralph Nicholas Wornum to which reference has already been made. Its title is
The Exhibition as a Lesson in Taste, and it consists of three parts, general considerations of the value of ornament, a consideration of the exhibits so far as they
are ornamented and, preceding this, a survey of the historical styles. This,
Wornum must have felt, was indispensable as an introduction to works which,
after all, were without exception based on the past. Wornum distinguishes nine
styles, three antique, three mediaeval, and three modern. The antique styles are
Egyptian, Greek and Roman, the mediaeval Byzantine, Saracenic and Gothic
(Lombard and Norman are to him only varieties of Byzantine, and the three
together are called Romanesque), and the modern Renaissance, Cinquecento
and Louis Quatorze.

It is obviously in these modern styles that his system comes to grief. He
explains 'that the Renaissance begins with the Conquest of Constantinople in
1204', but has nothing to say on the Ducento in Italy. The Trecento is his first
variety of the Renaissance (admitted perhaps because of Ruskin). It is 'chiefly a
mixture of Venetian and Siculo-Norman ornament, the Venetian being purely
Byzantine in its origin'—a piece of remarkable nonsense. There follows the
Quattrocento as the second variety. 'It was in this period', he says, 'that men
gradually introduced all those peculiar arbitrary forms, pierced and scrolled

*42 Boxwood cradle designed by W. Harry
Rogers for Queen Victoria*

43 Gas chandelier by Cornelius & Baker of Philadelphia

shields, or cartouches, and tracery, or strap-work, which eventually became the most characteristic details of the styles of the Renaissance, except during the short period of the prevalence of the Cinquecento in the earlier half of the sixteenth century, when they were very generally discarded, as was every element not found in ancient examples'. So Cinquecento Wornum calls the pure High Renaissance; what then does he call Renaissance? He says that a design 'designated . . . by the vague term Renaissance' may contain 'the classical orders and ornaments combined with conventional Byzantine scroll-work, Moorish tracery and interlacings [he probably means arabesques], scrolled shields, fiddle-shapes, and strap-work, and natural imitations of animal of vegetable forms of every description'. 'This peculiar style', he continues, 'flourished in the sixteenth century, simultaneously with the more definite Cinquecento, which was in fact an attempt at purification of style by the great artists of that period . . . The Cinquecento, therefore, . . . does not imply merely sixteenth century Art, but a particular art of the sixteenth century. The term Renaissance is sufficiently definite for the mixed style, more especially as this style belongs to several ages and countries, though more particularly to France . . . There are accordingly four Italian styles of the revival—the Trecento, the Quattrocento, the pure

44 Papier mâché panel by Jackson & Sons

Cinquecento, and the mixed Cinquecento or Renaissance; there is one French style of the period—the Renaissance, the same as the mixed Cinquecento of Italy, and there is one English style—the Elizabethan, which is the English Renaissance'. Wornum regards the pure Cinquecento as the culmination of ornamental art requiring for its practice 'a faultless taste', grants the Renaissance also 'well understood detail' but blames it for 'a prevalence of the bizarre and a love of profusion of parts' but has little to praise in the Louis Quatorze. This has nothing but 'a gorgeous effect as a whole'; it disregards detail and in its 'final debasement, the Rococo' also disregards symmetry. The Louis Quinze is to him only a variety of the Louis Quatorze.

Wornum's terminology from the point of view of today is certainly not very helpful. It was however more or less the accepted terminology at the time and is therefore of interest to the historian. Its validity is confirmed by Redgrave's *Supplementary Report on Design*. Just like Wornum he begins with some pages on principles of design and a brief historical survey. He is more outspoken than Wornum—a remarkable fact considering that he was writing an official document—blames the Italian Renaissance for going to Roman 'magnificence and barbarism' rather than to Greece for inspiration, calls Wornum's mixed Cinquecento 'a debased form of the Renaissance' and has not a good word for the Louis Quatorze. In the exhibition Redgrave finds the 'florid and gorgeous tinsel' of the Louis Quatorze still prevailing 'in three fourths of the works'. Wornum says more or less the same, only he says it a little less passionately. The Greek, we read, is almost absent, the Gothic rare and the pure Cinquecento also exceptional. The mixed Renaissance and the Louis Quinze dominate, 'the latter

45 Pianos, including a Rococo upright, by Collard & Collard

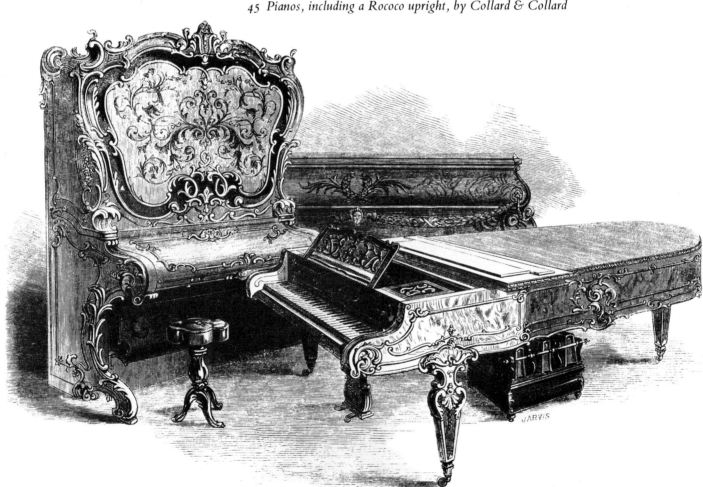

46 *'Elizabethan New Patent Grand Oblique Pianoforte' by P.O. Erard*

in quantity, the former in quality'. The Renaissance or mixed Cinquecento is 'the best understood style', practised by 'the most able designers of Italy, France, Austria, Belgium and England'.

With these weird categories firmly in one's mind, it will be easier to appreciate the style of the exhibits. It is psychologically understandable anyway that on the whole the Dixhuitième and the Elizabethan-cum-Jacobean come off best; for the former allowed for the highest degree of licence, and the latter was a bastard style in itself. The papier mâché panel of Jackson's combines leaf scrolls and birds as the French Early Renaissance might have used them, with Elizabethan strap-work, and is in this respect true Mixed Cinquecento, the sources belonging to the same century and being not too discrepant in intention; the Erard upright piano on the other hand is entirely Elizabethan in its motifs and the gorgeous piano of Collard & Collard's entirely Rococo and nothing else, although a Rococo in the usual and universally Victorian colour scheme of dark brown and green. The fact that upright pianos were not known either in the eighteenth or the sixteenth centuries did not worry the mid-Victorian manufacturer nor the mid-Victorian critic such as Wornum. A sense of congruity between the style of decoration and the object to be decorated returned only much later. An age which frankly applied art to objects instead of thinking in terms of aesthetic value from the beginning of the designing process, could hardly find fault more readily with the Elizabethan piano than with the Egyptian steam engine or the Gothic railway station.

If congruity had been demanded, then for such new purposes a wholly new style would have been needed, and most of the mid-Victorians were frightened of that. Pugin is a characteristic case in point. In 1843 he chastised the battlements and tracery of the new Great Western stations, but then described his own ideas of a grand, massive, simple and substantial railway architecture also in terms of buttresses and depressed pointed arches,* and Ruskin in the *Seven Lamps* calls a railways station as alien to architecture as a wasp's nest and a rat-hole,* and states that 'architecture does not admit iron as a constructive material'.* Hence his infuriated dislike of the Crystal Palace which was shared by Pugin.*

(margin references:) 44 · 46 · 45 · n.45 · n.46 · n.47 · n.48

Others saw further. Matthew Digby Wyatt, whom we have met before and who was Secretary to the Executive Committee of the Exhibition, said in a lecture in 1851 that the structure of Paxton's building would 'probably tend to counteract conventionality of style in architecture, and may be expected to produce, hereafter, important changes in the construction and appearance of many extensive buildings throughout the country'. It certainly did not produce any in his own extensive range of buildings, as we shall see in another essay. Not even Paddington Station is in any way influenced by Brunel's iron structure of the train-shed.

This discrepancy between clearsightedness in the abstract and muddled performance is a typical Victorian feature. It is connected with hypocrisy, with too well-founded a feeling of security, and also with visual deficiencies which will need more explanation later. Meanwhile the same discrepancy appears even more surprisingly in George Gilbert Scott's *Remarks on Secular and Domestic Architecture* of 1858, where even he, convinced champion of the thirteenth-century Gothic, assures his readers—actually talking of bridges—that 'it is self evident that the triumph of modern metallic construction opens out a perfectly new field for architectural development'.* This remark was meant no doubt as n.49 a retort against Ruskin who hurried an appendix (no. 17) into his *Stones of Venice*, just in time for its publication in 1851, to state that iron and glass are 'eternally separated from all good and great things by a gulf which not all the tubular bridges nor engineering of ten thousand nineteenth centuries cast into one great bronze-foreheaded century will ever overpass one inch of'.* But most em- n.50 phatically of all architects a minor but interesting architect, Thomas Harris,* in n.51 1862 made the claim for the Crystal Palace that with its design and construction 'a new style of architecture, as remarkable as any of its predecessors, may be considered to have been inaugurated'. This passage occurs in an article in a book which Harris called 'Examples of the Architecture of the Victorian Age'—a term still very unusual at that time.[51] Harris raises his voice to plead for nine- n.52 teenth-century buildings expressing 'the spirit of our times, its form and pres-sure'. He wants what he calls a Victorian Style—in opposition to Ruskin who had equally firmly said in 1849 that 'we want no new style of architecture', although 'a day never passes without our having our English architects called upon to be original, and to invent a new style.'* n.53

Now in the Great Exhibition those who shared Harris's beliefs were rare, except amongst the engineers and inventors. Semper in his pamphlet on the exhibition wrote: 'Only in products in which the seriousness of their use does not allow anything unnecessary, that is in coaches, weapons, medical instru-ments, etc., one can occasionally see a sounder way of decorating and improving form'.* Coaches are indeed amongst the few things shown which are convincing n.54 regardless of date. 47

47 Underspring step-piece barouche by Hallmarke & Aldebert

48-50 The Coalbrookdale grille: half the original design, and details from the re-erected gates

With such exceptions, however, imitations of the past dominated, and what we today can easily recognize as their Victorian style is far from Wyatt's and Harris's ideas (though not their buildings). We must now continue our survey of exhibits to illustrate these two points, period imitation and its thoroughly mid-nineteenth century treatment. This may perhaps best be done by trades.

The fireplaces discussed were of cast iron. The Coalbrookdale Company also showed a huge cast-iron park gate, designed by Charles Crooks. It proves the natural sympathy of the Victorians with the most Baroque manifestations of the Dixhuitième and also the coarsening which the age wanted and the substitution of cast for wrought iron necessitated. Yet the *Illustrated London News* called this gate 'light and elegant'. It was re-erected in a slightly different form close to the Exhibition Road entrance to the Park and the most impressive thing about it seems today just its massiveness and refusal to be elegant. Top-heaviness is also amongst its peculiar qualities—Redgrave wrote that the decoration at the top 'tends to sway down the gate'—and top-heaviness we have seen before as a typical quality of 1851.

1,
48-50

The same mixture of the ham-fisted and the fanciful appears in the huge cast-iron canopy or pavilion erected over John Bell's statue of the *Eagle Slayer*. 54 The statue stands now in front of the Bethnal Green Museum, but the canopy has 55 gone. It had its vertical supports in the shape of slender oak-trunks with leaves and acorns—no doubt under the influence of the German Knüttel style (as Wornum calls it) which was itself a revival in the thirties and forties (especially by the *Fliegende Blätter* in Munich, founded in 1844) of Dürer's light-hearted marginal decorations in the Prayer Book for the Emperor Maximilian. Inside the cast-iron canopy, right at the top one could see the eagle transfixed by an arrow, a somewhat childish effect which the *Illustrated London News* rather surprisingly called an 'absolutely inexcusable piece of bad taste'. The ironwork has all the scrolly heaviness and unashamed lavishness of 1851. Wornum said it would be desirable that 'more attention be paid to the production of ordinary articles of use in cast iron'. But that is just what so expansive and grandiloquent a style as that of 1850 was least able to do.

By and large it felt most at ease in the displays of silverwork of no utility whatever. Trophies and testimonials were amongst the favourites of the public. Few were as restrained as J. Wagner's fruit-cup in oxydized silver, which 51 Wornum calls 'a mixture of natural and conventional forms in the spirit of the Quattrocento' and 'the most beautiful work of this class in the Exhibition'. Mostly they go all out for a combination of bold ornament and wild figure sculpture. 'The Louis Quinze prevails in every phase of its development', says Wornum, 'from the symmetrical variety proceeding immediately to the most bizarre vagaries of the Rococo, which last very much predominate'. So, presumably, the flagons exhibited by Joseph Angell would have been called 53 Dixhuitième in spite of some Gothic polygonalities. Hunt & Roskell's Tweeddale Testimonial is more truly Rococo, at least in its upper parts. The mediaevalizing battle-scene below is curiously incongruous, but in outline as curly and spiky as the mixture of rocaille curves and thistle above. Alfred Brown was the sculptor of the Testimonial. Alfred Stevens in a letter speaks of the 'ready-made abortions from Hunt & Roskell'.* Fatter and more ebullient is the Emperor of n.55 Russia's Ewer by Garrard's representing the Eighth Labour of Hercules. The 56

51 *Centrepiece by J. Wagner of Berlin*

52 *The Tweeddale Testimonial by Hunt & Roskell*

53 *Flagons by Joseph Angell*

54 *Iron canopy by the Coalbrookdale Company, over John Bell's 'Eagle Slayer'*

55 *The 'Eagle Slayer' today*

56 *The Emperor of Russia's Ewer by Garrard's*

57 *Ice-pails and centrepiece by Hunt & Roskell*

spiral movement of figures and ornament is genuinely Baroque and in its coarse way effective. The same style in a version of feminine elegance appears in the clockcase modelled by John Bell of the *Eagle Slayer* and exhibited by Elkington's. 58 The seductive maidens sinuously floating round the clockface—Wagner's *Rheingold* was composed in 1853–54—represent the twelve hours. At the foot are allegories of morning and evening, a daring thing to introduce after Michelangelo. The tension of the Medici Chapel is, needless to say, lacking, and absence of tension is indeed a quality equally typical of mid-nineteenth-century sculpture and architecture. In the ice pails by Hunt & Roskell this same uninterrupted 57 undulating flow is expressed not in figures but in naturalistically applied big, fat lotus leaves. The pails as well as the centre-piece with the river Ganges behind belong to a service presented to the Earl of Ellenborough in India.

Now the naturalism of these leaves was something new in the mid-nineteenth century. It had Rococo precedents only in a minor playful way, but can be traced back to the huge silvered tobacco leaves on the ceiling of the Banqueting Room at the Brighton Pavilion. In fact surprisingly much that was to become characteristically Early and even High Victorian in design is heralded in Nash's work at Brighton and elsewhere. The generation of the exhibition—content to copy styles of the past—was prouder of nothing more, and considered nothing more an original achievement all their own, than this scientific naturalism of foliage carving and modelling. The theory of it is rooted deeply in the Victorian faith in facts. Even Ruskin takes no end of trouble to reconcile his moralist theory

58 *'Hours' clock by John Bell, made by Elkington's*

59 *'Narcissus' dessert dish by Smith &*
Nicholson

60 *Dessert dish by H.S. & D. Gass*

of art with constant emphasis on natural laws and a close study of nature. 'Whatever is in architecture fair or beautiful, is imitated from natural forms'.* Gottfried Semper also says that some of the best contemporary designs 'show a
laudable effort to borrow their forms immediately from nature'.* So the capitals
of High Victorian churches are carved with a large variety of leaves of the
countryside,* and in the more licentious medium of silver such dessert dishes
were possible as those shown by Smith, Nicholson & Co. The confitures here
were placed into flowery or leafy shapes — regardless of the fact, pointed out by
Wornum, that whatever was carried thus on delicate stems would be 'one
hundred times more than enough to crush them in their natural state'. But such
rational arguments were irrelevant to the designers and the public. Ouida, aged
eleven, had a much shrewder notion of what was the intention of such vessels or
or the inkstand with a deer and a fawn and stumps of trees holding the ink which
she so much admired. 'It did not look at all what it was, it was lovely' she writes. *
This admiration for the *trompe-l'oeil*, the cute disguise, the surprising gadget, is as
old as art and will always remain the privilege of the naïve, and the naïvety of the
visitors to the 1851 exhibition was beyond our conception.

So naturalism was welcome as a compliment to science and also as a dainty
costume to cover and embellish function. It was welcome aesthetically too, because the curves of stems and leaves in nature often possess the scrolly, nobbly,
swelling character the designers were aiming at. H. S. & D. Gass for instance
showed a dessert service of which they proudly said that it was 'modelled from

n.56
n.57
n.58
59
n.59
60

63 Tubular metal chair by Kitschelt

water plants in Kew Gardens (by permission of Sir W. Jackson Hooker, F.R.S., Director)'. The four dishes represent Nymphaea thermalis, Nymphaea rubra, Calladium and Dillenia speciosa. Fuchsias and anemones are used for curtain hooks by Winfield of Birmingham, the brass manufacturer, and called by the *61, 6* *Art Journal* 'graceful appendages of the elegant drawing-room'. Storks support a *64* table by Morant of London. The form here is slenderer and indeed more graceful and elegant than in the majority of exhibits. One can say that the naturalists or horticulturists were those whose taste tended more towards the refined. The coarser tastes enjoyed the inflated shapes of the Louis Quinze varieties. Two chairs show typically top-heavy, thin-legged specimens, one Austrian (by *63*

61, 62 Floral curtain-hooks of brass by Winfield's

64 Table by Morant's

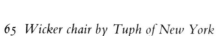

65 *Wicker chair by Tuph of New York*

65
67
66

n.60

August Kitschelt), the other American and of wickerwork. The dressing-table and chair by Clay have again the same qualities, this time a little purer in their Rococo. The papery flatness of the legs with their curly feet will be noticed; it is due to the replacement of wood by papier maché. The ribbon-like quality of the legs of a table shown by Thonet's of Vienna on the other hand is explained not by a new material but by a new technique. Michael Thonet was the inventor of bentwood furniture, that is solid beechwood bent under heat. He had in fact earlier still, about 1836, also experimented with bent strips of what can only be called plywood,* and the illustration looks as if the table might be made in that way but the *Art Journal* says that the legs are 'bent from the solid piece'.

66 *Bentwood table by Thonet of Vienna*

67 *Papier maché dressing-table set by H. Clay of London*

68, 69 Teapots by Cork & Edge

70 Vases by Wedgwood's

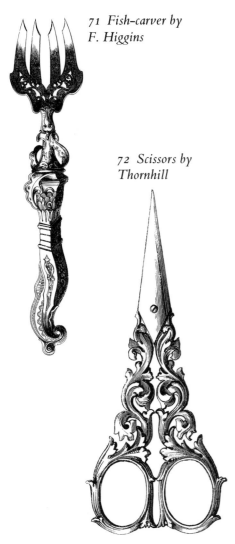

71 Fish-carver by F. Higgins

72 Scissors by Thornhill

After silver and furniture, pottery and porcelain. Wedgwood's remained   70
faithful to their classical shapes—and a serious critic such as Wornum said: 'The
best shapes remain Greek . . . All our vagaries end in a recourse to Greek shapes'
—but the vagaries of the other manufacturers are more eloquent of the taste of
1851. The Royal Worcester Porcelain Works are only slightly bulgier and im-   73
purer, with a touch of the Rococo in the handles. The teapots of Cork & Edge of   68, 69
Burslem are further advanced in debasement, and with the French compotière   76
by Charles Avisseau the wildest 1851-Art Nouveau is reached. The *Illustrated
London News* calls these things 'admirable imitations of the vases made by Ber-
nard Palissy in the sixteenth century'. This can only refer to the introduction of
elements taken over direct from nature. Jugs and a coffee set from Grainger's of   74, 75
Worcester are the English parallel of such undisciplined naturalism. Wornum
objected to it saying 'He is a poor designer [who] can do nothing more than
imitate a few sprigs or leaves wherewith to decorate'. Redgrave, needless to
say, agreed with Wornum, and Henry Cole himself had shown his agreement
some five years before by designing the Summerly tea-set. This is indeed of a   77
much sounder, simpler design. It is unornamented, and although its shapes show
to a certain extent the generous curves of the mid-nineteenth century, long years
of use have proved it to be serviceable and functionally sound.

It is one of the most noticeable characteristics of the exhibits of 1851 that
little attention was paid to ease of handling, ease of storing or ease of cleaning. As
for the latter two, the fact that there was no shortage of servants may account for
their neglect, although Redgrave stresses that silver made for use should be designed so as to stand up to 'constant cleansing; not at the hand of the silversmith,
but of the butler and his assistant'. But unserviceable shapes and decoration were
not due to thoughtlessness but to positive aesthetic desires. Mr Higgin's spoons
and forks were not only handled by butlers or housemaids but by the mistress   71
of the house herself and her guests. Yet nothing could be more excruciatingly
uncomfortable to hold and operate—nothing except perhaps Mr Thornhill's
scissors which the *Art Journal* mentions as 'highly to be recommended as ex-   72
amples of the taste of the designer'. The stylistic qualities in all these are the same,
whether in terms of naturalistic tendrils or of acanthus scrolls, and they are by
now familiar—all-over filling with decoration, open outlines, thick relief.

73 *Vases by the Royal Worcester Porcelain Company*

74 *Jug by Grainger's of Worcester*

75 *Coffee-service by Grainger's of Worcester*

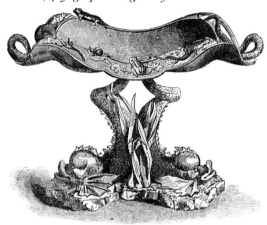

76 *Compotière by Charles Avisseau*

77 *Summerly tea-set by Henry Cole*

78 Decanter by Richardson's of Stourbridge

What is done with rounded forms in the spoons, forks and scissors, was done with innumerable jagged angles in many of the glass decanters and even drinking glasses. Redgrave had no difficulty in pointing out that the 'heavy and deep surface cutting to which glass is now so frequently submitted' obliterated one of the basic qualities of glass, its transparency, and thereby tended 'to vulgarize as far as possible the simple and beautiful material'. His criticism could not have an immediate effect, because heaviness and deep relief were just what the public wanted, and wanted so badly that it was quite ready to sacrifice comfort to it. Nowadays everybody seems to agree that functional perfection and ease of handling should be the primary consideration of purchaser as well as designer; 1851 can serve to remind us that there have been ages to which aesthetic considerations mattered more than utilitarian. And should we condemn them?

The textile section is a diagram in the flat of what the other sections have shown of the mid-nineteenth-century style in three dimensions. Problems can be entirely reduced here to surface decoration. Aesthetically interesting weaves were scarcely illustrated. But within the field of decoration the popular favourites are again bloated scrolls or imitations from nature. A group of five carpets demonstrates on the one hand the riotous effect of large bouquets of flowers, rank ferns and thick whorls, on the other the rarer manifestations of restraint, whether in terms of an imitation of Louis Quatorze or of a kind of subdued Renaissance. The latter in a design by Grüner however was criticized by Wornum for being derived from ceiling rather than floor decoration.

78

80–82

83, 79

79 Part of a carpet designed by Ludwig Grüner for Windsor Castle

80, 81 *(above and right) Details of carpets by Turberville Smith & Co. of London*

82 *Carpet by H. Brinton & Sons of Kidderminster*

83 *Carpet by Watson, Bell & Co. of London*

A similar survey can be made of table-cloths. Here again the range goes from the scrolly Dixhuitième to the naturalistic, and here also reticence of design is rare and represented outstandingly by Grüner. What is different from carpets and possible only in a light material is the introduction of bits of landscape. The Balmoral table cloth of linen damask has the castle in the centre, and in the border between thistle scrolls scenes referring to 'the healthy and manly amusements pursued by Prince Albert', as the *Art Journal* says. The jerky change-over from ornamental to realistic treatment, from the two-dimensional to the three-dimensional does not seem to have worried the public. It is especially confusing in the centre and its border where pictures set close to each other have to be viewed in four different directions.

Yet another group particularly suitable for comparison are the Cashmere shawls, an extremely popular article, it seems, imitated in Britain as well as France. The characteristic motif is what was known as the Indian pine. In original Indian work the ornamentation of the ground and the infillings of the cones all consist of small motifs of no distinguishing character in themselves.

84, 85
89
86

88

87, 90

84, 85 Table cloth and table cover by Beveridge's of Dunfermline

86 Muslin curtain by J.J. Sutter of Appenzell

88 *Centre of the Balmoral table cloth*

87 *Shawl by M.E. Hartwick of Paris*

89 *Table cloth designed by Grüner*

90 *Cashmere shawl by Roxburgh of Paisley*

Matthew Digby Wyatt in his folio illustrates two of these with approval and none of the mid-nineteenth-century imitations. These use grosser motifs, often of realistic flower bouquets and interlace them with large flag-leaf or similar sprays. Grapes may hang down from behind a pine, and altogether the even surface of the cloth appears to the eye broken wherever possible. Occasionally the ground suddenly reveals glimpses of park scenery.

The same ambiguity between landscape, naturalistic flowers in the border, and thick scrolls can be seen even in the ethereal medium of a Swiss muslin curtain. On the whole the landscape parts on textiles are very much less attractively done than the vegetable parts. There is indeed a freshness about the flowers and leaves on some of the dress and furnishing fabrics, woven as well as embroidered or printed, which we are only just able to appreciate once more.

87

86

1–93

91 *Printed chintz by McAlpin, Stead & Co. of Cummersdale*

92 *Furnishing damask by H.C. McCrea of Halifax*

93 *Embroidered waistcoat by J.W. Gabriel of London*

94 *Toast rack by Hall's of Sheffield*

One thing with regard to the ornamentation of textiles needs special emphasis. In spite of all the realism that went into decoration, we find nowhere parallels to what printers are doing to scarves today, no Sights of London, no ballet scenes, no sailing yachts, no foxhounds. In fact the associational element is almost entirely missing. That is all the more remarkable, because we have seen amongst the exhibits several examples of the importance of the associational as against the strictly aesthetic, and there are many more. Wagner's silver table centre for instance, represents the progress of mankind to civilization under the guidance of genius. At the foot of the base is man in the early stages of civilization, as a hunter and herdsman. The female figures above represent cultivation and husbandry. At the top genius is seen strangling the serpent of ignorance and standing on a palm tree rising high from within the agricultural civilization shown below. Similarly Fourdinois's walnut sideboard (France, No. 1231) is supported by six hounds. The pilasters are adorned with four figures representing the four quarters of the world. On the right is a hunter, on the left a fisherman, as brackets. On the top appears Abundance, to her left and right children reaping and gleaning. Another sideboard, by Cookes & Sons of Warwick, represents 'with sculptural relievos' the history of Kenilworth Castle. The description in the catalogue takes up a column and a half. A pretty toast-rack by Hall's of Sheffield has wheat-ears and leaves to support the slices of toast. John Thomas's fireplace has, as we have seen, a medallion of Chaucer and the figures of Dorigene and Griselda; John Bell's clock, the twelve hours around the dial. Ploucquet of Stuttgart, taxidermist, showed his stuffed animals 'in imitation of the attitudes, habits, and occupations of rational creatures' and H. Fitz Cook called his papier mâché chair *The Daydreamer*. It is described thus in the catalogue: 'The chair is decorated at the top with two winged thoughts—the one with bird-like pinions, and crowned with roses, representing happy and joyous dreams, the other with leather bat-like wings—unpleasant and troubled ones. Behind is displayed Hope, under the figure of the rising sun. The twisted supports of the back are ornamented with poppy, heartsease, convolvulus and snowdrop, all emblematic of the subject. In front of the seat is a shell . . . and on either side of it, pleasant and troubled dreams are represented by figures. At the side is seen a figure of Puck, lying asleep in a labyrinth of foliage . . . The style of the ornament is Italian.'

One may doubt this last statement, but it is in its woolliness as typical of the date as is the elaborate allegorical apparatus built up around so utilitarian an object as an easy chair. There must have been a great need for the interesting story amongst the public to account for this. We have seen that the need for the inflated and expansive form made people put up with discomforts. The need for

51

94

37
58
96

17

the story occasionally did the same. A. J. Jones of 135 St Stephen's Green, Dublin, for instance exhibited an armchair of Irish bog-oak and this had not only 'chivalric bustos of ancient Irish warriors' at the top of the back, but 'the arms formed by wolf-dogs—one at ease and recumbent', with the motto on the collar 'Gentle when stroked', the other irritated and sitting up, with the counter motto 'Fierce when provoked'. So here a piece of furniture even required mottos to be fully understood.

We are here, I think, close to the innermost core of mid-Victorian taste. The patrons of 1850 were no longer the patrons of 1800. A new class had come to the top and settled down smugly. The years between 1840 and 1860 or 1870 are a phase of assured possession between two phases of restlessness and revolt, in the economic life of the nation as well as the intellectual. Shelley and Byron had gone, Engels and Marx not yet gathered a following. Engels, it is true, had written on the *Condition of the Working Class* in 1845, Carlyle's *Past and Present* had come out in 1843 and Kingsley's *Alton Locke* in 1848. So the new socialist reform of the future, represented by two men under thirty years old when their books came out, and the old romantic idea of reform based on an unreal vision of mediaeval history, met at this juncture. But neither had very much immediate effect. Carlyle passed on much to Ruskin, whose social-reformatory work was begun only shortly before 1860, and to Morris whose firm started in 1861, and the first volume of Marx's *Das Kapital* came out only in 1867.

95 Irish bog-oak chair by A.J. Jones of Dublin

Meanwhile the decades of Peel and Palmerston succeeded in keeping the upheavals of 1848 from the English shores and in managing smoothly a nation basking in the sunshine of unprecedented prosperity. No country could touch Britain for industrial and commercial success. The imperialism of Disraeli—and also of Napoleon III and Bismarck—the new powers of a united Germany, a united Italy and a colonizing France had not yet appeared. There were in the years about 1851 few major worries for the wealthy, and there was noticeably growing wealth among the workers. The Corn Laws had been repealed in 1846. Faith prevailed in unlimited chances for the capable and the energetic to get rich, however humble their origins.

The Great Exhibition was to show the Works of Industry of All Nations. No visitor from abroad would have doubted what nation was leading in industry. In canals, in road surfaces, in steam navigation, in railway construction no one could compete with Britain. Here the first big factories had been built,

96 An ermine tea-party, by the taxidermist Ploucquet of Stuttgart

here the first industrial cities had grown. It was all enormously impressive, though much of it was not edifying to the eye. For the new masters had no time to bother about civilized appearances nor had they had a youth to make them demand what would look good. No education and no leisure, these two deficiencies explain nearly all that is aesthetically distressing about 1851. The appreciation of aesthetic values in architecture and design, of proportions, textures, harmonies of colours, requires training and time. The appreciation of the emotional values in painting and sculpture also requires a readiness to listen, to follow a lead and be captured, and this cannot be expected in one whose mind is occupied with machine and counting-house. Thus effects were bound to become louder and more obvious. A bulgy curve will be taken in more easily than a delicate one, richly glowing colours than subtle shades, and stories carved in relievo than sheer satisfying proportions. We can say that what appeals to the child, appealed to the big men with the heavy purses in 1851: Ouida's 'It did not look at all like what it was' for instance, or an Ottoman Coal Sarcophagus and a Cricket Catapulta, or indeed the Crystal Palace itself with its engineering courage and vast uniformity. Admiration for technics is easier than for aesthetics. Again accurate copying of period details could appeal strongly, and so could accurate copying of flowers from Kew. For whereas to risk verdicts on artistic merit seemed unsafe and also a little dubious, accuracy could be checked and hence evaluated. Thus the naturalism in the carving of the capitals of a Gilbert Scott church is as typical of 1850 as Ford Madox Brown's plea for meticulously correct historical costume put forward in 1850 in *The Germ*, the short-lived journal of the young Pre-Raphaelites, or Holman Hunt's journey to the Holy Land to paint the Scapegoat against a correct Dead Sea. The Pre-Raphaelites in this respect were exactly as High Victorian as their enemies, the popular and successful genre painters, and it is remarkable that Ruskin who valiantly defended the young Pre-Raphaelites in his letter to *The Times* of 1851 could have written only a few years before of Landseer's *The Old Shepherd's Chief Mourner* that it was 'one of the most perfect poems or pictures—I use the words as synonymous—which modern times has seen.' That passage appeared in the first volume of *Modern Painters* in 1843. Now Landseer's most popular pictures are of dogs, yet have such titles as Low Life and High Life, Alexander and Diogenes, Dignity and Impudence, A Distinguished Member of the Royal Humane Society. Their titles made their success, just as Wilkie's merry village subjects with their wealth of easily followed and understood incidents made him one of the most internationally famous of British painters. Waagen called him 'the first painter of our times', and Lady Eastlake wrote of the Raphael of the Cartoons now at the Victoria and Albert Museum that he appeared there to be 'as powerful as Michael Angelo, had his power stood alone; as activating as Rubens had his action taken precedence; as individual in character as Wilkie, had that been his sole object.'* n.61 The ultimate combination of a rich anecdotic interest with extreme accuracy of treatment came with Frith's *Ramsgate Sands* of 1854, *Derby Day* of 1858 and *Paddington Station* of 1862.

Prince Albert was a born reformer. He was high-minded enough to feel that after Raphael and Michelangelo Wilkie and Landseer were not an achievement one's conscience could be proud of. Art surely was to serve higher purposes. Had he not seen that it could be so, in the cartoons of the German Romantics at home, in Cornelius, Schnorr von Carolsfeld, in Schadow and the others? Westminster Palace had been consumed by fire in 1834. The new Houses of Parliament were built in its stead, in a national Gothic style, conscientious and decoratively sound in all the carved details, the wall-papers, the metalwork and so on for which Pugin was responsible. Painting was not to be left out of the interior decoration. In 1841 a Royal Commission was appointed 'to take into consideration the promotion of the Fine Arts of this country, in connexion with the rebuilding of the Houses of Parliament'. Prince Albert was made its chairman; it was his first appearance in such a job. He was only twenty-one years old. He took it as seriously as he was to take everything. A decision was reached quickly that the

97 *'Britons Lamenting the Departure of the Romans', by E. Corbould*

paintings should be illustrative of history rather than allegory, and done in fresco, that is in the mediaeval and Renaissance technique resuscitated by the Nazarenes, the early German Romantics, some thirty years before. Their shadow loomed large behind the whole scheme. Their leaders were still alive and powerful, Cornelius at Berlin and Overbeck in Rome, the one by then representing the most formal, official, academic side of high-minded art, the other its Catholic religious humility. In 1842 a competition was announced to obtain cartoons for the frescoes. Cornelius came over himself to advise. The cartoons were exhibited in 1843; there were a hundred and forty of them. Prizes went to Watts, Armitage, Cope, Horsley, John F. Bell, Townshend, Pickersgill and others. Benjamin Haydon who had worried about elevated history painting in England for longer than anyone else had sent two cartoons but obtained no recognition. Ford Madox Brown was no luckier, nor was Alfred Stevens. In the same year, 1843, Albert commissioned a number of artists (for instance Leslie, Maclise and Landseer and Etty) to paint frescoes in a garden pavilion in the gardens of Buckingham Palace. The pattern was obviously the casino of the Villa Massimi in Rome painted by the German Nazarenes in 1818. The Massimi frescoes were from Tasso, Albert's from Milton's *Comus*. Meanwhile a second exhibition of cartoons for the Houses of Parliament was held in 1844, and a third in 1847. Amongst those selected now was William Dyce who had spent quite a long time in Italy and met Overbeck there and who had later for the Government gone to study art schools in Germany. Maclise and Redgrave also obtained premiums. Amongst the cartoons shown were such subjects as Caractacus and Boadicea, St Augustine and the First Trial by Jury, Harold's Defeat and the Charity of Edward the Confessor. It was a noble effort and it led nowhere.

The spirit of reform was in the air no doubt, and where, in the same years, it took the form of religious reform, of a renewed earnestness of mind, it could become a real power. But in fine art it could not be but a failure. Aesthetic sensibility cannot be restored by decree. Nothing could be more characteristic of the uneasy position of the fine arts in the mid-Victorian *milieu* than the fact that they were excluded from the 1851 exhibition and yet included to an oddly limited extent. Class Thirty was called 'Sculpture, Models and Plastic Art, Mosaics, Enamels, etc.' The Introduction in the catalogue begins thus: 'The Exhibition having relations far more extensive with the industrial occupations and products of mankind than with the Fine Arts, the limits of the present Class have been defined with considerable strictness. Those departments of art which are, in a degree, connected with mechanical process, which relate to working in metals, wood, or marble, and those mechanical processes which are applicable to the arts, but which, notwithstanding this, still preserve their mechanical character, as painting in colour, come properly within this Class. Paintings, as works of art, are excluded; but, as exhibiting any improvements in colours, they become admissible. When admitted, they are to be regarded not so much as examples of the skill of the artist, as of that of the preparer of the colours. The admission, however, of objects included under the definition of "plastic art", has greatly tended to relieve the general aspect of the Exhibition; and their happy and judicious arrangement in the great structure forms one of its most interesting features.'

It is a curious document. As for painting, two illustrations appeared in the *Illustrated London News,* Edward Corbould's *The Britons lamenting the Departure* 97, 10 *of the Romans,* and Pickersgill's *The Origin of the Quarrel between the Guelphs and the Ghibellines,* the one characteristic of the high cartoon style in its less disciplined mid-nineteenth-century variety, the other of that pleasantly sentimental historical genre to which the young Pre-Raphaelites opposed their severer, more sensitively stylized interpretations. Corbould's painting was exhibited as an example of Miller's silica colours, Pickersgill's water-colour in a lithographic reproduction of Rowney's.

Of sculpture there was of course far more.

> There's statues bright
> Of marble white,
> Of silver and of copper,
> And some of zinc,
> And some I think
> That isn't overproper.

98 Thorvaldsen's 'Ganymede' in Copenhagen porcelain

Thus sang Thackeray's indefatigable Mr Molony in his account of a visit to the Crystal Palace. He was as right about the zinc as he was about a remarkable tendency to half-concealed impropriety, as we shall see presently.

Sculpture indeed as a rule kept within the restrictions proposed by the exhibition, in so far as in the nineteenth century very little large stone work was actually executed by the artist himself. He usually only made a model, and assistants then transferred it by mechanical means to the large block of stone. However executed, the display of statuary from the largest to the smallest was numerous enough to allow for a fairly accurate survey of the existing trends of taste about 1850. The Greek Revival whose disappearance from the world of design Wornum regretted could still be seen in a work by the great Thorwaldsen himself who had been born as long ago as 1770, had taught and inspired innumerable younger sculptors and died in 1844. However, his noble *Ganymede* had been translated by the Copenhagen Porcelain Manufactory into biscuit 98

99 *'Greek Hunter' by John Gibson*

100 *'Origin of the Quarrel of the Guelphs and Ghibellines', by E. Pickersgill*

porcelain and by another Danish manufacturer into ivory and his scale reduced to statuette size. The reduction of large sculpture to measures suitable for the mantelshelf was altogether at its most popular in the mid-nineteenth century, and English manufacturers had developed a special unglazed ceramic material

118 known as Parian or Carrara—the invention was contended by Herbert Minton and Alderman Copeland—to compete with the whiteness of marble. The most distinguished of all English sculptors of the period, John Gibson, who was born in 1790 and lived in Rome where visitors of all nations called on him, had sent to

99 the Exhibition his *Greek Hunter* of marble—obviously Grecian in taste, though the details about the dog tell of the approach of realism. Matthew Digby Wyatt in fact specially praised the well-observed contrast between the youth and the hound pulling vigorously in different directions, and called the piece 'unquestionably one of the most beautiful works of art contributed to the Exhibition'.

101–104 (left to right) 'King Alfred Taught by his Mother', by the Thornycrofts; 'Rosomonda', by John Thomas; 'Saher de Quincy', by J.S. Westmacott; and a Hero from the 'Nibelungenlied' by Fernkorn

Also still classical in composition though romantic and national-historical in its choice of subject is *King Alfred taught by his Mother*. This group is by Thomas and Mary Thornycroft, the latter a pupil of Thorwaldsen and Gibson. Thomas's and Mary's son was the better known Hamo Thornycroft. *101*

Individual statues from national mediaeval history were plentiful. John Thomas, who has been mentioned before, had a Rosomonda amongst other things, J. S. Westmacott a Saher de Quincy, Earl of Winchester (a piece which was to find a permanent place inside the Houses of Parliament), and Fernkorn of Vienna some heroes from the *Nibelungenlied,* which were inspired by the bronze figures of the Emperor Maximilian's tomb at Innsbruck, but executed small in cast iron. Fernkorn did indeed six large stone statues of German emperors for the Imperial Vault at Speier Cathedral on the Rhine. In this style were the largest works of sculpture exhibited, two equestrian statues, the Barone Marochetti's *Richard Coeur de Lion,* shown outside the western entrance, and now standing in front of the Houses of Parliament, and Eugène Simonis's *Godfrey of Bouillon,* now at Brussels. The Thornycrofts incidentally also showed an equestrian statue, but *102 104 105 106 103*

105 (left) 'Godfrey of Bouillon', by Simonis of Brussels

106 (right) 'Richard Coeur de Lion' by Baron Marochetti, in front of the Houses of Parliament

107 Queen Victoria on her favourite charger, by Hamo and Mary Thornycroft

108 'Sleeping Child and Dog', by Henry Weekes

this was a portrait, the young Queen herself placed gently on an elegant horse 107 evidently portrayed from life. The Queen wears a long flowing robe, the horse is seen prancing in the best Baroque manner. Baroque in a more robust way is August Kiss's famous *Amazon* which was made in bronze in 1839, in marble in 110 1842, and appeared at the Exhibition, true to Mr Molony's statement, in zinc. The figure which to Matthew Digby Wyatt was 'probably the noblest work of art now existing' is again still of the classical race, but the wild outline of the group and the realism of the nude show that we are approaching the middle of the century. The same turn towards realism in terms of a sentimental mediaeval subject can for instance be seen in Friedrich Wilhelm Engelhard's *Lore Ley*, 111 made in 1848. Engelhard also had been a pupil of Thorwalsden for a time.

More attractive than these figures which are neither wholly classical nor wholly romantic, nor wholly Victorian, are those in which a romantic theme is

109 'The Babes in the Wood', by John Bell

110 *'Amazon' by August Kiss, cast in zinc*

111 *'Lore Ley' by F.W. Engelhard*

112 *'Paolo and Francesca', by Alexander Munro*

treated frankly with the effective sentimentality of the mid-nineteenth century. John Bell's *Babes in the Wood* are clearly derived from Sir Francis Chantrey's monument to the Robinson children in Lichfield Cathedral which in its turn goes back to Thomas Banks's celebrated Penelope Boothby at Ashbourne church in Derbyshire. When this was first shown at the Royal Academy, Queen Charlotte burst into tears. Penelope Boothby died in 1799, the Robinson Monument is of 1817. Both, though romantic in their emphasis on innocence, were extremely restrained compared with Bell's grosser self-abandon, disorderly attitudes and naturalistic flowers and leaves. The motif was obviously popular. It appears again in Henry Weekes's *Sleeping Child and Dog*.

It was the self-indulgent sentimentality in such pieces which irritated the young Pre-Raphaelites so much. Genre-painting and genre-sculpture, they felt, were done only to entertain. There was no aesthetic discipline and no moral truth in them. Their own standards were to be more exacting. *The Germ* fought 'exaggerated action, conventionalism, gaudy colour, false sentiment, voluptuousness, poverty of invention' and preached 'entire adherence to the simplicity of nature', 'patient devotedness' and 'truth in every point of representation'. The Pre-Raphaelites were too young to make any difference to the character of the Exhibition. Ford Madox Brown, their mentor, though never a member of the Brotherhood himself, was only thirty, Holman Hunt twenty-four, Rossetti twenty-three and Millais twenty-two. But Alexander Munro, one of their closest followers, only twenty-six years old, had a group of *Paolo and Francesca* accepted which indeed represented Pre-Raphaelite principles in its intensity of feeling and simplicity of detail.

Voluptuousness is one of the vices of art to which *The Germ* took exception. But if one considers what one remembers of English art of about 1830 to 1850, it does not seem to be a frequent complaint. Wilkie, Leslie, Mulready, Maclise, Webster—the genre painters—kept well within the bounds of respectability, as

113 *'The Greek Slave', by Hiram Powers*

114 *'Circassian Slave in the Market at Constantinople', by Raffaele Monti*

115 *'Andromeda' by John Bell*

did Dickens and Thackeray and Trollope in their novels. Etty, it is true, had lived till 1849, but he belonged to another generation, to Lord Byron's to be precise (Etty born 1787, Byron 1788). Nudes, as we have seen, persisted in sculpture—but they were far from voluptuous; and in painting they were all but abolished. Yet at the exhibition surreptitious pleasures of the senses could be had in two highly characteristic contexts. You could see gleaming in polished marble how naked innocence was exposed to outrage, and you could obtain a glimpse of unobserved innocence, half exposing its charms. Hiram Powers's *Greek Slave* was certainly the most famous statue exhibited. Hiram Powers was an American, born in 1805. He was self-taught and had reached Italy in 1837. Thorwaldsen is reported to have said of him that his entrance upon the field constituted an era in art. In 1845 the *Greek Slave* was first shown in London. In 1849 a miniature statuette after it was brought out by Felix Summerly in Parian. In 1841 the *Art Journal* had written of his nudes that they had no tendency to introduce among our women foreign indelicacy'.* That is what it was. The figure was chastely and most attractively modelled, and there the poor girl, deprived of all her clothes, was offered in the market to some Turk. The concept appealed to the Victorian mind, and visitors to the exhibition could go through the same pleasurable if vicarious emotions in front of Raffaele Monti's veiled *Circassian Slave in the Market at Constantinople* and also John Bell's *Andromeda*. The other form of deflected High Victorian sensuality, Peeping Tom dreams as it were after the uneasy Pasha dreams, can best be analysed apropos John Bell's *Dorothea*. The statue is an illustration to Don Quixote. Dorothea is seen in shepherd's clothes, with her hair down, bathing her feet, when she is discovered by Don Quixote and Sancho. She is evidently only just becoming aware of the presence of the intruders and the state of her dress gives her every reason for being embarrassed. Yet we can really see only very little more than even a Victorian bathing costume would have exposed. But what we see is given us highly realistically, in fact, as the *Illustrated London News* said somewhat priggishly, 'more imitative than is consistent with the highest development of the art'. The effect anyway (especially in the woodcut), is surprisingly improper, just because any objection which might be raised could be countered by arguments of perfect respectability. *Dorothea* is the most convincing symbol of that bad conscience of the High Victorians which is wholly suppressed in the novels of the period but rampant in sculpture. She was indeed successful enough to be copied immediately in Parian by Felix Summerly and to be converted, with the addition of some highly realistic lilies and some dock-leaf, into a gas bracket .

113

n.62

114,

116–1

117

118
116

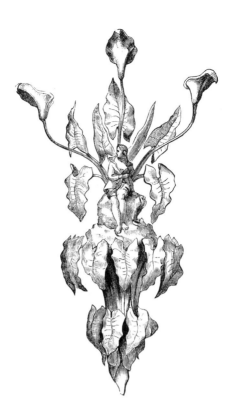

116–118 John Bell's 'Dorothea': right, in Parian marble; below, as illustrated in the catalogue; and above, as a gas bracket

119 Bread knife by John Bell

We have seen how intensely such critics as Redgrave and Wornum disliked naturalistic ornamentation. Of the direct application of works of sculpture to decorative purposes they were no more in favour. Indeed while Queen Victoria wrote in her diary just before the opening, on 29 April: '*Such* efforts have been made, and our people have shown *such* taste in their manufactures',* and while other equally well-disposed and naïve visitors were equally delighted, the promoters of the exhibition were not. They had had high hopes. 'Since the period of the Reformation', wrote one of them, 'we believe the prospects of Design . . . have never been so good as at the present time in England'.* Henry Cole had designed ornamental objects himself, as has been mentioned, and he had commissioned others to design for him. Amongst those working for Summerly's Art Manufactures had been Redgrave, John Bell, Maclise and Townshend. Cole had also been connected with the first exhibitions of design held on a small scale at the Society of Arts in 1846, 1847 and 1849, and with a remarkable publishing venture, the *Journal of Design and Manufactures,* which was edited by Richard Redgrave and began to appear in March 1849. The first number is dedicated to Prince Albert.* Amongst the contributors were Dyce, Owen Jones, Matthew Digby Wyatt and John Bell. A paper by Semper was reprinted and lectures by Wornum were announced. These men whose views of the Exhibition coincided in so many ways formed quite clearly a circle of friends and fellow-fighters in the cause of design. They were all in their thirties and forties at the time of the Exhibition (Semper born 1803, Redgrave 1804, Dyce 1806, Cole 1808, Jones 1809, Wornum 1812, Prince Albert 1819, Wyatt 1820), and they appeared prominently at the Exhibition in one function or another. Semper designed the Canadian, Danish, Egyptian and Swedish displays, Owen Jones the colour-schemes of the whole structural parts of the interior—in primaries: blue, yellow and red. Jones was also Superintendent of Class XXX, that is the class devoted to Sculpture etc., and of Class XVII, dealing with Paper, Printing etc. Wyatt was Secretary of the Executive Committee, and in addition responsible entirely for progress during the construction of the building. Dyce was a Juror for the iron and hardware class and a member of the prize-giving committee, Redgrave and Townshend sat on the Committee on Manufactures. Redgrave was also on the Jury for Sculpture etc., and wrote, as we have seen, the official *Supplementary Report on Design* to the Jurors.

Now the *Journal of Design and Manufactures* tried from its beginning to establish what its editor called 'sound principles of ornamental art'.* These principles were not entirely new. Behind them stands the reformatory work of Pugin. His *Contrasts*, it must be remembered, had come out in 1836, and his *True Principles of Pointed or Christian Architecture* in 1841. That was exactly the time when a feeling of uneasiness over the obvious decline of design became general. A Select Committee on Arts and their Connexion with Manufactures was appointed in 1836. It led to the establishment of the Government School of Design in 1837. Its director from 1838 to 1843 was Dyce. In 1840 grants were made for the creation of provincial schools at Manchester, Birmingham, Leeds, Glasgow and Paisley.* Their work did not prove satisfactory, and another Committee, in 1846, reported on their failure. The *Journal of Design* and the Exhibition must be viewed in relation to these developments.

Pugin's principles were clear and sound. Right at the beginning of *Contrasts* we read: 'The great test of architectural beauty is the fitness of the design for the purpose for which it was intended', and right at the beginning of the *True Principles* that 'all really beautiful forms in architecture are based on the soundest principles of utility'. Ornament should be no more than 'enrichment of the essential composition'. At present however 'glaring, showy, and meretricious ornament' alone is in vogue. Pugin curses 'the false notion of disguising instead of beautifying articles of utility'. Designers, especially those working in 'these inexhaustible mines of bad taste, Birmingham and Sheffield', 'conceal the real purpose' for which an article is made. 'Sheffield Eternal' is Pugin's name for a 'sprawling Rococo' which he specially detests. As for individual industries the

n.63

n.64

n.65

n.66

n.67

120 Summerly's Art Manufactures: from left to right, Henry Cole's teapot, 'The Flax' paper knife by John Bell, and a water carafe and christening mug by Richard Redgrave; behind, wine-tray of papier maché by Redgrave

furniture trade is taken to task as severely as the textile and wallpaper trades. 'All the ordinary articles of furniture, which require to be simple and convenient, are made not only very expensive, but very uneasy'. In wallpaper it is an absurdity to repeat 'a perspective over a large surface', in carpets 'to walk upon highly relieved foliage'.*

This set of principles and critical comments was accepted by Redgrave and the *Journal of Design*, though not Pugin's 'Gothicy' principles which 'to articles of modern invention' must be 'quite unsuitable'.* Wyatt in one of his contributions to the *Journal* explicitly pays 'a humble tribute to the truth and justice of many of [Pugin's] propositions'.* But the *Journal of Design* remains the first magazine created to serve the cause of industrial design exclusively, and not only to publicize but also to criticize. Its criticism is indeed of unparalleled outspokenness, especially at the beginning: 'We cannot praise the workmanship which is coarse, nor the design which is ugly', 'a pure abomination', 'this vulgar piece of absurdity'—such are some of the comments.* Even Felix Summerly, that is their own friends Henry Cole and John Bell, do not always escape blame (Vol. I, pp. 53, 55). And indeed much that Cole had brought out in 1846–48 was by no means in conformity with the standards of the *Journal*.

A survey of some of the Felix Summerly Art Manufactures can serve as a final confirmation of what High Victorian elements are present even in the designs of those most clearly aware of the deficiencies of popular factory production. Cole's own tea-set is, as has been said, much more sensible than tea-sets designed for the Exhibition, but in Redgrave's Camellia Teapot in Britannia Metal with a little figure in Parian on the top (executed by Dixon & Sons of Sheffield) the High Victorian sense of opulent curve is evident, and the Indian corn used as the motif for the handles of John Bell's bread knife (made by J. Rodgers of Sheffield) also spreads and bulges uncomfortably. Etched on the

n.68

n.69

n.70

n.71

120

77

121

119

121 Camellia teapot by Richard Redgrave

blade are a boy sowing and a boy reaping. The purpose of the object must be shown less by a serviceable shape than by literary association. For the same reasons H. J. Townshend calls his remarkably slender and elegant champagne glass (made by Christie's) 'Bubbles bursting' and his beer-jug (made by Minton's) 'The Hop Story'. The description of this reads: 'The bas-reliefs represent the picking, packing, and storing the hop, and the cooper at the beer-cask; "Labour refreshed" is one, and "Intemperance" the other supporter of the handle. "John Barleycorn" surmounts the lid'. So Cole and his friends, although they did from the beginning revolt against the wildest formal excesses, shared the universal High Victorian faith in the telling of stories by things made for day-to-day use. Three more examples to bear this out: a shaving-pot (made by Wedgwood) with the inscription:

> By the length of his beard can you measure a man?
> Poet or Hero? I doubt if you can.
> Bearded or shaven—Wit comes from Heaven;

a match-box designed by John Bell in the form of a Crusader's Altar Tomb (made in Parian by Minton's and in ormolu by Dee & Fargues*) and a door weight also designed by John Bell and given the shape of Cerberus with the three heads of a bulldog, a bloodhound and a deer-hound made by Stuart and Smith of Sheffield). The inscription here is on the base. It reads 'Welcome to come but not to go.'

122
123

124

n.72
125

122 *Champagne glass, 'Bubbles Bursting' by H.J. Townshend*

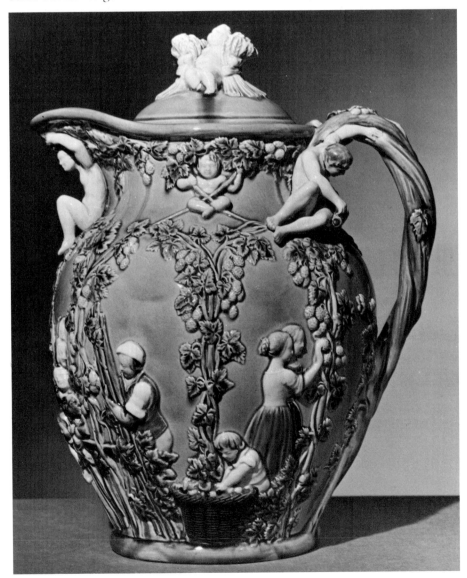

123 *'The Hop Story', beer-jug by H.J. Townshend, made by Minton's*

124 *Shaving mug by Richard Redgrave, made by Wedgwood's*

125 *Door weight by John Bell*

126 Chintz by Owen Jones

*127 Simplification by Dyce of a design
he found too naturalistic*

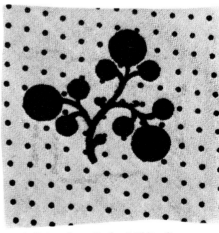

128 Printed textile by Liddiard's

No wonder the *Journal of Design* had its doubts about the propriety of some of these products of Henry Cole's. Others it showed without comment and with approval. On the whole it was indeed the object of the *Journal* to show what was best and to praise it. In this respect it is the most welcome corrective of the impressions transmitted to us by the catalogues and publications of 1851. It is known that exhibits on such occasions tend to be somewhat high-pitched. Every manufacturer and craftsman wants to show his finest and most elaborate things—not his workaday products. Some of the textiles and wallpapers to be seen in the *Journal*—and it had the unprecedented feature of including actual samples and patterns, not only illustrations of them—are indeed delightful, neither as coarse and florid as so much at the exhibition nor in any pedantic way correct according to whatever principles. Illustrations of work by Cole's own circle, are, however, also of interest, and designs by Dyce or Owen Jones, illustrated in the *Journal* are indeed flat, symmetrical and yet decorative, though in a somewhat ascetic way. The same had been true of Pugin's designs which could also be seen in the *Journal*. Wyatt in his folio on the best at the Exhibition also illustrates several things designed by Pugin, jewellery (made by Hardman), a big stove (made by the same, with Minton tiles), a carpet, an altar. Of his own power as a designer a bookbinding does not convey the highest opinion. Nor does a fireplace by Owen Jones illustrated in the *Journal*. Redgrave on the other hand designed a christening cup which was shown in the *Journal* in 1850 and then at the Exhibition, and which is a fairly simple, prettily sentimental piece.

The tenets of the *Journal* circle are very similar to Pugin's except that they are based on the current Victorian optimism rather than on Pugin's retrospective romanticism.

'Ornament is not . . . principal, . . . it must be secondary to the thing decorated',* there must be 'fitness in the ornament to the thing ornamented',* wallpapers must give 'the proper impression of flatness',* carpets must not have 'Louis Quatorze scrolls, gigantic tropical plants, shown in high relief, and suggestive of anything but a level or plane',* glass must show the clearness of water, 'Greek, Arabic, Indian, Louis Quinze ornament' must not be all 'printed on the same hanging',* shams in woven and printed fabrics are objectionable, * ironwork must be treated in harmony with 'the material and its manufacture' * 'the stucco abomination' must not hide 'honest brick'* and so on. Candlesticks 'supported on the toes of leaves and ends of flowers' and any 'rude adaptation of nature' are also violently resented. *

All these passages from the *Journal of Design* were printed before the opening of the Exhibition. Judged by such exacting standards, how much in the Crystal Palace could be accepted? Critical comments have been quoted as we went along. They came from Wornum, from Redgrave, from Wyatt, and from Semper. But the earliest outspoken condemnation of the taste displayed at the Exhibition was an article in *The Times,* no doubt written by one of the Cole group. The article, which speaks of 'the sins committed against good taste', and the 'most glaring . . . faults and short-comings' and 'the vulgarities of our manufacturers', was partly reprinted in the *Journal*, and Redgrave added 'the absence of any fixed principle in ornamental design is most apparent in the Exhibition'.* In his official *Supplementary Report on Design* Redgrave was no more guarded. 'It will be readily allowed that the mass of ornament applied to the works . . . exhibited is [meretricious]'.* Wornum's essay on *The Exhibition as a Lesson in Taste* came out before Redgrave's report. 'The taste of the producers in general' he sums up, 'is uneducated'. Wyatt used another, less aggressive form of criticism. His lavish folio with over 150 plates shows in its gorgeous chromo-lithography only what Wyatt approved. Much is Indian, Turkish, North African, Chinese, and little is British. His selection is evidently less critical than the others', as indeed his own architecture would lead us to expect.

Taken together, however, the *Journal* and these various publications are certainly a valiant effort to help matters. Moreover, thanks to Cole, there developed out of the exhibition a special Department of Practical Art within the

*128,

126,

130
38

120

n.73
n.75

n.76

n.77
n.79
n.80

n.81

n.83

Board of Trade (of which Cole was secretary) and a Museum of Manufactures, first housed in Marlborough House and then, from 1857 onwards, at South Kensington. At Marlborough House Cole had the courage to establish a Chamber of Horrors for the display of bad design. Dickens has described this short-lived adventure in *Household Words*. It is Mr Crumpet of Crump Lodge, Brixton, who speaks. 'I could have cried, Sir. I was ashamed of the pattern of my own trousers, for I saw a piece of them hung up there as a horror. I dared not pull out my pocket-handkerchief while anyone was by, lest I should be seen dabbing the perspiration from my forehead with a wreath of coral. I saw it all; when I went home I found that I had been living among horrors up to that hour. The paper in my parlour contains four birds of paradise, besides bridges and pagodas'.

Yet with all their zest and ingenuity Cole and his friends achieved nothing. The standards at the 1862 Exhibition were just as confused and the taste just as inflated. Yet their reform at the time was one of many, and the others accomplished more. Everywhere the earlier *laissez faire* began to give place to serious principles and a feeling of responsibility. Newman, Pusey and Keble must be seen in conjunction with Cole—Tract XC came out in 1841—and also the factory and housing legislation (Baths and Washhouses Acts 1846, 1847, Factory Act 1847, Town Improvements Act 1847, Public Health Act 1848, Lodging Houses 1851, Burials 1852). But while a religious conscience was still strong in England, left over from the earlier evangelicals, and while a social conscience was growing, aesthetic conscience was still bound to lag behind. I have tried to explain why fundamental improvements became possible only when imaginative power and aesthetic sensibility started to take design seriously. Alfred Stevens had done it, but only for a few years. Ford Madox Brown tried it, too: he did designs for furniture and also for household articles, and he wanted to exhibit designs for furniture at the Hogarth Club in 1859 and was not allowed to do so,

n.84 whereupon he resigned.* The change came only with William Morris, simply because Morris was the biggest man, though perhaps also because by then a new and different spirit of reform had developed in other fields as well. The first furniture which Morris designed—in 1857 for his room at Red Lion Square—was as Rossetti said, 'intensely mediaeval', 'tables and chairs like incubi and

n.85 succubi'.* Then, in 1859, came the building of Red House and more furniture, competently and sensitively designed by Philip Webb, and finally, in 1861, the establishment of Morris, Marshall and Faulkner. Here was a firm much more promising than Felix Summerly's because it was the creation of a man who loved to make things himself and knew how to make them, and because his friends were artists to whom decoration did not mean flamboyant ornament but a functional discipline. Morris himself was a lover of nature undoubtedly no less ardent than those who copied lilies for vases and lamps, but he insisted on training nature into pattern.

Finally there is the social aspect of Morris's reform. This is perhaps his most important achievement. Yet to the superficial glance just in this aspect Morris was wrong and the Cole circle had been right. The Cole circle believed in design for the masses, Morris in handicraft which, though meant 'for the people', could only be for the few because what is made by hand is bound to be costly. But Morris had seen what Cole and Redgrave and Semper and Wyatt had not seen, that design is not only an aesthetic problem, but also an integral part of a larger social problem, and therein lay the future.

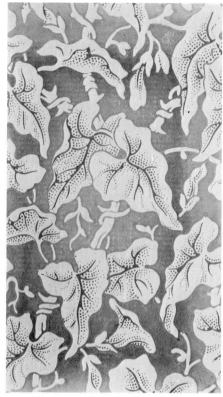

129 Wallpaper by Hinchliff & Co.

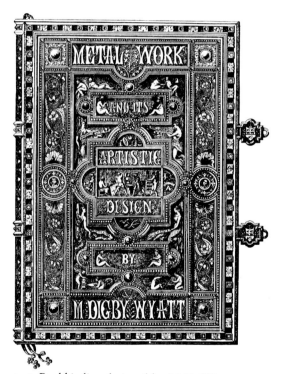

130 Bookbinding designed by M.D. Wyatt

1 *Design for a new National Gallery in London, 1866*

Cambridge University Press, 1949

IV
Matthew Digby Wyatt

This essay was my inaugural lecture as Slade Professor of Fine Art at Cambridge in 1950 and I have left it substantially as it was delivered, only making a few cuts where it overlapped with the previous essay in this volume.

Mr Vice-Chancellor, Ladies and Gentlemen,

'In addressing you for the first time from this chair it is natural that I should feel a certain amount of embarrassing emotions.' These words, you will agree, are a very proper beginning for an inaugural lecture. But they are not mine. They are Sir Matthew Digby Wyatt's, the first sentence of his inaugural lecture, when he had been made Slade Professor of Fine Art in 1869. At about the same time Ruskin had become Slade Professor at Oxford. Ruskin was—I suppose one would have to say—an author and journalist. Wyatt was an architect, a member of a family which has produced at least nine other architects, and among them such ornaments of the profession as James Wyatt of Fonthill, Ashridge and the Pantheon in Oxford Street, Jeffry of Sidney Sussex College and the Gothic modernization of Windsor, and Thomas Henry, Matthew Digby's brother, whose Wilton church of 1844 was one of the most famous examples of a revived Early Christian style.

Matthew Digby did not design anything quite so prominent, and the aesthetic quality of his buildings is distressing indeed, as I shall have occasion to show. But he was a successful man, though more in administration and organization than in art: Honorary Secretary to the Royal Institute of British Architects from 1855 to 1859, Gold Medallist and Vice-President of the R.I.B.A., Hon. M.A. Cambridge, Knight of the Legion of Honour, and so on.

He was forty-nine when he was elected to the newly founded Slade professorship, on the strength of his writings no doubt more than his buildings.* He had been articled to his brother Thomas Henry, who was thirteen years his elder, and had then, as was almost *de rigueur* amongst architects at that time, travelled on the Continent and published the results of his journeys. His chief interest had been the adornment of church interiors, an interest aroused no doubt by his brother, who had, when Matthew started on his travels, just completed the much-discussed and much-praised decoration in mosaic of Wilton church. So Matthew's first book was *Specimens of the Geometrical Mosaic of the Middle Ages*. It came out in 1848, and was followed later by others on polychromy in decoration, on metalwork, textile art, and the applied arts in general (see Appendix, p. 266).

The next year, 1849, was decisive in Wyatt's career. The Society of Arts commissioned him to write a report on an exhibition of French industrial products held in Paris. He went over with Henry Cole and thus won the friendship of that most remarkable Victorian.* Cole joined the Society of Arts in 1846, three years after Prince Albert had accepted the Society's presidency. The two men, equal in 'indomitable energy and perseverance', to use William Whewell's

n.1

n.2

2 *Byzantine Court for the Crystal Palace, Sydenham, 1854*

3 *Detail of Paddington Station, 1854*

words,* got on splendidly, and one result of their co-operation was the Great   n.3
Exhibition of the Industrial Products of All Nations which opened on 1 May
1851 with Wyatt as the Secretary to the Executive Committee. That the organization of the great show worked without a hitch and that it was a huge popular
success need not be said once again; that the exhibits had much that is aesthetically questionable or indeed bad by any criteria of judgment needs no re-iterating
either. What does concern me here is the fact that Matthew Digby Wyatt in
his own buildings fully shared the failings of the exhibits, and that in spite of this
he could be critical of the latter with well considered and well developed arguments.

As for his buildings only a few can here be looked at, just enough, I hope, to
come to a judgment on his gifts as an architect. Among his earliest architectural
designs is what he did for the Crystal Palace at the time of its re-erection at
Sydenham, that is in 1854. The Byzantine Court we know in a state of ideal   *2*
freshness from a water-colour at the Victoria and Albert Museum. It is quite
enjoyable as a water-colour,* painted in hot colours under a smiling blue sky,   n.4
with fat dark green and *sang-de-boeuf* columns and a general rotundity characteristic of the mid-nineteenth century. There is not much fantasy in the design itself,
no doubt because of the educational purpose of the structure. As for the Byzantine style one must, of course, not take this as in any way representing a personal
predilection of Wyatt. He also designed for the Crystal Palace the Pompeian,
English Gothic, French Gothic, Elizabethan, Italian Renaissance and some other
Courts and Vestibules.

While this catholic assortment of styles introduces us to Wyatt the architectural scholar and the future professor, we can see him at Paddington Station,
also in 1854, taking time off as it were to enjoy himself. The ground-floor of the
central feature of Platform One, with the Queen's apartment behind, is vaguely   *3*
of the French Dixhuitième, while on the upper floor two Quattrocento windows flank a debased Palladian or Venetian window. There is in addition plenty
of incised and fretwork ornament all along the platform, and at the old south end
of the station too. It is all very jolly in a ham-fisted way, as near as Wyatt ever got
to the style of the Victorian music-hall, that is the folk-art or popular art of the
nineteenth century. It has—no doubt deliberately—none of the classical gravity
and discipline of Hardwick's Euston Propylaea. In fact the most striking feature

of Wyatt's work at Paddington is the lack of self-discipline, the relief at being for a change off one's best behaviour, the relief at relaxation. One must examine the whole building to get the flavour of this completely relaxed tensionless trailing on of ornament. One consequence of this brief abandon of best behaviour is that Paddington is emphatically not period imitation. That makes it so particularly important for an understanding of Wyatt's own taste.

We find the same weakly flamboyance appearing more timidly in the Royal Engineers' Crimean War Memorial at Chatham. The design is in adapted Italian Renaissance forms with the addition of a few original decorative bits, such as the volutes. The arch was erected in 1861. In 1862 Wyatt did one design for the Albert Memorial as a classical temple and another as an Italian Gothic Cross. I don't know what they looked like, but I do know that in the same year, for an office building in Grafton Street, Dublin, he chose the Italian style of the fourteenth century.* Again certain details, such as the shop windows below and the attic story with its stumpy piers above, are deliberately incorrect, that is, mark a conscious or unconscious improvement by the Victorian architect on his Trecento predecessors. And it is quite obvious that they succeed in making the building look High Victorian. If one tries to analyse what else is here specifically High Victorian, I would point to three qualities. First, the all-over covering of the whole façade with motifs, second, the fact that all the motifs used are rather

4 *Offices in Grafton Street, Dublin, 1862*

5 *Royal Engineers' Crimean War Memorial, Chatham, 1861*

6 Courtyard of the India Office, Whitehall, 1867

7 Pitt Club, Cambridge, c.1865

rich and robust, and third, the lack of any resolute accents. This general even pitch of oratory is especially characteristic. The eighteen-thirties and forties still believed in contrasts of emphasized and unemphasized parts, though obviously not as much as the Georgians. That is evident, for instance, in the Fitzwilliam Museum at Cambridge by Basevi and Cockerell which was begun in 1837. The coming men in the eighteen-seventies believed in accents again, as one can see in Waterhouse's work at Girton (begun in 1873) and Champney's at Newnham (begun in 1875)—to stay at Cambridge.

After Wyatt's Tuscan Gothic, some Genoese Cinquecento of his. The job this time was a government building, the courtyard of Gilbert Scott's India Office in Whitehall.* So Wyatt was more restrained, but he did not give up what splendour he regarded as appropriate. The detail is uncommonly carefully designed, and the effect undeniably one of festive public display.

In the case of private display, Wyatt felt considerably less inhibited. For the Salon at Ashridge (1864), for instance, he designed huge doorways in aedicule surrounds with heavy broken segmental pediments and fireplaces supported by life-size labouring caryatids. Even more Gargantuan was the fireplace in the Hall of Clare College, Cambridge, redecorated by Wyatt in 1870–2. Willis and Clark tell us that it cost £3500 and was 'ornamented with large oak figures, supporting a bust of the foundress, the woodwork enriched with arabesques and festoons'. The plaster ceiling hung from iron girders is still *in situ* though regrettably simplified.

6

n.6

8 Eveline Rothschild Mausoleum, 1867   *9 Alford House, Kensington, 1872*

8   The odd combination of the festive with the turgid which characterizes these fireplaces is also exhibited in Wyatt's mausoleum for Eveline Rothschild at the Jewish Cemetery, West Ham. Mrs Rothschild died young in 1866. The mausoleum is circular with a dome of eighteenth-century detail on attached Corinthian columns. The panels between the columns with their naturalistic flower motifs in the centres and the ornamental ironwork above the panels deserve the attention of the student of mid-Victorian detail.

9   Alford House, Kensington, of 1872 is also classical, but with an admixture of the Parisian of Henri IV. The French roof is unmistakable. However, the red brick, the swags and the setting transfer one's thoughts from France to England and in particular Christopher Wren's England.

10   Purely English, but in the Tudor style, is Wyatt's most spectacular country mansion, Possingworth Manor built for Mr Huth, the celebrated collector. The design is of the accepted asymmetry, with decoration even extending into the roof—Wyatt had himself designed ornamental roof-tiles in several colours for a manufacturer. The Gothic version of the Venetian window in the middle gable should be specially noted. A similar carefree confusion of motifs reigns supreme

10 Possingworth Manor, Sussex, 1868

11 *West front of Addenbrooke's Hospital, Cambridge, 1864–5*

in the Hall of Possingworth. The fireplace is Gothic, the ceiling Jacobean, the *12*
upholstery in its unmistakably bulgy curves Victorian and nothing else. But
again the essential feature is the all-over covering of everything from floor to
ceiling with ornament of some sort, a monotonous process without emphasis or
punctuation.

Nowhere else in Wyatt's *oeuvre* does this embarrassing lack of concentration
come out more distressingly than in Addenbrooke's Hospital at Cambridge of *11*
1864. It is sufficient to look at these symmetrical wings with their buttresses
holding up an arcade with closely set columns, and the two broader arcades with
a third above displaying vaguely Gothic lintels which connect the wings with a
weakly recessed Tudor centre, and one cannot fail to feel that deliberation must
have dictated to the architect this covering of his whole surface with whatever
motifs, but that the quality and juxtaposition of these motifs shows him to have
been a highly insensitive architect.

Surely, you might say, it is perverse to exhume Wyatt on the occasion of so
special a lecture, and it would be, if there were nothing to him but this display of
architectural thick-skinnedness. In fact, however, his buildings are no more than
a foil to his achievement as a critic and theorist of design and architecture.* n.7

To give one early example, he wrote in 1850 apropos design in ironwork
that

'no successful results can be attained . . . until either 1st the manufacturer and
designer are one individual doubly gifted, or 2nd the manufacturer takes the
pains to investigate and master so much of the elements of design as shall at least
enable him to judiciously control the artist; or 3rd the artist by a careful study of
the material and its manufacture shall elaborate and employ a system of design
in harmony with, and special to, the peculiarities so evolved.'

This sounds like Morris, but Morris's lectures did not start until twenty-
seven years later. In fact it was published in Henry Cole's *Journal of Design and
Manufactures*,* the journal whose scope and sound critical principles we have n.8
already met. It is worth quoting more passages from it because they anticipate
Morris, and also sound remarkably topical even today.

'Chaos and disorder' rule in art to-day.* 'Everyone elects his own style. . . . n.9
We all agree only in being wretched imitators.'* Yet it is a 'vain and foolish n.10
attempt to make the art which faithfully represents the wants, the faculties and
the feelings of one people, represent those of another people under totally different conditions'.* Hence all our attempts at revivals have 'signally failed' and n.11

'the universal thirst' for a style 'in harmony with our institutions and modes of
n.12   thought' cannot be denied and 'must ultimately be satisfied'.* To satisfy it
n.13   'principles and not results' of the arts in the past must be heeded.* What are these
permanent principles of design to which industrial art of the nineteenth century
must return? First of all, every object 'to afford perfect pleasure must be fit for the
n.14   purpose and true in its construction'.* Its ornamentation must be related 'to the
n.15   process by which (it) is to be executed'* and to the position in which it is to be
seen. Thus a wallpaper made to cover a wall must give an 'impression of flat-
n.16   ness.'*

n.17   The same principle applies to floor coverings.* Moreover, 'a carpet, whilst
it covers the floor, is also the ground from which all the furniture . . . [is], as it
were, to rise: it should therefore be treated as a flat surface and have none of
n.18   those imitations of raised forms and solid architectural ornaments so often seen'. *
There must be no 'Louis Quatorze scrolls, gigantic tropical plants, shewn in high
n.19   relief, and suggestive of anything but a level or plane'.*

To see how Digby Wyatt had devoured and digested all these theories, we
must look at what he said in a lecture of 1852 called *An Attempt to define the*
n.20   *Principles which should determine Form in the Decorative Arts.** In nature 'form is,
in every case, if not dependent on, at least coincident with, structural fitness'.
'Ornament appears the offspring of necessity alone.' 'Without due attention to
n.21   simplicity, fitness has never been adequately carried out.'* In designing an
object we have to be fully aware of 'all essential particulars concerning its
material, its method of construction, and its uses'. Exactly the same is true of designing a building. Here also consideration of its purpose must come first, and all
materials must be used 'according to their nature'.

12 Hall of Possingworth Manor, Sussex, 1868

Now this insistence on truth in architecture, 'plain and manly truth', had been preached three years before Wyatt's lecture, by a man in no way connected with the Cole circle, in a book called *The Seven Lamps of Architecture*. One of the seven lamps is the Lamp of Truth, and Ruskin, in the enthusiasm of his thirty years—he was just one year older than Wyatt—thundered against 'architectural deceits' consisting of 'a mode of structure or support, other than the true one' and the endeavour to make surfaces 'represent some other material than that of which they actually consist'.*   n.22

Wyatt knew the *Seven Lamps* of course and even reviewed it in 1849 in the *Journal of Design*.* He was impressed by 'this thoughtful and eloquent book'   n.23
and its 'denunciation of shams', which corresponded so well to what the *Journal of Design* had established as one of its own functions. But he was critical of other aspects of Ruskin's preaching, and here we are watching the beginnings of a conflict which is of high interest to us here, not only because it happens to be one between the future first Cambridge and the future first Oxford Slade Professors, but also because the two positions held by the two men are still of great significance for our own day.

The points of disagreement were chiefly two. One seems at first quite a small point, but is psychologically interesting enough: the attitude of Wyatt and Ruskin to their predecessor, Augustus Welby Pugin; the other concerns the much wider issue of the possibility of a genuine style of modern architecture in the nineteenth century. As regards Pugin, Wyatt in a somewhat later review of Ruskin's *Stones of Venice*,* blamed Ruskin for his attack on Pugin and for con-   n.24
cealing the influence which Pugin had evidently had on him.* And it is indeed   n.25
true that Pugin, who after a hectic life of only forty years, died insane in 1852, was the fountain-head of all the reform movements in design and architecture during the nineteenth century. In his writings of 1836 and 1841, besides establishing fanatically that to build in the Gothic style only was a matter of orthodoxy and a point of honour, he also insisted that 'the great test of architectural beauty is the fitness of the design to the purpose for which it is intended',* that 'con-   n.26
struction . . . should vary with the material employed',* and that it is thus   n.27
absurd in wallpapers to repeat 'a perspective over a large surface' and in carpets to use 'highly relieved foliage'.*   n.28

Wyatt, an honest man, felt strongly that Ruskin should have done what he himself did,* namely, paid 'a humble tribute to the truth and justice' of many of   n.29
the propositions put forward by that 'most earnest and earliest' amongst reformers, 'the late Augustus Welby Pugin'.* Wyatt's charge against Ruskin is,   n.30
in my opinion, only too well justified, and to have recognized the questionable personal character of Ruskin at so early a date is a sign of considerable shrewdness in Wyatt. Equally shrewd is his criticism of Ruskin's 'half-views' on the problem of architecture and design under nineteenth-century conditions. This is what he writes*—and he was, I think, the first to recognize this valid objection to   n.31
Ruskin as well as Morris:

'Instead of boldly recognising the tendencies of the age, which are inevitable . . . instead of considering the means of improving these tendencies . . . he either puts up his back against their further development, or would attempt to bring back the world of art to what its course of action was four centuries ago. Our course in this nineteenth century may be hateful, if you please; denounce it, but as it *is* our course, wise men should recognise the fact.'

The inadequacy of Ruskin's argument, says Wyatt, comes out most clearly in his lack of a 'consistent theory of mechanical repetition as applied to art', that is of machine-art and in his 'very lop-sided view of railways and railway-architecture'. And it is true that in the *Seven Lamps* Ruskin lists 'machine-made ornament of any kind' amongst the architectural deceits, and owing to his almost exclusive concern with ornamentation as the source of architectural beauty* never considers the aesthetic possibilities of machine-shaped forms. And   n.32
as regards railway-architecture, that is the new architecture of iron and glass,

Ruskin was indeed at first painfully confused and then bluntly hostile. In the *Seven Lamps* he says on the one hand—a unique remark, I think, in his vast *oeuvre*—that 'the time is probably near when a new system of architectural laws will be developed, entirely adapted to metallic construction',* but on the other hand, he calls 'the iron roofs and pillars of our railway stations . . . not architecture at all'.*

Wyatt, in his turn, wrote an article in the *Journal of Design* which he called *Principles and Treatment of Ironwork** and which contains a juster appreciation of the architectural values of metal structures—and an appreciation moreover which must be amongst the earlier and most generous.* Here is what he wrote, in 1850, it must be remembered: 'It has become difficult to define where civil engineering ends and architecture begins.' Bridges such as the tubular Britannia Bridge across the Menai Straits and the Conway Suspension Bridge are amongst the 'wonders of the world', and as for Isambard Kingdom Brunel, the designer of the Clifton and Hungerford Bridges and Wyatt's fellow-designer later on at Paddington Station, 'his independence of meretricious and adventitious ornament is as great and as above prejudice as his engineering works are daring in conception and masterly in execution. From such beginnings', Wyatt continues, 'what glories may be in reserve, when England has systematized a scale of form and proportion—a vocabulary of its own, in which to speak to the world the language of its power, and freedom of thought and feeling, we may trust ourselves to dream, but we dare not predict. Whatever the result may be,' he concludes, 'it is impossible to disregard the fact, that the building for the Exhibition of 1851 is likely to accelerate the "consummation devoutly to be wished" and that the novelty of its form and details will be likely to exercise a powerful influence upon national taste'.*

When Wyatt wrote this manifesto—a document not, I think, hitherto known and yet of just as much importance in the history of taste as the *Seven Lamps*—he was already secretary to the Exhibition, and Paxton's design for the Crystal Palace had been made, approved and published.*

That in this crucial case again Wyatt was right and Ruskin was wrong we have already seen in the preceding essay. Instead of presenting Ruskin's wrong-headed remarks again, here is what he wrote in a special pamphlet when the Crystal Palace had been re-erected at Sydenham in 1854 (with Wyatt's various courts inside): after three hundred years 'of the most curious investigation' all that architecture has been able to produce for this 'national museum' is a 'magnified conservatory';* and in *Praeterita* again he refers to the Crystal Palace as a 'cucumber frame'.* Wyatt on the other hand, in a factual and restrained address to the Institution of Civil Engineers in 1851, said that the Crystal Palace 'may be expected to produce, hereafter, important changes in the construction and appearance of many extensive buildings throughout the country'.*

So, to say it again, in respect of contemporary architecture and industrial design, Cambridge undeniably scores over Oxford. However, I know only too well that it would be unwise for me from this chair to carry too far specific comparisons between the first Cambridge and the first Oxford Slade Professors. For Ruskin, though perhaps more often wrong than Wyatt, and though no doubt the less acceptable character, was a man of genius, and Wyatt was not. Ruskin was, moreover, of burning eloquence and high sensitivity, and in both these qualities Wyatt was somewhat defective. We need only compare a few passages referring to painting and architecture. Here is first as much as Wyatt in his Slade course does in the way of analysing a Giottesque painting, the *Marriage of Saint Francis with Poverty* at Assisi: 'A vivid and graceful embodiment of that incident.'* And here is Ruskin on Giotto's *Meeting at the Golden Gate* in the Arena Chapel at Padua:

'It is full of the most solemn grace and tenderness. The face of Anna, half seen, is most touching in its depth of expression, and it is very interesting to observe how Giotto has enhanced its sweetness by giving a harder and grosser

n.33
n.34
n.35
n.36
n.37
n.38
n.39
n.40
n.41
n.42

character than is usual with him to the heads of the other two principal female figures, and by the rough and weather-beaten countenance of the entering shepherd.'*   n.43

And, secondly, here is a typical Ruskin remark on the nature of the Gothic style in architecture:

'The feelings and habits in the workman must be understood. There is first the habit of hard and rapid working; the industry of the tribes of the North, quickened by the coldness of the climate, and giving an expression of sharp energy to all they do, as opposed to the languor of the Southern tribes.'*   n.44

Again, as a criterion of good Gothic work the following could hardly have been improved even by the late Professor E. S. Prior, the best English interpreter of Gothic and—let it be said—a Cambridge Slade Professor:

'See if it looks as if it had been built by strong men; if it has the sort of rough-ness, and largeness, and nonchalance, mixed in places with the exquisite tender-ness which seems always to be a sign-manual of the broad vision, and massy power of men who can see past the work they are doing, and betray here and there something like disdain for it. If the building has that character, it is much already in its favour; it will go hard but it proves a noble one.'*   n.45

Partiality forbids me to match this with a detailed quotation from Wyatt's Slade lectures on the history of architecture with their rare dim remarks about 'a lighter scale of parts', or 'a beauty of refinement in the execution of foliage [and] mouldings'.*   n.46

However, perhaps one should not be shocked by this deficiency in our Wyatt. For since all his signal contributions concern the principles of design and the appreciation of a new technological architecture, why should he be ex-pected to have been a man of any special sensibility? Here also lies, of course, the explanation of the fact how so undeniably remarkable a man can have been so undeniably bad an architect. Such a contrast between theory and performance is frequent amongst Victorian architects. It occurs in Pugin and Gilbert Scott, even more blatantly in Viollet-le-Duc, and in many others.

Very generally speaking one can perhaps say that harmony between theory and performance must be rooted in a much deeper harmony between thought and feeling.* This harmony returned only into the arts of design with William   n.47 Morris. Morris, it is known, appreciated Owen Jones; Wyatt he will hardly have noticed much. The man to whom he owed most was Ruskin. From Ruskin he received his romantic backward-looking enthusiasm for the Middle Ages. From Ruskin he received his faith in art as 'a happiness for the maker and for the user', *   n.48 and from Ruskin his hatred for his own century, its machines, its commerce and its grimy cities.

Wyatt would have approved no more of Morris than he did of Ruskin. Wyatt worshipped industry and 'the comparative annihilation of time and space, through the railway and telegraph'. He firmly believed in 'free trade . . . free press, free navigation, free education . . . comparatively free postal com-munication' and 'that ruthless destroyer of conventional restrictions—Com-petition'.*   n.49

Morris on competition is as telling: work in the Middle Ages was intelligent work and pleasant to do. Work now is unintelligent and 'irksome and degrad-ing'. 'The immediate cause of this degrading labour which oppresses so large a part of our people is the system of competitive commerce'; for 'machine-organized labour is necessary to competitive commerce'. *   n.50

The contrast here between the Cole circle and Morris goes to the very foundations of their feelings and convictions, and hence, when you read the venerable past-Master of Trinity, the Rev. William Whewell, a man in symp-athy with the Cole circle, Prince Albert and the ideas behind the exhibition of 1851, pronounce that art ought to be created 'not to satisfy the tastes of the few,

13 Ironwork of the suspension bridge formerly in St James's Park, 1857

n.51 [but] to supply the wants of the many',* and then find that Morris said exactly
n.52 the same—'what business have we with art at all, unless all can share it'*—then
you will be suspicious at once of this seeming concordance. In fact, Morris of
course meant something utterly different. His aim was to make all work and all
art a joy for the maker and the user. To Cole and the others the aim is, as Wyatt
put it in 1849, to provide 'the enjoyments of taste to the enormous and now all-
n.53 powerful Bourgeois class'.* I will not dwell on the class aspects of this. What
matters to me is that Wyatt thinks of the industrialist and the designer for industry, not of the craftsman. And he thinks not of the clientele that can afford the
work of the craftsman—Morris's clientele, whether he liked the fact or not, had
to be of a certain affluence—but of art which everybody can afford.

Hence Cole's Art Manufactures of the forties, hence his activities as Secretary
to the Department of Practical Art, and later as Director of the Victoria and
Albert Museum, and hence Redgrave's job as Inspector General of Art.

Looking at it from the point of view of today, Wyatt, Cole, Redgrave are
the predecessors of our Councils of Industrial Design and Art Councils and all the
other governmentally—and perhaps academically—aided means of promoting
art. They were just as convinced as we are, and as Morris was, that not all is well
in the realm of art and architecture, but they believed that by better training and
by lecturing and exhibiting, art, architecture and aesthetic understanding might
be re-established within our own society, whereas Morris believed that a complete change of heart, if not a complete upheaval of society, would have to
n.54 precede the re-establishment of an art worth having.*

Who in this argument is right? We have to ask ourselves just as urgently
now as they had to in 1851. Who is right? Ruskin and his disciple Morris, or
Digby Wyatt?

In asking this question in this form, I have cunningly placed Wyatt on the
same level as Ruskin and Morris. If you are ready, after having listened to me,
to be taken in by this, I shall have succeeded in my humble intention of making
the first Cambridge Slade Professor appear for an hour more interesting than he
really was.

An appendix listing Wyatt's works will be found on pages 266–268

1 William Morris (1834–1896)

Journal of the Royal Institute of British Architects, 3rd Series, LXIV, 1957

V

William Morris and Architecture

n.1 THE FASCINATION of any reading of William Morris, be it his letters or his lectures or any monograph on him* is to feel in the presence of an exceptionally powerful human being, a being with plenty of contradictions and incompatibilities, but all forged into one impetuous whole, forceful, wilful, single-minded. 'I am a boor and the son of a boor', he communicated to a man at their
n.2 first meeting.* A maid at the Burne-Joneses one day took him for a burglar, so
n.3, 4 slovenly, or unplaceable, was his dress*—dark blue suit, lighter blue shirt, no tie,*
n.5 and a 'great capacity for producing and annexing dirt'.* His restlessness, the fact that he couldn't sit still even at meals, that he got into tempers which made him run his head against the wall, or bite his teeth into the edge of a table, these things
n.6 are familiar.*

Less familiar perhaps but equally illuminating is the fact that with all this violence he remained yet a detached character, to a remarkable degree managing to keep out of emotional entanglements that might endanger his work. 'I must confess it . . . I am living my own life in spite of . . . anything grievous that may
n.7 happen.'* 'I have ever been loth to think that there were no people going through
n.8 life . . . free from binding entanglements. Such a one I want to be.'* Wilfred Scawen Blunt summoned this up immediately after Morris's death. 'He is the most wonderful man I have ever known, unique in this, that he had no thought for any thing or person, including himself, but only for the work he had in hand. . . . He was too absorbed in his own thoughts to be either openly affectionate or actively kind. . . . I have seen him tender to his daughter Jenny and nice with her and with his wife, but . . . his life was not arranged in reference to them. To the
n.9 rest of the world he seemed quite indifferent . . .'*

And this of a man who gave up painting because it was too unconnected with the promotion of the well-being of others, who gave up architecture because work in an office, as architecture mostly is, was too detached from life, and whose ever-guiding maxim was: 'What business have we with art at all,
n.10 unless all can share it.'* His socio-aesthetic principles are familiar: art must be for the people, not for the connoisseur; it must be by the people not by 'unassisted
n.11 individual genius'.* This is how the conditions of art were in the Middle Ages, and unless such conditions can be restored to our age, there is no hope of a decent art or a decent life.

It is from these principles that one must start to understand Morris's faith in
n.12 architecture. His faith was indeed of the highest: 'the master-art' he calls it,* and
n.13 'one of the most important things which man can turn his hand to'.* His hand, it should be noted, not his mind. It may be an accidental turn of phrase, but it is very telling all the same. The crafts that make up architecture were closer to

Morris's heart than the intellectual power of designing. So the aspect of architecture which interested him most is that, according to him, 'every work of architecture is a work of co-operation'.* And so it is, of course, though not necessarily always in the sense in which Morris meant it. What he meant is the outcome of his veneration for the Middle Ages. 'The ancient buildings of the Middle Ages' were indeed 'the work of associated labour and thought of the people'.* Today, on the other hand—that is, in Morris's day—'the great architect' is 'carefully . . . guarded from the common troubles of common men'.* How true this was of an age in which an architect of repute designed churches, public buildings, country houses and villas but scarcely ever houses for the common man need hardly be stressed. Yet this is not really what Morris was pleading for. He was a born craftsman, and so he turned his plea at once from architecture in the direction of craft: 'Noble as that art is by itself, and though it is specially the art of civilisation, it neither ever has existed nor ever can exist alive and progressive by itself, but must cherish and be cherished by all the crafts whereby men make the things which they intend shall be beautiful and shall last somewhat beyond the passing day. It is this union of the arts, mutually helpful and harmoniously subordinated one to another which I have learnt to think of as Architecture.'* We today may have our doubts about the word crafts here, irreplaceable as it was to Morris, but the wide view taken of the duties and privileges of the architect will strike a sympathetic chord. In a passage immediately preceding the one just quoted, Morris said more comprehensively that architecture 'embraces the consideration of the whole external surroundings of the life of man; we cannot escape from it if we would . . . for it means the moulding and altering to human needs of the very face of the earth itself'.* That surely was bold in the days of Scott and Butterfield, or even Norman Shaw and Philip Webb, and its logical consequence was that to Morris 'unless you are resolved to have good and rational architecture, it is . . . useless your thinking about art at all'.*

But so far this has been architecture in the abstract. Now how do these principles link up with the actual building that surrounded Morris? His enthusiasm was for Gothic architecture, and his dislike of Renaissance architecture was intense, both tastes fostered by his great admiration for Ruskin. He discovered the Gothic style for himself first at Oxford and then when travelling in France at the age of twenty-one. 'O! the glories of the Churches we have seen!' he exclaimed in a letter to a friend,* and at the age of twenty-two he wrote in an article in the *Oxford and Cambridge Magazine*:* 'I think those same churches of North France the grandest, the most beautiful, the kindest and most loving of all the buildings that the earth has ever borne.' He would have written almost the same at the age of sixty-two. In the same youthful letter there is also a reference to a church 'Deo gratias not yet restored'.* So Morris's great preoccupation with protection instead of restoration started early too and was of course also stimulated by Ruskin.* It led in the end to Morris being instrumental in bringing about the Society for the Protection of Ancient Buildings, the Anti-Scrape, as they called it, and in formulating the principles for the treatment of old buildings which are to this day valid. They include two important new points: an intense appreciation of the surfaces of buildings, and tolerance for the incongruity of their furnishings, as accumulated through the ages. 'The natural weathering of the surface of a building is beautiful, and its loss disastrous.'* In another place Morris adds to this aesthetic the historic interest in 'the sentiment attaching to the very face which the original builders gave their work'* —a fallacious argument because weather ruins an original face as thoroughly as the nineteenth-century builder's workmen. Now for furnishings: 'In my opinion there is no remedy . . . but for the public to make up its mind to put up with "comparatively recent" incongruities in old churches . . . and to be content with keeping them weathertight.'* Hence Morris's hatred of Gilbert Scott whom he once called 'the (happily) dead dog'* and hence his defence of Wren's City Churches menaced with destruction,* although he obviously could not like them. He called St Paul's, 'on the grounds of beauty', hardly acceptable 'as a substitute for even the

n.14

n.15

n.16

n.17

n.18

n.19

n.20
n.21

n.22

n.23

n.24

n.25

n.26
n.27
n.28

latest and worst Gothic building', and accepted Wren churches only either as 'proper', respectable and showing 'the due amount of cultivation . . . of a
n.29   decent unenthusiastic ecclesiasticism' * or, from the historian's point of view, as 'a destined link in the history of the ecclesiastical art of this country'. All the same, in some cases he was ready to acknowledge the 'architectural beauty' of English
n.30   Renaissance work, e.g. in the staircase of Ashburnham House.* But these cases are rare, and his dislike was really constitutional, in the sense that it applied to all Italian Renaissance art as well. In a letter to Lady Burne-Jones from Verona he confessed in the same year in which he wrote to *The Times* in favour of the City Churches: 'With the latter [i.e. post-Gothic] work of Southern Europe I am quite out of sympathy. In spite of its magnificent power and energy, I feel it as an enemy. . . . Even in these . . . wonderful towns I long rather for the heap of
n.31   grey stones with a grey roof that we call a house north-away.'*

But all this is still only Morris's reactions to the old, even if extremely lively reactions. What now when it comes to building afresh and for his own age? The first principle is this: 'Today there is only one style of architecture on which it is
n.32   possible to found a true living art . . . and that style is Gothic architecture. * However, in practice things worked out much more complicatedly. For neither was Morris an advocate of the Gothic Revival, as it was accepted by many estimable contemporaries of his, nor was he entirely an enemy to Georgian domestic architecture. So his actual position was very different from, e.g. Scott's who had advocated the Gothic style as the most suitable for 'domestic architecture, present and future', and denounced Baker Street and Gower Street
n.33   as 'utterly intolerable'.* Morris, on the other hand, called J.P. Seddon's neo-
n.34   Gothic St Paul's Parish Church at Hammersmith 'an excrescence'* and Water-
n.35   house's Assize Courts at Manchester 'a dreary pretentious heap'.* So it looks as if the pleading for Gothic architecture meant no more than that 'an architectural style' for our age must be 'the growth of our own times, but connected with all
n.36   history'.* Nor was all history to Morris simply tantamount to Gothic forms. That results as clearly from a study of Morris's designs for textiles as from such
n.37   sayings as 'I by nature turn to romance rather than classicalism'.* His friend
n.38   Webb said the same about him: 'W. M. . . . used any "strain"* which came
n.39   through his wide knowledge of many ways and manners.'* In fact and in spite of all these strains, i.e. these allusions to Persia, Turkey, Gothic tapestries, Jacobean embroidery in Morris's designs, Burne-Jones was right in saying: 'All his life he hated the copying of ancient work as unfair to the old and stupid for the
n.40   present.'* He said the same himself once, inveighing against 'the trick of mas-
n.41   querading in other men's cast-off clothes'.*

So while, according to Morris, a style of the late nineteenth or twentieth century ought to be founded on the Gothic it ought not to imitate it. So far this sounds perfectly consistent and convincing. Unfortunately, however, Morris continues the very passage quoted above, about the founding of all living architecture on Gothic architecture, by adding: 'As to the form of it'—that is, of living architecture 'in the future'—'I see nothing for it but that the form, as well as the
n.42   spirit, must be Gothic'.* Here then is a conflict, and in order to understand how it could arise we must look more closely at Morris's conception of the development of the Gothic Revival in the nineteenth century. In several pages of his lecture on *The Revival of Architecture* he describes how the early Gothic revivers
n.43   built 'ridiculous travesties of Gothic buildings',* how the 'genuine study of mediaeval architecture' began, how 'it was slowly discovered that it was not, as was thought in the days of Walter Scott, a mere accidental jumble of pictures-queness consecrated by ruins . . . but a logical and organic style' and how 'those principles' discovered in the Gothic style 'belonged to the aesthetics of all art in
n.44   all countries'.* The next step after that was to see—regretfully perhaps—that the nineteenth had too little in common with the finest Gothic, that of the early fourteenth century, to make it at all possible to link the one with the other. So architects, Morris says, turned first to the Perpendicular as a 'more workaday'
n.45   style* and then even to the late sixteenth and the first half of the seventeenth

2 Mid-seventeenth century staircase of Ashburnham House, London

3 Bedford Park: design for the Tabard Inn and stores, by Norman Shaw

centuries, because the style then valid 'drew what vigour and beauty it had from this impulse of the period that preceded it'.* After this 'semi-Gothic survival' * followed the change to classical architecture.

Classical architecture has so far only been considered in terms of Wren and Italy, but how did Morris react to the workaday Georgian buildings in the streets of England? Here his attitude is curiously ambiguous. That he did not like them is certain. But beyond that he wavered between abuse and tolerance. His remarks range from 'pedantic imitations of . . . the most revolting ugliness'* and 'the feeble twaddle of the dilettantism of the latter Georges' to the admission that this feeble twaddle still 'had a kind of life about it, dreary as that life was',* and to occasional much more surprising admissions. To give one example, George Gilbert Scott, as we have seen, found Gower Street utterly intolerable. Morris says: 'One is beginning to think with regard of the days of Gower Street.'* Now what architecture of his own day could have made Morris say that? Two things evidently. The 'sweltering dog-hole' of the workman on which he felt naturally very strongly, 'surrounded with miles of similar dog-holes',* but also the wealthy house which he called 'simply blackguardly' and built for 'ignorant, purse-proud digesting-machines'.* In fact he made very little difference in aesthetic value between poor, medium and rich. He said: 'The murder of art that curses our streets from the sordidness of the surroundings of the lower classes, has its exact counterpart in the dullness and vulgarity of those of the middle classes, and the double-distilled dullness, and scarcely less vulgarity of those of the upper classes.'* So what made the Georgian house acceptable was its simplicity and solidity. Morris said they were 'stupid and unimaginative enough', but 'creditably built . . . and without pretence'* and hence 'at the worst not aggressively ugly or base'.* He called them 'bible and port-wine houses',* and that surely means a modicum of praise for their 'commonsense and convenience', the sign of a moment 'when, though art was sick and all but dead, men had not quite given it up as a bad job'.*

Now in this same passage there is also a curious remark on the houses 'built about the reign of Queen Anne', which still 'stretch out' a hand towards the Gothic times'. How can this be understood? Surely the style of Queen Anne's reign is the simplest, straightest, least ornamental of all. The one possible answer is that Morris did not really mean it. Queen Anne at the moment when the lecture was given in which this passage occurs—that is in 1878 or 1879—was a term used to denote the recent revival in domestic architecture led by Norman Shaw and with its gables, bay windows and short pilasters indebted more to the Dutch and English mid-seventeenth century than to the early years of the eighteenth. How imprecise the use of the term Queen Anne was can be read in many places. For instance in a book called *Les Merveilles de l'Exposition de 1878* there is one illustration of Norman Shaw's British Pavilion, half-timbered, with asymmetrically placed gables, the friezes of short blank arches so familiar in Elizabethan and Jacobean woodwork, and oriel windows on brackets; in short, pure early or mid-seventeenth century, and the text says that it is 'construite dans un style très charmant et surtout très-aimé des Anglais, le style du temps de la reine Anne'.*

n.46,
n.48
n.49
n.50
n.51
n.52
n.53
n.54
n.55,
n.57
n.58

Another quotation, and this from London and not from France and hence, one would think, better informed about English events and taste, is the delightful anonymous *Ballad of Bedford Park,* Norman Shaw's revolutionary garden suburb of 1875–80, which is quoted in Sir Reginald Blomfield's biography of
n.59   Shaw.* This is what it says:

> 'Here trees are green and bricks are red,
> And clean the face of man.
> We'll build our houses here, he said,
n.60 > In style of good Queen Anne.'*

'He' was Jonathan Carr, the promoter of Bedford Park. And sixteen lines earlier we hear this:

> ' 'Tis there a village I'll erect
> With Norman Shaw's assistance,
> Where men may lead a chaste correct
> Aesthetical existence.'

3   Now the cottages of Bedford Park are again certainly not in the *style de la reine Anne* and in addition, it will be noticed that here the whole so-called Aesthetic Movement is taken in, and to this Morris himself as a designer and decorator no doubt belonged. The immediate source of the ballad is of course Gilbert and Sullivan's *Patience.* Everybody remembers the lines:

> 'Be eloquent in praise
> Of the very dull old days
> Which have long since passed away,
> And convince 'em if you can
> That the reign of good Queen Anne
> Was Culture's palmiest day.'

And everybody also remembers that the piece ends:

> 'You will rank as an Apostle
> In the High Aesthetic band,
> If you walk down Piccadilly
> With a poppy or a lily
> In your mediaeval hand.'

That alluded of course to Oscar Wilde, but, once again, Wilde, Norman Shaw,
n.61   Morris—it was all lumped into one about 1880 and called Queen Anne.* Here
n.62   for instance is what Colonel Edis, the architect, said in a lecture in 1880:*
'Then came the Gothic revival, and in furniture we exchanged the curule chair for the "narrow seat and knobby back", not more comfortable or pleasant to our persons than the ancient "sedilia"; nor can much be said for the carved cabinets, ponderous sideboards, and imitation mediaeval furniture, constructed of course "on unexceptionable authority after the true fashion of our ancestors". And now has set in a fashion, dedicated to her most sacred Majesty, Queen Anne, a fashion which has developed much of really good art character, and which, after all, properly applied, is really bringing us back to old English work. Amongst the more educated professors of the style, we find at present many pretty conceits, which are not worthy of the name of art; but we also find good construction and carefulness of design, which we may hail as forerunners of better times, and more artistic work. It is but fair to say that to Messrs. Street, R.A., Norman Shaw, R.A., Waterhouse, A.R.A., E. W. Godwin, W. Burges, P. Webb, and other architects, and to Messrs. Morris and Co., Messrs. Crace, Messrs. Gillow, Messrs. Jackson and Graham, Messrs. Jeffrey, and other well-known firms, much praise is due for their efforts in the cause of artistic design.'
    Morris must have felt himself in an ambiguous position. Philip Webb who was the architect most after Morris's own heart and Morris's own architect had
4   indeed already in Red House—built for Morris in 1859—used real Queen Anne windows, slender, with segmental heads and close white glazing bars, and had

placed them in his Gothic brick setting, and this could indeed be regarded as the proof of Morris's assertion that in the Queen Anne style—the real Queen Anne style—'there was yet left some feeling of the Gothic . . . joined to forms such as sash windows, possible to be used in our times'.* This remark can refer only to   n.63
Philip Webb, his lifelong friend. Webb came from Street, the best type of the high-minded, but also openminded, High Victorian Gothic Revivalist, and the man under whom Morris also had worked for a short time as an assistant. Webb's is a harder, rougher, more robust style than Shaw's. It has in his best work those 'massive, direct and simple qualities of the "barbaric" saving element of breadth' which he praised in early buildings.* This Morris must have appreciated.   n.64

Yet the fact remains that he nowhere in his lectures and writings explicitly proclaimed Webb the great architect of his day. So it does look as if to Morris even Webb's actual buildings were not a solution and that the baffling remark about the Gothic forms of the future quoted above remained his negative answer to the whole architecture of his day. The remark was in fact made three years before his death. The possibilities for a twentieth century future which we can see in Webb, in Shaw, in some of Shaw's followers, in Voysey's earliest houses he did not recognise. He could not extricate himself from the dilemma of Victorian historicism.

His uncomfortable feelings are most clearly seen in his attitude to Norman Shaw. He did not really like Shaw. Yet Shaw and Shaw's clients liked him. He furnished for instance Shaw's Swan House. One can indeed say that the Arts and Crafts Movement was spiritually the work of Morrisites though physically of Norman Shavians. Yet to promote 'pretty conceits' (to use Colonel Edis's term) was clearly not what Morris and Co. had been built up to do. What then was his personal reaction to the Shavian style? The most important statements are in the lecture of *c.* 1879 called *Making the Best of It* and the lecture of 1888 on *The Revival of Architecture*. It is here that Morris in the words quoted before traced the development of the Gothic Revival from the imitation of forms to the recognition of principles and then led on to the sixteenth and seventeenth centuries and so to Queen Anne and Norman Shaw. He praises the 'ringleaders of the rebellion',* he calls their designs 'experimental', and holds 'that they are . . . born   n.65
of thought and principle' as well as of 'great capacity of design',* and he admits   n.66
that 'at first sight the Queen Anne development has seemed to conquer modern taste more or less'.* But at this point his doubts become noticeable—not only   n.67
in so far as in another place he (rightly of course) calls these houses still 'the exceptions',* but also in the attributes he grants them and the terms he uses to   n.68
describe them. Where he refers to Norman Shaw by name, he speaks of his 'elegantly fantastic Queen Anne houses in Chelsea'* and in another place of the   n.69
'quaint and pretty architecture' of Bedford Park.*   n.70

Now anyone familiar with Morris's terminology can only regard 'pretty, elegant, fantastic' as damning with faint praise,* and what Philip Webb says   n.71
about Norman Shaw corroborates that view. Webb calls the neo-Queen Anne 'dilettante-picturesque' and 'exceedingly artificial'.* 'Artificial' is the operative   n.72
word here. Shaw's is indeed a more sophisticated architecture than Webb's, and that to Morris must at once have linked him up with the whole artificiality of his century. Moreover, Webb was his man also in so far as he never ran an organised, commercial office like Shaw;* that he designed every detail himself* and that   n.73
he believed that 'the beginning of training for building and design must be on the works and in the shops'. That is of course the counterpart of Morris's belief in the craftsman and his dislike of the designer, or 'squinter on paper' as he called him.*   n.75

Morris would not be Morris without this undying hatred of nineteenth, or one may just as well say, twentieth-century methods of production, the production of the design, then the production of the article, and finally the production of the building. This horror of the machine and horror of the big city anchor Morris in the Victorian age just as firmly as his ultimate faith in Gothic forms. It is indeed true that a juster appreciation of what the machine might do for

4 *Entrance front of Red House, Bexleyheath, built for Morris by Philip Webb in 1859*

civilisation began only at about the time of Morris's death and gathered strength —with the aid of both reasonable and unreasonable arguments—in the first decades of our century.*   n.76

But while disgust with the machine even to the extent of the 'nasty, brim-stone, noisy, shrieking railway train',* and disgust with the big city and London   n.77 in particular—'this beastly congregation of smoke-dried swindlers and their slaves'*—'a whole county covered over with hideous hovels',* 'masses of   n.78, sordidness, filth, and squalor, embroidered with patches of pompous and vulgar hideousness'*—while these magnificent vituperations belong to Morris the   n.80 Victorian,* there is plenty in the same lectures and letters which belongs   n.81 squarely to the twentieth century, and these pioneering or prophetic utterances deserve to be catalogued and commented on in conclusion. First simply a string of short quotations. 'Until our streets are decent and orderly', it is no use to speak about the prospects of art.* So do away with 'the sluttish habit' of throwing   n.82 away sandwich papers 'as if it had been snowing dirty papers'.* Improve 'the   n.83 daily increasing hideousness of the posters',* see to it that 'we have clear sky   n.84 above our heads'*—a compliment is paid here in passing to Saltaire and Sir   n.85 Titus Salt's 'huge chimney . . . as guiltless of smoke as an ordinary domestic kitchen chimney'.* Then, and this turned out to be a particularly effective plea: n.86 'What do you do with the trees on a site that is going to be built over? Do you try to save them? Do you understand what treasures they are in a town or a suburb? . . . In London and its suburbs we always begin by clearing a site till it is as bare as the pavement'* and not, as Morris well knew, because their disap-   n.87 pearance is necessary for the builder to lay out his new estate, but 'because it will take him too much trouble to fit them into the planning of his houses'.* And   n.88 then, as for the house itself, Morris pleads for the bare floor: 'It is a great comfort to see the actual floor'* with just a rug here and there, he pleads for natural oak   n.89 showing in the woodwork of a room, just as it comes from the plane,* and for the   n.90 dining table without a cloth and only with mats.* No wonder then that he also   n.91 makes the typical Werkbund or D.I.A. statement that the kitchen as a rule is a more reasonably and pleasantly furnished room than the drawing-room or parlour.*   n.92

The philosophy on which this was based is all of a piece, and Morris was honest in saying that he would rather live 'in a tent in the Persian desert, or a turf hut on the Icelandic hillside' than in the England of his time.* Yet here we are   n.93 faced with a conflict, a conflict which goes through all his working and preach-ing. Clearly there is another side to this plea for extreme simplicity. There is for instance the passage where he speaks of the utilitarian, solid, unpretentious Late Georgian town architecture as 'the fallow of the arts before the new seed could be sown'.* And there are other places where *tabula rasa* is taken far more seriously.   n.94 They are in fact among the most frighteningly prophetic of his sayings: 'How often it consoles me to think of barbarism once more flooding the world and real feelings and passions, however rudimentary, taking the place of our wretched hypocrisies.'* And 'Perhaps the gods are preparing troubles and horror for the   n.95 world (or our small corner of it) again, that it may once again become beautiful and dramatic'.* And 'Maybe man may, after some terrible cataclysm, learn to   n.96 strive towards a healthy animalism, may grow from a tolerable animal into a savage, from a savage into a barbarian, and so on; and some thousands of years hence he may be beginning those arts which we have now lost'.*   n.97

That is pure Spengler: the disappearance of a civilisation and its replace-ment by another, starting from scratch—the disappearance of our civilisation and its future replacement. But did Morris really mean that? He may, but he was much too active, too busy a person to be paralyzed by such thoughts. And so there are other passages where he speaks of doing 'our best to the end of pre-paring for change, and so softening the shock of it; to leave as little as possible that must be destroyed to be destroyed suddenly and by violence'.* He called   n.98 that 'reconstructive' as against destructive socialism. But while his lectures may indeed be accepted as serving at least that purpose, can the same be said of his work as a designer and decorator? There surely the conflict was much more acute, and consequently the work itself, socially speaking, is much more of the nineteenth than the twentieth century. Morris's products were costly; they were only accessible to the few, the select, those who according to him don't matter. His products were neither by the people nor for the people, and the recognition of this fatal limitation in his own writings is very rare indeed. I can only think of one, a late passage on the possibility of inexpensively produced books being yet n.99   fully beautiful, purely on the strength of their 'fitness for use'.*

But then, not the least of the thrills of reading William Morris is the surprises his writings give. They call for a final random sample—all bits connected with architecture and planning. On Oxford: 'the little plaster houses in front of Trinity College . . . are in their way as important as the more majestic buildings n.100   to which all the world makes pilgrimage'.* Then an Outrage—Outrage in the Nairn sense: 'Most true it is that when any spot of earth's surface has been marred n.101   by the haste or carelessness of civilization it is heavy work to seek a remedy'.* On the spec. builder: Don't 'lay the fault upon the builders, as some people seem inclined to do: they are our very humble servants, and will build what we n.102   ask for'.* So it becomes a matter of education, and there is Morris saying in n.103   1880 that 'the twentieth century may be called the Century of Education'.*

This is amazing enough, but what of the following two ultimate quotations, two of the most profound? Apropos of gardens in towns Morris suggests not to apply too much ingenuity and complexity to the planned details, but to n.104   leave 'Nature to do the desired complexity'.* Surely that could be the motto of all the best recent housing, i.e. the Roehampton Estate. And of the church or civic hall in a town Morris says that they 'to a certain extent make up to town-n.105   dwellers for their loss of field, and river, and mountain'.*

This alone should be enough to bear out the truth of that astonishing remark by—of all people—Toulouse Lautrec: 'Je crois qu'il n'y a qu'à regarder William n.106   Morris, pour avoir une réponse à toutes vos questions.'*

1 *An interior of 1880 by Edis: the chair (left) is by Godwin, the frieze by Stacy Marks, and the wallpaper by Morris*

VI
Art Furniture of the 1870s

'I WAS TALKING with a lady friend of mine the other day who was puzzled as to what to do with her growing son, and we discussed the possibility of his taking to one of the crafts . . . say cabinet making . . . We were obliged to admit that . . . the thing could not be done; it would make him either a sort of sloppy amateur, or an involuntary martyr to principle . . . At first sight the thing seems monstrous . . . Why in the name of patience should a carpenter be a worse gentleman than a lawyer? . . . And yet, you see, we gentlemen and ladies durst not set our sons to it . . . Amongst other things the lady said to me: "You know, I wouldn't mind a lad being a cabinetmaker if he only made Art furniture." Well there you see!'

WILLIAM MORRIS: Art, Wealth and Riches (*Coll. Works, Vol.* 23, *p.* 154).

I have found the term Art Furniture applied for the first time in 1868. In that year the *Building News* of December 25 had a plate called Art Furniture showing pieces designed by Walford and Donkin Architects. The furniture is in the Gothic style. In the same year Charles Lock Eastlake published his *Hints on Household Taste* in which the term occurs twice, once used by Eastlake himself and once as the name of a firm, the Art Furniture Company, with which apparently Arthur Blomfield was connected. Eastlake, three years later, brought out the standard history of the Gothic Revival; Blomfield was one of the most successful, if certainly not the most inspired of its representatives. In the same year 1871, the *Building News* had a plate illustrating furniture designed for the Art Furniture Company by Edward Godwin, the architect of Whistler's house in Tite Street, Chelsea.

The word is significant. It is proof of a split which had occurred during the second third of the nineteenth century between art and craft, and between art and manufacture. Furniture in the days of Sheraton had been accepted without questioning as art—of its own kind and within its own limits. Now, unless an artist condescended to *apply* art to a cupboard or a table, they could no longer be art. We know of this development through William Morris whose one aim in life was to undo it. The term Arts and Crafts was coined to express the illusion that peace between the two could be restored in terms of the nineteenth century. The Arts and Crafts became an accepted term chiefly through the Arts and Crafts Exhibition Society which began its activities in 1888. But William Morris started thirty years earlier, with the 'tables and chairs like incubi and succubi' of which Rossetti speaks as parts of the furnishing of Morris's first London rooms in Red Lion Square.* When two years later, in 1859, Morris had got

n.1

2 Talbert: 'A Study of Decorations and Furniture', 1869

married and needed a house of his own, Philip Webb, the architect, his friend and former colleague in Street's office, designed for it an oak dining table, chairs, a cupboard and even table glass, candlesticks and firedogs.* Morris's firm, it is n.2 known, was started in 1861. In its prospectus we read: 'The growth of Decorative Art in this country, owing to the efforts of English Architects, has now reached a point at which it seems desirable that Artists of reputation should devote their time to it.'* And so in 1861 and 1862 Morris's produced to the n.3 designs of Madox Brown, Rossetti, Philip Webb, J. P. Seddon, Morris himself and others, tiles, wallpapers, table glass, stained glass, and also furniture. Of the furniture the pieces usually known to people are very ornate; cupboards such as the one at the Victoria and Albert Museum which Seddon, then about thirty-four years old, designed for Morris to hold his drawings and which was painted with stories of King René's Honeymoon by Madox Brown, Rossetti and

3 Seddon: 'King René's Honeymoon' cabinet, 1861

3

4 Webb: table for Morris & Co., c.1865

Burne-Jones. But we hear from Mackail also that Webb's furniture comprised 'specimens of most articles of common use . . . the greater number quite plain and depending for their quality on their simplicity and elegant proportion.'* The Victoria and Albert Museum has one such table and Lethaby in his book on Webb* says that in Webb's notebooks for shortly after 1860 a dining-room table, a round drawing-room table, washstands, a dressing table, towel-horses and so on are mentioned as designed for Major Gillum, an art-minded business-man, one of the founders of the Hogarth Club in 1858, the owner of the small version of Madox Brown's *The Last of England,* now in the Fitzwilliam Museum, Cambridge, and the client for whom Webb in 1861 designed the remarkable warehouse in Worship Street, London, which still exists.* Major Gillum's nephew, Colonel W. Gillum, possesses several of these pieces. One is a round table, the other an oblong table. The round table is an extremely simple, rustic piece, with short rounded legs, panelled construction, hinges demonstratively big and exposed, and the timber unstained. The oblong table has spindly turned legs, a thin top with a long drawer with a gracefully curved front and metal rings as handles, and the timber is polished. It is remarkably different from any one style of the past, although the top shows sympathy with the eighteenth century and the legs with the seventeenth.

These four pieces of Morris-Webb furniture introduce all those questions under which the most interesting furniture of the sixties and seventies must be contemplated: sympathy with the Middle Ages, simplicity, rusticity, and also lightness, and independence of period precedent. With the exception of the first all these qualities are the opposite of what one would expect High Victorian furniture to have been like.

Pugin's, Carlyle's, the Pre-Raphaelites', Ruskin's, Morris's sympathy with the Middle Ages are known. Morris derived his from his reading of Ruskin and his architectural training in Street's office; Ruskin believed in Italian Trecento Gothic first and foremost; Street, who won the competition for the Law Courts in 1868, kept 'a decided adherence to the earlier phase of Gothic,'* that is the Early English.

A dedication to Street appears on the first page of a book brought out by a man in 1867 who was not an architect but a designer of furniture and metal-work, Bruce Talbert (1838–81).* In the introduction to this volume he declares it to be his intention 'to present furniture modelled on the best style of the past, mainly the twelfth and thirteenth centuries,' and then emphasizes that 'domestic work of early date . . . demands a certain amount of invention before it could . . . fulfil the purpose or give the comfort now necessary to us'.* The results are sturdy and massive, with rich, flat surface decoration.* Yet when it comes to whole interiors by Talbert, they are not necessarily all that heavy and Gothic. Especially for drawing-rooms Talbert recognized that they call for more 'elegance and lightness,'* and so at least the cupboards are slimmer, and the busy forms of the surface decoration, in the coving in particular, also help to create a slightly less ponderous effect.*

n.4
4
n.5

n.6
6

7

n.7

n.8

n.9
n.10
2

n.11

n.12

5 *Talbert: dining room cupboard, 1866*

6, 7 Webb: tables designed for Major Gillum about 1861, made by Morris & Co.

8 *Eastlake: bookcase, 1868*

9 *Burges: chimneypiece at Melbury Road, 1875*

Talbert at his most cyclopic is remarkably similar to William Burges (1827–81), the last upholder amongst architects of the Early English style for domestic furnishings.* In his own house in Melbury Road, London, he has as late as 1875 the short columns, the oppressive trefoil arches and so on which occur all through Talbert's book. Here at least, as far as weight goes, there is nothing to contradict our prejudices regarding the High Victorian style.*

10

9, n.1

n.14

This is perhaps not quite so when we examine the plates to Eastlake's *Hints on Household Taste*. Eastlake, who fully acknowledges his debt to Pugin and Ruskin, designed pieces which, although Gothic, do not look as primeval as Talbert's and Burges's, while being much more elaborate than Webb's.*

8

n.15

But Eastlake's book is more remarkable today for its text than its plates. We are still used to regarding Morris as the one and only reformer of Victorian taste and ascribe to him the whole campaign against over-elaboration, sham display, dishonesty in the use of materials, and so on. In fact, as we have seen in the preceding essays, the first to plead for purer ideals was Pugin, and he was almost immediately followed by Henry Cole, Owen Jones and Matthew Digby Wyatt. To them no doubt Eastlake owed such remarks as these: 'Every article of manufacture . . . should indicate by its general design, the purpose to which it will be applied' (p. 81). 'So far from good design being under any circumstances incompatible with strong and sturdy service, it is only in bad design that use is not kept in view as the first and guiding principle' (p. 122). At present it is 'far better to choose the very plainest and simplest forms of domestic furniture procurable in the shops' (p. 156) than to indulge in any luxuries in furnishing; for it is a fact that 'the most commonplace objects of domestic use . . . are sure to be the most interesting in appearance' (p. 53). And so Eastlake goes on to recommend the unvarnished exposing of the natural grain of wood (p. 159), as Morris was to do later, strict flatness in wallpaper design (p. 103), and the use of iron or brass for bedsteads (p. 184).

Talbert, oddly enough, agreed on all these points with Eastlake—the same remarkable contradiction between theory and performance which appears in Pugin, Wyatt, Scott and others. Talbert in the introduction to his *Gothic Forms applied to Furniture* recommends the Early English style because of its 'great breadth and simplicity,' calls the later Gothic 'lavish display of ornament . . . quite undesirable for Cabinet Work,' praises solidity, 'construction honestly shown,' and 'tenons, pegs, iron clamps,' etc., frankly exposed, and disapproves (not without qualification) of the staining and of too much veneering of wood.

To return to Eastlake, another seeming contradiction is that he contrasts (*Hints*, p. 173) the bad taste in all 'fashionable establishments devoted to decorative art in London' with the far superior taste of 'those nations whose art has long been our custom to despise,' his one and only example of such nations being the Japanese. So here, in Eastlake's book, appreciation of the Gothic style appears, at least for a moment, side by side with appreciation of Japan. The earliest stages of the fashion for *Japonnerie* have often been described: how the etcher Bracquemond discovered in Paris in 1856 some Japanese woodcuts, how their clear, light colours appealed at once to those who were working towards the ideals of an Impressionism to come, how Madame de Soye, back from the East after ten years, opened a shop in the rue de Rivoli in 1862 and called it *La Porte Chinoise*, how the Exhibition of 1862 had a much noticed Japanese section, how Whistler painted his *Princesse du Pays de la Porcelaine* in 1864, how Rossetti collected blue and white china at the same time, how Manet painted Zola in 1868 against a background of Japanese woodcuts, and how Farmer and Rogers's Oriental Warehouse was established about 1862 as a shop in London where Chinese and Japanese goods could be purchased. Farmer and Rogers's manager was Sir Arthur Lasenby Liberty (1842–1917) and so in 1875 Liberty's came into being. In addition, Dudley Harbron in his book on Edward Godwin* showed how surprisingly early Godwin was in the field with his admiration for Japan. Godwin (1833–86) who was, just at that time, making a name for himself with designs for public buildings in the Gothic style and who was a close friend of

n.16

10 *Burges: painted bookcase,*
1862

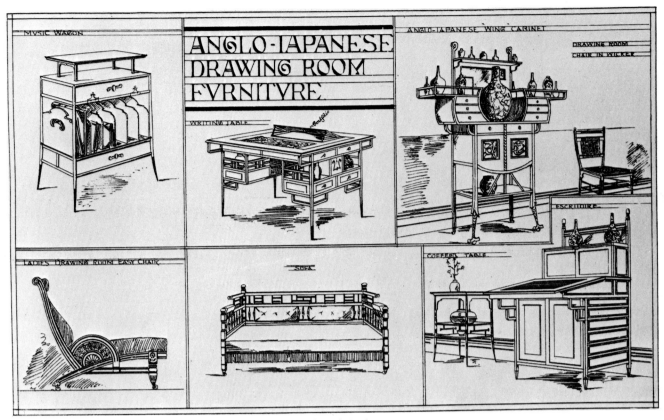

11 Page from William Watt's catalogue of furniture by Edward Godwin, 1877

12 Godwin: detail from a sketchbook

Burges, decorated his own Regency house at Bristol in 1862 in a very different taste. This is how Harbron describes it: 'His scheme consisted in painting the walls of his rooms in plain colours, hanging thereon a few Japanese prints and laying some Persian rugs on the bare floors.' Godwin presumably knew of Japan through the exhibition of 1862, and he may also have heard of Whistler's enthusiasm*—the fact remains that the spindly thinness and the non-permanent look of Japanese furniture inspired Godwin in the design of what was later to become fashionable under the name Art Furniture. Thus it is called in an oblong quarto volume which Godwin brought out with the manufacturer William Watt in 1877. The pieces in this catalogue—for that is no doubt what it was meant to be—are all very much in the same style, and Godwin calls it on one page Anglo-Japanese. These precariously projecting shelves, these thin curved brackets, these spidery tapering legs all seem to be more closely allied to the Art Nouveau style of twenty years later than to Victorian architecture of the sixties and seventies. For although the catalogue came out only in 1877, we have seen that Godwin's Art Furniture (for the Art Furniture Company) was illustrated as early as 1871, and Godwin in an introductory letter to the catalogue of 1877 says that, for instance, one particular coffee-table was first made for him 'nine or ten years ago' which would take us back to 1868, the year with which this essay began. Godwin complains in this introductory letter of imitations of his work, and one such imitation made by the distinguished firm Jackson and Graham is indeed illustrated in a book of 1881.* Godwin goes on to explain that such effortless looking designs as those shown in his volume yet 'demand no inconsiderable amount of thought' and cannot be made 'by any happy-go-lucky process whatsoever.' Godwin's furniture bears this out. The table illustrated was designed as early as 1867 or 1868, and the wardrobe is as simple in outline. Its combination of units, moreover, is so rational that few would hesitate to date it in the early years of the twentieth century. The table is Godwin at his most elegant, of a lightness and playfulness which comes out even more sparklingly in his sketches. The drawing comes from a sketchbook of Godwin's and suggests how one should look at his furniture.*

n.17

11,1

16

n.18

16
13

n.19

13 *Godwin: wardrobe*

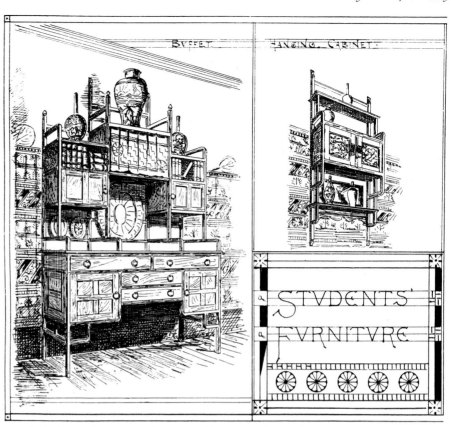

14 *Godwin: multi-purpose buffet, and hanging cabinet, from Watt's catalogue*

15 *Godwin: ebonized sideboard with Japan paper insets, c.1877*

16 *Godwin: coffee-table, c.1868*

Equally original and unforeseeable are Godwin's 'Greek' chairs, the parallel *17*
in his furniture design to his keen interest in Greek plays and their production.
To get the full, seemingly post-Victorian flavour of this style, one must also take
its colour character into consideration. Godwin was Whistler's friend and designed his house for him in 1877, the White House in Tite Street, Chelsea. Later
Whistler married Godwin's widow. Now Whistler painted the walls of his
house, and later the walls of exhibitions (in 1883 and 1884) in such colours as
lemon-yellow, white, rose. So here were interiors which in their delicacy of
colour and the fine-limbed grace and somewhat *outré* scaffolding-transparency
of their furniture pronounced total opposition to what had been known as art
furniture a little earlier, the monuments of early Webb, Talbert and Burges.

The year of the Godwin catalogue was also the year of Morris's first lecture
and of the beginnings of his grand series of textiles. The creation of the Hammersmith carpets followed a little later, and then the opening of the Oxford Street
shop. In the same years—and, it must be realized, by no means only under
Morris's influence—a whole spate of books appeared all dealing with furnishing,
interior decoration and furniture. Here are the titles:

> W. J. Loftie: Art At Home Series, 1876, etc. (*A Plea for Art in the House*,
> by W. J. Loftie; *The Drawing Room*, by Mrs Orrinsmith; *The Dining
> Room*, by Mrs Loftie; *The Bedroom and Boudoir*, by Lady Barker; *Sugges-
> tions for House Decoration*, by R. and A. Garratt).
> Mrs H. R. Haweis: *The Art of Beauty*, 1878.
> Mrs H. R. Haweis: *The Art of Decoration*, 1881.
> R. W. Edis: *Decoration and Furniture of Town Houses*, 1881.

17 Godwin: 'Greek' chair, 1875

Of these book Edis's is the most ambitious. It runs to about three hundred pages
of text and is well illustrated. It gives us the best idea of what artistic furnishing
meant at the end of the period with which this essay is to deal—or at least what
it meant to those who were not exclusive adherents of William Morris. Colonel
Sir Robert W. Edis (1839–1927) was a successful West End architect and a man
equally successful, it seems, in his military career and as a big game hunter. He
designed the Constitutional, the Junior Constitutional and the Badminton Clubs
in London, the Conservative Club in Glasgow, the Inner Temple Library, the
Great Central Hotel (now British Rail headquarters) in Marylebone Road, the
Ballroom at Sandringham. His book is the text of his Cantor Lectures to the
Royal Society of Arts in 1880. It deserves a fairly full summary.

Although Edis takes his motto from Ruskin, he establishes at once in his
foreword that he is not a Gothicist. He says that it is his intention to avoid 'the
trammels of any particular school' whether it be the 'Classic, the Gothic, or so-
called Queen Anne.' The addition of Queen Anne to Classic and Gothic in 1880
cannot be a surprise to anyone aware of William Morris's remarks quoted in the
preceding essay and of the other passages quoted there. Edis like Queen Anne,
including incidentally Chippendale, Adam and Sheraton (p. 31), just as for instance Loftie liked it.* But Mrs Haweis has her objections against the 'Queen   n.20
Anne mad decorators' (1881, p. 52), for a reason which is not without interest.
To her Queen Anne and Chippendale 'cannot be called beautiful. Their virtues
are merely negative. They are a reaction against vulgarity, and that is all' (1878,
p. 242, etc.).* Similarly Mrs Orrinsmith can recommend only to those 'whose   n.21
taste has not been properly developed' that 'Quaker uniformity, the reverse of
vulgarity' which has suddenly become fashionable (p. 27).

The greatest difference between Edis and Morris is that Edis was not a
pessimist with regard to his own time. Morris as late as 1888* saw all the good   n.22
in architecture in his own day as no more than 'the result of a quite self-con-
scious and very laborious eclecticism'.* Edis says that gradually by such means as   n.23
exhibitions, all classes have become filled 'with a desire and love for beautiful
form and colour and a distaste for crude vulgarities and hideous forms' (p. 4). So
here from the beginning is comfortable optimism as against Morris's heavier-
going social criticism. In his vision of the deep roots of art in social life Morris
remained alone.

But while Edis likes Queen Anne (p. 14) and is ready to accept Gothic or rather a general Mediaeval in the new meaning which Morris had given it, he has hard things to say against the 'mediaeval examples of Wardour Street' (p. 37), 'the fashion of so-called mediaeval furniture' (p. 31) and 'bookcases plastered over with gothic buttresses.' The Garratts agree with him and call the type of furniture to which they object more specifically 'Early English' (p. 49). This must be directed against Talbert and Burges. But Edis is even more outspoken in his dislike of 'the flimsiness of furniture imitated from Japanese examples' (p. 7). That sounds as if he meant Godwin; but he cannot because in another place he mentions Godwin specially, together with Street, Shaw, Waterhouse, Webb and others (and incidentally Burges) amongst the praiseworthy architects. If he paints so unattractive a picture of 'rooms decorated with imitation Chinese bamboo work and tinted sealing-wax and gold with splashes of blue and green in imitation of Japanese lacquer' (p. 9), he is probably referring to the com- n.24 mercialization of Godwin's style which had already begun in 1880.* And one can hardly blame him for that if one reads in Mrs Orrinsmith's book the serious suggestion of placing above the fireplace 'a picture surrounded by dried ferns— or perhaps Christmas greenery and Japanese fans huddling amongst all' (p. 47).

If we now try to get an idea of Edis's own views we see at once that he carries on the Pugin-Henry Cole-Owen Jones-M. D. Wyatt-Eastlake tradition of criticism. He preaches that 'all things that show what they really are, and do not pretend to be something else, are in the end best' (p. 23). We must set our 'faces against all pretensions, shams and conceits' (p. 284). That includes that 'our houses should speak the language of our day' (p. 284), and that furniture of the past should not be imitated (p. 17). The language of our day for furnishing seems to be, according to Edis, 'simple and plain' without 'overloading . . . with
18 heavy and scrolly furniture' (p. 109). He illustrates a Morris buffet – contrasting it with the usual 'twisted and curled and carved' sideboards (p. 112) – and
9, 20 Morris's so-called Sussex chair and the long seat developed by Morris from it. These simple, sensible, traditional cottage chairs had been discovered by Morris's friend and business manager Warington Taylor sometime between 1865 and 1868. They have humble rush seats and slender legs, arms and stretchers, a
n.25 quality obviously emphasized specially in Edis's drawings.* In this attitude of Edis to honesty and fitness for use today again the other writers concur. Mrs Orrinsmith says that in good furniture of the past 'fitness was desired before beauty' (p. 82), the Garratts also call 'fitness the one great source of beauty' and Mrs Orrinsmith goes on to describe what to her the 'Victorian style in furni-ture' should be: 'Resign all ideas of wood carving as a decoration.' Instead of that insist on 'honest material, little glue, and good sound workmanship, even if a sparsely decorated apartment be the temporary result' (pp. 97, 109).

18 *Morris & Co.: buffet, illustrated by Edis in 1881*

19, 20 *Morris & Co.: settle and chair first produced in the 1860s*

21 *Edis: dining room with a classical frieze and 'Puritan' chairs, 1881*

22 *Edis: drawing-room furniture, 1881*

It was unavoidable that these preachers of plainness and simplicity should get into trouble with their own liking for Queen Anne and Georgian furniture. And indeed the discrepancy between Edis's own taste and his recommendation of 'plain polished or painted deal furniture' in preference to 'the elaboration of Chippendale fretwork or Queen Anne ornamentation' (p. 16) remains unsolved—as so much in the relations of theory and performance amongst the Victorian reformers in art including William Morris.

While most of Edis's arguments so far discussed* go straight back to the reformers of 1851—Owen Jones is in fact quoted more than once* —we find one other trend in Edis's book which must reflect readings of Morris's lectures. It sounds very odd in a book so obviously written for a wealthy clientele to be told that 'the aim of all true art should be to produce good work for the million' (p. 250) and that the urgent problem of the day is therefore 'good and artistic furniture at a moderate cost so that it might be within the reach of all the classes' (p. 26).*

The answer is that Edis was not a strong character. He had no mission as Morris had. He was ready to pick up whatever convinced him at first sight and put it into his lectures without much bothering about the consistency of his views. There is no system behind his book. That comes out most clearly in his attitude to colour and in his illustrations. As regards colour first, one finds that he wants it 'bright and cheerful' (p. 40) in town houses. But then, in specifying colour-schemes, they invariably come out sombre and hot, 'warm golden brown and yellow' on the staircase (p. 159), 'a good dark tone' dado with walls of 'chocolate colour' in the dining-room (p. 171), 'golden-yellow walls with a golden-brown flower pattern' in the drawing-room (p. 202) and so on. These colour-schemes, which tally with what one feels was the Victorian taste, find a parallel even in Morris, although Morris went in for dark blues and peacock greens rather than Edis's brown and gold.* The timbre, however, is the same in Edis and Morris, and also incidentally in Mrs Haweis (who recommends for instance a red room with a black ceiling starred with dull sea-green and yellow, p. 251), and in Mrs Orrinsmith ('low tones, twilight shades, olive greens, peacock blues, cloudy reds,' p. 61).*

The most curious thing to us nowadays is the regret of the Mid-Victorians at the large size of windows in most town-houses. Mrs Orrinsmith says explicitly that they should be reduced in apparent size by leading parts of them with small quarry panes, because light is only healthy if 'distributed in discrete doses' (p. 64), and even William Morris in his lecture *Making the best of it* (1879 or earlier) says that 'windows are much too big' in most houses.*

n.26
n.27

n.28

n.29
n.30

n.31

Edis's eclecticism appears everywhere in the choice of his illustrations. The
22   furniture in his Plate 7, an arrangement from Jackson and Graham's, he recommends as combining 'general artistic merit of design with simplicity and practical
commonsense' (p. 103). It consists of a sideboard and a small table nearly as
spindly as Godwin's, and a Morris-type chair. In spite of his censures against heavy
Gothic furniture he shows a sunflower wallpaper by Talbert, the chief mis-
sionary of that style (p. 61), and he also shows a 'Modern Jacobean Hall' by
Gillow's, the decorators (Plate 15). His own interiors are specially interesting.
They combine furniture emphatically no longer heavy and no longer imitative
of any style of the past, with a few eighteenth century allusions (small square
21   glazed panes of a cupboard door, delicate garlands in a frieze and so on), and an
all-over decoration with foliage wallpaper, and figure or bird or fish panels
obviously in the style of William Morris, Walter Crane and Stacy Marks.
Indeed the picture which forms the frontispiece of Edis's book has actually a
n.32   frieze by Marks and Morris's Pomegranate paper.*

Now such interiors perhaps more than Morris's give an all-round idea of
accepted artistic furnishings about 1880. It is—to emphasize it once more—much
less stodgy than most people would imagine and also much less imitative. Its
covering of all surfaces with ornament is Victorian, but the ornament is not
ponderous. And the furniture certainly possesses much more lightness than ten
24   or twenty years before. Compare with Edis's an interior from Godwin's catalogue and you will at once observe how the seventy years between them and us
have covered over the differences between the individual tastes of the two
designers.

In this connection it is worth noting that in one plate of Godwin's catalogue
a cabinet looking much like the others and much like Edis's is called 'in the
23   Queen Anne style'. The overlaps are even more curious than that, and they prove
that progressive decorators then as now were a small set at one in fundamentals.

*23 Godwin:
'Queen Anne' cabinet*

24 Godwin: design for a drawing room, from Watt's catalogue of 1877

25 Burmantoft Faience tiles

There is for instance Maurice B. Adams (1849–1933), Technical Editor of the *Building News* from 1872–1923, and a close follower of Norman Shaw with whom he worked on the Bedford Park Estate, where he designed the Art School. He was the leader of the fashion for imitation eighteenth-century furniture about 1880, a fashion which one would think would have been distasteful to a man like Talbert. Yet Talbert in publishing a second part of his album of furniture designs eight years after the first, that is in 1876, thanks amongst others Adams for help and indeed goes out of his way to state that 'in the intervening eight years ideas . . . have greatly changed. . . . At present there is no style without admirers; even the English Rococo has its worshippers, and we find that those who were once believers only in the thirteenth century Gothic now imitate the Tudor, the Jacobean or the Georgian—at least so far as domestic work is concerned'. He goes on, it is true, to warn against commercialized Chippendale, just as Edis had warned against commercialized Japanese. But in fact there were no real hatreds between the various schools of thought amongst the moderns.

Adams's furniture is particularly interesting in that it demonstrates the step from the new grace of, say, Godwin to full-dress Georgian imitation. Here again *26* the resulting style looks much more 1900 than 1880. But again when it comes to complete schemes for interior decoration, period imitation is silenced and the style appears entirely original and basically in sympathy with Morris and Godwin and Edis. Adams was the designer for Messrs. Wilcock of Leeds Burmantoft Faience, tiles which were much used to achieve that overall covering with flat decoration which was so dear to the period. Edis illustrates it in Plate 1 of his *25, 2* book and recommends it.

And now in conclusion, having shown how theory, forms and colours in the work of Morris and Webb, and Godwin and Whistler, and Edis and Adams assume a distinctly Late Victorian character at a surprisingly early date, a last aspect must be given a few lines, a proto-Art Nouveau of the seventies, i.e. earlier even than Mackmurdo's by now famous title-page to his book *Wren's City Churches*.* The Art Nouveau sense of slender, undulating leaf-shapes in their *n.33* sway appears to a certain extent already in Adams's tiles on the one hand and in such woodwork as Lewis F. Day's cabinet of 1879 on the other. Day (1845–1910) *28* was one of the founders of the Arts and Crafts Exhibition Society and the Art-Workers' Guild—and so we are back with the Morrisites whom we started from.

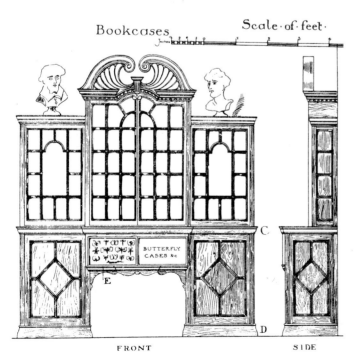

Bookcases

Scale·of·feet·

FRONT   SIDE   *26 Adams: bookcase, 1881*

STAIRCASE   FIREPLACE   COSEY·CORNER

27 Adams: entrance hall tiled in Burmantoft Faience

Upper portion of Cabinet   Example . of Inlay

Lewis F. Day 1879

28 Day: painted cabinet, 1879

1 *Mackmurdo's title-page for his own book on Wren's City Churches, 1883*

VII
Arthur H. Mackmurdo

2 Arthur Heygate Mackmurdo (1851-1942)

3 Wrought-iron sign of the Century Guild

MACKMURDO'S great evolutionary importance lies between that of Morris and that of Voysey. Morris was born in 1834, Voysey in 1857, Mackmurdo in 1851. Morris & Co. was founded in 1861; Voysey's early buildings date from the late eighties: Mackmurdo began work in the seventies, and reached full maturity as early as 1880. Some of his works between 1880 and 1890 were more advanced, more original, more adventurous than those of any other British architect during that decade (which is tantamount to saying the work of any European architect).

Arthur H. Mackmurdo was of old Scottish stock. His father had at one time read for the Bar, but later became a successful manufacturer of chemicals and a very wealthy man. When his son had expressed his desire to become an architect, he was apprenticed in 1869 to T. Chatfield Clarke, a minor London architect, and as he found that he could not learn much from Clarke, he chose his own master and induced James Brooks to accept him as a pupil. Brooks (1825–1901) belongs to the generation of Philip Webb and Norman Shaw, of Street, Burges, Bodley and Sedding. He is the architect of plain, almost blunt, but noble churches —the Ascension in Lavender Hill of 1874 is perhaps the finest—but he was also unusually interested in ornamental details and did not like to leave decoration to less sensitive collaborators. While acquiring his professional equipment, Mackmurdo read much, attracted particularly by works on social problems. He was fortunate in having as a guide Herbert Spencer, a friend of his father. Ruskin he discovered for himself and felt so profoundly moved by his books—it was the time of the first issues of *Fors Clavigera*—that he decided to graduate at Oxford in order to attend Ruskin's lectures. Ruskin seems to have recognized at once the exceptional qualities of his new pupil. He took him to Italy, travelled with him, induced him to sketch wherever they went, and to pay as much attention to nature as to the works of man. Sketches made in 1874 and 1875 exist at the William Morris Gallery in Walthamstow. In 1875 Mackmurdo set up a practice in London, first at 28 Southampton Street, Strand, and after 1880 at 20 Fitzroy Street, where his hospitable house was known to many an art lover and many a young artist (as is referred to in Sir William Rothenstein's recollections). It was also in these years that he was introduced to and became a friend of the Morrises at Kelmscott House, Hammersmith; I well remember Mackmurdo saying to me in 1938: 'She was a remarkable girl, was May . . . I used to row her up the river.' As to his work during these decisive fifteen years between 1875 and 1890 one should bear in mind into what artistic situation Mackmurdo came when he started on his own. What are the great public buildings in London representing the tendencies of the seventies? There is the Romanesque Natural History

4, 5 No.6 Private Road, Enfield, c.1873: the tile-hanging, polychromy, timbering and Gothic window show Mackmurdo as a fashionable architect of the moment

Museum of 1873–79 (by Waterhouse), the pompous Renaissance façades of the new Burlington House of 1873 (by Banks and E. H. Barry), Street's Gothic Law Courts of 1874–82; and there was also—smaller, but of great influence—Norman Shaw's New Zealand Chambers, built in 1873. Even more important for future development were Norman Shaw's private houses. One of Mackmurdo's first buildings, a house at Bush Hill Park, Enfield of about 1873, shows the impression which Norman Shaw's early works, such as Leys Wood, Sussex (1868–71) had made on him. About 1883 he designed another house at Bush Hill Park, Enfield, (No. 8, Private Road),* and now he had found a style all his own. Where did these proportions originate, or the plain wall of the upper storey with its three horizontal windows placed on top of the pilastered ground floor? Where can he have seen anything resembling these clear-cut cornices, or the ornamented bands that run along the windows? There is no doubt some faint recollection of the North Italian Renaissance in it, but it is ingeniously re-shaped. The feeling of this first-floor design is that of Frank Lloyd Wright if anything, and it was well over twelve years before Wright started work.

Alongside this rapid development of his architectural style we find an equally surprising progress in the field of design. Morris's style was really the *dernier cri* at the moment when Mackmurdo began, and yet, impressed as he was by Morris's theories (Morris's lectures started in 1877) he did not succumb to Morris's form. The proof of this lies in his work for the Century Guild and the *Hobby Horse*, and in his early textiles and wallpapers.

Mackmurdo saw, just as Morris had seen before founding his firm, that it was impossible to buy well-designed and decently made objects through the

4, 5

6, 7

n.1

ordinary channels. So he combined with a group of artists and craftsmen to produce what they regarded as good quality work and to offer it to the public. The enterprise was started probably in 1882 and called the Century Guild—the term guild being an outcome of Ruskin's ideas and not really appropriate. This is the first of many cases in which schemes of Mackmurdo's have influenced or even originated later activities which, as time went on, became more famous or popular and overshadowed the original example. Among the co-operators in the Century Guild were Selwyn Image, whose power of design Mackmurdo deeply admired, also De Morgan, and Benjamin Creswick the sculptor. Clement Heaton specialized in cloisonné; Heywood Sumner in stencilled decoration; George Esling in copper, brass and pewter work. They all worked to their own as well as to Mackmurdo's designs. His wallpapers were printed by Jeffrey's and Essex's, his textiles woven by a Manchester firm. The agents to the public were a firm called Wilkinson's of 8 Old Bond Street. The sign of the Guild, which was

3   designed by Mackmurdo early in the eighties, is of the same astounding independence as his contemporary architecture. Only very little in it is reminiscent of mediaeval tradition, but there is no connexion either with the favourite Morris motifs. Instead the consistent emphasis on long, undulating lines, flame-like or seaweed-like or even like women's long hair, points straight forward into Art Nouveau, as the Continent started on it ten years later, inspired indirectly—that can now be regarded as certain—by Mackmurdo. The most telling of all his

1   proto-Art Nouveau designs is the title-page to his book on *Wren's City Churches*,

n.2 illustrated as such in all the recent Art Nouveau books.* The same drifting

10   curves Mackmurdo used as a decorative adornment for chair-backs and more

6, 7 No.8 Private Road, Enfield, c.1883: the mouldings, seen from the side, already project in thin slabs foreshadowing the Liverpool exhibition stand

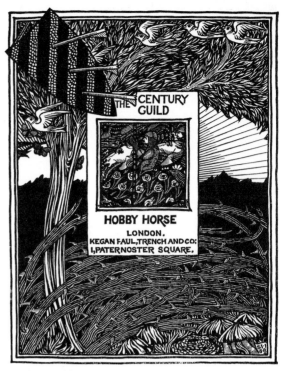

8, 9 *Century Guild, 1884: Mackmurdo's 'Single Flower' fabric, and the cover of the 'Hobby Horse', by Selwyn Image*

10 *Chair, about 1883*

sweepingly in his designs for wallpapers and printed textiles. Their dates and *8* those of the chairs are not absolutely certain. Before 1885 is likely, since, after all, the Wren book is clearly dated 1883, but before 1883 must remain doubtful. On the other hand, whatever the dates, they are early enough to have profoundly influenced Voysey in his much more successful designs* (see pp. 144–5). *n.3*

While engaged in the Guild work, Mackmurdo thought out another plan and again hit upon an idea of far-reaching influence. There was at that time no journal of artistic distinction in existence. Mackmurdo resolved to start one. He looked round and found in the Chiswick Press a printing press of unusually high standard and in Emery Walker a man to whom the reproduction of drawings and other works of graphic art could be safely entrusted, and ideal book-decorators in Selwyn Image and Herbert Horne. By printing the *Hobby Horse*— *9* this was the name of the magazine—on hand-made paper, by carefully choosing a good traditional type, and by conscientiously setting and spacing the type, a production was achieved far above anything available at the time. 'Never before,' says Aymer Vallance in his article on Mackmurdo published in *The Studio* (vol. 16, 1899), 'had modern printing been treated as a serious art.' A first issue came out in 1884 and more numbers were published regularly from 1886 onwards. Seven volumes in all exist. Mackmurdo showed them to Morris, and he and Emery Walker, together perhaps with Cobden Sanderson, induced Morris to start a printing press. Thus the Kelmscott Press and even more the Doves Press may be regarded as an outcome of Mackmurdo's initiative.* The *n.4* same must no doubt be said of John Lane's *Yellow Book* which began to appear in 1894, and it can, we now know, also be said of van de Velde's early endeavours in printing and book decoration. When his friend Max Elskamp in 1893 received the second number of *Van Nu en Straks* he wrote to van de Velde: 'C'est vraiment plus beau que le Hobby Horse'.* *n.5*

In the first issue of the *Hobby Horse* Mackmurdo wrote on the idea of the Guild and also on Early Italian Painting, and it remained a characteristic of the journal to include regular contributions on Italian art. In fact it was at the time the most evident difference between Mackmurdo's and Morris's style that whereas Morris never found anything appealing in Italy, Mackmurdo—guided by Ruskin—passionately admired the musical element in Renaissance design and architecture.

The contrast showed itself in the early days of the Society for the Protection of Ancient Buildings (founded in 1877). Morris's interest came primarily from what he had seen of Gilbert Scott's misdeeds in restoring cathedrals, Mackmurdo's from the danger with which the development of the City of London threatened Christopher Wren's churches. But whereas Morris's sympathy with mediaeval art is clearly reflected in the forms which he himself created, it is surprising to see that Mackmurdo's plea for Wren's churches was brought out with that page already discussed which is neither classical nor medievalizing but Art Nouveau.

The Society for the Protection of Ancient Buildings was only one of the societies with which Mackmurdo was closely connected. Another was the Home Arts and Industries Association, started by Mrs Jebb in 1885. Mackmurdo had for a long time been interested in a revival of rural England, a problem which was even more in the centre of his thoughts in his late years. Equally topical is an enterprise of the eighties, the Art for Schools Association, discussed in the first issue of the *Hobby Horse*. The aim of this society, which later carried on as the Fitzroy Picture Society, was to supply schools with well-printed chromolithographs of valuable old and modern pictures. Burne-Jones, Watts and Walker were among those who contributed.

It was the same quick grasp and independent judgment of what was promising that made Mackmurdo discover Frank Brangwyn, whom he saw one Sunday morning wildly painting somewhere in the City. He gave him a studio in his house and introduced him to Morris. In the same house incidentally he had a collection of old musical instruments and encouraged Arnold Dolmetsch to give his first English concerts of sixteenth- and seventeenth-century music on contemporary instruments.

Mackmurdo's pioneering zest comes out most boldly, however, in his
11 architectural work of the eighties. The project for an artist's house illustrated in the first issue of the *Hobby Horse* carries on from the second Enfield house and combines Queen Anne windows and a Renaissance pediment with a general composition and certain details surprisingly independent, and the exhibition
12 stand for the Century Guild at the Liverpool International Exhibition of 1886 is totally and in every detail independent. Its slim white pillars and its sharp

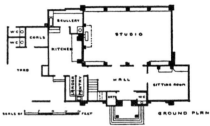

11 'House for an Artist', 1884

12 Century Guild exhibition stand, Liverpool, 1886

13 No. 25, Cadogan Gardens, London, 1899

mouldings anticipate Voysey and Mackintosh. Voysey indeed was fully aware of the debt he owed Mackmurdo (see below, p. 141). When first Voysey and then Baillie Scott, Mackintosh, Ashbee and Smith & Brewer appeared on the scene, Mackmurdo began to fade. There were several reasons, but not inferiority of design. A house like No. 25 Cadogan Gardens, built in 1899 for Mortimer   *13* Menpes, may, it is true, show in its façade with the three long and narrow bay windows Mackmurdo's growing sympathy with Norman Shaw's Anglo-Dutch style of the seventeenth and eighteenth centuries, but the side towards Cadogan Gardens, with the first and second floor windows sunk between unadorned brick strips and with the graceful outward-curving cornice, is in its delicacy of proportion and detail again an entirely personal achievement.

And besides the architectural qualities of Mackmurdo's façades, there is his interest in questions of planning and technical equipment. He was among the first in this country to think of the problems of regional planning and garden cities. It was his idea, set forth about 1881 in discussions with Patrick Geddes, to establish 'regional communities' with a Civic Hall and a Spiritual Hall as their centres, with workshops having direct access to roads, railways and waterways, and workers' houses close to the factories and also to the countryside, the school and hospital being placed at expedient intervals outside the ring of dwellings.

Another interesting project was Hogarth Cloisters planned at Ealing about 1892. Mackmurdo suggested the erection of a vast quadrangle 1140 feet in length surrounded by cloisters which were to be open in summer and enclosed with glass and heated by steam in winter. The individual houses and flats were to open on to the cloisters. They were all to be lighted with electric light. A central club house should form the centre of one side of the quadrangle, including a dining-hall, a dining-hall for children, and private dining-rooms, kitchens, steam laundry, billiard rooms, gymnasium, swimming baths, entertainment rooms and a nursery.

Amongst buildings carried out which introduced unusual technical problems was a cold store at 111–113 Charterhouse Street, erected in 1900, and a gymnasium built for the Gordon Institute for Boys in Liverpool about 1890. This building measures 110 feet by 56 feet, and cost only £1,000. The area is spanned by ten semi-circular wooden arches rising directly from the ground. They carry the roof as well as the gymnastic apparatus, an ingenious arrangement, as the curves of the arches distribute all strains, and the elimination of angular joints makes the construction ideally safe.

14 Mackmurdo's largest building in London is the Savoy Hotel, erected in 1889 while he was in partnership with Herbert Horne. Here and in other works of the same period he preferred a richer decoration to the simplicity of the earlier period. However it must be stressed that at no time had he been a purist. Although there are more columns and curved cornices, and manifold mouldings, and more festoons in his houses built in the nineties and after 1900 than in those built before, he had always been anxious to introduce somewhere what he calls 'a touch of music'.

At the beginning of the new century Mackmurdo left London and settled in Essex where he had bought an estate. In 1904 he started building the large house of Great Ruffins, Wickham Bishops. Later on, financial circumstances forced him to give this house up. But even then he did not return to his profession but preferred the quiet of his cottage. He now concentrated entirely on economic research, which led him to his ideas of State-Socialism. He pleaded for living wages and pensions fixed by the State, and for replacing a monetary system based on gold by a system founded on food vouchers.

When I first met him, my attention being drawn to him and his secluded cottage-life by Voysey, he was enthusiastically pursuing these utopian researches. *2* He was eighty-six years old, but no less active and agile for that. He walked with me and talked of his economic conceits, his light blue eyes glittering, his wavy white hair blown by a breeze, a black coat slipped on over his butcher-blue blouse or blue shirt—the kind of blue blouse which William Morris wore, and which Voysey wore. The shirt being in this case—as in other cases—a profession of faith.

14 River front of the Savoy Hotel, London, 1889

1 The Orchard, Chorley Wood, 1900

VIII
C.F.A. Voysey

CHARLES F. ANNESLEY VOYSEY was born in 1857 in Yorkshire where his father was a parson. The Rev. Charles Voysey was a man of gentle manner but firm conviction and suffered later the misfortune and humiliation of being deprived of his living for heresy. The Voysey case of 1871 was a *cause célèbre* of ecclesiastical policy. The future architect was the eldest son. He went to Dulwich College, after the family had moved to London and, not being a success at school, nor having shown scholarly leanings under a private tutor later, he was articled to an architect. The architect was J. P. Seddon, friend of the Morris circle and a medievalist of some power and individuality. The hotel at Aberystwyth—now the University College—is his best-known building, the church at Hoarwithy in Herefordshire perhaps his best. Voysey stayed with Seddon from 1875 to 1879, had then a short spell with Saxon Snell, a hospital specialist, and in 1880 joined George Devey, a domestic architect of far greater n.1 interest and importance than is realised today.*

2 C.F. Annesley Voysey (1857–1941)

About 1882 Voysey set up in practice on his own. There were no architectural jobs coming along for a number of years, and so, advised by Mackmurdo, he began to design textiles and wallpapers, as Mackmurdo was doing successfully in the early eighties. Mackmurdo, it will be remembered, was six years older than Voysey, and between 25 and 31 there is quite a difference. Mackmurdo was the greatest single influence on Voysey's style. Of course he knew William Morris as well—that goes without saying. Who in the 1880s, interested in architecture, interior design and furnishing design could have avoided knowing the shop in Oxford Street and at least hearing of the lectures? But from the first Voysey was out of sympathy with much of what Morris represented. He was repelled by Morris's 'atheism' and by his ebullient temperament ('like that of a drunken sea-captain', someone who knew him once said to me), and looking as an architect at Morris he felt a lack of a sense of space. Mackmurdo on the other hand had just that. It came out not so much in the house he built at Enfield about 1883 (see p. 135) and the house for an artist he designed in 1883 and published in the first volume of the *Hobby Horse,* the journal of the Century Guild, as in the exhibition stand for the guild at the Liverpool exhibition of 1886 (see p. 137). The façade of this stand, with its thin, widely spaced white wooden posts and its curious flat and thin architrave slices on top of each post is the foundation of Voysey's furniture and internal fitments, as Mackmurdo's textiles with their 36, 8 bold curvaceous, sea-weedy lines are the foundation of Voysey's wallpapers and textiles, though both Voysey's architecture and his designs achieved originality and maturity very soon. The inspiration from Mackmurdo implied a contradiction which stands at the start of Voysey's as of Mackmurdo's work, the

COTTAGE FOR M H LAKIN·Esqre
AT·BISHOPS ITCHINGTON NEAR WARWICK
C·F·A·VOYSEY·ARCHt·45 TIERNEY Rd STREATHAM HILLS W·

3 House at Bishops Itchington, Warwickshire, 1888–9

contradiction between designs unmistakably Art Nouveau—proto-Art Nouveau, since they are several years older than those of any Continental creators of Art Nouveau—and an architecture so convincedly rectangular that it was soon found suitable to be used as a weapon against Art Nouveau. The contradiction is of considerable importance, as we shall soon see once more, and it is only one of two which run through Voysey's work.

The years before 1888 are of interest for designs only,* the years between 1888 and 1892 saw the beginning of his architectural practice. Voysey was ready for it; that is proved by the fact that already the small house at Bishops Itchington of 1888–9 has most of the characteristics of his later houses, the characteristics

n.2

3

4 No.12 The Parade, Bedford Park, 1891

which make them look comfortable, at ease in the landscape and not exacting to live in: roughcast walls, decorative buttresses with pronounced batter, a big reassuring roof and horizontal mullioned windows. The English yeoman's house of the seventeenth century was his pattern—there can be no doubt about that, and Voysey himself confirmed it to me more than once—but the total *ensemble* is not just period imitation but introduces a simplicity, a bareness of surfaces and a consistent emphasis on horizontals which pointed the way out of historicism altogether. Innovation is even more patent in the often illustrated and discussed house of 1891 in Bedford Park, Norman Shaw's garden suburb (see above, pp. 112–13). The house is, except for one broad bay window, a plain rectangle in plan, and the elevation stresses this fact emphatically. It was a blunt statement against Norman Shaw's adjoining prettiness—more radical than any other statement of Voysey's—more so certainly than that of the two houses in Hans Road in London which followed in 1891–2. The staircase in one of them* has the same thin wooden posts as Mackmurdo's exhibition stand. The exteriors of the two houses are made into one composition, linked by a porch decorated with delicate flowing patterns. The traditional bay windows are kept but set close into the façade and pierced by a row of uniform window openings prophetic of the window bands of the twentieth century. The interplay of the decorative motifs above the entrances is repeated in the two oriels starting on the first floor and rising to the third and is caught finally in the twice curving-up parapet.

The change to success came in 1893, the year in which Perrycroft at Colwall was built, one of Voysey's most familiar houses, and the year in which *The Studio,* itself in its first year, illustrated wallpapers and metalwork and also furniture of his. He was then already on the move away from Art Nouveau to the kind of effects in design which had from the beginning been those of his

5 *Houses at 14 and 16 Hans Road, London, 1891–2*

6 *Staircase landing at Hans Road, 1891–2*

7 Morris's 'Strawberry Thief' chintz, 1883

8 'Cereus' wallpaper, 1886

9 'Trees and Birds' chintz, 1895

architecture. A proof is a design of Trees and Birds of 1895. If one compares this with an earlier design of his, the contrast is at once obvious. The tension is relaxed, the coverage of the surface sparser, the motifs closer to nature, and a prettiness is aimed at and achieved which some years before had not been the younger man's aim. But one should also compare such a design of 1895 with one by Morris, say his *Strawberry Thief* of ten years before; for only then the novelty of what Voysey was now doing can become fully visible. Morris's design covers the surface as closely as Voysey's had done in the eighties. Morris's colours are sombre, Voysey's light and cheerful. Morris harks back to late medieval tapestries, Voysey has no forerunner at all. But one thing Morris and mature Voysey have in common. Both were at home in nature, in the woods and fields and gardens, and both succeeded—more happily than any designers ever—in combining faithfulness to nature with a perfect stylization in two dimensions. As regards other qualities, Morris undeniably possessed an abundance in everything he did which Voysey lacked—any comparison of photographs of the two men will make one expect that, Morris with his beard and his shock of hair, Voysey in his quaint Quaker-like dress—but this abundance Voysey may not have envied. Or what else did he mean when he said to me that he found Morris too sensual?

One more word on this comparison of a Voysey and a Morris design. Such a comparison is not, this must be fully realised, a comparison of the famous with the new and only just up-coming. Already in 1896 *The Studio* wrote that Voysey's wallpapers were as familiar to connoisseurs as Morris's chintzes. Van de Velde, for example, according to what he told me, must have come across them already about 1894–5. That he was thrilled by them is understandable; for their freshness meant to Continental artists a new spring after the stuffiness of the Victorian winter.* But van de Velde must have been thrilled for more special reasons by those earlier designs which Voysey himself in 1894–6 no longer considered valid statements, by the designs of the eighties which must have been an encouragement to anyone moving in the direction of Art Nouveau. The same is true of Voysey's metalwork. The tea kettle and stand which were illustrated in the first volume of *The Studio* might even be called Art Nouveau by critics today. Voysey himself, however, would have hated that. He wrote in the *Magazine of Art* in 1904 (p. 259): 'I think the condition which has made Art Nouveau possible is a distinctly healthy development, but at the same time the manifestation of it is distinctly unhealthy and revolting'. The contrast which Voysey makes here between condition and manifestation is important, and we

9
8

7

p. 10
2

12

n.4

8, 12

10

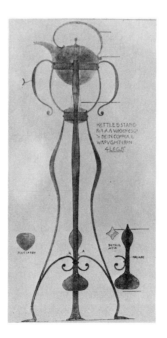

10, 11 Metalwork: kettle and stand of 1893, and fire-irons of c.1902

12 'Water Snake' wallpaper, c.1890

shall have to return to it a little later. Meanwhile the fact remains that the sinuo-
sity of Voysey's early designs for wallpapers, textiles and metalwork was an
encouragement for Belgian Art Nouveau and also for what, as we shall see, can
with a measure of justification be called Glasgow Art Nouveau. On the other
hand the fire-irons, which were made by Thomas Elsley's probably in 1902, or
shortly after, show all the moderation and charm of the chintz pattern of 1895.
A slight swelling enlivens the shafts, and the heart-shaped ends are a particularly
pretty conceit. Indeed, to appreciate Voysey's position he must be seen as a
friend of decoration, but not of the dominance of decoration over structure, and
as a friend of sound structure but not to the degree of a sweeping elimination of
decorative enrichment such as the true revolutionaries of 1900 were doing on
the Continent and in America. If he wrote under one of the first publications of

13 A Voysey house in its setting: Perrycroft, Colwall, of 1893

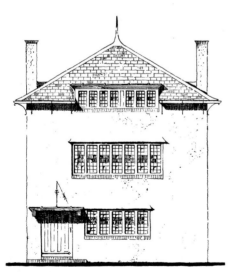

14 'Cockney villa minus ostentatious jimcrackery', 1890

a design of his—for a villa: 'Cockney Villa minus ostentatious jimcrackery',* *14, r* he meant Victorian decoration rather than Morris and Mackmurdo decoration. That becomes perfectly clear in an interview with *The Studio* given as early as 1893, where he said: 'Let us begin by discarding the mass of useless ornaments and banishing the millinery that degrades our furniture and fittings. Reduce the variety of patterns and colours in a room. Eschew all imitations and have each thing the best of its sort'.* This in conjunction with a scathing reference to   n.6 'gloomy drab and chocolate or dirty black green' and a praising reference to 'bright hopeful cheeriness', both in an article in the *Journal of Decorative Art* of 1895,* shows that his polemics were anti-Victorian in the first place.   n.7

Yet Voysey was no revolutionary nor did he ever want to be one. Intrepid innovation without the ruthlessness of revolution gives his best houses, those of the years immediately before and after 1900, their unmistakable personal character. By the end of the nineties, in fact, he had become one of the most sought-after domestic architects in England. For country houses especially, potential clients soon realised that it would be difficult to find an architect who had more feeling for the character of a setting, for unobtrusive and yet visible comfort, and who was capable of handling all the details in such a sensible and sensitive way. Moreover, he was meticulous about the business side of his commissions, and it is typical of him that whenever any of his designs was published he liked to state the exact cost. It would probably now be impossible to list all the country houses that he built since 1893, were it not for the fact that he noted them all in a little black book in his clear and careful handwriting, and that he had arranged all his photographs and designs into an excellent collection which is now at the Royal Institute of British Architects.* All his important works   n.8

were also illustrated and discussed in English magazines at the time, particularly in *The Studio, The British Architect* and *The Architectural Review*, and—largely due to Hermann Muthesius's early understanding of the value of his art—in the German magazines *Dekorative Kunst* and *Deutsche Kunst und Dekoration.**

Two houses will have to serve here to give an idea of Voysey's mature style. It is the style of Bishops Itchington fully developed rather than that of Bedford Park and Hans Road. It leans on seventeenth century English country traditions but handles them with an originality never showy but the outcome of deep feeling. He never wants to impose his own personality on the region, the landscape, or the house itself. One of the most perfect, and also the best-known of the houses is The Orchard of 1900 at Chorley Wood, on the edge of the Chiltern hills north-west of London. Voysey's own description of it in *The Architectural Review*, X, 1901, and the pictures chosen for that article, clearly reveal what his principal aim was: a unity between nature and the house in which the latter is subordinated to the former. At the centre of the whole design is the great cherry tree on the right, which is over 50 feet in circumference. The composition also includes other trees, as well as the high hedges around the house and the flowers in the unmown fields. The walls are whitewashed, the woodwork is pale green and the slate roof silvery-grey. The ground-plan of the house is basically rectangular. The dining room and the nursery face south, the study faces north because of the even light, as do the offices. Three of the five bedrooms on the first floor face north. A large, airy attic space—a rarity in an English house—has not been forgotten. For the walls in the living room Voysey chose a smooth purple fabric below broad white friezes, and only the bedrooms were hung with his wallpapers. Almost all the inside woodwork is natural, unstained oak. Outside you see again the high roofs and Tudor windows, but the smooth walls and particularly the large blank gables show that a new style is on its way.

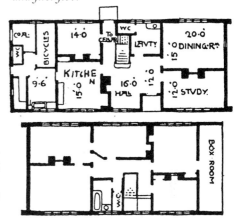

15, 16 The Orchard, Chorley Wood, 1900: façade (above), and plans of ground and first floor

17 Lounge-hall of The Orchard, Chorley Wood, 1900

This is even more patent in the façade towards the lake of Broadleys built *20* in 1898 for A.C. Briggs on the edge of Lake Windermere. To take in as much as possible of the view, the design incorporates three bow windows in a row, which rise to the edge of the high roof. Behind the middle window lies the large hall, occupying both floors; the bay window on the left belongs to the dining room below, which is linked at the back of the house with the extensive kitchen wing. On the right, also below, is the drawing room, leading off into a conservatory. The absence of compromise remains astonishing for 1898. There were no models in the past either for the boldly curved bows or for the meeting of totally un-moulded horizontal and vertical members in them. Voysey comes here amazingly close to the twentieth-century concrete and glass grid.

Surprisingly modern features appear inside the houses too, particularly after 1900. An outstanding example is the staircase of Garden Corner in *18* Chelsea, which was done in 1906 for E. J. Horniman; it combines domesticity with the utmost simplicity of detail. The walls are plainly panelled, and instead of banisters there are the high and closely-set vertical posts which Mackintosh used in the Glasgow School of Art in 1898, and George Walton at The Leys in 1901. The same excellence and sobriety characterize Voysey furniture of these years, for example a seat in Garden Corner of 1906 which has exclusively *19* verticals and horizontals, linked by quadrant brackets supporting the little end tables. Yet the seat looks friendly and inviting. The same is true of two small tables also designed for Garden Corner. Here, grace is combined with the *21* greatest conciseness of detail. In the same year, 1906, *The Studio* published a lovely ebony clock with ivory inlay, bronze balls as feet and one bronze ball on *22* the top. Here perhaps more than anywhere one realises how important a part Voysey played in the creation of the twentieth century. And yet even this lacks all dogmatism. The hands and the numerals have no rigidity. Decoration in its place remains decoration and should be enjoyed as such. Equally the silver table-ware made in 1907 is rational in shape to a degree not achieved anywhere before, *25* and yet is not harsh in the least. The toast-rack in particular, designed entirely out of circles and semicircles, is an astonishing achievement and could so easily have become pedantic or ponderous.

18 Staircase hall of Garden Corner, Chelsea, 1906

19 Settee of unstained and unpolished oak, 1906

20 Broadleys, on Lake Windermere, 1898

21 Interior showing one of Voysey's folding tables, 1905–6

22 Ebony clock decorated with ivory, bronze, and yellow silk, 1906

In designs for textiles the same stage in Voysey's development is marked by the Deer and Trees of 1908. It is the direct descendant of the Birds and Trees of 1895, but in the scattering of motifs, large and small, all pretty and all true to nature in spite of their unfailing two-dimensionality, it is more mature, indeed a perfect manifestation of Voysey's character.

For from whatever angle one looks at Voysey's work, one is never far from Voysey as a person. There is first of all the fact that as an architect he confined himself almost entirely to private houses, most of them in the country. He did no public and very few commercial buildings; one office building (Essex & Suffolk Equitable Insurance Company, Broad Street, London, 1906), one shop (Atkinson's, Bond Street, London, 1911) and one small factory (Sanderson's, Turnham Green, 1902). Apart from these, Voysey seems to have concentrated all his attention on the home, and this once again, is not a rebel's attitude. Voysey's attitude was inconsistent—that one has to face—just as so much in Morris is inconsistent.* In 1895 he slated 'the lazy and contemptible practice of relying

24

23

n.10

23 *Sanderson's wallpaper factory, Turnham Green, 1902*

24 *'Deer and Trees' chintz, 1908*

25 Silverware, designed in 1907

upon precedent for justification', but added immediately a warning against going to foreign styles for inspiration (i.e. Art Nouveau), because they are bound to be 'out of harmony with our national character and climate', and he was cross with me for having discussed his work as pioneer work of the twentieth century style. He disliked the twentieth century style, and his argument as he put it to me, when he was eighty-two, is so typical of the whole man that I want to end with it: 'This new architecture cannot last. The architects have no religion. They have nothing exalted which they could try to approach; they are like designers who draw flowers and trees without remembering and honouring Him who created them'.

1 Glasgow School of Art: the main entrance, 1897–9

IX
Charles Rennie Mackintosh

This introduction to Mackintosh, his life, his character and his work came out as a small book in Italian in 1950. In 1952 Thomas Howarth's Mackintosh book came out, a volume of over 300 pages with well over 200 illustrations. It is an admirable piece of work; however, I still think that my approach to Mackintosh differs sufficiently from Professor Howarth's to make an English translation and publication in the context of n.1 *this volume not totally useless.* *

2 *Charles Rennie Mackintosh (1868–1928)*

BEFORE 1890 no one living outside Glasgow could possibly have heard of the city as a centre of art. It may have been famous for its industries, especially its shipyards, for its trade, and its magnificent surroundings, the bare mountains and the lakes among trees, and the wide, majestic estuary of the Clyde. Artistically, Glasgow was completely provincial. Apart from M'Taggart, the solitary Impressionist, there were no original or influential painters. Architects had abandoned the Grecian austerity of the early nineteenth century, and the bold and impetuous originality in the use of Greco-Egyptian material that had characterized the work of Alexander Thomson, for a genuine and fruitful, if rather dull, imitation of the Northern Renaissance, with its high gables and its n.2 inflated details which were also the rule at that time in other British towns. *

There was a sensation, therefore, first in Great Britain and then on the Continent, when paintings by artists soon to be called the Glasgow School or the Glasgow Boys were shown, in the Grosvenor Gallery in London, in 1890, and then in the Glaspalast in Munich. These painters had obviously been inspired, apart from M'Taggart whose surprisingly independent technique was evolved shortly after 1880, by the painters of Barbizon and the Dutch Impressionists such as Mauve, Mesdag, Jongkind and the Marises. A great exhibition of the work of these had taken place in Edinburgh in 1886. Besides such examples, there was what Whistler painted in London. He, probably more than anybody else, impressed the group of the Glasgow Boys, that is James Guthrie, John Lavery, E. A. Walton, Roche, Cameron, Stevenson, Henry, Hornel, Paterson, Kennedy, Hamilton, Ferguson and others. In 1898, Lavery and E. A. Walton were made corresponding members of the Sezession, the famous Viennese artists' association, and by then their works were to be found in museums and art galleries in Paris, Brussels, Budapest and Prague. Glasgow itself was at first amazed, but at least in a few people bewilderment gave way to admiration. Glasgow Corporation bought Whistler's portrait of Carlyle as early as 1891.

Whistler and the Glasgow Boys naturally excited the greatest interest among the students of the Glasgow School of Art, to which an enterprising new director had recently been appointed, the painter Francis Newbery. It was not only the painters at the School of Art who were encouraged by the new climate; it also inspired architects and decorators. Among these were several who were soon to achieve an international reputation. They were a small group of men and women, whose talent was controversial but unmistakable, impetuous in their approach to problems and unshakable in their faith in the ideals of the aesthetic movement, which had been formulated as 'art for art's sake' in France in the middle of the nineteenth century and publicized between 1880 and 1890 by

Oscar Wilde. Among them was only one who possessed genius of the highest order. He was Charles Rennie Mackintosh, and his genius burst into sudden brilliant flame in the nineties and then burned itself out within twenty years. The other members of the group were George Walton, younger brother of the painter E.A. Walton, Herbert McNair, the two Macdonald sisters, of whom Margaret was to marry Mackintosh and Frances was to marry McNair, Talwin Morris, E.A. Taylor, and others.

Charles Rennie Mackintosh was born in 1868. He entered the Glasgow School of Art in 1884, and in 1889 he joined the successful firm of Honeyman and Keppie as a draughtsman. One year later, when he was still only twenty-one, his exceptional talent was already so patent that *The British Architect*, the most intelligent architectural journal of the time, published a project for a museum which he had done for a student scholarship, and another for a Public Hall,* n.3 done for the Alexander Thomson Travelling Scholarship which in fact he won. The plan for the Public Hall is still conventionally classical, but the draughtsman- 4 ship already shows signs of the unmistakable intensity in which Mackintosh was to excel. In 1892 he designed a Chapter House for the Soane Medallion of the 3 Royal Institute of British Architects.* His idiom here was still the current n.4 mixture of the Italianate with the Gothic of the Arts and Crafts Movement.

In 1893 he seems to have been promoted from the position of a draughts- man in Honeyman and Keppie to that of a designer. In the design for the new offices of the *Glasgow Herald* done probably in 1894,* Mackintosh's hand is un- 5, n.5 mistakable in the long curves of the corner turret below its top. These long curves place Mackintosh's position in the years of his beginnings as an architect. Their ancestry is found in certain passages in William Morris's textile designs and certain details in Rossetti and Burne-Jones, and in addition in the new freshness and lightness of weight and colour in Whistler and his friend, the architect Godwin. Add to this the Mackmurdo of the eighties (see pp.132–7), Beardsley who was to die prematurely in 1898, Voysey whose simple, clean and picturesque houses were just in the mid-nineties getting the appreciation due to them (see pp. 140–51) and, of non-British artists, Jan Toorop whose enigmatic picture *The Three Brides* was painted in 1892 and reproduced in the first volume of *The Studio* in 1893.* The Arts and Crafts ingredients are less easily defined. n.6 They go beyond what could be seen illustrated in the magazines, and so it is likely that the young Glasgow designers visited the 1893 Arts and Crafts exhibi- tion in London.

One result of all this was the tower for the *Glasgow Herald*, and another was some watercolours of the same year, 1894, which were done for an odd book, apparently an unsuccessful magazine of the School of Art. Its only title is *April Number, 1894*. It contains a short essay by Mackintosh entitled *Cabbages*, with a

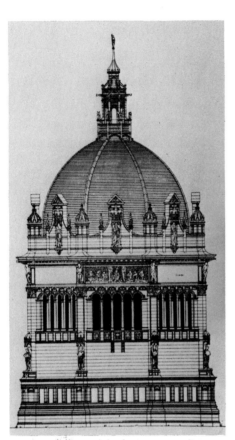

3 Design for a Chapter House, 1892

4 Design for a Public Hall, 1890

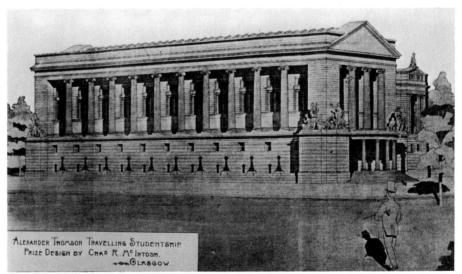

5 *Design for the 'Glasgow Herald' building, probably 1894*

remarkable illustration, and a reproduction of two panels by Frances Mac- *6, 9*
donald. The drawing is extraordinarily fresh and original, an amazing anticipation of twentieth-century art. On the other hand, the lines of the panels are
already over-elongated, with that tendency towards abstraction and excessive
tension which characterizes the Mackintosh-Macdonald interiors of the next few
years, and which gives the *Glasgow Herald* tower its originality. We must not
underrate this originality. In 1894 there were very few architects in any part of the
world who would have dared to use motifs in ways which historical precedent
had not sanctioned. Sullivan in America, Horta in Brussels, Mackmurdo,
Voysey and Baillie Scott in Britain, were among them, and Mackintosh followed
their example.

6 *'Cabbages in an Orchard', watercolour, 1894*

7 *Settle shown at the Arts and Crafts Exhibition, 1896*

The School of Medicine of Queen Margaret College in Glasgow, planned *10*
in 1894–6, was built, like the *Glasgow Herald* building, by Honeyman and Keppie,
but was designed, down to the details, by Mackintosh. The first floor windows
are his most characteristic contribution. In 1896, the Glasgow painters showed
their works at the Arts and Crafts Exhibition in London. *The Studio* reproduced,
among other things, a settle by Mackintosh, and a clock and some metalwork *7, 8*
panels by the Macdonald sisters. The clock-face shows for the first time those
curious mannerisms of linear design which were the most widely imitated
feature of the Mackintosh-Macdonald style. The principal elements are long
lines, sometimes spiralling, more often almost but not quite parallel, and sometimes intersecting though never at acute angles. Their origin very probably lay
in the Celtic style of Irish and Northumbrian illuminated manuscripts and the
carvings of the High Crosses which at that very time were becoming more
widely known.* Mackintosh's settle has Mackmurdo's and Voysey's spindly *n.7*
posts or shafts reaching right up to the top rail.

Mackintosh's great opportunity came in 1897, when he was twenty-eight,
and he rose to it. Miss Cranston, an enterprising and far-sighted Glasgow lady,
had decided to open some tea-rooms in the city in order to introduce the public
to more civilized drinking habits than those of the public house. She asked
George Walton, Guthrie and Mackintosh to design the first of these tea-rooms. *p. 17*
It was in Buchanan Street, and nothing of it now remains. In the same year
Francis Newbery entrusted the new building of the Glasgow School of Art in
Renfrew Street to Mackintosh.

A surviving photograph of Mackintosh's room in the Buchanan Street tea- *11*
rooms shows us chairs with ladder-backs of the sort made popular by Morris
and his followers, and a large painted frieze with tall upright figures of women
seen in profile and entwined in a tangle of roots, stalks, and flowers, in a style
midway between Celtic and Art Nouveau.

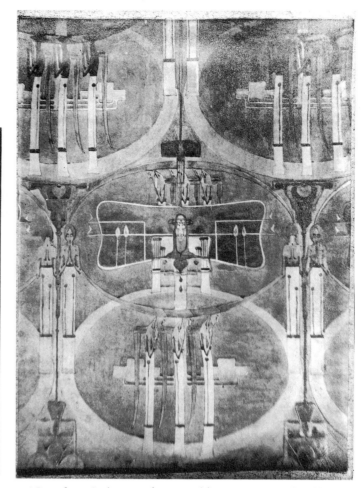

8 Metalwork by the Macdonald sisters, 1896

9 'Crucifixion', drawing for a panel by Frances Macdonald, 1894

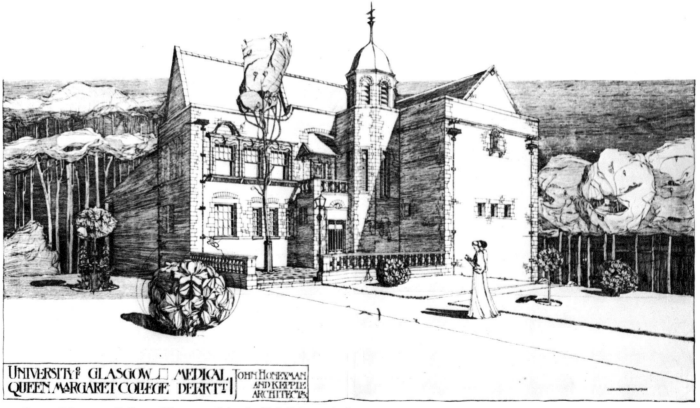

10 Queen Margaret College, Glasgow: School of Medicine, 1896

11 Buchanan Street tea-Rooms, Glasgow, 1897; the frieze is by Mackintosh, while the chairs and panelling are by Walton

12, 13 Glasgow School of Art: the complete building, 1897–1909 (right), and Dalhousie Street elevation, 1897–9

n.8   The first stone of the School of Art* was laid in 1898; the first section of the building was finished in 1899. The main entrance is placed demonstrably asymmetrically, with three bays on the left and four bays on the right. This

1   entrance is certainly sensational. The stonework around the door uses some themes of Margaret Macdonald's, but the subtle spatial undulation is all Mackintosh's. A small oriel window is on the immediate left of the entrance, a motif reminiscent of Norman Shaw and Voysey, and on the first floor there is a similar but even smaller oriel, which contrasts with a large double window surmounted by a heavy, curved pediment, of the kind favoured by the more traditional architects of the moment, but concavely curved in plan in a very characteristic Mackintosh way. Above the pediment is sheer wall, rising irregularly on the left and the right and an asymmetrically placed polygonal turret, which, in its bareness, points to another important source of Mackin-

n.9   tosh's inspiration, Scottish baronial architecture of the Stuart period.* This influence is even more apparent in the turreted elevation at the corner of Dal-

12   housie Street, which appears to be much higher than the rest of the building, on account of the sharp rise from the city centre to Renfrew Street. The subtle modulation of planes from this point must be seen to be appreciated.

13   To the right and left of the Renfrew Street entrance, on the other hand, Mackintosh's design is of splendid simplicity, unashamedly functional, nothing but the huge and regularly-placed windows of the studios, with the completely unmoulded mullions and transoms which Voysey liked so much. The only relief is the thin but far projecting top cornice and the enchanting metal work.

16   The iron brackets in front of the first-floor windows are functional; they support the boards used when the windows are cleaned. But the area fence with its slender verticals and its elegant curves at the top and filigree spheres with leaf motifs and birds (again of Voysey inspiration) is purely decorative and exquisitely detailed.

19   The interior of the school has the same mixture of the functional and the

15   decorative. The plan is quite straightforward. The lighting and a few other details show Mackintosh's interest in practical things. But there are other details which are nothing but a free play with space, e.g. screens of thin wooden verticals

14 Glasgow School of Art: main stair, 1897–9

15 Glasgow School of Art: plan

16, 17 Glasgow School of Art, 1897–9: wrought-iron window brackets, and director's room

instead of a staircase handrail (a Voysey motif), and the unnecessarily prominent *14*
posts supporting the balcony above the staircase, the bold curves of the secondary
staircase, and the way in which, in the director's room, the top cornice of the *18, 1*
panelling is carried right round the oriel window. Colours everywhere are light,
and the woodwork is mostly painted white, although that on the main staircase *19*
is black. On the landing there is a decorative panel of steel, a material which, at
the turn of the century, was not yet regarded as aesthetically acceptable. However, in spite of such occasional experiments Mackintosh cannot be considered a
designer truly in sympathy with the nature of materials. This is patent from the
way in which he insisted on painting wood, and on forcing it into the shapes
which his aesthetic ideas demanded.

18, 19 Glasgow School of Art: museum, 1897–9 (right), and later concrete fire-escape stair with tile inlay

20, 21 Queen's Cross Church, 1897–9: exterior from the north-east, and interior showing wooden vault and iron tie-beams

The School of Art persuaded Mackintosh to stay in Glasgow. A decade followed of ambitious and successful enterprises into which he launched himself with great enthusiasm. John Keppie, of Honeyman and Keppie, made him a partner in 1904. In 1897 Queen's Cross Church (consecrated in 1899) was begun, on a simple rectangular plan but with a most interesting east end, where the choir is combined with a short tower of unorthodox outline. The interior is wide and spacious with a wooden tunnel-vault, exposed iron girders acting as tie-beams, and an east window with tracery in the shape of a heart; the glass is white and an unusual blue.

Then came two exhibitions which made the successful local architect the man of the moment in certain European architectural circles. The first was in Vienna, at the Sezession towards the end of 1900, and the second at Turin in 1902. During the Vienna exhibition, Franz Wärndörfer, one of the principal founders of the Wiener Werkstätte, probably bought some of the furniture for his dining-room; alternatively he may have commissioned it from Mackintosh afterwards.* This furniture had a considerable influence on the Sezession and on the Wiener Werkstätte. How Mackintosh's art struck sensitive Continental observers can best be seen in a passage in Friedrich Ahlers-Hestermann's book *Stilwende**: 'Here we found the strangest mixture of puritanically severe functional forms and lyrical sublimation of the practical. These rooms were like dreams: everywhere there are small panels, grey silks, the slenderest vertical shafts of wood, small rectangular sideboards with upper edges that jut out, so smooth that their different parts merge into one, so straightforward that they look as innocent and serious as young girls about to receive Holy Communion—and altogether unreal. There was also a decorative piece like a jewel, destined for some place or other, and it seemed inconceivable that its lines should be anywhere broken, lines of a shy elegance like a tenuous and distant echo of van de Velde. The fascination that these proportions exerted, and the aristocratically spontaneous certainty with which a piece of enamel or stained glass or wrought iron was placed, enchanted all artists . . . Here were mysticism and aestheticism, although far removed from the Christian sense of the former word, and with a strong scent of heliotrope, and a feel of well-cared-for hands, and of delicate sensuality. As if in contrast to the exuberance of what had gone before there was scarcely anything in these rooms except two upright chairs, with backs as tall as a man, which stood on a white carpet, looking at each other over a slender table, silently, like ghosts.'

22 Mackintosh's stand at the Sezession Exhibition, Vienna, 1900

23, 24 'Haus eines Kunstfreundes', 1901: view from the south-east, and dining-room

In order to understand Mackintosh, it is essential to grasp the fusion in his art of puritanism with sensuality. The enchanting curves of Art Nouveau have the same importance as the austere verticals of the incipient Modern Movement, and the blacks and whites are as essential as the soft pinks and violets.* Every-   n.12
thing is extremely seductive, but far from pure. In this questionable spiritual atmosphere lies the difference between Mackintosh's interiors and those of Voysey. In order to see the expression of Mackintosh's style, free from all the obligations which commissions naturally imposed, one must look through the pages of the book called *Haus eines Kunstfreundes* which is an imaginary house   23, 2
designed for a competition by the famous German publisher of art books, Alexander Koch.

That was in 1901, but by then Mackintosh had already received the first commission to build such a house in reality. It was Windyhill at Kilmacolm for   25, 2
W. Davidson, begun according to Professor Howarth in 1899 and completed in 1901.* In 1902 followed the commission for Hill House at Helensburgh for   n.13
Walter Blackie, the publisher (completed in 1905). Both houses show magnifi-

25, 26 Windyhill, 1899–1901: exterior, and entrance hall

27 *Hill House, 1905, from the south-east*

cently how Mackintosh was able spontaneously to combine the delicacy of lines
with the robustness of the Scottish countryside. Take Hill House. The house
must be seen from all sides: the south side is comparatively plain, but it has a
shallow oriel on the first floor on the left, and a delicately detailed closed-in
veranda on the ground floor further right. Above this there is no window at all,
and the whole fenestration is indeed not axial. The south east corner on the other
hand is extremely varied in plan as well as in skyline, with a round turret, roofs of
different heights and chimneys of different shape. On the west side is the curiously
small and insignificant entrance and one huge chimney with battered contours.
It is doubtful whether one will derive more delight from the study of the building itself or of Mackintosh's drawings; for he was without any doubt one of the
greatest architectural draughtsmen ever. His strokes are of great force, he is
boldly original in the conventionalized signs he invented to indicate trees,
clouds, etc., and his lines and chiaroscuro are powerful enough to allow his
drawings to be considered as works of art in their own right.

    As for the plan of Hill House, the main living rooms are on the ground floor
facing south, with a fine hall behind and two more or less matching wings on the
east and west sides, one for the kitchen and services, the other for the main staircase and the billiard room. The staircase has again the characteristic slender up-
rights which, being at one and the same time a source of separation and of communication, make the space so eloquent. This staircase leads to the first floor,

28 *Hill House: the main entrance*

where the principal bedrooms are above the living rooms, a straight corridor is above the hall, and subsidiary bedrooms are in the wings and in the attic floor. Colours are as characteristic as shapes: the living-room for example has black furniture, a black ceiling with the black continued down the walls to the top of the wall panelling which has a silver framework and panels with pink flowers, pink   *31* textiles, and a fireplace decorated in pale purple. The main bedroom is of course   *33* white and has a little violet in the decoration. The furniture ought to be examined   *30* very closely; for example, the Henry Moore-like forms of the mirror and the   *32* contrast between the strict verticals and horizontals (don't overlook the various floor patterns) and the organic curves. The back of the black chair between the two wardrobes is an unmitigated grid but the wardrobes have exquisite linear decoration with just enough unexpected curves.*   n.14

His talent for sensitive, original and unfailingly charming interior design made Mackintosh the ideal architect for the Cranston tea-rooms which followed after those in Buchanan Street. Miss Cranston had complete faith in Mackintosh. She also got him to design the interior of her house (or rather that of her husband, Mr Cochrane), Hous' hill, at Nitshill. Unfortunately there is nothing left of it today. In the middle of the music-room was a deliciously curved white screen,   *35*

29 Hill House: entrance hall

30 Hill House: main bedroom, looking out from the bed alcove

31 Hill House: bay window of the living room, with a black ceiling and stencilling in pink and silver

32 Hill House: main bedroom mirror

33 Hill House: detail of fireplace

34, 35 Hous' Hill, c. 1906: the remodelled music-room, showing the screen and (left) built-in settles

'a segment'—this is Professor Howarth's description—'of a complete circle of about eighteen to twenty feet in diameter . . . to which the side walls of the room were tangential. The curved end wall of the room', Professor Howarth continues, 'and this inner circle were concentric.' The relation was re-iterated by the drum-shaped light fitting, and there were of course Mackintosh's built-in cupboards and wall-seats, the latter quite essential to the spatial ingenuity of the *ensemble*. Neither Frank Lloyd Wright nor Le Corbusier has brought internal spaces more boldly to life.

34

In the Cranston tea-rooms effects of this sort are lavished on settings of no intrinsic appeal. None of the tea-rooms were expressly built as such. The Buchanan Street tea-rooms were followed immediately by ones in Argyle Street

36, 37 Argyle Street tea-rooms, 1897: the Dutch kitchen, with furniture by Walton and decoration by Mackintosh

38, 39 Willow Tea-Rooms, 1903–4: façade, and the Room de Luxe showing Mackintosh's leaded glass and chandelier and a panel by Margaret Macdonald

(furnishings and fitments 1897), then in Ingram Street (work on and off between 1900 and 1911) and then by the Willow Tea-Rooms in Sauchiehall Street (1903–4). Of all these only the ones in Ingram Street remain fairly completely. They are in a disgraceful state while this book is going to press, and Glasgow Corporation ought to reinstate them. Of the Sauchiehall Street tea-rooms the façade and some of the interiors form part of a store. One of the Argyle Street interiors, with its rigid verticals and horizontals and its delicate black and white motifs of minute proportions, might well remind one of the most modern work of the same date by Austrian architects (Josef Hoffmann's Palais Stoclet, e.g.) if it were not for the sonorous curve towards the fireplace supported by its densely packed shafts of columns like billiard cues. In Sauchiehall Street the lighting is amazing, with chains of glass balls that hang from long metal threads. The ground floor contained one of Margaret Macdonald's most splendid works (dated 1903), in a wide white frame with a double curve, flanked by shafts which

8, 58
36
37
39

40 *Cutlery, for the Newberys (above), the Davidsons (below left) and Miss Cranston*

41 *Chinese Room at Ingram Street, looking towards the ceiling, c. 1912*

42 *Scotland Street School, 1904: the stair-turrets are above the girls' and boys' entrances, with the gymnasium in the centre*

43 Design for Liverpool Cathedral, 1902–3

taper for purely decorative reasons and which support a thin canopy directly beneath the ceiling. The spatial ingenuity of Mackintosh goes far beyond verbal description. The climax was the Ingram Street interiors and the library of the School of Art. The Oak Room and the Chinese Room in Ingram Street dating from *c.* 1906 and *c.* 1912 have a fabulous interplay of transparent screens of wooden fins. Mackintosh keeps the galleries a little way away from the walls, supported on posts, so as to leave a space which allows one to look up from the ground floor and down from the gallery.

Mackintosh, like Voysey before him, also designed cutlery—for the Cranston tea-rooms, for private clients and for his friends. These pieces too are highly original in shape, although not always functionally convincing.

The architectural commissions of these years were more of an official nature and less frequent. Mackintosh's plan for Liverpool Cathedral (1902–3) was not accepted: the commission was given to young Giles Gilbert Scott. Mackintosh proposed a building of traditional form, rather similar to York Minster, but with details so freely Gothic and with so much Art Nouveau, that they would have left Sedding's and Henry Wilson's most daring projects far behind. However Sedding's style must have had a great influence on Mackintosh's Liverpool design, his only attempt to return to ecclesiastical architecture. The Scotland Street School for Glasgow City Council was begun in 1904. It is symmetrical, with two projecting staircases and, in the centre, on the ground floor, a gymnasium covered from top to bottom with white tiles set off by a little black and bright green. The staircases are iron-framed, the iron being mostly visible, and

44 *Glasgow School of Art, 1907–9: library gallery*

in the raised part at the back there is an intricate interplay of the metallic members, every detail of which has been thought out with the utmost ingenuity. The windows are worth special study. Only large-scale drawings could do them justice.

From 1907 to 1909 the School of Art was enlarged on the east side along the steep slope of Scott Street, by the building of a wing to house a library. Here, for 46 the first time, we see signs of a change of style. Mackintosh's external forms become squarer. It would no longer be so easy to find undulating lines, or projections or recessions with organic resemblances. The windows are in angularly projecting oriels. The decoration of the entrance also has mainly angularly pro- 45 jecting motifs. However, the resourcefulness and the originality have remained, and the interior of the library is a great masterpiece of spatial composition. The 47 framework is extremely simple—a square room, with three polygonal oriel windows and a gallery. But the posts have been most ingeniously placed; they stand forward from the gallery, which is connected to them only by the horizontal beams on which it rests, and by balusters of oddly scalloped outlines and no practical purpose. Even where the gallery meets the oriel windows it does not 44 cross them but, on the contrary, is drawn very slightly inward, as if to leave the verticals without any horizontal interruption from floor to ceiling.

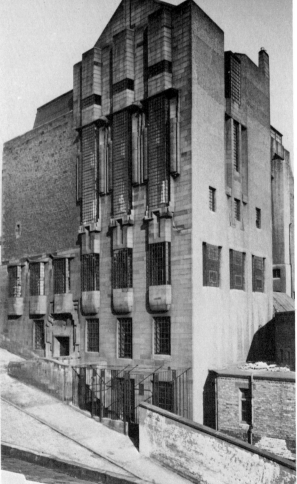

45, 46 *Glasgow School of Art, 1907–9: Scott Street entrance and elevation*

47 Glasgow School of Art, 1907–9: interior of the library, with its original furniture

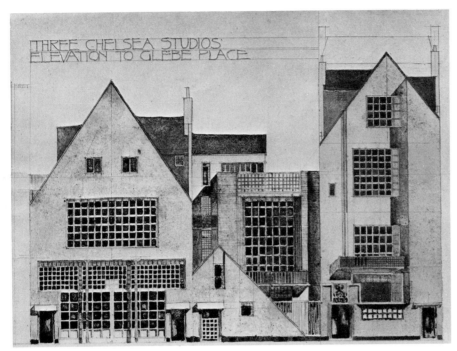

48, 49 Design for studios in Chelsea, 1920: in Glebe Place (left), and for the Arts League of Service

50 Smokers' companion, 1916

We find the same new angular style in the extraordinary ruthlessness of the design (never executed) for three studios in Glebe Place, Chelsea,* of all Mack-   n.15
intosh's designs that which will find the readiest enthusiasm among the younger   48, 49
architects of the 1960s. In the interiors of Mr Bassett-Lowke's house in Derngate,
Northampton (1916), which were Mackintosh's last important work, this
angularity becomes a manner. In the bedroom the most characteristic touches   51, 52
are the black and white materials used for part of the ceiling and the walls,
and the vivid touches of royal blue there and in the fabrics.* The staircase is   n.16
again screened, but this time by a chequered trellis instead of the slim verticals of   55
earlier projects. Much of the decoration is no longer reminiscent of Art Nouveau
but seems to hint strangely and prophetically at the German and French Ex-   50, 5_
pressionism of 1920.

51, 52 No. 78 Derngate, 1916: guests' bedroom, in black, white, royal blue, and grey, with oak furniture

53 No. 78 Derngate, 1916: the lounge hall, painted black with stencilling in brilliant colours

54, 55 No. 78 Derngate, 1916: lounge hall and chandelier and trellised staircase

56 Dressing table with aluminium handles

In 1913 Mackintosh broke off his connection with Honeyman and Keppie of Glasgow and went to live in London. Here, far from well-off, since he no longer received architectural commissions, he mostly painted—forceful landscapes, with sharp and energetic lines and cubic forms, and intense, naturalistic *57* flower studies. The end came in 1928, after years of hardship, during which his wife proved a tower of strength. It was a frightful end; Mackintosh died of cancer of the tongue.

Why these years of hardship? What had gone wrong? What had driven him from Glasgow and from his successful career? In photographs Mackintosh has an immediately striking face, with a sensuous mouth and eyes flashing under *2* bushy eyebrows, an expression both intense and vague, which attracts at the same time as it repels. He was ruined by drink. Those who knew him still talk a lot of his time in Glasgow, and a few old friends tried to deny the irregularity of his life. But there is no need for them to try. Van Gogh would not have been van Gogh if he had not cut his ear; Rembrandt would not have been Rembrandt if he had not gone bankrupt; Caravaggio would not have been Caravaggio without his brawls in the taverns. Mackintosh—the historian might as well accept this—would not have realized his visions of spatial intricacies, nor would he have designed as he did and drawn as he did, if he had not been Mackintosh, whisky and all.

He could be gentle, but also violent and cynical, and he was prone to fits of anger. He adored children, and wild flowers, of which he had a rare knowledge. During his best years, I have been told, he sometimes arrived at the office in the evening with piles of sheets of paper, ready to fill them during the night either with sketches or with large-scale details drawn with the greatest possible accuracy. In the morning they would find him exhausted and drunk, and the sheets of paper covered with drawings so perfect that they might have been jewels. The details were then left to the draughtsmen who were accustomed to his manner

57 *'Tile Roofs', watercolour, c.1927*

58 *Wrought-iron work on the gallery of the Willow Tea-Rooms, 1903–4*

59 Panel from the plaster frieze in the Willow Tea-Rooms, 1903–4

and style. They were excellent men—first of all W. Moyes (*c.* 1904 and after) who later went to Australia, then R. France who went to Canada. France worked out the details of the School of Art Library, and A. Graham Henderson those of some parts of the Ingram Street tea-rooms. Then began the crises over the work Mackintosh was doing for his firm and which he did not get done in time, and over other things too, so that in the end relations broke down. John Keppie, a former partner, was already dead, but had certainly not been entirely without blame. He too drank a lot, but he could take it, and he never fully appreciated the power and the instability of Mackintosh's genius.

For he was a genius. He had a spatial imagination as fertile and complex as those of Frank Lloyd Wright and Le Corbusier, and discovered the necessity and the possibilities of abstract art in his wall-panels several years before Picasso and Kandinsky had begun their efforts to liberate art from nature, and he discovered abstract metal sculpture of a transparency in which outer and inner space are made to merge when Moholy Nagy was only eleven, and Alexander Calder five. I never knew Mackintosh, but at the same time I have never met anyone—and I have approached many of his friends and contemporaries—who did not speak of him with a light in their eyes.

59

6, 58

1 Fireplace in the ante-hall
of The Leys, Elstree, 1901

Journal of the Royal Institute of British Architects, 3rd Series, XLVI, 1939

X
George Walton

GEORGE WALTON was born in Glasgow on 3 June 1867. His father, Jackson Walton, born as early as 1808, was a painter. He had been a wealthy man when he was young, but his financial position had gradually so deteriorated that his son, the youngest of his twelve children, after going to a grammar school until he was fourteen, had to start as a junior clerk at one of the Glasgow branches of the British Linen Bank. The love of beauty and craving for aesthetic expression hereditary in his family made him attend evening classes at an art school (probably the Glasgow School of Art), the only art training he ever had. Then, at the age of twenty-one, he decided to throw over what looked a fairly safe future and to set up in business as a designer and interior decorator. Now this decision was much more remarkable at the time when Walton took it than it would be now. What made him do it, we shall probably never know exactly. He must of course have heard of William Morris who, in 1877, had begun to preach his inflaming gospel of craft and beauty as social ideals. Before 1888, the date when Walton's firm was opened at 152 Wellington Street, Glasgow, Walton had apparently been to London only once for a fortnight, in 1884 or '85. Besides, London would not have offered much to encourage the establishment of a firm of this kind. Apart from Morris's work, there was that of the Century Guild, A. H. Mackmurdo's foundation of 1882, which could be seen at Wilkinson's in Old Bond Street (see p. 135). Voysey had only just started designing wallpapers, and the Arts and Crafts Movement did not attain much publicity until the first exhibition of the Arts and Crafts Society was held in 1888. All this being so, it can merely be assumed that young Walton apart from hearing about Morris's ideals had seen some of his printed textiles—the earliest of these came out in 1883—which had found their way to Glasgow.

For Glasgow in the late eighties was far from backward or provincial in matters of art. The 'Glasgow Boys' have been referred to earlier on, and one of them, E. A. Walton, was George Walton's brother, and he above all was a fervent admirer of Whistler. Now it is noteworthy in this connection that Whistler was not only revolutionary as a painter but also as a decorator. His famous Peacock n.1 Room of 1874,* and also the way in which he furnished his own studio in Chelsea in 1878, and decorated two exhibitions of the Fine Art Society in 1883 and 1884, was novel in the extreme. Those white dados and light walls—extremely different from Morris's grave colour-schemes—pleased E. A. Walton, the painter, so much, I am told, that he called his white cat Dado. Lightness—of touch and colour—was, more generally speaking, what distinguished the new Glasgow pictures from the work of Victorian artists. Whether we examine the grey and silvery green landscapes of E. A. Walton, or Lavery's white, grey and

2, 3 Café for William Rowntree's, Scarborough, 1897

4 Hoarding at the Buchanan Street tea-rooms, Glasgow, 1896-7

black full-length portraits, or Henry's and Hornel's Celtic fairy world of gem-like impasto—there is nothing stodgy, nothing conventional about Glasgow painting of 1890.

This bracing atmosphere is no doubt responsible for George Walton's adventure. Success was with him almost at once. It is surprising to see how many decorating and redecorating jobs fell to this young untrained designer between 1889 and 1896, the year when his reputation began to transcend Glasgow.* In n.2 these years he visited London more often. It is there that he met his first wife. They were married in 1891, and as she was a Londoner, and his brother, the painter, had moved to London in 1893, it can be assumed that George Walton now kept in close touch with what went on in town in matters of design and decoration. This may be of some importance for the understanding of Walton's development round about 1895.

Walton's first work to obtain a considerable amount of publicity was Mrs Cranston's tea-rooms at 91 Buchanan Street, Glasgow, the ones in which Mackintosh did his first public scheme of decoration. Walton designed first the p. 1 hoarding around the shop front during the alterations in 1896 and '97, probably 4 one of the earliest if not the earliest hoarding ever treated as a work of aesthetic significance, and then the billiard room and other rooms. Almost concurrently another café was commissioned from Walton. He had in some of his Glasgow jobs worked together with a young architect Fred Rowntree, a great admirer of his. Thanks to his recommendation the firm of Rowntree and Sons, of Scarborough, now asked Walton in 1896 to decorate their café at 20 and 21 Westborough, Scarborough.* Unfortunately neither this (for John Rowntree's) nor n.3 the Cranston tea-room survives, and a similar but smaller job carried out in 1897 for William Rowntree's at 32 to 39 Westborough is now recorded only by 2, 3 photographs and a water colour in the possession of the firm.

The range of Walton's activity had by then widened considerably. In 1897 and '98 he furnished a house for Mr J. B. Gow at Leadcameroch*, and another 16, 1 one for Mr S. Leetham, Elm Bank, in York,* the two most complete domestic 20, 1 jobs entrusted to him before 1900. He opened a subsidiary shop at 15 Stonegate, York, in 1898, and in the summer of 1898 decided to move to London. His most prosperous years followed. In Glasgow, besides his headquarters in Wellington

5 Remodelled back of Kodak's shop in the Strand, c.1900

Street, he had his workshop in Buccleugh Street, and for a short time—1899 to 1900—a showroom at 278 Sauchiehall Street. In London he lived at 16 West-bourne Park Road until 1901, and then at 44 Holland Street. He designed glass for a firm called Clutha Glass, for which at a much earlier date Christopher Dresser had worked; furniture,* and textiles (carried out by Alexander Morton's); he showed at the exhibitions of the Arts and Crafts Exhibition Society in 1899 and the following years—as he had done once before in 1890—and he decorated an exhibition for the Royal Photographic Society at the Dudley Galleries in 1897. It is through these that he met the principal patron of his late life, Mr George Davison, head of the European Kodak sales. In 1897 he arranged an Eastman Exhibition in London for Davison. He then refurnished the Kodak offices in Clerkenwell Road, and soon after that started on a chain of new Kodak shops, in London in the Strand, Regent Street and Brompton Road, in Glasgow,

6 Clutha Glass, designed about 1897-8

7 Hoarding during the building of Kodak's shop in the Strand, c.1900

*8 Interior of the Kodak shop in Brussels,
c.1900*

9 Stand at the Glasgow Exhibition, 1901

Brussels, Milan and Vienna.* These shops, as well as his excellent stand at the great Glasgow Exhibition of 1901* and the publicity given to his work in German periodicals helped to make his name known abroad. He furnished for Mr Goshawk a house in Vienna of which photos only survive; he took part in an exhibition in Budapest in 1902 for which he received a diploma from the Hungarian Ministry of Education. In 1905 a living room designed by him was on show in the Berlin art gallery of A. S. Ball.* The most mature achievement of these years of progress and success is The Leys, a house of comfortable size, built and completely furnished in 1901 for Mr J. B. B. Wellington at Elstree near London.*

8, n.7
9, n.8

n.9
21, 2

n.10

10 Interior of the Kodak shop in the Strand, c.1900

11 Wern Fawr, Harlech, 1907–10

12 St David's Hotel, Harlech, 1910–11

13 Sign for the Central Liquor Traffic Control Board, 1916–21

Of work carried out during the ten years before the war, not much need be said here. There were some big and important jobs such as the White House at Shiplake for Mrs Davison (1908)*, Wern Fawr, the Harlech home of Mr George Davison (1907–10)*, and the St David's Hotel at Harlech (1910–11), unfortunately burnt down in 1922; smaller houses, e.g., The Philippines at Brasted in Kent (1902),* Alma House, Cheltenham*, and Finnart House, Weybridge (1905), and shopfronts and interiors (W. Judd, Queen Victoria Street;* Wellington & Ward, High Holborn, 1910; Waterer & Dickins, Bromley).

Then the war intervened, and George Walton—now 47 years of age—was called as assistant architect and designer on to the Central Liquor Traffic Control Board. Between 1916 and '21 he did well over 100 surveys of public-houses, designed furniture, interiors and some unusually pleasant inn-signs. His headquarters were at Carlisle, where, as will be remembered, public-houses were put under Government control. It was in connection with this work that Sir James Morton came into close touch with Walton. His firm had woven some Walton designs before 1900. Now when Sir James had taken over—in addition to his large combine, Morton Sundour Fabrics—the small firm of Edinburgh Weavers in order to establish an outpost of modern design in weaves and prints, he went to Walton to obtain designs. There was something tragic in this episode. Walton, who had never been much of a business man, had not found a safe footing after the end of his Carlisle work. Only few and small jobs were forthcoming, such as a War Memorial for St Peter's, Glasgow (1920), stained glass windows for Boreham Wood church, commissioned by Mr J. B. B. Wellington (1923), for whom he also added a wing, a lodge and gate and some wall paintings to The Leys (1923–24), the reredos for St Anne's Derby (1927), the layout of the remodelled garden inside the Bank of England, now replaced by Sir Herbert Baker's new building (1921), the redecoration of Mr John de la Valette's house at 12 Little Stanhope Street, W.1 (1921), alterations to Mr W. O. Hutchinson's country house the Old Vicarage at Leatheringham, Suffolk (1929), and a row of four small suburban houses in Sterne Street, Shepherd's Bush (1923), in one of which he himself lived (No. 53). The only larger jobs after the war did not come until a few years before his death. They were once again commissioned by the Davisons; the complete decoration of Davison's 'Château des Enfants' at Cap d'Antibes, in connection with one of his generous and curious charitable schemes, and the Memorial Chapel for Davison erected by his widow at Cap d'Antibes in 1931.

Thus Sir James Morton's offer appeared as a boon to Walton, and between

1926 and 1931 he did well over sixty textile designs. However, only a few of them were executed and put on the market, and this is precisely where the remarkable encounter between George Walton and James Morton reveals its tragic note—truly tragic, because no clash between right and wrong occurred, nor, in fact, any clash at all. Sir James Morton had a genuine love for, and a forceful appreciation of, the most perfect examples of design of his own generation, Voysey's, Walton's, Mawson's works. At the same time it was one of his favourite plans to make Edinburgh Weavers the pioneer centre of the most up-to-date design and weaving in Britain. With this aim in mind he appointed in Mr Antony Hunt a manager of exceptional susceptibility to post-war tendencies and of a wholly twentieth-century outlook. Mr Hunt had studied the Paris exhibition of 1925 and understood its message. He could not help more and more concentrating upon a type of designs quite different from any Walton could be sympathetic to. And yet he, too, was a great personal admirer of Walton's 'big and magnanimous' personality. Walton on his part, while he conscientiously endeavoured to see the point of view of a new generation, was far too sincere and thoughtful a character to remodel himself according to standards of novelty which he could not fully appreciate. He was too strong to adapt his hand successfully to that new bluntness, or severity, or dash; and while he thus seemed to stand out for tradition, he was, on the other hand—just like Voysey, just like Baillie Scott—not traditional, or rather conventional, enough to return to that unproblematic Neo-Georgian into which English twentieth-century architects had converted domestic building, or to that British Empire Palladianism which just then became the curse of public architecture.

For he was strong and unswerving in his ideals, despite his quiet and friendly manner. Voysey has thus described him in an obituary note which is equally telling of his own and of Walton's character.* 'May one who has known George Walton for 40 years intimately be allowed to testify to his lovable nature. He could not say an unkind word about any man. If there were any he did not like he was silent. He was sensitive to an exceptional degree, and a beautiful colourist. His ingenuity was such that he could have made a fascinating design out of Hell fire. He was the most gentle of men, with strong feeling always under control.'

He died on 10 December 1933.

14 *Textile design for Sir James Morton, 1930*

15 *Cottages in Sterne Street, London, 1923*

16 *Fireplace in J.B. Gow's house at Leadcameroch, 1897–8*

Walton, during the years from 1895 to 1905, was one of the most brilliant of that group of British architect-designers who progressed beyond Morris towards a new style of the twentieth century without ever quite reaching it. Voysey and Mackintosh are the most important of the group. Walton's work around 1900 therefore deserves a detailed examination, whereas his work after 1905 can be treated more summarily.

There is a great difference between Walton's decorative schemes in the early nineteen and the hoarding for Mrs Cranston's tea-rooms in Buchanan Street or the fireplace in Mr Gow's house at Leadcameroch of 1896 and 1897–98 respectively. What has happened is in short this: Walton at the beginning of his career was an ardent follower of William Morris, whose textiles he actually used a good deal for upholstery. His own designs with symmetrical pairs of animals or monsters and closely spreading leaves have an 'all-over' quality similar to Morris's. He freely incorporated pieces of antique furniture and the old-world effect of dark beams along white walls and across white ceilings. One may recognise, knowing which way Walton was going to develop, that a certain flow of lines sometimes distinguishes his designs of furniture or fireplaces from those of the true partisans of the Arts and Crafts. On the whole, however, the difference is not great. The hoarding, on the other hand, and the fireplace at Leadcameroch are designed as a deliberate challenge to tradition. Where is the boldness of the startlingly big ornament on the hoarding derived from? Where from its happy and clear colours, and the irregularly heart-shaped spots on the background?

17 *Interior for Whitelaw Hamilton, 1890–91*

18 *Large-patterned silk tapestry, c.1897*

19 *Stencilling for E.A. Walton, 1891*

20 *Furniture at Elm Bank, 1898*

And what is the origin of the wilful curves of the fire dogs? To discuss this is to define Walton's position in the evolution of Art Nouveau in Britain.

Considering the part played by Mackintosh in the decoration of the Buchanan Street tea-rooms, the first supposition would probably be that Walton evolved his style under Mackintosh's influence. This, however, can hardly be so, although details will have to remain doubtful so long after the events. Walton was not only a little older than Mackintosh—which would in itself not mean much—but he was a successful decorator when Mackintosh was still a student of architecture, though an exceptionally successful student winning one prize and one scholarship after another. I am told that Walton's attention one day was drawn by Mr Keppie to the young draughtsman working so brilliantly in his drawing office 'very much in your style. You should meet him.' How can the actual dates be ascertained? Mackintosh's earliest work, the Glasgow Herald Tower of 1894, foreshadows already in some details those violent lines driven, as it were, by inherent energies, which characterise his later style. They get more concise and forceful in his drawings of 1895 and 1896 with the strangely elongated female figures of Toorop derivation. When did Walton arrive at the style of the fireplace? Most of his work of before 1896 seems more traditional than Mackintosh's. And yet, amongst the photographs which chance has preserved, there is that of a stencilled wall decoration for his brother's, the painter's, house, and this, done in 1891, proves him capable of entirely unconventional work at such an early date. Now this has no doubt nothing of Mackintosh's frenzy, and it may well be that for a short time about 1896–97 Walton fell under the spell of Mackintosh. Walton's own idiom was probably gentler, more amiable; determined but not wild. It is to be seen in the wall decoration of 1891 just as clearly as in that of the Rowntree café of 1896 and that of the Leadcameroch house. Subtly and exquisitely drawn individual motifs against a plain or very lightly patterned background, a tulip, a butterfly, some stray long-stemmed flowers and leaves (as in the silk tapestry shown here, which was used as stencilled wall decoration at Leadcameroch).

These Walton motifs have nothing to do with Mackintosh. Their source is London. There first Mackmurdo (see pp. 132–9) and then Voysey (see p. 140 ff), both already before 1890, had achieved the very lightness and simplification which Walton was aiming at. Voysey's influence grew, and is more marked on work about 1896 than on the stencilled pattern of 1891. In 1893 *The Studio* in its very first volume had illustrated pieces by Voysey. And there is one more name to add, the most important perhaps. In a letter to the *Architectural Review*, published only a few months before his death, Walton stated himself that his work was 'influenced considerably' by Whistler, and that the 'arrangement and colour' of Whistler's exhibitions in London were 'the most remarkable events of his time'.*

So much as an attempted explanation of Walton's early style. For a short time he seemed to join forces with Mackintosh, and the two together created a Glasgow style of 1900 so full of character and definition as was to be found in very few European centres. However, they were really of widely differing human qualities. Mackintosh's genius thrust him into unforetold spatial adventures, Walton with all the fervent intensity and integrity of his character endeavoured to disentangle himself from what might be more novel than genuine. The front of his little shop in York (1898), modelled to a certain extent on Georgian lines, was a first indication of a change from youth to maturity. Furniture such as that illustrated (Elm Bank, 1898) points in the same direction. How violent, how ruthless, appears Mackintosh furniture in its distortion of timber, if it is compared with the gentle slenderness of this chair, the straightforward surfaces of this wardrobe. The stand of Walton's firm at the Glasgow Exhibition of 1901 and the exterior and interior of Mr Wellington's house The Leys are perhaps Walton's most accomplished works. It is surprising to see how he seems to have cut out all vagaries from the façades. It is only the lettering that tells in the exhibition stand, only the restrained motifs of the porch in The Leys.

p. 15

p. 15

19

2, 16

18

n.15

20

9

23

Otherwise this designer, who had never had an architectural training, expresses himself (in his first job of the kind incidentally) in the purest terms of architecture. The placidity and serenity of the building is entirely dependent on the right proportions of roof to walls and windows to walls. Who else was able in England at that date to combine sobriety so successfully with charm and a feeling of comfort? Very few indeed.

Voysey, we know, kept his gentle hold over Walton. The billiard room in the centre of The Leys can serve to prove that. With its lovely light fittings, its slender metal balustrade round the gallery, and its enchanting transparent screen of narrowly spaced upright wooden bars separating the staircase entirely from the room, it is one of the most delightful interiors designed by Walton. This type of screen is first to be found in Voysey's houses in Hans Road, Kensington (1891–92). He used it again, e.g. in the most famous of his houses, The Orchard, at Chorley Wood (1900), and Mackintosh almost at once took it over with the utmost enthusiasm, as the ideal medium for his spatial endeavours (Glasgow School of Art, 1897–99, Hill House, Helensburgh, 1902–5, etc.). One detail needs some further comment: the tapering wooden posts with their bold entablature. They are so typical of that particular moment in the evolution of the new style, not wholly new as a feature but wholly new in their meaning, wilfully elongated, as slender as the curves of Art Nouveau and as challenging too, with their widely projecting tops held up without any visible effort. Voysey used these posts, and before him Mackmurdo at the Liverpool Exhibition of 1886 (see p. 137). It is for this front, so amazingly ahead of its time, that Mackmurdo seems to have invented the motif, which was then, owing to Voysey's influence, repeated everywhere, even in commercial furniture of about

21 *Billiard room in The Leys, Elstree, 1901*

23 The Leys, Elstree, 1901

22 *The White House, Shiplake, during its construction in 1908*

1900. By no means did Walton, however, repudiate ornament at this stage, nor at any other. Only he now kept it under close control. It blossomed out in the transparent, genuinely imaginative metal work above the light fittings, it gathered round the fireplace of the hall, and—to mention another room at The Leys—it emphasized some of the panels around the otherwise bare fireplace of the small ante-hall.

Walton's buildings, after this stage had been reached, are ever-changing solutions of the same problem, the encounter of an imaginative, entirely unconventional architect with the external and internal requirements of jobs which he is too honest and conscientious to disregard. Thus there is a decidedly Late Georgian flavour about the White House at Shiplake without Georgian forms being anywhere copied. It is the atmosphere of the Thames banks acting upon the architect, just as the atmosphere of the Welsh coast had acted upon him when, during the same years, he built Wern Fawr and the St David's Hotel at Harlech. The local stone in its colour and weight and the massiveness of the square blocks re-echo the menacing severity of the hills and the grey sea. Neo-Romanesque some people may call the Memorial Chapel at Antibes. In fact, the personal transformation goes here as far as in the previous buildings, and how precise Walton was in the formal interpretation of the emotional or functional requirements of a task is most clearly proved by the Sterne Street houses of 1923, where a straightforward job finds a perfectly straightforward answer. The *Sachlichkeit* of these small houses makes the surrounding builder-built houses with their bay-windows and their half-timbering look all the more false and fussy.

It is perhaps this concentrated and thoughtful approach more than anything that enabled the untrained designer to become what he became. George Walton was, as his friends tell you, a quiet man, kind and silent. He was happy in his work, not a fighter. Thus he never broadcast his ideas in writing, nor did he—as far as I know—more than once publicly speak of them. This only lecture of his, delivered in 1898 or 1899 to the Scottish Architectural Association, contains, however, so much of importance to an understanding of his attitude to art and design that it must, in conclusion, be mentioned. A few quotations may suffice: 'There is no reason why machinery should not be used in certain cases provided always that no attempt is made to use it as if it had brains.' 'The use of material in its natural state is delightful.' Walnut without French polish, and yellow pine in its true colour are recommended. If timber is to be painted, let it be white for bedrooms, or otherwise grey or green. Amongst colour schemes, the following are suggested, and they are all typical harmonies of 1900: walnut, grey, silver and rose; satinwood, ivory and canary; mahogany, crimson and gold.

The most interesting remark stands right at the beginning of the lecture. Walton emphasizes that he is not a craftsman himself, but 'a great deal is to be learned from the craftsman who intelligently executes one's own designs.' Now, in point of fact, those who knew Walton say that although not a creator with his hands like William Morris, he was a genius at understanding the nature of materials and their handling by craftsmen. In this again he stands precisely where his style places him, right in the middle between the Arts and Crafts and the Modern Movement. Morris believed only in salvation by hand work, the designer of today regards craft only as laboratory work for the preparation of standards for machine production. Walton—just like Voysey—no longer made, but what he designed was conceived in terms of craft production. His metalwork as well as his furniture needs the skilled worker. This combination of designing with an unerring sense of materials was necessary if a new style, a new grammar of form, was to be created. George Walton played an important part in this development, important enough to justify a paper devoted exclusively to him.

24, 25 St George Memorial Chapel, Cap d'Antibes, 1931

Part Two
Twentieth-Century Themes

1 *Frank Pick (1878–1941)*

XI
Patient Progress One:
Frank Pick

IF we remember the reluctant scepticism which delayed modern architecture and design on its way into and through England, the consistency of the London Passenger Transport Board in developing a strictly modern idiom of the greatest aesthetic integrity for its buildings, equipment and rolling stock is both surprising and highly encouraging. Here, obviously, enterprise and perseverance have been at work, logic and discipline, civilized urbanity and humane common sense. And here consequently an orderliness and unpretentious harmony have been achieved on which the eye does not tire to rest, a style as near in spirit to that of Gray's Inn, the squares of Bloomsbury, early Wedgwood tea sets and Georgian cutlery as our age can hope to get.

That all this is so, that the L.P.T.B. stands for an architecture unequalled by
n.1   transport design in any other metropolis*, and that it has by means of its buildings and publicity become the most efficacious centre of visual education in England, is due to one man. Without Frank Pick, London's transport system might have developed into something no less extensive and well-working than we know it to-day (although this is doubtful too), but it would certainly not be the civilizing agent—to use Christian Barman's happy expression—that it is.

The L.P.T.B. was founded in 1933 as the head organization of London's transport concerns. The Act of Parliament creating it marked the end of a long development towards concentration. Here are a few dates to recall it:

1829 Shillibeer's first horse buses from Marylebone to the City
1829–1843 Brunel's first Thames tunnel
1850 first horse-buses with roof seats
1855 foundation of the Compagnie Générale des Omnibus de Londres in Paris, the later London General Omnibus Company, or 'General.' (The General gradually bought out most of the small enterprises running bus services)
1863 Metropolitan Railway—the world's first underground railway—opened between Paddington and Farringdon Street
1868 opening of the Metropolitan from Baker Street to Swiss Cottage
1868–74 gradual opening of the District from Hammersmith to Mansion House
1870 first horse-drawn trams (all trams were later acquired by the L.C.C.)
1890 opening of the first electric tube railway: the City and South London Line from King William Street to Stockwell
1899 first motor buses
1900 opening of the Central London tube from Shepherd's Bush to the Bank
1900–1907 gradual extension of the City and South London Line from Clapham Common via Bank to Euston; and gradual opening of the Hampstead tube from Strand to Highgate and Golders Green

1901 first electric trams
1902 incorporation of Underground Electric Railways Ltd., a holding concern controlling the District and since 1910 also the Bakerloo, Piccadilly and Hampstead Lines
1904 first General mechanical (steam) buses
1906 opening of the Bakerloo Line and of the Piccadilly Line from Hammersmith to Finsbury Park.

In 1906 Sir George Gibb became general manager of Underground Electric Railways. He had been with the North Eastern Railway before, and brought with him as his assistant Frank Pick, then twenty-eight years old. In 1907 Pick was transferred to the staff of Mr Stanley (later Lord Ashfield), who at once recognised his latent genius. In 1909 he became Traffic Development Officer, in 1912 Commercial Manager. In the same year his company assumed control of the 'General,' in 1913 of the Central London and the City and South London lines. So by then unification was well on its way. Frank Pick was made Joint Assistant Managing Director in 1921, Assistant Managing Director in 1924, and Managing Director in 1928. Meanwhile the Underground Common Fund had been established in 1915 (pooling of receipts of all the members of the Underground group and distributing of funds on an agreed percentage), the Ministry of Transport had been founded in 1919, the Railway Act had concentrated the railway system into four companies, and the London Traffic Act of 1924 had made more drastic changes in the administration of metropolitan transport possible. The result was the formation of the L.P.T.B. in 1933. Frank Pick was its Vice-Chairman from 1933 to 1940.

His task in developing, under Lord Ashfield, an organization which carried every day as many passengers as the whole population of Canada, and employed a staff of over 75,000 was formidable. He proved equal to it in whatever emergency. So at least friends and respectful foes assure you. The quiet mastering of rush work from morning till evening had to him become a matter of course, long before his responsibility covered the whole of London's transport policy, and left a surplus superior to the sum total of many a successful man's energy. How he employed this surplus and for what reasons he employed it, as indeed he did, it will be for the following pages to show.

In his last years, disappointed but wise, he knew what he had been working for all his life. How far he had a clear picture of his aims, when at the age of twenty-four he entered the transport business, must remain doubtful. Yet he could not have chosen a more promising field, had he selected it in the full light of future understanding. Transport caters for all, transport organization and transport design affect all. Moreover it is a modern enough trade not to be encumbered by outworn traditions, and hence easily spurred to adventure, technically, and aesthetically too. Thus the very first tube ever built, the City and South London one of 1890, is of a functional soundness of design, untouched by any but engineering considerations, which it took Frank Pick a good deal of effort, twenty-five years later, to reintroduce and improve upon. The same is true up to a point of the earliest 'General' motor buses of 1904. But it is not true of station buildings. Here, where the engineer was not concerned, the meanest of architecture was still accepted as a matter of course. Improvements had, however, begun before Pick appeared, and it is historically entertaining to note the Art Nouveau ornament on, for instance, some of the original Piccadilly Line stations (*sang-de-boeuf* faience), the subdued Palladianism of the early twentieth century Metropolitan stations (white faience), and the then very up-to-date brick Neo-Georgian of the Golders Green station of 1907.

Two years later, in 1909, Frank Pick was promoted to the post of Traffic Development Officer of Underground Electric Railways. His job does not seem to have been clearly defined. It was apparently meant to cover anything that this young man might choose to undertake for the development of transport: the planning of new routes as well as improvements to, and publicity for,

2 *Poster by Fred Taylor, 1914*

existing ones. There was no separate publicity department, and so for the first ten or fifteen years of Pick's activity in London, the time, in fact, until he became Assistant Managing Director and then Managing Director, publicity absorbed most of the energy left over from the daily routine of a prodigiously growing
n.2 combine.*

The art of the poster and the art of lettering were the first that he tackled. Here he won his spurs as a patron. It was a sound start, for the English poster as well as English lettering had achieved a remarkably high level. Pick could here build on a firm foundation. Since the Beggarstaff Brothers had created their style of bold, flat surfaces and simple clear colours in the mid-nineties, and since Morris's Kelmscott Press and Emery Walker's Doves Press, the posters and press-work of England had been accepted as leading by the other European nations.

2 Among the artists who designed posters for the Underground between 1908 and World War I, Fred Taylor and Gregory Brown are the most notable. Their work, especially that illustrating the London countryside, is of an excellent standard, sound, forcibly telling its story, and no doubt convincing to the man in the street. Pick might have kept to this type of poster for many years, as the railways did, if his had been exclusively the point of view of the salesman of transport commodities. But it was not. He for his part, in an article in *Commercial Art* (vol. 2, 1927, p. 137) insisted that it was, and that the only difference between his attitude and that of average salesmen was that he took a slightly wider view, rating more highly 'the establishment of goodwill and good understanding between the passengers and the companies.' Thus, one surmises, Pick must have talked to his directors and others whom he regarded it as expedient to convince. But could they not have answered that, if goodwill was all he was after, he should have stuck to the poster style of 1910? What happened instead was that he met younger artists, saw them struggle for new and less easily appealing ideas, and decided to support them in their struggle, although his own balanced and weighty mind must often have doubted the revolutionary methods which they favoured. So McKnight Kauffer appeared on the scene in 1915, at first sight none too different from Taylor, though evidently bolder and more sweeping in his stylization. In his poster for Oxhey Woods, for instance, the forms of the trees are reduced to abstract shapes. What is only just discernible in his poster of 1915 had, by 1924, become the all-pervading quality of his art. His posters and those of a few others, such as Austin Cooper, looked in 1924 already exactly like the kind
3 of thing that we are now used to calling 'Paris-1925,' rather wild and jazzy, but exciting and stimulating. And still, Pick supported them. Here for the first time in his career, the business man in him came up against his real self, the educationalist; and the business man was defeated—to the extent that McKnight Kauffer's
4 mature and even more daring posters appeared more frequently on L.P.T.B. hoardings than those of any other artist. Pick was decidedly catholic in his taste in posters. He knew for how many classes of people transport caters. And he knew that for every one of them something could be offered that was suitable. Whether he was at that time, or ever, conscious of this educational bias or not, it can safely be said that no exhibition of modern painting, no lecturing, no school teaching can have had anything like so wide an effect on the educatable masses as the unceasing production and display of L.P.T.B. posters over the years 1930–1940.

However, there is one other field in which Pick's influence has been even more universal. It is lettering. The story is this: the Victorians, while abandoning the quiet distinction of English eighteenth century printing for a more florid and finicky ornamental kind of lettering, had, forced by the rapid growth of advertising, devised display types quite new and as daring as their contemporary
n.3 architecture in iron and glass. Such were* the Egyptian or Antique with bold letters of even thickness throughout and heavy slab serifs, the Fat Face with very thick strokes and exaggeratedly thin serifs, and the Grotesque with no serifs at all. The latter became popular very suddenly during the 1830s. Even a lower case appeared as early as 1834. Of these new types the Egyptian was the most original,

3 *'Poster Cubism' by McKnight Kauffer, 1924*

4 *McKnight Kauffer's mature style, 1932*

5 *'Unreformed' Underground panel, with Grotesque lettering and a solid bull's-eye*

ABCDEFGHIJKLMNOPQRSTUVWXYZ abcdefgh
ijklmnopqrstuvwxyz 1234567890£ (&.,:;'!?""''/-*),

6 *Edward Johnston's alphabet for London Transport, 1916*

strong and full of character, but the Grotesque possessed the highest readability and directness of appeal for large-scale work.

When Pick took over, Grotesque was the favourite lettering of the Underground lines. Examples can still be seen in some of the unreformed stations, such as South Kensington. There were cruder and more refined Grotesques, and Pick was careful to choose the best that were available. Beyond that at first he did not go. A good Grotesque was a sound, clear, reasonable letter. But by degrees, as his sensibility sharpened and his experience widened, he realized that Grotesque had certain deficiencies which he felt it his duty to overcome—again not because they were in the way of sales, but because they jarred on his sense of harmony and orderliness. Grotesque had no module to regulate depth and width. If this could be introduced, a happier balance would be attained. So, about 1912 or 1913, he began to play with compasses and ruler, trying to work out a new type face. He could not succeed, because he was not an artist. But he busied himself sufficiently to know precisely what he wanted. He also discussed his ideas freely with men who knew more about lettering and printing than he did. It was Gerard Meynell apparently, then of the Westminster Press, who had also taken an active part in enlivening Underground posters about 1914, who first suggested Edward Johnston as the right artist to satisfy his wishes. He introduced Johnston to Pick, and with that flair that had made him recognize McKnight Kauffer, Pick entrusted the job to Edward Johnston.

Johnston worked on the script for a long time. When it was at last ready in the summer of 1916 (in capitals as well as lower case), it was far more harmonious and balanced than Pick can have visualized during the preparatory stages—a truly twentieth century Sans, logical and consistent, based as far as possible on squares and circles, and thus of convincing and restful proportions. It was meant from the beginning as a display type. No fount of it exists smaller than 36 point, i.e. $\frac{3}{8}''$ letters. For text printing it has never been extensively used. It was, of course, confined to the L.P.T.B.*; hence its effects could not be instantaneous. But they must have been strong all the same. We can first discover them in Central Europe, just as Mackintosh influenced Austria before he acted on Britain. In Germany especially, where the years 1922–28 had brought a most exciting revival of Egyptian and Grotesque, some of the best new sans serifs can hardly be understood except as the result of a careful study of Johnston Sans. While these new German type faces, however, appealed only to a very small section of the printing trade in their own country, and a smaller still over here, things changed to a degree and at a speed not experienced in printing for a long time, when Eric Gill created Gill Sans for the Monotype Corporation in 1928. This machine-set type, both modern and pleasing, became in a few years the favourite with all those who were or wanted to appear modern-minded. It kept the field for many years without any serious competitor and will no doubt, for the historian, be one day the hallmark of 1930–40 publicity. And since Gill frankly admitted that his alphabet was not more than a judicious revision of Johnston's, and Johnston might never have started on his but for Pick's initiative, it is no exaggeration to say that Pick's vision changed the face of British printing. Station names, by the way, were originally written across a plain red diamond and later across a disc. Then the subtler, crisper-looking ring was designed. Again Pick had a hand in this. He had seen the triangle of the Y.M.C.A. and asked for something of that quality, but more balanced. Edward Johnston supplied it.

As for architecture, he was to play a part hardly less important, though important in a different way. But that was fifteen years later. The station buildings of the Golders Green–Edgware extension, gradually opened in 1923–1924, have a pleasant but not very exciting appearance. No attempt was yet made by the company's architect, S. A. Heaps, to get beyond accepted Neo-Palladian forms.

Then the southward extension of the same line to Morden was built (1925–1926). Here the engineers have more interesting solutions to spatial problems (e.g., the octagonal booking hall at Morden disguising the odd angle of track and main street). As for the façades of the station buildings, a new architect now introduced new forms, as bold though not of as undated a beauty as Johnston's lettering. Pick had met Charles Holden* on the committee of the DIA (on the DIA see the following essay) and had, with his insight into human qualities, sized him up as rightly as he had sized up Johnston and McKnight Kauffer. Holden for this first batch of station buildings designed a standard pattern adaptable to as many modifications as the various sites required. Its bare white walls of Portland stone and unrelieved angular concrete cornices, and its curious pillars crowned in lieu of capitals by balls with horizontal slabs across are a highly original expression of the 1925 spirit—more progressive than any other contemporary English building except Thomas Tait's Adelaide House.

7 Underground panel with the new Johnston lettering and station name across a ring

8 Edgware extension, 1923–4: Brent station by S.A. Heaps

9 Morden extension, 1925–6: Clapham South by Charles Holden

Shortly after the completion of the Morden line, Holden was at Pick's request entrusted with the plans for the Underground headquarters building in St James's. It was opened in 1929 and has the same cubic qualities as the preceding stations, but is of special interest mainly because of its sculptural decoration. As for this, including, it will be remembered, works by Epstein and Henry Moore, Pick did not at first like it. But Holden convinced him, and once he was convinced, he supported it, with his committees, and had his way.

As soon as the many problems concerning the Underground Building were solved, a new job on an equally large scale turned up. It had been decided to extend the Piccadilly Line. Stations in the west had to be remodelled to take tube trains, and new ones had to be built from Finsbury Park to Southgate and then to Cockfosters. They were situated in surroundings far more countrified than those of the Morden extension. Pick felt that therefore a different type of building was required. But what should it look like? Much thought was given by Holden and Pick to this question, and, since lately the architectural papers had said much and shown a little of a new style developed in Sweden, Denmark, Holland and Northern Germany, Pick went on a journey there with Holden (June 20—July 7, 1930). They were impressed by what they saw, but did not lose their heads (see their illustrated report to the Company, printed for private circulation). What they liked and what must have influenced their future attitude towards building was the simple, comfortable and civilized new brick buildings of Sweden, Holland and Hamburg (neither Hoeger's Teutonic romanticism of the Chilehaus, nor Dudok's Dutch romanticism of the Hilversum town hall). This style they recognised as suitable for English surroundings and in accordance with English traditions.

They did not go on from Hamburg to Berlin, where they might have seen the then most up-to-date transport architecture of Europe. Alfred Grenander's underground extension had been designed in 1929 and was opened in 1931. It is interesting to compare his buildings with Holden's. The general appearance is strikingly similar, but detail in Berlin is less personal and less sensitive.

10–12 Head office at 55 Broadway, by Charles Holden, and its sculpture: Night, by Epstein (above), and the North Wind, by Henry Moore (below)—all of 1928

13 *Sudbury Town in 1916*

14 *Sudbury Town of 1931, by Charles Holden*

When a general idea had taken shape in his head as to what he and Holden wanted to convey in the new stations, Pick suggested taking one of the buildings to be re-done along the South Harrow–Uxbridge line and erecting it as a complete sample. Sudbury Town was chosen. It was begun on December 13, 1930, and opened on July 19, 1931. It is a landmark not only in the history of Pick's work but also in that of modern English architecture. For it should not be forgotten that by then the new Continental style, shorn of its Paris-1925 or Dudok or German expressionist excrescences, had no representatives at all in this country, except for Peter Behrens's New Ways at Northampton, built in 1925–26 for Pick's friend, W. J. Bassett-Lowke, Frederick Etchell's premises for Crawford's of 1930, and Trent and Lewis's Victoria Cinema of the same year.* Moreover, Sudbury Town had nothing tentative or demonstrative. It is natural and easy, precisely right in its proportions and thoroughly functional in its layout. It stands firm and yet graceful, telling in its honest exterior that it is not intended to be more than a seemly casing for certain traffic functions. The diagram shows what these functions were: 1 indicates the main inward traffic; 9 the main outward traffic; 2 is the bookstall (note the rounded corner because of the outward traffic from 8, the refreshment room); 3 are the ticket machines, 4 the booking booth, 5 the place where the ticket collector stands, 6 the up-platform, 7 the waiting room, 10 staff quarters. The station has two entrances side by side, each with two openings separated by a slender brick pillar. The footbridge stands as a band boldly stretched across, against the brick rectangle of the booking hall. The excellent relation between height of parapet and height of roof-supporting pillars connects it for the eye with the proportions of wall and cornice in the station building.

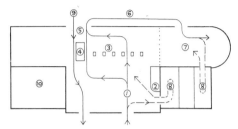

15 *Station layout and traffic at Sudbury Town*

The completion of Sudbury Town station marks the opening of the 'classic' phase of underground architecture; 1930–1935 can be considered the 'classic' years. Sudbury Hill, Alperton and Acton Town on the same line followed immediately, and then in 1932–1934, Manor House, Turnpike Lane, Wood Green, Bounds Green, Arnos Grove, Southgate, Enfield West and Cockfosters; and, towards Hounslow: Chiswick Park, Acton Town, Northfields, Boston Manor, Osterley and Hounslow. Rayners Lane and Park Royal on the Uxbridge branch came a little later. Some of them were carried out under Holden's immediate control, others by S. A. Heaps; for Enfield West Holden worked with James, Bywaters & Pearce, for Rayners Lane with R. H. Uren. The plans of all these stations are dictated by function, by the lay of track and adjoining streets, by necessary subways and the stream of passengers in and out. This also determined their general shapes, a central cylinder here, a curved front there, a rectangle along the street, or right across the track in other cases, or again a narrow rectangle to cover the distance between the required site for the station and a main road not in its immediate neighbourhood. The repertory of forms used, on the other hand, was kept very much the same for all of them, once it had been found and found good.

16 *Arnos Grove station, 1932*

17 *Alperton station, 1933*

18 *Arnos Grove booking hall, 1932*

Sudbury Hill looks sturdier with its one centre window on each side and the wide expanses of unbroken wall. The rhythm of brick wall and concrete cornice, a leitmotif of L.P.T.B. architecture, is carried from the booking hall in steps right down to the platform. Alperton, like Sudbury Town, has the two entrances again, but as the pillars are missing, quite a different rhythm results. There are, moreover, the low shopping wings to enrich the picture at Alperton, whereas Sudbury Town has a concrete ramp on the left for prams to pass across the line. Arnos Grove is perhaps more impeccably satisfactory than any other. There was ample space, traffic approaches were from two sides, meeting at a right angle. The cylindrical shape was thus appropriate. The low square parts spreading out beneath the cylinder link up with the main directions of track and streets. Everywhere simplicity of outline is combined with a remarkable delicacy of detail. To relieve the band of concrete beneath the ground floor cornice, for instance, bands of blue tiles are inserted, a feature already to be found in the Morden extension of seven years before. They add colour and form a convincing background for the station names. The lighting standard, and the standard combination of the L.P.T.B. bull's-eye with the flag-staff should also be noted. The curved walls of the interior are of the same beauty and clarity of proportion. Nor does simplicity deteriorate into dullness. One's interest is kept busy by the interplay of verticals and horizontals: first floor against ground floor, and windows with their sub-divisions against brick walls with their attached concrete shafts. The only criticism of the interior of Arnos Grove is that the ticket booths develop not very convincingly round the central pillar.

17

22

16

18

19 *Southgate station, 1935*

20 Bounds Green station and ventilation tower, 1933

21 Chiswick Park station, 1933

20   At Bounds Green the engineers asked for a ventilation tower, and the site for the station was small, close to two streets. So a shallow building with cham-
19 fered corners resulted. At Southgate, on the other hand, there was enough space and buses were to circulate round the station. So the surrounding sites were bought up, and shops were built to form an orderly background for the low circular station building. Shops were also incorporated into the composition of Turnpike Lane. Here, furthermore, the booking hall is below ground by a number of steps to indicate the fact that at Turnpike Lane Station the tube line just emerges to the surface. A ventilation tower is successfully inserted between
21 station and shops. At Chiswick Park (1932–3) the tower seems a little inarticulate, somehow reminiscent of the Morden Extension. The semicircular booking hall expresses the confluence of three street approaches. The problem at Northfields lay in the position of the track and an old station unusually far away from the main street with which the new station had to be connected. So Holden designed a wide forecourt and a booking hall, long and somewhat narrow with the long axis connecting forecourt and track, a combination of booking hall, in fact, and passage. Enfield West, (now Oakwood), designed with James, Bywaters & Pearce, has the main road meeting the track at an odd angle. The forecourt conceals this. The booking hall incidentally is here immediately above the track. Similarly it had been placed right across the track at Acton Town, where two entrances at right angles correspond to the two main streets. Chiswick Park has
33 one of the rounded booking halls, and again the proportions of ground-floor pillars to the windows and the posts separating them are singularly happy.

22 Sudbury Town platform and footbridge by Holden, 1931

23 *St John's Wood station by S.A. Heaps, 1938–9*

24 *Warren Street station by Heaps, 1939*

25 *Litter basket in Piccadilly station, 1930*

Spaces for advertisements are an integral part of the design. Cockfosters is of quite a different nature, because here concrete is the material and not brick. The resulting forms, which will be recognised later in some of Holden's platforms too, are closely reminiscent of those used by the French. But that is in all probability—just as the similarly between Holden's brick stations and those of contemporary extensions on the Berlin Underground —due to identity of function entirely, and not to influence. The clerestory arrangement at Cockfosters is as genuine an expression of concrete as the windows of Enfield West or Chiswick Park are an expression of brick.

The aesthetic danger in the L.P.T.B. style is, of course, dullness. Holden and Pick were convinced that novelty is no merit, and that a good thing remains a good thing, however often you do it. Hence the uniformity of style permeating all their work. But no architect of such educational leanings as Holden can always be equally inspired. The buildings erected by the L.P.T.B. at Leicester Square and Warren Street stations bear witness to this. Nor could his personal touch be easily replaced by the detailing of others. The Leicester Square and Warren Street buildings were carried out by S. A. Heaps, the L.P.T.B.'s chief architect. St John's Wood station of 1938–1939 was designed entirely by Heaps— an attempt at further modification of the Holden scheme, without giving up its prevailing character. At Boston Manor, on the other hand, and Osterley features are introduced deliberately, it appears, for novelty's sake. In this the architect and his patron could not be successful. The dash of the Mallet-Stevens forms in the Boston Manor tower, and the quaintness of the Osterley tower did not come

26 *An early interior: Bank station*

27 *Total planning: Leicester Square, 1935*

28 *Boston Manor by Holden, 1934*   29 *Osterley Park by Holden, 1935*

naturally to two such serious and honest men as Holden and Pick. The brilliancy of Tecton (of the Penguin Pool at London Zoo, and Highpoint flats) was inaccessible to Pick and bound to displease his educational mind.

Parallel with the architecture of station buildings there ran a great deal of other major and minor architectural work, office buildings on station sites, underground booking halls such as Leicester Square and Piccadilly Circus, platforms below and above ground, the latter of a clearly visualized and expressed brick or concrete character, and all such details as subway entrances, lighting standards, platform seats, clocks, kiosks, ticket machines etc., down to the concrete posts holding the cables along the lines. Even they were by Holden.

The architectural problem of the underground platform is one of combining tubular shape with spaciousness, and plenty of advertising space with clear visibility in what concerns the passenger. In the later stations these requirements were closely studied. But platforms as satisfactory as that at St John's Wood (by S. A. Heaps) are still few. Light fittings, for instance, are better at St John's Wood than on most other platforms. Seats and automatic sales machines are recessed so as to preserve a complete flushness of the curved walls, and the name of the station can be seen at once, out of whatever carriage window you look. Above ground a large variety of possibilities were offered to the architect. There was first of all—just as in station buildings—the difference between a style appropriate for brick and a style appropriate for concrete; and there were, furthermore, combinations of the two. The platform of Chiswick Park Station is a typical piece of concrete architecture with the bold cantilevering that concrete

30 *Lamp standard, 1933*

31 *Cantilevered concrete platform at Chiswick Park, 1932–3*

32 *Streamlined 'tube' shape at St John's Wood, 1938–9*

33 Brick: Chiswick Park booking hall, 1933

34 Concrete: platform at Cockfosters, 1935

alone can achieve. It was designed in 1932. The covered platform at Cockfosters   *34*
is again of a frank concrete character. The introduction of the clerestory was
functionally and aesthetically successful.

The same style was also adopted for bus and tram architecture: country
coach stations, garages, shelters, waiting-rooms and the like. There again a vast
variety is happily combined with a general unity of idiom. The L.P.T.B. style is
everywhere at once recognizable—the first principle of sound publicity—but the
forms chosen never seem imposed upon the expression of the functional peculiarities of a job. The bus shelters, for instance, were one of the most gratifying   *36*
additions made by the L.P.T.B. to the pattern of London's suburbs. They were
originally designed in 1933. Surely these clean and friendly looking structures
must have done a great deal to convince the man in the street of the acceptability
of a style that, if introduced with a Tecton impetus, might have roused his
opposition. Object lessons are the best lessons. Those who have experienced the
functional advantages of these shelters, the advantages of so much glass and so
little in the way of roof support, will be prepared to welcome something of the
same kind at home. When it came to station seats, once more patient progress
marks the development. A large number of designs were tried out and kept or
discarded, from straight-forward, comfortably shaped seats to attempts at a
combination of back-to-back heavy garden seat with station name-plate, or at   *38*

*35 'Leaf' upholstery moquette by Marion
Dorn, 1937/8*

36 Bus shelter of 1939

37 Terrazzo bench, 1937

38 Combined bench and station sign

37 Aalto shapes in a terrazzo-looking concrete material used frequently and for various purposes.

Nor were designs, in cases where jobs were identical in their functions or had to be repeated very often over a number of years, allowed to become stagnant. Research went on all the time, guided and supported by Pick. A characteristic example is afforded by the bus stop signs. Nothing more than a post and a sign were required. The sign had to be conspicuous and easily legible. But the post should, according to Pick's vision, be more than just a post. It should at a glance appear the modest representative of an organization promising comfort and visual pleasures. So here the question of decoration came in, a question that occupied Pick's mind a lot, especially in later years. The experiments with ornamental tiles and plaques on some platforms are one proof of this, and the drive for better upholstery materials for tubes, buses and trams, that went on during Pick's last year or two with the L.P.T.B. is another. He could easily find out the best textile designers—having for years been Chairman of the Board of Trade Council for Art and Industry—and he chose those who did not only think in terms of designing on paper, but knew enough of industrial production. His correspondence with artists and manufacturers is highly instructive. In spite of all his administrative work he took no end of trouble in explaining everything to everybody concerned and coaxing everybody into doing what he wanted. His patience in such cases was prodigious.

More instructive still as an illustration of this faith in patient progress is the history of London Transport rolling stock from 1907 to 1940. As to tubes and surface trains, the wooden Piccadilly Line coaches of 1907 were by no means bad. Metal panels had been used on wooden strutting early in this century, but their sizes were still those of wood panels. The first steel-framed carriages ran on the District in 1911. The early tube carriages of 1906, etc., had pantograph doors at both ends. They were closed in later on. The design was still that of railway carriages. To the 1920 stock a new section was given, a bulging out of the sides to obtain more foot space. One could thus do away with footboards sticking out, an ugly and dangerous feature. The seemingly streamlined section of the underground carriages introduced on the Piccadilly Line in 1937 is caused by the same considerations. The sole function of the curve is to cover the footboard so that it can be used at stations, when the doors are open, but not as soon as doors close and the train starts. Automatic doors, incidentally, came in in 1906, but were given up and re-introduced in 1919. Development ever since has been towards wider door space—it is now twenty-five per cent. of the side wall—wider window space with thinner pillars separating the windows, and smoother surfaces, obtained by means of larger panels and flush welded joints.

39, 40

35

41

42

39, 40 Concrete bus stops of 1935 and 1937

42 Car of 1937 with flush automatic doors and ventilator hoods

41 French Piccadilly Line stock of 1906

43 Interior of 1906 Piccadilly Line stock

Similarly with interiors. In 1906 every part of the equipment seemed 43
separately stuck on. The 1920 stock was a tremendous advance. Yet, compared 44
with 1937, it appears still finicky. In the latter such features as ceiling lights and 45
rails for strap handles have become part of the architectural composition. By
means of a great deal of technical ingenuity the piers between the windows too
have been made flush. Visible screws have been all but abolished. The alternation
of lengthwise and crosswise seating was introduced in order to obtain the widest
standing accommodation by the doors and taper it down away from the doors.
The results put the Paris Metro to utter shame, and made the Berlin U-Bahn
appear heavy and pedestrian.

44 Interior of 1920 Piccadilly Line stock

45 Interior of 1937 stock

51
6,47
48

The same exactly is true of buses and trolley-buses. Up to 1923 no change of aesthetic significance is to be noticed. Then the tidying up began. The NS type could, thanks to the provision of a lower centre of gravity, have a covered upper deck. It also has a more orderly grouping of parts along the back end with its open staircase, and a cleaner treatment of the radiator and the canopy to the driver's seat. LS and LT (1927–1930) had sixty instead of fifty seats, six wheels and sprung seats. Enclosed staircases, introduced in 1927, became standard with the ST of 1929; this was a smaller type, on the whole very similar to the LS. The canopy in the front, however, is more satisfactory in outline, the route number is in a more organic position, and the relation of window to body is brought

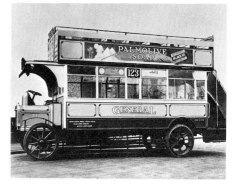

46 *The standard S type bus of 1920*

47 *NS type bus of 1925*

48 *ST bus of 1929/30: an enclosed staircase and fully pneumatic tyres*

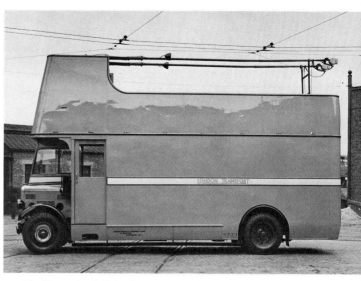

49 *Experimental trolley-bus, 1930: six wheels and a completely new shape*

50 *Trolley-wire lubricating car, 1938*

more into accordance with Pick's changing architectural views. These come out, however, more clearly in the first experimental design for a trolley bus. It dates *49* from the year of Sudbury Town—1930—and shows an immense advance over all the previous buses. Tram cars in Copenhagen had especially impressed him. The details of the front should be noted in particular, and the curved window above the staircase. The STL buses of 1933—fifty-six-seat four-wheelers— adopted most of the innovations of the first trolleys. Tubular metal seats were introduced in 1934. In the seventy-seat trolley-buses of 1935 and the RT buses of *52-54* 1939 this new flush and crisp design was essentially kept, though minor improve- ments were still made. They are wider windows with fewer separating pillars,

51, 52 *Bus interiors: above, NS of 1923 with wooden seats and exposed roof struts; right, RT of 1939 with tubular seating, flush roof and crank-operated windows*

53, 54 The RT bus of 1939, with larger windows, smooth treatment of the front, and a new placing of the route numbers

more curves, a different placing of route number and route indicator, and different details where body front, driver's seat and radiator meet.

And while patient progress thus gave the public ever better and ever more pleasing vehicles, Pick did not take less interest in design for vehicles, buildings or pieces of equipment which did not concern the public at all. In the case of the *50* overhead wire lubricating cars, one can perhaps argue that the public sees them and in fact likes looking at them, and that therefore their beauty of shape and cleanness of surface will be an asset from the business point of view. This does *55* not, however, apply to the interiors of sub-stations, signal cabins, factories and *56* workshops. Here the only people to benefit by care for interior beauty are the

55, 56 Behind the scenes: signal cabin at Acton Town, 1934 (left), and locker room at the Acton works, 1933 (above)

IT'S A CHANGE YOU NEED

MOVE TO EDGWARE

33 MINS FROM CHARING CROSS SINGLE FARE 8ᵈ QUARTERLY SEASON 62/6
36 MINS FROM BANK – – – – SINGLE FARE 9ᵈ QUARTERLY SEASON 67/6

TRAINS EVERY 9 MINUTES

UNDERGROUND

57 Social propaganda combined with business, 1925

employees of the Board. Yet Pick was anxious to give to the places where they work just as much beauty as to the places of daily communication between the passenger and the Board.

In this more than anything else Pick's attitude comes out as that of the reformer. His primary impulse was a desire for honesty, harmony and order. Others might help to bring a more honest and orderly world into being by political and social measures. If they did not sufficiently try to, if they seemed to lack honesty or accuracy or discipline, he was scandalized. Hence his failure at the Ministry of Information. What he had forgotten, in taking up the job of Director-General there, was that the L.P.T.B. had made him happy only in so far as (and as long as) it had given him a free hand to combine large-scale organization and administration with large-scale propaganda for the visual expression of honesty, harmony and order. He thought in terms of visual propaganda whatever he did. His new buildings, his rolling stock, his innumerable pieces of excellent industrial design, helped to make streets better and ultimately towns better. This and this alone was their *raison d'être*. For better towns stood always before his mind's eye, towns more beautiful and more orderly, and also more human than any of to-day, true communities in shape and social structure, which their citizens would be proud to serve.

He wrote two pamphlets at the end of his life, which it is necessary to know, if one wishes to understand his mental make-up. One is called *Britain must rebuild* (London, 1940), the other *Paths to Peace* (London, 1941). Here are a few sentences from the later of the two: 'If we are to achieve our hopes and forge the armour of light, everyone will have to work for the community in some way or other for nothing. What we seek can only be gained by voluntary work, which is work of love.... What excuse is there for relieving anyone of his share of tidying up his street; protecting his park or public garden; caring for his neighbour in misfortune; watching against abuse amongst those in authority; doing something to beautify and adorn his surroundings, which all may share....'

Now this is immensely revealing. It is a religious mind that speaks, developed in the puritan atmosphere of England, but freed from puritan fetters by a new humanism and an utterly unpuritanical love of visual beauty. Frank Pick was made of the stuff of Carlyle, Ruskin and Morris: energetic as they were, passionately educational as they were, always in earnest as they were, and also a little heavy-handed as they were, and as you must be, if you want to move masses. He has been called a dictator. He has been called cruel and formidable, reserved and aloof. He was nothing of the sort. Those whom he liked and respected knew him as generous, open and exceedingly lovable. And as to dictorial appearances, he only shared the dictator's drive and the dictator's faith in order. But no dictator has even been a humanist. A dictator need not be like Hitler. He can have a high moral goal. He can devote himself—this is Cromwell's case—to forcing men into living better lives. He does not care, however, for lives and men to be happier in this world. In this Pick was just as unpuritanical as in his delight in architecture and design.

However, he was too sharp-sighted a man to overlook the fact that while the passenger appreciated a smoothly working transport system and grumbled if he did not get it, he did not quite so readily appreciate the improved beauty of a ticket machine. If in spite of that Pick insisted to such a unique extent on giving him beauty in buildings, equipment and everything, he did so because of his faith in the ultimate soundness and goodness of human nature. If the man in the street—and Pick regarded himself entirely as one of them—could not at once see the ethical, the vital value of these improvements, he must be made to see it, gently but firmly. To surround him with the right things was, of course, the best approach to visual education. But exhibitions had a job to do, too. The D.I.A. had convinced him of that, and so, in 1932 he allowed the D.I.A. to show a selection of exemplarily designed British goods in the Charing Cross booking hall. It was followed by exhibitions of L.N.E.R. and then of S.R. posters, Shell-Mex posters, Design in Modern Life (D.I.A.), New Houses for Old (Housing

58

58 DIA exhibition at Charing Cross in 1932. Its credo was Pick's: 'fitness for purpose and simplicity are the key to good design'.

Centre), Noise Abatement, Milk Marketing, the workings of the G.P.O., the evening classes of the L.C.C., the Highway Code, the *News Chronicle* Better-Schools competition, the work of students of the London Central School of Arts and Crafts, Smoke Abatement, the Green Belt projects, etc. Now it would certainly be reasonable to say that a station hall where nobody goes but in a rush is not a suitable place for exhibitions. Yet Pick, the educationalist, felt the need for small, free popular exhibitions on such themes, and so Pick, the patron, made them possible.

For he was, to add a last word, the greatest patron of the arts whom this century has so far produced in England, and indeed the ideal patron of our age. Christian Barman in his obituary in *The Architectural Review* said that Pick had been described 'as a modern counterpart of Lorenzo the Magnificent. . . . But the novel and remarkable thing about him is just that he was the very opposite of a Lorenzo. You could apply the term Lorenzo very aptly to Jack Beddington or to Sir Kenneth Clark. To both these men the art they serve is the main thing. . . . To Pick, art was always a means to an end. . . .' Quite true—but so it was to Lorenzo the Magnificent. The end then was personal enjoyment and self-glory. Patronship with such an end is no longer possible to-day. Granted that Sir Kenneth Clark probably derives a kind of intense joy from the works of Henry Moore that would have been inaccessible to Frank Pick, even he as a patron bought mainly with public funds for a public purpose. No—if a Lorenzo can be conceived nowadays, it can only be in terms of big business or big administration, in terms of no leisure and no private glamour and also—and this is perhaps the most important point of all—in terms of architecture with all the other arts serving her, and thus serving the community.

1 Inlaid writing cabinet designed by Gordon Russell, 1927

XII
Patient Progress Two:
Gordon Russell

S. B. RUSSELL, Sir Gordon's father, moved to Broadway in 1904, having bought the Lygon Arms, in the conviction that the motor age would revive country inns and there would be scope for inns of the highest standards. Among these there should also be the furnishing of the rooms with genuine antique furniture. The buying of furniture necessitated a repair shop at the back. Soon it had customers also from the village and the country around. 'Any necessary repairs [are] carried out by skilled craftsmen in the workshop on the premises,' says the first booklet of the Lygon Arms, a remarkably well printed and well got-up production called *The Story of an old English Hostelry.** By 1914 about ten men were working in the shop* and antiques were also bought for re-sale. Americans discovered the hotel and the shop, and before 1914 considerable shipments of antiques left Broadway station. Gordon Russell, then twenty-two, had had a grammar school education and a practical education in the inn including a close interest in the repair shop. This included the making of pieces for the Lygon Arms, some beds, single and double, and some towel rails. Gordon Russell designed them, if that is the right term for what work preceded the making of these solid, rustic, extremely heavy pieces which still exist.

They are evidently naïve work, from the point of view of design as well as of craftsmanship. This needs some emphasis; for in the Cotswolds, and not far from Broadway, some of the most sophisticated artist-craftsmen of England were working at that very time. William Morris, by the products of his workshops founded in 1861 and even more by his addresses and lectures delivered between 1877 and his death in 1896, had given a new meaning to craft in England. He had taught with enthusiasm and fanaticism that all healthy art in all healthy periods had been craft, that industry had ruined craft and that only by artists choosing to be craftsmen could art, and with it civilization, be rescued. He was an ardent lover of nature and of honest country building and country craft. What he preached he lived. He learnt to carve, to illuminate, to weave, to dye, and he designed as easily as he rhymed. He lived in a Georgian house in London, but in a stone manor house in the country, at Kelmscott, near Lechlade, a mere thirty miles from Broadway.

Nearer still, at Sapperton, less than twenty miles away, one of Morris's most faithful disciples, Ernest Gimson (1864–1919), had begun in 1903, one year before S. B. Russell bought the Lygon Arms, to design furniture and metalwork and have it made in his own workshops. Gimson was trained as an architect at Leicester. He moved to London in 1886. Among his first London friends were Ernest and Sidney Barnsley, Ernest working under Sedding, one of the most original church architects of those years (Holy Trinity, Sloane Street), Sidney

n.1
n.2

2

2 Oak bed by Gordon Russell for the Lygon Arms, Broadway, c.1910

under Norman Shaw. Gimson had met Morris already in Leicester. He now met Webb, Morris's closest friend among architects, as well as Emery Walker and Lethaby. Gimson, apart from working architecturally, learned to do plaster decoration with his own hands and to make chairs.

For a while Gimson apprenticed himself to a chairmaker near Ledbury. Lethaby also was interested in furniture. He, together with Mervyn Macartney and Reginald Blomfield, ran a firm, Kenton & Co., during the years about 1890, for which they designed furniture. They did not make anything. The furniture was shown in 1896 at the exhibition of the Arts and Crafts Exhibition Society, a body which had been formed in 1888. Work by Gimson had already been in the exhibition of 1890, by Gimson and by Sidney Barnsley in that of 1893. Ernest Barnsley appeared for the first time in the exhibition of 1896. Later in the nineties Gimson and the two Barnsleys decided to leave London and move into the country. They looked round and finally found Pinbury in Gloucestershire. In 1903 Gimson changed Pinbury for Sapperton. The Barnsleys went on with their honest, well designed and excellently made furniture until they died, Ernest in 1925, Sidney in 1926. Gimson, whose workshop was at Daneway House, did much in the same honest rustic style, but also a good deal that was more elaborate, sophisticated and original. Among his work one remembers turned chairs and chairs with ladder backs, tables with chamfered legs and rails of many shapes and patterns, cabinets of square shapes with drawers of varying shapes and sizes rhythmically alternating with small doors to cupboards, cabinets on high stands, cabinets with dainty bands or frames of small-scale inlay. These cabinets were by no means imitated from, or sometimes even inspired by, the past. They were pure Arts and Crafts; i.e. an original early twentieth-century contribution. The same can be said of his metalwork, firedogs, altar-crosses and the like. They are indeed particularly imaginative and subtle.* In the furniture shop the fore- n.3
p. 23.
man was Peter Waals, a Dutchman by birth and upbringing. Waals carried on after Gimson's premature death—perhaps more in the Barnsley than the Gimson spirit. His workshop was at Chalford in Gloucestershire, and he died only in 1937.

S. B. Russell knew Gimson. Gordon Russell however never met him. But he knew the members of another equally interesting group which had settled down even nearer Broadway, at Chipping Campden, only five miles away over Broadway Hill, in 1902. The head of this group, the Campden Guild, was C. R. Ashbee (1863–1942), also a fervent follower of Morris, but a man very different from Gimson, much more sophisticated and in the style of his products much less single and concentrated. Ashbee was the son of a wealthy father, a business-man and book collector of curious tastes, and a German mother from Hamburg. He went to King's College, Cambridge, but had to fend for himself, as his mother had left his father and he had stood by her. In 1888, when he was twenty-five, he started the Guild and School of Handicraft at Essex House, Mile End Road, in the East End. The idea of a guild came from Morris and Ruskin, and in his various books Ashbee recognized his indebtedness to both.* His first book was n.4
called *A Few Chapters on Workshop Reconstruction and Citizenship,* and his second *An Endeavour towards the Teachings of John Ruskin and William Morris.* They came out in 1894 and 1901.

The guild occupied itself chiefly with furniture and metalwork, but in 1898 a private press was attached to Essex House. Ashbee also worked as an architect and built several houses in Chelsea (Chelsea Embankment and Cheyne Walk) which are amongst the best and most original of their date in England. Ashbee believed in the village as much as in craft, and so — in spite of obvious commercial disadvantages—he moved his guild in 1902 to Chipping Campden. He tried to establish for his craftsmen a life both rural and culturally stimulating. Theatricals played an important part. Guildsmen also had their own small-holdings. Ashbee was unable to make a financial success of the guild at Campden, and it went into liquidation in 1908. He succeeded in reviving it, but the First World War finally killed it. Guildsmen however stayed on at Campden, notably Alec

Miller, the carver and sculptor, and the brothers Hart, one a silversmith, the
n.5 other a carver.* Ashbee's style differed from Gimson's in being always a little
closer to Art Nouveau. He liked floral and foliage elements in long, undulating
curves and used them not only in his metalwork but also in wood or metal panels
or mountings on furniture. The Guild worked at Campden while Gordon Russell was at school there. Locals disapproved of these Londoners and perhaps also
of their activities, although these certainly had nothing in the very least scandalous.

Finally, one more artist must be mentioned, Fred Griggs (1876–1938), who
first came to see the guild and then stayed, until in 1926 he began to build himself
Dover House, a Cotswold dreamhouse, large, rambling and hidden away from
the street. He did not finish it till 1934, and died four years later. He was a wood-engraver primarily, and his illustrations in the *Highways and Byeways* series of
county books, and also a few in Morris's *Collected Works,* teem with medieval
fantasy and are translucent with a true understanding of Cotswold building
craft. He knew a good deal about this kind of architecture and designed his own
house in all its details. In 1919 he intended to go into partnership with Gimson,
but Gimson died before anything came of it.

So around Broadway in the early years of this century the spirit of William
Morris was very much alive, and work of a solid, honest, but also delicate and
imaginative kind was being done, in furniture and in metalwork. Technically,
these artist-craftsmen and designers were ready to remain the pupils of their pre-decessors of a few centuries ago, but formally they were original and refused to
be satisfied with imitations of the past—a strange mixture of revival and pioneering, characteristic of the best of those years in design as well as architecture and in
Britain as well as abroad.

But—and this is the most curious fact about the beginnings of furniture
making at Broadway—the humble new beds of about 1910 made for the Lygon
Arms are in an odd way survival rather than revival and not at all pioneering. S.
B. Russell knew the Campden Guild as well as Gimson. But no reflection of this
appeared yet at Broadway. Just as the blacksmith still clinked away in his shop in
the village street, so the Lygon repair shop still did naturally and without re-flection what it was called upon to do.

When war broke out in 1914, Gordon Russell was called up at once, and
when he came back he was anxious to build up something of his own, attached
to Broadway but not exclusively to the Lygon Arms nor to antiques. Gimson
and the Barnsleys had proved that good honestly-made furniture not designed to
imitate furniture of the past was a possibility, and incidentally Heal's in London
had proved that it could be designed, made and sold commercially. At Broad-way the craftsmen were there, the showroom was there. So Gordon Russell
went to London in order to show a few designs he had made to two men whose
judgment he valued: to Percy A. Wells, the head of the cabinet-making depart-ment at the Shoreditch Technical Institute, and to John Gloag, who had become
assistant editor of *The Cabinet Maker.*

Percy Wells (1867–1956) was a distant relative of Mrs S. B. Russell. Gordon
Russell had met him before the war, when Wells had walked over to Broadway
after a visit to Ashbee's guildsmen at Campden. Wells was the author of the
'cabinetmaker's bible', *Modern Cabinet Furniture and Fitments,* written jointly
with J. Hooper and first published in 1909. He was a craftsman who had learnt
the trade from the bottom, first as an apprentice and then as a journeyman. He
was bluff and sincere; his judgment could be trusted, and it was encouraging.
That made a great deal of difference to Gordon Russell, and a little later he could
privately dedicate a copy of the fourth edition of the *Hostelry* book which came
out in 1924 and was the first to have a chapter on the new venture of furniture-making: 'To Percy A. Wells without whose help and encouragement the last
n.6 chapter might have remained unwritten'.* Percy Wells indeed, after 1920,
visited Broadway regularly several times a year and advised.

John Gloag also encouraged, and in addition he illustrated some of the work

3 *Cabinet by Gordon Russell of walnut, laburnum and ebony, 1923*

4 *Cabinet by Gordon Russell of walnut inlaid with ebony, box and laburnum, 1924*

of the young firm, first in *Cabinet Maker* in 1923,* and then in the year books of n.7
the Design and Industries Association which had been founded in 1915 and
which Gordon Russell speedily joined. John Gloag, as we shall see in the following
essay, was editor of the year books, and the issues for 1923–4 and 1924–5 had
illustrations of Gordon Russell pieces.

The enterprise indeed began to make its mark. If the fourth edition of the
Hostelry, to which reference has already been made, says that the cabinet workshop had 'not as yet had much time to become known', that was an understate-
ment; for by 1924 it employed about thirty. On the advice of Percy Wells the
repair shop had been separated firmly from the shop making new pieces, and also
on Wells's advice Edgar Turner, son of Jim Turner who had from the start been
in charge of the repair shop, had gone for six months in 1923 to a good Shoreditch firm to learn the finer points of cabinet-making. Moreover, Wells also
sent improvers from his institute to Broadway, and among them in 1924 arrived
W. H. Russell, seventeen years old then, and later chief designer of the firm.* n.8

At Cheltenham in 1922 an Exhibition of Cotswold Arts and Crafts was held,
and here Gordon Russell showed for the first time. Major Longden, of the Department of Overseas Trade, who was responsible there for exhibitions, happened to see this and in 1923 invited Gordon Russell to furnish a model café for
the Second Annual Exhibition of the recently founded Institute of Industrial Art
in the north court of the Victoria and Albert Museum. Heal's were the other firm
asked to furnish a room. As a result of this the first complete dining-room was
ordered by a private patron, Mr A. Hartley, of Rochdale. Also in 1924 an invitation was received from the Wembley Exhibition to show in the Palace of Art,
and the cabinet made by Edgar Turner for the exhibition was sold to Lord Duns- 3
any for £200. An even more elaborate cabinet made by C. Marks was shown 4
at the Paris Exhibition of 1925 and received a gold medal. The firm received two
silver medals as well. Such a cabinet would have taken a craftsman six months to
make.

The style of these early pieces was closely modelled on that of Gimson, the 5
Barnsleys and Peter Waals. English woods were used throughout—oak, walnut,
cherry, chestnut, cedar, yew, laburnum. They were left in their natural colour.
Legs and handles were heavy, chamfers deep, panels bevelled. Simple stools,
sold at 39s. 6d., were made side by side with elaborate pieces with inlay. When
early in 1926 Percy Wells wrote on Gordon Russell in *The Architects' Journal** the n.9
craftsman was mentioned by name against every illustration.

But Gordon Russell was not wholly satisfied with these spectacular suc-
cesses of only five years' work. He soon began to realize, as indeed Lethaby had
done, and Voysey, Ashbee and others, that craft on its own was not enough, that
the greatest strides in the prodigious progress of English design which the late
nineteenth and the early twentieth century had seen had been due to architects
not to craftsmen, and that this movement now, being left in the hands of craftsmen, even such admirable craftsmen as the Barnsleys and Peter Waals, was in
danger of stagnation. The wider viewpoint of architecture ought to be brought
into the workshop, and so in 1924 R. D. Russell, the youngest son of S. B.
Russell, aged twenty, was despatched to the Architectural Association in London
to train as an architect. He stayed until 1927. Rarely has the dictated choice of a
profession been so successful.

The years 1924–7 were years of confusion in English design. The Arts and
Crafts movement had influenced the trade only to a very small degree. Heal's,
under (Sir) Ambrose Heal (born in 1872), was almost the only example of a large
and prosperous, old-established firm taking up the Arts and Crafts innovations
intelligently and developing them with originality. The furniture shown at
exhibitions of 1900 (Paris) and 1901 (Glasgow) by Heal's is, with its cubic shapes
and dainty inlays, as fresh as any designed—indeed a little later—by Gimson.
Heal's could not afford to specialize in such pioneer work. But they popularized
simple oak 'cottage' furniture successfully, and they also went on with furniture
of Georgian inspiration. Nothing could be more telling than the catalogues p. 23

which, from 1921, they brought out regularly year after year and which they called 'Reasonable Furniture'. In these and other catalogues natural oak suites of frame and panel construction in the Arts and Crafts tradition appear side by side with semi-Georgian sideboards and a few pieces in which the pretty square patterns on the veneered carcasses are still in the spirit of the pioneer work of 1900. These pieces of Heal's, such as for example the sideboard C809 of 1921* and the bedstead C365 of 1924 are perhaps the most original designs produced in England during the quinquennium after the war.*

n.10

n.11

Then, however, the Paris exhibition of 1925 came. It was a great event, and its effect on decoration and furnishing was on the whole disastrous. The exhibition might have been the triumph of that sound, crisp new style of architecture which had grown between about 1900 and 1925 in America, in France, in Germany and Austria. This new style was not entirely absent at Paris—Le Corbusier's *Pavillon de l'Esprit Nouveau* was certainly the most exciting individual building, and Mallet Stevens's cubism was startling—but it was smothered by chiefly French displays of arbitrary cubic and arbitrary streamlined shapes and by jagged, jazzy applied decoration—modernistic vagaries only too easily adopted as clichés. Their origin was Expressionist experiments conducted during and immediately after the war first by architects and then by designers in Holland (de Klerk) and Germany (Mendelsohn) and also a little later in Sweden and France.

England on top of all that had exhausted its impetus from the Morris and the Arts and Crafts years and had settled down to a comfortable, reasonable, uneventful neo-Georgian which in furnishing meant genuine eighteenth-century pieces or copies of them. In 1925 concurrently both the genuine modern style and the bogus modernistic one entered the country. The earliest house in the new twentieth-century style, New Ways at Northampton, was designed in 1926 by Peter Behrens for W. J. Bassett-Lowke and has a share in both trends. *The Architectural Review* illustrated it in the same year. It also reported on some of the fantastical post-war Expressionism in 1922 and 1923 (de Klerk, Taut, Dudok, Mendelsohn at his most streamlined, and the Gothenburg Exhibition). In 1924 it wrote on Østberg's Stockholm City Hall but also on Gropius, in 1925 on the Paris Exhibition, in 1926 and 1927 on Le Corbusier.

235,
9–20

The mannerisms of French decoration at and after the Paris exhibition are however, reflected in *The Architectural Review* too, and their repercussions in England can be followed in the volumes for 1927 and 1928, but more fully in the *Studio Yearbook of Decorative Art* of the same years. The designers and firms involved included the Bath Cabinet Makers, Betty Joel, Stark Brothers, and also the architect Joseph Emberton who has just been mentioned on the side of the gods and who was to come forth on the same side even more decisively in 1930 with his design for the Royal Corinthian Yacht Club at Burnham-on-Crouch. But in 1927–8 he certainly wavered.* Even in the catalogues of Heal's about 1930 modernistic suites found entry. They appear, it is true, side by side with their 'reasonable' furniture, just as in *The Architectural Review* and *The Studio Yearbook of Decorative Art* the Barnsleys, Peter Waals, and now of course also Gordon Russell went on being illustrated. The only thing that was still lacking everywhere was furniture to correspond with the style of Behrens and Gropius and Le Corbusier, furniture such as, for example, Adolf Schneck was designing about 1927 for the Deutsche Werkstätten; that is, nothing extreme and nothing as daring as Breuer's and Mies van der Rohe's tubular steel chairs, but chairs, tables and sideboards without mouldings and frills, of an uncompromising un-period appearance, and moreover making use of veneering on solid boards or on plywood.

n.12

Illustrations of such furniture could in 1927 just be seen in some of the continental magazines.* But who saw them? Certainly not Gordon Russell, and also—curiously enough—not those teaching or studying at the Architectural Association. The Architectural Association schools were in fact untouched. R. D. Russell was impressed by Steen Eiler Rasmussen who at the time taught for a

n.13

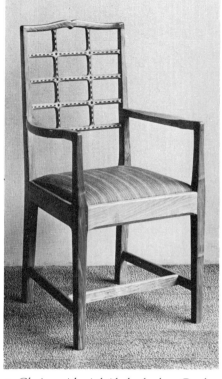

5 *Chair with inlaid back by Gordon Russell, 1925*

6, 7 Boot cupboard and sideboard by Gordon Russell of Cuban mahogany, with brass handles on ebony back-plates, 1925

short period. Rasmussen is familiar now as the author of the most sensitive book on London (*London, the unique City*); his gentle and persuasive pedagogic genius is better known in his own country. It was his feeling for materials and workmanship which R. D. Russell admired. Inspiration from Le Corbusier or Gropius or indeed Dudok neither he nor his three friends who were at the AA at the same time remember: Marian Pepler (later Mrs R. D. Russell), D. W. Eden Minns and David Booth.* All these three, from 1930–1 onwards for a few years, n.14 worked for Gordon Russell's too, as will be seen presently.

At Broadway meanwhile the workshops went on their own way, their style not materially changing, but their production methods beginning to take notice of the possibilities of some machinery. The first planer was bought in 1924 or 1925, and it was followed by a circular saw, a band saw, an Elliott wood-worker, and a dimension bench. Two morticers, two spindles, a tenoner and a thicknesser came in 1929. By then timber was roughly planed before being handed out to the craftsmen, according to a timber-list made out by the fore-man. But the craftsman still made his individual pieces throughout. Suites (that is, sets of dining-table, sideboard and chairs, or dressing-table, wardrobe and chest-of-drawers) were still unknown at Broadway. This was a workshop, not a factory. Customers commissioned whole rooms only very rarely, and contract work was as rare.* n.15

Prices varied a great deal. They were not at all high for small utilitarian pieces, but a writing cabinet such as No. 614 of 1927, of which six were eventually *1* made, sold at £120. A 6 ft. oak dining table (No. 318 of 1925) was priced at £9 18s. 6d., the 4 ft. 9 in. sideboard to go with it at £13 18s. 6d. A Spanish chestnut dressing chest of 1925 (No. 219) sold at £18 18s., but a 6 ft. wardrobe of walnut (No. 518 of 1926) at £70. These prices can be gathered from printed catalogues, an innovation of about 1926.

It was said a little earlier that the style did not yet change at Broadway, but there are, among the pieces illustrated or recorded, two which contradict this statement. They are a boot cupboard of Cuban mahogany (No. 365 of 1925) and *6* a Cuban mahogany sideboard (No. 383 of 1925). Instead of frame and panel *7* construction, both have flush fronts. The cupboard even has doors of veneered blockboard. The two designs clearly belonged together, as the use of the same ring-handles indicates. On the other hand the cupboard has broad feet which repeat in contemporary style Gordon Russell pieces of the normal Arts and Crafts type (e.g. the cupboard No. 435), but the sideboard—and the circular table which goes with it—have finely moulded, almost reeded, slender legs. Did Gordon Russell, when he designed these pieces, realize how far he departed from the tradition he had himself established? He told me that, as far as he can remember, he was guided by certain eighteenth-century precedents—wardrobes with flush veneered doors built up of reversed mahogany strips — and by occasional flush Gimson pieces, such as a chest of about 1916. The sideboard incidentally is remarkably similar to some of the work of Ambrose Heal at the same moment n.16 and a little earlier.* The origin in the case of Ambrose Heal, it will be remembered, is a compound of Sheraton inspiration with the great originality of Heal's pioneer work of about 1900. So these square, flush shapes are a continuation of the English eighteenth century and the English style of 1900 rather than an effect of Continental 1925. However that may be, Gordon Russell's two mahogany pieces remained an exception for the next four or five years.

In the years between, the only important trend to be noticed is that towards simpler, less costly pieces. Typical examples in a simplified Arts and Crafts style are the Gunstock table (794, 1928; in oak £3 10s.; in mahogany £3 15s.), the Coxwell Bedroom (oak, 836–41, 1929; dressing table £4 18s. 6d.; bed 8 £3 17s. 6d.) and the Weston Dining Room (oak, 853, etc., 1929; table £4 18s. 6d.; sideboard £12 12s.; single chairs £2 15s.). They remained

8 Weston Dining Room in Japanese oak by Gordon Russell, 1929

9 Unit bookcases by Gordon Russell, about 1930

10 Circular table in black walnut and sycamore by R.D. Russell, 1930

popular right through the 1930s. Of the Gunstock or the Weston table a dozen or more would be made at a time. It will be noticed that the Coxwell and Weston were designed and handled as suites, and this was an innovation too. The trend for simple suites had of course been acknowledged by Heal's even before 1928. But then Heal's was a big shop, and it was in London. It is said that in connection with an exhibition held at the Arlington Galleries in Bond Street in 1928, Gordon Russell began to feel the disadvantage which it was to his firm to be confined to Broadway; that is, confined to one outlet and to a village. After all, the firm now employed about 120 people. It was clearly outgrowing Broadway—not as a domicile but as a trading centre.

So the decision was taken to open showrooms in London, and in 1929 a shop at No. 28 Wigmore Street was rented. At that time the shop's retail trade was already no longer confined to furniture but included glass from Powell's and Stevens & Williams (some designed by Gordon Russell) and textiles from Donald Brothers, the Old Bleach Linen Company and Wardle's. Nor was the trade altogether confined any longer to retail. Gordon Russell believed in the suitability of furniture of the Weston type for schools and colleges, and substantial contract orders were indeed received in 1929 and 1930. Bolton School ordered 1,700 chairs and 450 desks, Bryanston, Dartington Hall, King's College Aberdeen, The Downs School Colwall, Emmanuel College Cambridge, and others followed.

The year 1930 was the *annus mirabilis* of Gordon Russell's. Of the four revolutionary events in the history of the firm, two belong to 1930. The first had been the decision to make new instead of repairing and selling old furniture. The second concerns style, the third production methods.

Style first. The remarkable fact is that in 1930, without any preparation but the greater simplicity of the rooms of 1928 and the mysterious boot cupboard of 1925, Gordon Russell furniture suddenly turned modern in the sense and on the aesthetic level of the best of Continental furniture. Nor can it be said—as might be tempting to suggest—that the cause of the change was the celebrated Stockholm exhibition of 1930, the one in which Asplund was responsible for the buildings. They taught Sweden and other Continental countries that within the new style solutions were possible, lighter, more airy and more metallic than the chunky cubistic houses of the twenties had been. But for the change of heart in Gordon Russell's the exhibition came too late.*   n.17

And just as no external explanation for the change seems convincing, so no single prime mover within the firm can be named. The fact is that Gordon Russell himself may well have been responsible in the first place. He certainly designed the completely straightforward unit bookcases (No. 913), which   *9* aesthetically as well as programmatically set the tone. On the other hand, being in personal charge of the drawing office he now encouraged others to design, and they designed in the new way. They were of two kinds: on the one hand W. H. Russell, who from being a learner in the shop had gradually become chief draughtsman; on the other hand R. D. Russell and Eden Minns both back from the AA—trained in, and in close touch with, London. Yet no difference in style or even handwriting can be discovered between them. Eden Minns designed the low fireside chair (No. 917)—one can assume that by and large the   *11* numbers represent the order in which designs were produced—and this chair again shows no sign of harking back to the character or the detail of the Weston and Coxwell rooms of the year before. R. D. Russell's circular table No. 966 is   *10, 1* a specially beautiful piece. The angular supports rising out of the cross-shaped stretcher are broad flat bands of sycamore, the two-tier tops are of walnut. Later in the year Eden Minns designed a walnut dining room, Kineton (Nos.   *13* 982, etc.), and W. H. Russell a bedroom, Shipton (Nos. 989, etc.), and an adjust-   *12* able fireside chair (No. 998).* The chairs of the Kineton room were by R. D.   *14, n.* Russell and were distinguished by the curve of the tops of the arms. One of the most memorable facts about this production of 1930 is that there seems to be so little hesitation. The confusion into which the Paris *artistes décorateurs* and jazz

11 Chair and settee by Eden Minns and table by R.D. Russell, 1930

12 Shipton dressing-table in black walnut and chrome by W.H. Russell, 1930

n.19 modernism had plunged the English furniture trade left hardly any traces.*

This new style posed one problem. The flush surfaces, the square legs, the exact unmitigated angles partook of the connotations of machine precision which played such a significant part in the modern style of architecture. Yet the furniture was all hand-made, by the same men who had done the elaborate pieces of the past years and with the same meticulous care. However, the style once accepted, the lure of the machine was bound to make itself felt. And not only could it be argued that the style called for the machine, but there was also the additional attraction of reduced cost, if machines were to be given a greater share in the production, and of a wider market. This was a commercial attraction, but it had its social implications too. Gordon Russell must have felt a mission. He was the only one in his country yet to believe in this new style. Could others be converted to it? Clearly the most likely converts were not the rich, but professional men and then the enlightened, enterprising and underpaid class of school-teachers, librarians, scientists in laboratories and so on. The fact that one desk brought out in 1930 (No. 948) had handles not of brass but of stainless steel and red erinoid plastic was a sign of how Gordon Russell's mind worked.

But the change of manufacturing methods, the step into quantity pro-duction, might have taken many years, if it had not been for another event of 1930, the event which led to the third of the revolutionary moves. The story is is one of pedagogic significance. If Gordon Russell's had not moved in the direction they did move, Frank Murphy would not have rung up Gordon Russell one day to ask him to undertake the designing and making of wireless cabinets for him, and if Gordon Russell had not believed in the necessity and the advantages of trying his hand at mass production, he would not have accepted the offer. Frank Murphy was an engineer. He had been in the General Post Office before the war, and then in advertising. He had just started in the radio trade. The day after the telephone call he and E. J. Power came to Broadway and met Gordon and R. D. Russell. Shortly afterwards the Russell brothers went to see the Murphy factory at Welwyn Garden City. The collaboration was established, and it resulted in great advantages to both sides, to Murphy's because they got the best wooden radio cabinets then existing in any country in the world, to Gor-don Russell's because they learnt what real engineering precision meant and how the most intelligent use can be made of machinery.

13 Kineton Dining Room in walnut by Eden Minns, 1930

14 Bookcase and adjustable chair in black walnut by W.H. Russell, 1930

15-18 Radio cabinets for Murphy's by R.D. Russell, of 1931 (15), 1934 (16), and 1936-8 (17, 18)

Radio cabinets at that time were either period or jazzy; that is, either imitation-Georgian with cabriole legs and the function carefully hidden, or with sound-holes decorated by a fretwork tree with gnarled branches or a fretwork rising sun. The first of the new cabinets came out in 1931. It was simple and straightforward, tripartite with the two narrow outer parts plain and in the centre part the controls and a square soundhole with a grid dividing it into nine small squares. In 1932 the same type was continued. It was supplemented by two cabinets with slightly modernistic soundholes and in 1933 with a circular soundhole decorated with the three-ray motif of the Mercedes cars. The models of 1934, especially the console ones, achieved a greater independence from even the more general characteristics of the other cabinets, and since then year after year brought new and interesting designs.* They were all done by R. D. Russell. By 1939 the design of the Murphy cabinets had changed the attitude to design of quite a number of radio manufacturers, a gratifying case of one firm's enterprise leading to improvements in a whole industry.

15

16

n.20,

The production of the Murphy cabinets was at the beginning beset with all kinds of troubles. The initial order was for about 1,000 cabinets. They were made in batches of 250. Broadway had no experience of that kind of work nor a factory to do it in. It was doubtful whether it should have one. Gordon Russell felt a responsibility to the village and its character and of course also to the Lygon Arms. After all, in 1934 Gordon Russell's had more than 400 employees and so Broadway must have seemed blatantly inadequate. So the radio makers emigrated. Geoffrey A. Jellicoe designed a factory on the Guinness estate at Park Royal, and in July 1935 it was occupied.

19 Desk by Gordon Russell in black walnut with black cellulose top and rustless handles, 1933

At Broadway R. D. Russell took charge of the drawing office in 1931 and remained until, in 1932, he joined Murphy's and did his—by no means reduced—work for Gordon Russell furniture as an outside designer and consultant. At the same time, from 1931 to 1933, Gordon Russell himself continued to design, and
19 the desk (No. 1080) is his. It was conceived for quantity production, with $\frac{1}{2}$ in. walnut-veneered plywood panels tongued into the posts. David Booth also was
20 designing at Broadway. Due to him are, for example, a fine desk (No. 1051, walnut with a sycamore drawer front), a fall-front desk (No. 1030) and the Evenlode bedroom of 1933 (Nos. 1063, etc.). When R. D. Russell and David Booth left, W. H. Russell finally took over.

Gordon Russell's had found their style in 1930. From 1931 it was developed. No new departures have to be listed, except for one, not connected with the production of the firm. In 1933, on the suggestion of Gordon Russell himself, the shops began to stock Alvar Aalto's new bent-plywood chair. Aalto had invented (or in fact re-invented) this technique of furniture-making only in 1932.
n.21 In 1933 an exhibition took place in London* and Gordon Russell must have
21 seen the stools and tables there, ingeniously simple pieces which could be sold at very low prices. The decision of a firm, famous by then for fine cabinet work, to offer such mass-produced pieces not made by themselves shows a remarkable objectivity and a remarkable appreciation of the distinct aesthetics of hand-made and machine-made furniture. In the same spirit, in 1936, the best designed of
2, 24 Thonet's famous bent beechwood chairs were admitted to the shop, and in 1937
2, 23 Marcel Breuer's bent plywood chairs made for Isokon,* the factory started by Jack Pritchard, London friend of Walter Gropius and promoter of the Lawn Road flats.

As for Gordon Russell's own output, production remained as before in batches of six or twelve. The most interesting work was certainly R. D. Russell's. In 1934 he designed the Welbeck dining-room of Honduras mahogany (Nos. 1096, etc.) with rounded corners and inlaid lines of sycamore on the table top and with rounded legs repeating to the outside the curvature of the corners of the
24 top. From the planning point of view the Finstock dining-room and bedroom (Nos. 1114, etc.) of the same year ought to be recorded, because it was an attempt at a consistent design for the furniture of a whole flat or at least bed-sitting room.

20 Desk by David Booth, 1932, armchair by R.D. Russell, 1933, and stainless steel-framed mirror by Eden Minns, 1930

21-23 Stool by Aalto, chair by Thonet, and Isokon chair by Breuer, sold by Gordon Russell's

24 Finstock Dining Room by R.D. Russell, 1934, with Thonet bentwood chairs

25, 26 Thirty-Four I bedroom (left) and easy chair, both of 1934 by R.D. Russell

The desk and dressing-table for instance were identical. The Thirty-Four I room   *25*
(Nos. 1100 etc.), as its curiously unromantic name indicates, tried to achieve a
standard product at a price lower than any that had been made before. Dressing-
table, chest of drawers and wardrobe cost £31.* The settee and easy chair (Nos.   *n.23*
1110 and 1150, again of 1934) were the *ne plus ultra* of that cubism which these   *26*
years of the Lawn Road flats liked. The width of the arms across the top was
eight inches.

   But R. D. Russell's finest work during 1934 and indeed the following years
was on the contract side, and especially for private offices. Only one or two   *27*
examples can here be illustrated, for instance one for O. T. Falk & Co. For   *28*
much of the soft furnishings which now appeared in the showroom Marian
Pepler (Mrs R. D. Russell) was responsible, occasionally as a designer, mostly as
a buyer. Marian Pepler, side by side with Marion Dorn, was the best textile   *p. 20*
designer in England. Marion Dorn's work was more striking and varied, Marian
Pepler's had a sensitivity and quiet perfection not surpassed anywhere in Europe.

27, 28 Office furniture by R. D. Russell, c. 1934, with rugs by Marian Pepler and curtains by the Welsh Tweed Mills

29 Woburn sideboard by R.D. Russell, of Bombay rosewood with elm lines

30 Sudeley sideboard of African rosewood by W.H. Russell

As a buyer she and her successor from 1936 onwards kept in close touch with Edinburgh Weavers for fabrics to be specially designed and made for the show-
27 rooms, with the Welsh Tweed Mills for which Marianne Straub was designing, with Helios (a subsidiary of Barlow & Jones), with other British manufacturers and with certain Continental suppliers. There was, of course, also Swedish and Dutch glass, Wedgwood pottery and much else to be provided. Geoffrey Jellicoe designed larger showrooms at No. 50 Wigmore Street which were occupied in 1935. The shop was a joy to move about in. Speaking from personal memory I would say that the furniture of between 1935 and the war, in its entirely con-temporary, never mannered, and never showy style, equalled the best on the Continent, and its workmanship was more perfect than any I saw in the Con-tinental shops I visited. The fact that the men who made these pieces, however much of the rough and preliminary work machines were gradually taking off them, were still the same men who had been the craftsmen of the 1920s bore fruit. The other fact that at Broadway the drawing-office was in constant touch with the cabinet-shop also bore fruit.

    The range of furniture was now extended to include some more luxurious suites such as the Hazleton bedroom of sycamore with a little ebony inlay and a
29 large curved dressing table (Nos. 1134–41), the Woburn dining-room of Indian rosewood with the remarkable sturdy circular and banded table legs (Nos. 1165,
30 etc.) and the Sudeley dining-room of African rosewood with its gentle curves to the centre part of the sideboard (Nos. 1260–1). They sold at £150, £94 10s. and £115 respectively. There was here clearly a policy of trying to retain the market for the best in material and finishes and lead it towards modern design. But Gordon Russell himself was still sufficiently attached to the ideals on which the firm had originally been built up to suggest to W. H. Russell a dining-room and a bedroom of oak with reminiscences of the Arts and Crafts in its general character and such details as the corner posts and handles (Enstone dining-room, Nos. 1162–3, Ilmington bedroom, Nos. 1156–8). They were not as much of a success as he must have wished.

    1937 was the year of the next Paris exhibition. W. H. Russell designed a
34 large living-cum-dining room for it. This was done at the invitation of the Board of Trade and represented Britain excellently. The only other firm in-vited was Heal's. The two parts of the room were separated by a curved fitment, and the bold hangings were designed by Marian Pepler and made by Edinburgh Weavers. The room was intended to appear sturdy and reliable and in that res-pect rather marks the climax of the style of the thirties than the beginning of the new more delicate style which was to culminate in the fifties.

This new style made its appearance in 1937–39, with the Aston bedroom by W. H. Russell (Nos. 1299–1304, 1938), an inexpensive walnut job selling at £44 10s. for the usual three pieces. The dressing-table and the bedside table had   31
slim tapering legs and the handles were of light grey plastic. A second example of the new elegance was a drinks cabinet of African rosewood and ebony designed   32
by J. Wilson (No. 1317, 1938). The black stand had tall circular legs and a gently concave front, and the interior of the cupboard was lined with grey plastic. A third example may be added, because it was a very special piece, a long side-board by R. D. Russell which was shown at an exhibition of the Arts and Crafts   33
Exhibition Society held at the Royal Academy in 1938. It was of pearwood with a front of coromandel ebony inlaid with irregularly shaped rings which were in fact sections of beef bones polished.*   n.24

As interesting socially as this piece was aesthetically, and at least as signifi-cant, was Gordon Russell's own initiative in the same year, 1938, in convening a group of like-minded retailers and suggesting to them the manufacture by Gordon Russell's of standard suites which would not be sold to anyone else. They would carry the Gordon Russell name, but they would be machine-made, and they would, owing to this and to larger orders than Gordon Russell's own retail trade could ever place, be cheaper than such furniture had been hitherto. The members of the group, calling itself the Good Furnishing Group, were Beattie's of Wolverhampton, Elsa Booth of Oxford, Elizabeth Denby, Dunn's of Bromley, Gane's of Bristol, Mummery & Harris of Frinton, Rowntree's of Scarborough, Schofield's of Leeds, and Wells of Bedford.

The fact that Gordon Russell believed in this scheme is of considerable significance. The Murphy cabinets had been his company's first step in the direction of manufacturing for others and of manufacturing on a large scale.*   n.25
This new venture was a logical extension. The war deprived it of its effects.

The war meant the closing of the London showrooms, bomb damage to the Broadway showrooms, the making of ammunition boxes, model aircraft, wind-tunnel models, Mosquito wing nosings, instrument cases and so on. But to Gordon Russell is meant a widening of the range of his activity in perfect con-tinuation of the direction which he had in his mind and which had led to the Murphy and then the Good Furnishing enterprises. About the middle of 1942   35
Hugh Dalton, then President of the Board of Trade, set up a committee to advise him on the introduction of standard furniture to supply wartime needs sensibly and speedily. The chairman was (Sir) Charles Tennyson. Gordon Russell was one of the members. The first pieces appeared early in 1943, rather undiplomatically called utility furniture.

31 Aston dressing-table by W.H. Russell, 1938

32 Cocktail cabinet by J. Wilson, 1938   *33 Sideboard by R.D. Russell with inlay and handles of polished bone*

34 Room for the Paris Exhibition of 1937: the furniture, of English woods, is by W.H. Russell, the textiles by Marian Pepler

They were the only furniture which was permitted, and they were well made, as far as circumstances allowed—much better made than the hire purchase stuff which a large part of the public had bought before—and they were decently if not excitingly designed. They did not have to face the problems of design for mass production as they had to be manufacturable by moderate-sized and small firms. The large firms were as a rule busy on aircraft parts. In the end about 600 firms made this utility furniture. As a result of the experience gained with the first ranges Gordon Russell suggested to Sir Charles Tennyson the forming of a permanent design panel, and after the acceptance of the suggestion became its chairman. The later ranges of utility furniture designed under Gordon Russell were a considerable improvement and approached the style, if of course not the craftsmanship, of the Gordon Russell furniture of before the war.

In 1944 Hugh Dalton set up the Council of Industrial Design. In 1947 Gordon Russell became its director. In 1955 he was knighted, in 1960 he retired from it. The work for the Council was a final achievement. Making the best furniture by hand, making the best modern furniture by hand, selling the best modern fabrics and other furnishings with it, making the best-designed modern furniture by machine, selling it through others, designing modern furniture on a national scale, and so in the end directing the whole national movement towards good modern design—no personal development could be more logical and more satisfying. Sir Gordon Russell, being able to look back on this achievement while building a dry wall or a brick-vaulted store-room at his house and in his garden on the hill above Chipping Campden, must regard himself as a lucky

n.26   man.*

35 Dining room in walnut plywood by J. Wilson for the Good Furnishing Group, 1939

DESIGN for to-day

SEPT. 1935 ONE SHILLING

1 *Cover of the DIA magazine in 1935*

XIII
Patient Progress Three:
The DIA

I T IS familiar that the pattern for the DIA was the German Werkbund. The Werkbund was founded in 1907 and after seven years had established itself so firmly that it could hold a large exhibition at Cologne, on the scale of national exhibitions. It was the exhibition which is now famous mostly for Gropius' model factory and Bruno Taut's glass house, two truly epoch-making buildings. The war broke out shortly after the opening and deprived it of much of its potential effects. But, as the story of the DIA shows, not all of them. For meanwhile, this

n. 1 is what had happened in England.* In 1912 one of the Arts and Crafts Exhibitions had been held which had taken place every four years in London since the Arts and Crafts Exhibition Society had been founded in 1888 and which continued in the traditions of William Morris. The exhibition had been a financial failure, and some younger members began to ask themselves whether there was something basically wrong with the society.

The most active of them was Harold Stabler, craftsman in metals. His thoughts on craft, design and industry were met by those of a few who had seen the Cologne Exhibition of the Werkbund. They were Ambrose (later Sir Ambrose) Heal, his cousin the architect Cecil Brewer (Smith & Brewer were the

2 designers of Heal's store in Tottenham Court Road, an outstandingly modern job considering its date 1916) and H. H. Peach, founder of Dryad's, who made

3 cane furniture under German and Austrian inspiration.

A working committee was formed consisting of Stabler, Heal, Brewer, Peach, Ernest Jackson, a painter and lithographer, J. H. Mason, the printer and

n.2 typographer who taught so admirably at the London Central School,* and Hamilton Temple Smith, later a director of Heal's. He and Brewer were secretaries. Hamilton Smith was the last of the seven founders to survive. He died only on 30 December 1961. Behind the group, not at first one of them, but a tower of strength, stood W. R. Lethaby, head of the Central School and the greatest of the followers of Morris' teachings. When Brewer shortly after the visit to Cologne showed friends photos of recent German work, Lethaby did the

n.3 explaining, so he tells us in his obituary notice for Brewer.*

The committee of seven in January 1915 presented a memorandum to Sir Hubert Llewellyn Smith who was Permanent Secretary to the Board of Trade from 1907 to 1919. It pointed out that the menacing expansion of German trade before the war was due to the 'untiring efforts which the Germans have made to improve the quality of their work'. The Werkbund was specially mentioned and the signatories included Lord Aberconway, chairman of the Metropolitan Railway and of John Brown's steel mills, Kenneth Anderson of the Oriental Steam Navigation Company, Brangwyn Burridge, Lethaby's successor as head of the

2 *Heal's store by Smith and Brewer ('Year Book', 1922)*

3 *Cane chair by Dryad's ('Year Book', 1922)*

Central School, B. J. Fletcher of the Leicester College of Art, St John Hornby of W. H. Smith and *Imprint*, J. Marshall of Marshall & Snelgrove, James Morton of Morton Sundour, Frank Pick, Gordon Selfridge, Frank Warner and H. G. Wells. A committee was also mentioned. It consisted of Ambrose Heal, H. H. Peach, Hamilton Smith and Harold Stabler. So that is the DIA *in nuce*.

The memorandum was acted upon remarkably speedily, and in March an exhibition was arranged by the Board of Trade in Goldsmiths' Hall called 'Exhibition of German and Austrian articles typifying successful design'. H. H. Peach kept a copy of the brief pamphlet issued on fine paper for the occasion. Much of the exhibition seems to have been devoted to the Wiener Werkstätte.*   n.4
In the pamphlet Germany is praised for 'methods . . . co-ordinating education, production and distribution' and promoting 'co-operation between the manufacturer and the designer'. 'The need for the employment of machinery', the pamphlet adds, 'has been thoroughly appreciated'. 'The founders of the modern movement' in Germany succeeded not by 'redundancy of ornament' but by 'appropriateness, technical perfection and honest workmanship'. The pamphlet ends with this sentence: 'The establishment of a well organised association with similar objects in this country is much to be desired'.

It all sounds DIA and may well have been formulated in collaboration of the group of friends with the Board of Trade. The group, fortified by the blessings given in the pamphlet, now acted quickly and in May 1915 brought out a pamphlet of the same format and on the same paper called *A proposal for a new body*. The paper, the *mise-en-page*, the black and red printing and especially the dark greyish-blue paper cover tell of the Emery Walker-Cobden Sanderson tradition.

The new body was to encourage 'a more intelligent demand amongst the public for what is best and soundest in design', to insist that 'machine work may be made beautiful by appropriate handling' and to prove that 'many machine processes tend to certain qualities of their own'. It emphasises the influence of the English Arts and Crafts on the Continent, especially on German typefounding, and blames England for leaving her own arts and crafts 'to struggle hopelessly' while favouring a 'sort of curiosity shop ideal'. 'We need an Efficiency Style' say the signatories. They were more or less the same as those of the memorandum. The address given was 6 Queen Square, i.e. Cecil Brewer's office, which was also the premises of the Art Workers' Guild. The ties with the Arts and Crafts were strong at the beginning, despite the insistence on the potential value of the machine. We shall hear more of that.

May 1915 is the date of the formation of the DIA. In July the first propaganda leaflet was issued. It was called *A New Body with New Aims* and was presented in the same way as its predecessors. It contained articles by A. Lys Baldry, painter and writer, A. Clutton Brock, art critic of *The Times*, who had characteristically enough only a year before written a book on William Morris, Sir Robert Lorimer, the Scottish architect, F. Morley Fletcher, director of the Edinburgh College of Art, and Sir Leo Chiozza Money, a politician specially interested in trade and labour questions. Chairman was Kenneth (later Sir Kenneth) Anderson. On the council were Lethaby, Burridge, W. B. Dalton, the principal of Camberwell, Morley Fletcher, St John Hornby, James Morton, Frank Warner, Charles F. Sixsmith of the Bentinck Cotton Mills near Bolton, and John Marshall. The articles were reprints, e.g. from *The Times* and *Country Life*. Clutton Brock's contained the memorable phrase: 'Where an enemy has a noble lesson to teach, it can only be learned from him nobly'. Lorimer referred to Muthesius's stay in England as an instance of intelligent German promotion of good design and to Messel's façades of Wertheim's store in Berlin as an instance of truly modern architecture.

At the same time (or even a little earlier) Lethaby's article on *Art and Workmanship*, published in *Imprint* No. 1 (January 1913), was issued as another pamphlet. It contains phrases worth remembering in perpetuity, whether they stand up to close investigation or not. 'A work of art is a well-made thing, that is all.' 'Art is not a special sauce applied to ordinary cooking.' It is 'the well doing of what needs doing'. It is 'the humanity put into workmanship; the rest is slavery'. All this is patently William Morris, and it is not surprising after it that Lethaby grants machine-made products only goodness 'in a secondary order'. Here clearly was a conflict looming, and we shall have to watch it through the early years of the new body.

The proper prospectus came out in November. The council had in the meantime been joined by James Burton of Pilkington's, William Foxton who became foremost in promoting cheap, modern, printed textiles, H. P. Gee of Stead & Simpson, E. Scott Nicholson of Hudson, Scott & Sons, colour-printers, and Harry Peach. Manufacturers among the original members included Boots, Cadbury's, Early's of Witney, A. E. Grey the potters, Hollis the spinners, Lord Leverhulme of Lever's, Osler's and Worcester Royal Porcelain. Among the printers who were members were the Baynard Press, the Chiswick Press, Eyre & Spottiswoode and Spottiswoode Ballantyne, among the stores Debenham & Freebody, Crofton Gane of Bristol and Gordon Selfridge. There were several art schools led by Edinburgh and Leicester—Bath, Bradford, Brighton, Camberwell, Cork, Hessle, Huddersfield, Ipswich, Nottingham and Woolwich. There were a number of architects—Forbes & Tate, Theodore Fyfe, J. A. Gotch, Charles Holden, Morley Horder, Keay of Leicester, Basil Oliver, J. H. Sellers, F. W. Troup, E. Warren and R. S. Weir. Frank Pick who does not fit into any one category, was a member, as were the designers W. A. S. Benson, Gordon Forsyth, Graily Hewitt, Selwyn Image, Minnie McLeish, Joseph Thorp (if he can be called a designer), and Percy Wells, the artists Anning Bell, Lucien Pissarro and Noel Rooke, and James Bone the journalist.

In October 1915 already the DIA had shown its youthful energy. At the Whitechapel Art Gallery an exhibition of Design and Workmanship in Printing was opened. The signet designed by Ambrose Heal was already in prominence. There were good reasons why the first exhibition was one of printing. England in her best work was foremost in the world in that field, and the exhibition found wide interest. In 1916–18 it travelled to Liverpool, Leicester, Leeds, Edinburgh, Dublin, Belfast, Derby, Perth, Ipswich, Northampton and in the end to Johannesburg, Durban, Port Elizabeth, Cape Town and Bloemfontein. It must have done a great deal to make the young struggling body known. In 1916 also the *Deutscher Werkbund* published a translation of the foundation documents of the DIA, all the articles by Lethaby, Clutton Brock, etc.—a pretty piece of give and take.

Membership of the DIA rose in 1916 from 244 to 391 and reached 583 in 1917.* The Werkbund, however, had 1319 members at the beginning and 1870 by 1914.* But it must not be forgotten that there was a war on. Considering that, the DIA was remarkably active in its first three years.* Branches were founded at Manchester, Edinburgh* and Glasgow* and lunch meetings were arranged in London.* In October and November 1916 the Arts and Crafts Exhibition Society held a show at Burlington House, and the DIA had one room of this. The *Burlington Magazine* called the room 'anti-Ruskin in that it welcomes machinery and seeks to give it designs worth making in ten thousand lots'.* Special praise was given by a number of journals to the cotton fabrics in high colours made by the Bentinck Mills for the West African trade. To include them was certainly a stroke of genius. The DIA after that held a competition in conjunction with the Calico Printers' Association, and on the short list for the prize appeared the names of Mrs Maufe and of Lovat Fraser who was to die so soon after.* In May and June 1916 a textile exhibition was held at Manchester. The DIA had written to sixty manufacturers. Only three replied. It was still an uphill fight. In the end members themselves went round and found much more than they had expected. The exhibition was held at the Art Gallery. In selecting and discussing the members gathered valuable experience of the snares of textile designing: fabrics which appear clear from nearby but muddled at a distance, fabrics whose colours speak at daytime but go dead by artificial light, fabrics convincing in design when seen flat but not when seen draped and so on.* The pottery trade was also tackled, and the reception was no warmer. A conference was held at Stoke on Trent concerning the Burlington House exhibition. The exhibition was strongly criticised locally. No process-work had been shown. What had been shown was coarse and did not do justice to the high skill of the factories. 'Expert craftsmanship', Hamilton Smith retorted, 'does not always go hand in hand with fine design', and H. H. Peach stressed that the exhibition was deliberately confined to 'things of our own day'.* Another conference followed   n.14 in October 1917, and the establishment of a Pottery Trade Group. Not much is heard of it after.

The ups and downs of the association can be followed closely in the *Journal*, started in 1916 with two odd numbers called *The Beginnings of a Journal* and *More Beginnings,* and established properly in 1917. Some themes run through the twelve numbers. The last came out in summer 1919. One theme of course is that of the DIA principles by then well and truly handed round, discussed and formulated. Fitness for purpose had become the slogan. But there remained worries. Sturge Moore the poet* in a letter contrasted the beauty of a rose, neither neat   n.15 nor tidy, with the DIA criteria of beauty (as formulated for instance in Lethaby's *Art and Workmanship*). 'Comely utensils won't do instead of roses.' 'Worthy work never equals Michaelangelo.' 'Morris cannot touch Burne-Jones.' We have not yet found an answer to this letter today, even if we disagree on the superiority of Burne-Jones over Morris. Sturge Moore ends with a plea for 'the luxurious and capricious displays of the unmerited kindness of the universe', and one is grateful to him for the reminder.

From the other side an anonymous editorial in answer to a Morrisite article by the painter Harold Speed in the *Fortnightly Review* of May 1918 wrote aggressively that men will never be content if they have to do humdrum work, for example at a stamping machine 'making perfect buttons for the commonwealth' and that, in spite of that, a machine civilisation such as the DIA accepts according to its terms of reference, must face the fact that 'work, in most walks of life, will be a curse for ever'. Speed answered, but here again the debate is still as wide open as ever.

Then there was the worry of well-designed things not being cheap enough for those who would want them, those with incomes of £150 to £300 a year. Members did not doubt that the demand existed, e.g. Ambrose Heal who asked in 1918 for 'plain, straightforward, stoutly made, properly planned and thoroughly useful furniture'.* But in fact the DIA style, if one can speak of a   n.16 DIA style, was still close to that of the Arts and Crafts, whatever compliments were paid to machinery, i.e. quantity production. This came out for instance in the passages the *Journal* chose to reprint from writers of the past.

Herbert Spencer and his *Study of Sociology* of 1872 are introduced because they stress functional soundness and criticise thoughtlessly designed objects;*   n.17 Gladstone (at the opening of the Wedgwood Institute at Burslem in 1863), because he spoke of 'the greatest possible degree of fitness and convenience for [the] purpose', even if he added (unaware of Lethaby's plain cooking and sauce) that beauty comes after and only to the 'highest degree which, . . . compatibly with that fitness and convenience, it will bear'.* Ruskin's address of 1859 at Bradford   n.18 (printed in *Two Paths*) is the first the DIA reprinted with his still entirely topical plea to the manufacturers: 'You must remember that your business, as manufacturers, is to form the market, as much as to supply it'.*   n.19

The longest passage is from an address by J. D. Sedding of 1883, and this is entirely in the Morris spirit, although the machine received some kind words. Sedding singles out three evils in English manufacture: 'bad design, bad materials, and bad housing of the operatives'. He pleads against smoke, against products which appear to be of materials innocent of them and against 'borrowed inspiration', i.e. period styles. He sees 'a pale society of ghosts' stand at the elbow of the designer. And the end of the passage is: 'Art can never live a wholesome life . . . that is not related to the people at large'. Similarly Lovat Fraser in a letter cursing the bad influence of the cinema (which he already calls The Pic-

n.20 tures) speaks of himself as 'an old-fashioned William Morris affair,'* and Baillie Scott in an interesting paper called *Good and cheap* attributes the passion of people for what is 'flashy and smart-looking' to 'something wrong with the social organism', and to 'labour and capital pulling in opposite directions'. In fact while the Werkbund had had its great battle between the individualists—those with craft ideals—and the standardisers at their conference in 1914, ending, though without a vote, in victory for standardisation, the DIA was still un-
n.21 decided in 1918* when an editorial stated: 'The last thing we should father is this idea of standardisation'.

Side by side with this runs an equal distrust of forms entirely cut off from tradition. This appears only once in the early journals, but very characteristically. It is a note against 'barbarous patterns', the Russian ballet (which had had seasons in London in 1911, 1912, 1913 and 1914) and 'Coon music'. Does that mean Roger Fry's Omega Workshop? It is likely. The remark came out in Summer
n.22 1919* and the Omega operated from 1913 to 1920, and its textiles were thor-
n.23 oughly Expressionist in pattern.* The layout of the *Journal* is indeed very subdued and not at all anti-traditional. To understand these years it must always be kept in mind that a campaign for simplicity and fitness could point to Georgian precedent as justifiably as to the Arts and Crafts and to the Arts and Crafts as justifiably as to the Werkbund. The result in Germany was revolution, first rational in the Cologne Exhibition, then anti-rational in Expressionism, then from 1924 or so onwards rational again. The result in England was, with few exceptions, as we shall see, the Georgian Revival, and printing in the hands of men such as Mason and calligraphy in those of Johnston joined forces with the Georgians. The DIA did not for a long time know exactly where it belonged. John Betjeman's *Ghastly Good Taste* (of 1933) was the first revolt against the effects of DIA propaganda.

To the end of the war the propaganda had gone well, and its success was evident. The principal fortress, Government, seemed to be on the point of surrender. In 1919 the Ministry of Reconstruction published a pamphlet called *Art and Industry*, and this in its tenets and its whole tenor was 100 per cent DIA: 'A low grade supply will induce a low grade demand'. 'We have no style, but are nauseated with "styles".' 'Art is indispensable in life, and therefore in education and work.' Ruskin's and Sedding's speeches were duly quoted. At the end hopes were held out for the formation of a British Institute of Industrial Art, a permanent exhibition of good design, and a bureau of information.

The bureau was duly formed, Major Longden became its director, and the DIA joined up with it. But the co-operation must have been disappointing to the DIA; for in 1924 the connection was severed. Indeed after an initial spurt the institute did little. As for the DIA, disénchantment was earlier and deeper. Already in 1919 the *Journal* carried an editorial in which we read: 'The millenium is not yet' and the DIA must 'make up its mind what details of improvements are within its power'.

It was the editorial to the last issue. The *Journal* could not be continued. After an interval of more than two years it was replaced by a monthly *News*
n.24 *Sheet,* and of this only four numbers came out.* From it we learn that a register of approved designs was being compiled and that some furniture was being designed by the DIA for the Office of Works (acting through the Royal Society of Arts). The DIA was probably asked on the strength of a 'little specimen collection' of well designed furniture shown at the Shoreditch Institute in May 1919 and sponsored by the LCC and the DIA. Percy Wells, head of the furniture
n.25 department at the Shoreditch Technical Institute* from 1902 to 1935, was behind it. Otherwise the DIA held an Exhibition of Household Things, subtitled 'designed primarily to serve their purpose'. It was again at the Whitechapel Gallery (October to December 1920) and included eight completely furnished rooms. In 1921–22 an attempt was made to have smaller shows at 6 Queen Square. They dealt, one after the other, with printing, textiles, furniture, pottery, household appliances and lighting.

4 *Print cabinet by Peter Waals*
(*'Year Book'*, *1922*)

5 *Bookcase by Heal's ('Year Book', 1922)*

6 *Plate by Truda Adams*
(*'Year Book'*, *1922*)

7 *Teapot by Joseph Bourne of Denby*
(*'Year Book'*, *1922*)

When in 1922 the DIA found it possible to return to issuing a bigger publication it was due to the co-operation of Benn Brothers the publishers, and the result was the first of a series of year books, larger in format, bound and mostly consisting of illustrations. This is what the Werkbund had done in 1911–15. As one turns over the pages of the volumes for 1922, 1923–4 and 1924–5, one has at last an opportunity to see for oneself what the DIA at that time meant by good design.

The first volume was introduced by C. H. Collins Baker, keeper of the National Gallery. Furniture is either (and mostly) in the Gimson tradition (e.g. by Peter Waals and later Gordon Russell) or approaching Georgian (e.g. by Heal's and also by Charles Holden), but in pottery, side by side with Carter, Stabler & Adams's spiky decoration *à la* Munich and Stockholm, the plain blue and white of T. G. Green's appears, and the plain Joseph Bourne things, and in textiles Foxton's have a touch of the Expressionist. On the other hand, at the end are cars, trains and aeroplanes, motor boats and radio masts. Much stress is laid once again on printing, both letterpress and posters and labels. Here again the range goes from the Georgian to McKnight Kauffer's spiritedly Expressionist forms.

The one thing still totally missing is the simple, uncompromisingly rational style which was to be the so-called International Modern of the 1930s. This was just about 1924 beginning to defeat Expressionism in Germany, whereas in France the Paris Exhibition of 1925, in spite of Le Corbusier's pavilion of the *Esprit Nouveau*, propagated a new version of decoration, non-period but fanciful and rather lusher than Munich and Stockholm were practising. The first sign of awareness in England of the change to the Bauhaus style, to give it that name (the Bauhaus at Dessau was built in 1925–6), is an article in *The Architectural Review* on Gropius which came out, remarkably early, in 1924.*

The DIA was not so quick in reacting. One of its early members however was Bassett-Lowke who in 1926 commissioned Peter Behrens to design him a new house, New Ways at Northampton. In fact there is one yet earlier building in England which one may well call 'modern', and that is the offices in Red Lion Square for Austin Reed by Joseph Emberton. This dates from 1925, is quite unassuming, and was illustrated in the DIA *Year Book* for 1926–7. However, the source of this was Olbrich in his Düsseldorf store of 1906–8 rather than the Bauhaus.

The *Year Book* in 1926–7 changed its format to a smaller size and its illustrations to smaller sizes too. It was followed by a 1929–30 volume (no 1927–8), and that was for a long time the last of them. 1926–7 was edited by John Gloag,

(Marginal reference numbers: 4, 5, 6, 7, 12, 8, 9, n.26, 19, 2)

8 *Rolls-Royce ('Year Book', 1922)*

9 *Aeroplane interior ('Year Book', 1922)*

1929–30 by H. H. Peach and Noel Carrington. Gloag had become a member in 1924, Carrington in 1927. In the earliest volume Frank Pick wrote on *Design in Cities* with a remarkable sensitivity to the character of London ('London is an accident. It is full of variety . . . It represents the English policy of patching and compromising'); which is doubly remarkable seven years before Rasmussen's classic *London, the Unique City*, and remarkable also in its appreciation of the character of Piccadilly Circus ('I care little about its garishness'). Among the illustrations there were still georgianising houses side by side with buses and Orrefors glass.

The 1929–30 volume was wholly devoted to the disfigurement of town and country. Clough Williams-Ellis had by then become president, and this was his principal concern. The whole volume is indeed Ian Nairn's *Outrage* antici-pated by twenty-five years. Thanks to Williams-Ellis the DIA for a short time concentrated on the Outrage problem. The main result were the excellent *Cautionary Guides* to St Albans, then to Carlisle and to Oxford. There was also one called *The Village Pump*, on filling stations. The captions were splendid ('First depressions on arrival') and altogether the negative position was clear

14–16
10, 11

10, 11 *'Wild west' garage at Dunstable, and 'good architecture' at Dorchester ('The Village Pump')*

12, 13 *Textiles for Foxton's by Gregory Brown (left), and Claud Lovat Fraser ('Year Book', 1922)*

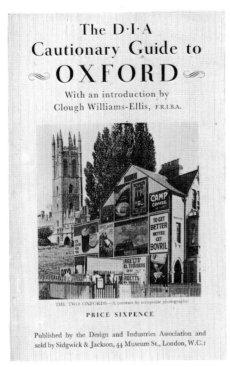

14 *A Cautionary Guide, 1930*

15 *'Oxford's Arc de Triomphe'*

16 *Oxford: 'dignity and efficiency—
a good example set by the Post Office'*

enough. The positive was still neo-Georgian more than modern—see the illustrations of Holden's classical Underground stations at Edgware and Morden and of a highly praised new post office at Oxford.*   *16, n.*

Meanwhile the *Journal* had been resuscitated as the *Quarterly Journal*. The format and character remained the same, though the contents began to change, even if at first hardly perceptibly. It is worth following its course for a while. In 1927 the Leipzig Fair had introduced a special section on good design. It was housed in the Museum of Decorative Art (Grassi Museum) and took in the first year the form of an international exhibition.

Britain was represented. The direction was in Peach's hand. Minnie McLeish wrote an appreciation. She told her readers that the programme of the exhibition was 'to show modern tendencies' which 'practically speaking do not exist in England', and she added: 'We do not understand this modern movement in design and do not like it'. Miss McLeish was a weaver and textile designer. But she did recommend all the same to study 'what goes on at Dessau'. The Weissenhof Estate at Stuttgart was also mentioned, and in No. 2 (December 1927) Bassett-Lowke described it in detail and with illustrations calling it 'a wonderful experiment'. In No. 3 (March 1928) New Ways came in and was called 'unique in England for its uncompromising modernity'. There was also Thomas Tait's Ideal Home concrete house, 'very like some German houses'.   *17, 18*   *19, 20*

Meanwhile, however, illustrations went on of traditional (Arts and Crafts) pieces such as Gordon Russell furniture (Russell & Sons had become members in 1924).* Also in 1928 Shoolbred's of Tottenham Court Road—who can still remember the store?—held an exhibition of modern furniture. The *Journal* (No. 3) writes that the exhibits were either in the Gimson tradition such as Gordon Russell's or of the Modern Movement, meaning however the Paris 1925 variety and not what *Journal* No. 5 called the Bauhaus style.   *n.28*

But this also entered the London stage now. The decisive date is that of an exhibition at Waring's held in 1928 and designed by Serge Chermayeff. This, John C. Rogers writes in the *Journal* No. 6, is 'by far the best thing yet done in this country', because it is 'not at all on the lines followed by those whose creed is the teaching of Gimson and Barnsley'. He recommends that the English should 'lay aside insular prejudices' and do likewise. In the same number consequently the Arts and Crafts Exhibition is blamed for a 'churchy, homespun, medieval atmosphere'. Also in the same number, at the end, Crittall's advertise their windows by showing a white and cubic house. The advertisement was not a draughtsmans' fantasy. Crittall's estate at Silver End (by Tait) had in fact been started in 1926. It was visited by the DIA in 1930*, but the houses were even then still called 'foreign-looking in England'. No wonder—in 1929* the new ICI building in Millbank and Carrera's factory at Mornington Crescent still received unquestioning praise. *The Architectural Review*, praised in the same year* as 'one of the most alive reviews of the day', was decidedly aliver at that moment. So was Jack Pritchard commissioning an exhibition stand for Venesta from Le Corbusier in 1930 and Sir James Morton founding Edinburgh Weavers in 1930, and Gordon (now Sir Gordon) Russell who in 1930 turned resolutely to the International Modern in furniture, and did it with a *noblesse*, a sensitivity and a restraint which had few parallels even on the Continent.   *n.29*   *n.30*   *n.31*

In fact, the DIA was in danger of being left behind, with other bodies making use of its pioneer work and going beyond it. The exhibition of Industrial Art for the Slender Purse, an important initiative, since the DIA was permanently blamed for recommending almost entirely costly things, was arranged not by the DIA but by the British Institute of Industrial Art at the Victoria and Albert Museum in 1929.* In 1930 the Society of Industrial Artists was founded. In 1930 also the LCC published a report on handicrafts in elementary schools, according to Percy Wells 'an almost complete acceptance of DIA principles'. 'No amount of prettiness', said the report, 'can compensate for the loss of utility'. In 1931 the Board of Trade appointed a committee on art and industry under the chairmanship of Lord Gorrell. In the same year an exhibition of Swedish Arts and Crafts   *n.32*

17, 18 Weissenhof Estate, Stuttgart; left, a house by Scharoun ('Quarterly', December 1927)

was held at Dorland Hall, and Gregor Paulsson apropos of it gave a memorable talk on the alliance between designer and manufacturer in Sweden. In Dorland Hall also in 1933 an exhibition of British industrial art was staged, organised by private initiative, not by the DIA.

In the same year again, and already in 1932, the BBC had taken hold of modern design and arranged talks with accompanying pamphlets. The first series was given by J. E. Barton, headmaster of Bristol Grammar School, the second by Gordon Russell, Francis Meynell, Wells Coates, A. B. Read, Elizabeth Denby, Frank Pick, John Gloag, Robert Atkinson, Maxwell Fry and others. Finally, in 1933 too, the Council on Art and Industry was established with Frank Pick as its chairman. It went on meeting and publishing occasional reports, until the war put an end to it.

All this sounds as if the air in those years had been buzzing with activities promoting good modern design. That is far from true. The way for all concerned, including the DIA, went steeply uphill. At Buenos Aires an official exhibition of British industry in 1930 was housed in an imitation Norman castle with a Tudor barn,* in the same year the new Union Castle steamer Winchester Castle had its main hall in the Flemish Renaissance style with copies of paintings by old masters, and as late as 1935 the Royal Academy, staging a grand exhibition of modern industrial art, made—to use the words of the DIA— 'a grotesque failure' of it, an embarrassment, I remember, to anybody who had foreign visitors during those months.

n.33

19, 20 New Ways, Northampton, designed by Peter Behrens for W. J. Bassett-Lowke ('Quarterly', March 1928)

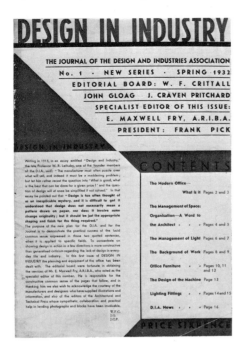

21 First issue of 'Design in Industry'

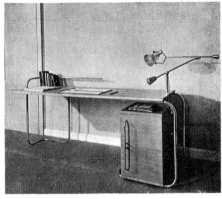

22, 23 Office desk by Wells Coates and pressed steel writing table by Heal's ('Design in Industry', Spring 1932)

Meanwhile, overshadowed by other organizations, the DIA went on and had no easy time. These were the years of the slump, and though membership rose steadily from 602 in 1923 to 820 in 1930 and, after a slight fall, to 865 in 1935, activities tended to be in a minor key.* A DIA exhibition was held at Gane's of Bristol in 1930, at Barrow's store in Birmingham in 1931, a Birmingham branch started in 1931, and was followed by others. At a meeting in 1931 Beresford Pite called the modern style barbarous and at another in the same year B. C. Joseph, an aluminium manufacturer, was facetious at the expense of modern French printed materials. These remarks were reported in the *Quarterly Journal* for May and January 1931. n.34

January 1932 was the last number. A new journal, *Design in Industry*, was started in Spring 1932, edited by W. F. Crittall, John Gloag and Jack Pritchard, larger in format and provided with a somewhat modernistic jagged cover. It reached only two numbers—both sold out at an edition of 1,500—and died, although the contents had been excellent: one edited by Maxwell Fry was devoted to the modern office, the other to modern kitchens. 21 22, 23

The journal was replaced in 1933 by another, *Design for To-day,* which was owned and run by a commercial firm but remained to the end of 1935 the official organ of the DIA. At the end they broke off and once again tried their own luck. *Design for To-day* was a monthly and, as one turns over its pages, one gets a fair survey of the events in architecture and design, even if the standard of inclusion is less discriminating than in the same years in *The Architectural Review*. Both periodicals show that the so-called Modern Movement was gaining ground. The Murphy radiograms (see p. 220) appear in *Design for To-day,* as did the new Welsh tweeds, interiors by Geoffrey Boumphrey, Raymond McGrath, Wells Coates and David Pleydell Bouverie, Clough Williams-Ellis's charming restaurant by the lake at Cobham and Russell Page's and G. A. Jellicoe's Cave Man Café at Cheddar Gorge, Keith Murray's designs for Wedgwood's, wallpapers by Bawden and others for Curwen's. Rugs by Marian Pepler are dealt with, a committee on traffic signs on which Noel Carrington reports, and Paul Abbatt toys, the furnishing of small houses at Welwyn (by Mrs C. G. Tomrley) and then at Birmingham, for £200, the new underground stations of the Piccadilly line, and Aalto's bent plywood furniture as shown at Fortnum's, Plan furniture as adapted by Chermayeff from Franz Schuster of Vienna, the Peckham Health Centre and the pithead baths and every so often a white cubic house, the designers being Lescaze, Roger Smithells, Wells Coates (who had designed the Lawn Road flats for Jack Pritchard in 1933) Connell & Ward, Skinner & Tecton, Holford & Gordon Stephenson, Marc Hartland Thomas, and Marcel Breuer. Then there are streamlined cars and engines, and Flaherty's *Man of Aran* and the experiment of Foley China to commission and market designs by John Armstrong, Vanessa Bell, Duncan Grant, Milner Gray, Ben Nicholson and Graham Sutherland. 1, 26,

This survey has taken us to the end of 1935. The annual report called it a year of 'sharp financial crisis', and membership indeed fell from 865 in 1935 to 649 in 1936. This was not a good omen for *Trend,* the ambitious journal which M. L. Anderson, E. O'Shaughnessy and James Shand started as their own enterprise but also as the DIA organ. It was a splendid paper, $13\frac{1}{2}$ by 10 inches, lavish in layout and setting out on its ill-fated career with a message from Edward VIII.

The first number came out in Spring, the second in Summer; there were none to follow. The contents were bright and intelligently chosen: zip-fasteners (invented by one Aronsen in 1893), refrigerators, camping, open spaces in towns, plastics (sixteen pages by Walter Landauer—now Landor), furniture shown by Heal's and designed by Maxwell Fry and Jack Howe, Breuer, McGrath, O'Rorke, and Christopher Nicholson and Hugh Casson.

But there were ominous signs too, a message for instance from Sir Kenneth Clark telling the DIA that 'it is not true that beauty and efficiency go hand in hand. Many perfectly efficient objects in everyday use, such as the typewriter, cannot be made beautiful, and almost all the highest forms of beauty are quite

24 Breuer & Yorke's ideal city: housing along a traffic-free waterside promenade ('Design for To-day', May 1936)

useless. I see no reason why the industrialist should prefer beautiful objects to ugly ones unless he has good taste. I believe that experience has found that, on the whole, the public prefer ugly objects'. A good deal could be answered to this at the time and can be now. The message showed however that the battle was not won, and that on the contrary there was a danger of the most intelligent getting bored with it.

Sir Kenneth Clark here uses good taste meaning good taste, but McKnight Kauffer in his message blamed the DIA for having had 'too much good taste' and for having 'done very little to help new design forward'. To him good taste meant clearly John Betjeman's *Ghastly Good Taste*. It was an involved situation, with Sir Kenneth Clark ready to give up and retire into an ivory tower, a tower however from which he would make courageous forays in defence of Henry Moore, Graham Sutherland and many other artists, and McKnight Kauffer wanting the DIA to do more in defence of what would correspond in design to Moore and Sutherland; but what would correspond?

Even more ominous had been some messages in a feature called 'Design and the Manufacturer' and published in *Design for To-Day* in 1935. There one could read that in Sir Josiah Wedgwood's opinion 'simplification and pure function-alism has reached its zenith' and 'some revival of eighteenth and early nineteenth century styles' is likely, and in William Turnbull's opinion the Regency cult was already upon us. Other statements were more positive, pleading for greater standardisation and the elimination of redundant patterns in furniture (J. M. Cohen) and for cutting down textile ranges by half (Turnbull).

25 Offices and multi-storey shopping centre in the 'Garden City of the Future'

Trend, we have seen, was a financial failure, and *Design for To-Day* also, after running on precariously through 1936, stopped publication—not without having illustrated one of the most interesting large-scale architectural schemes of the pre-war years: Breuer and Yorke's modern city commissioned by the Cement and Concrete Association and in its traffic planning and variety of grouping still entirely up-to-date.

, 25

The DIA resigned itself to retrenchment. *Trend* was replaced by a *News Sheet*. It had not much to report. Exhibitions had been in retail shops, first Barrows in 1935, then through 1936 at Kendal Milnes of Manchester, Dunns of Bromley, Rowntrees of Scarborough and Harrods, and in 1937 at Furlongs of Woolwich. Travelling exhibitions were sent round to go with renewed BBC programmes, and at Olympia in 1938 the DIA had a chance of arranging the whole ground floor of the Empire Hall in connection with a Woman's Fair. The DIA co-operated on this with the British Colour Council, the Institute of Industrial Psychology and the Institute of Adult Education. Displays were by McGrath, Misha Black, Riette Sturge Moore, John Grey, Edric Neel (who died young), R. D. Russell and Jesse Collins, and H. T. Cadbury Brown won the competition for the 'feature illustrating the importance of design in domestic objects'—not an enviable task. However, the most popular feature of the whole exhibition was a bogus Scottish Clachan to show tweeds in. That was the situation in 1939.

The war silenced the DIA, as for a while it silenced all cultural activities. In the field of design, as we have seen, this meant the breaking off at a point of high promise. Anthony Bertram in 1938 had introduced the subject to the TV screen, and in 1939 he introduced it to Penguin readers. So the mass audiences were alerted, but for the time being they had other things to think about. The DIA valiantly issued two duplicated news sheets in 1940 and then printed one in 1941 and another early in 1942. The first of them had to report the loss of the association's records in the bomb wreckage of the Building Centre. About the middle of 1942 people had settled down to the prospect of a long war, and so the DIA went back to a nicer production for its *News*. It was a miniature journal, 5 by 4 inches, printed by the Kynoch Press, and the first of the four which were brought out had its front page in Ultra Bodoni italics. The *News* read pathetically, but one admires the pluck and tenacity of those who worked on: activities in London and the branches, even travelling exhibitions, two joint exhibitions with the Army Bureau of Current Affairs (Homes to Live In, arranged by Elizabeth Denby and Noel Carrington, and Living in Towns, arranged by Ralph Tubbs), essay prizes for school children (one of the two first prizes in 1942 going to a Nottingham boy who is now a partner in Skidmore, Owings & Merrill) and, in these years of the Foreshaw-Abercrombie plan for London (1943), the Scott Report and the Uthwatt Report, a burning faith in the future: 'With peace will dawn the golden age of our opportunity'.

Did it? A tentative answer can only be given at the end of a survey of the post-war years—after all twenty of the total fifty. The first five of them were disappointing for the DIA, but not for the cause of design; for already before D-Day the Council of Industrial Design had been established, 'the richly endowed child of a self-supporting parent', as Goodhart-Rendel resignedly wrote in the *Almanack* for 1949–50. But the DIA, reduced to some 575 members—a figure which all efforts did not raise to much above 720 even by 1960—kept on a modest scale to the activities it had been busy on before and during the war. Secretary in those difficult years and after better times had dawned (1946–61) was Mary Harvey.* It was largely through her charm, enthusiasm and perseverance that the DIA continued to go ahead. A *Year Book* came out in 1946, and three *Almanacks* in 1947–50. The DIA helped to a limited degree in the Council of Industrial Design's 'Britain can make it' Exhibition in 1946, the exhibition which made the Council of Industrial Design known to the public and was the first sign of its potential. The second sign was the start of the COID'S magazine *Design* in 1949, taking over one responsibility from the DIA which had in the past proved irksome, but also keeping one whole set of possibilities of expansion out of the association's reach. But the more favourable atmosphere found its reflection in DIA activities too. n.35

The post-war re-establishment of the *Year Book,* financially self-supporting for the first time, was largely due to the energy and resourcefulness of V. V. Tatlock of the Architectural Press, the co-operation accorded by many of his AP colleagues, and the regular advertisement support he received from DIA member-firms. In 1950 the *Year Book* could speak of 'a growing feeling of power and enthusiasm', and the *Year Book* for 1951 was much more promising all round. It was the year of the Festival of Britain which Sir Colin Anderson, president 1951–4 and incidentally the second generation of Andersons to be president,

26 In 'Design for To-day' of September 1933 Maxwell Fry illustrated and praised the European small house

27 'Design for To-day' of May 1935 examined progress in design since 1835, as well as recent films

rightly called 'a triumphant vindication of all that our association has stood for since its foundation'. The festival was a tremendous success all round, and it established the word 'Festival' as an international term in Germany, France and Italy, just as the first International Design Congress, also held in 1951, had established the word 'design' as international currency. In fact, what with these events and what with the Hertfordshire schools and the LCC housing estates, Britain for the first time since pre-DIA days became a country to visit, to respect and to learn from in visual terms. The COID's *Design Review* was started in 1954 as a revival of the stock-list established before and for the Festival of Britain, and the Design Centre, another international success, opened its doors in 1956.

Naturally this progress was reflected in internal DIA terms as well, though for some time only to a very limited degree. The *Year Book* for 1951 is the first with considerably fuller contents. It contained among its articles Hamilton Smith's tale of the beginnings of the DIA with its characterisation of some of the first leaders: Peach, 'a man with fire in his belly . . . hitting out lustily on all sides', Brewer of 'austere intellectual scepticism', John Marshall with a 'deep religious and artistic sensibility', Jackson 'observant, witty and detached' and Burridge 'of the planning type', 'admirable at framing unambiguous rules' and in this so different from Lethaby, his predecessor at the Central School, 'who distrusted all systems, reformed or unreformed'.

The article was followed by an extremely useful bibliography of DIA publications. Altogether the *Year Book* had nearly sixty pages of text and thirty-two pages of illustrations, taken from the stock-list of the COID.

Among other DIA activities in the fifties the Ashridge weekends deserve to be recorded, nine of them from 1949 to 1957, and two exhibitions: 'Register your choice' in 1953 and 'Make or mar' in 1957, both held at Charing Cross Underground Station, the first a tested comparison between a DIA room and a room of conventional best-sellers. Over 30,000 votes were cast, and 60 per cent turned out in favour of the DIA. 'Make or mar' involved a subtler choice, between two rooms with more or less the same furnishings, one harmoniously and the other brashly arranged. The year books continued in their new fuller and more serious manner; 1956 has the first articles on automatic computation.

In 1958 came a new editor, Robin Mudie, and at once a sharp wind of change. The unmistakable Pop voice of Reyner Banham is heard, once very indignantly and thought-provokingly on the meaning of vernacular, once on commercials in TV. Ian Nairn ends a brilliant analysis of Rye Lane, Peckham, a street of no particular merit and certainly no DIA merit, with a challenging *Vive le chaos!* Now the typography and layout changed every year and owing to the efforts of designers like William Slack and, more recently, Ian Bradbery the *Year Book* has achieved a high standard graphically. Funnies appeared at the end, and in 1962 a new general secretary took over: Michael Farr of COID and *Design* magazine experience, who introduced himself with an article called *Bloc Busting*. It all tended to be a little shrill, and some of the old members no doubt did not like it. But the new men were right and they could prove it with an unanswerable argument. Membership went up at an unprecedented rate to an unprecedental total. It was about 700 in 1962, rose to 1,130 in 1963 and 1,400 in 1964. There were two regions (apart from London) in 1961, there are now eleven.

What were they started for? What did the new members join for? What do they now expect from the DIA? Or—in other words—what functions has the DIA, now that the COID, the Society of Industrial Artists and other bodies have taken over so much of the DIA's traditional work? To answer this question is not the historian's job, but this historian thinks he has found some answers in his study of the records of the DIA, answers which are not new, but nevertheless fully valid. Here, in conclusion, they are.

One can start at the beginning, with Plato's *Republic:* 'May we not say generally that the excellence or beauty or rightness of any implement . . . has reference to the use for which it is made? . . . It follows then that the user must know most about the performance of the thing . . . and must report its good or bad points to the maker.'* So we must listen to the consumer, i.e. consumer re-   n.36 search, etc. On the other hand Clutton Brock in his *Modern Creed of Work* had stated already in 1916 that 'the public does not know what it wants . . . Public taste is plastic . . . Producers in the mass can . . . persuade the public that it likes what they choose to give it'. So it is the manufacturers who carry the responsibility and who, as Ruskin had said, ought 'to form the market, as much as to supply it'. But is that true? Can the manufacturer enforce an improvement, if the buyers are not with him? Was the DIA not right in 1922 to stage a mock-trial of John Buyer 'for wilfully misrepresenting the public taste'?* So there is the   n.37 vicious circle, today's as much as yesterday's, and in the end one is thrown back on education. Education first, and most narrowly, in the functional and aesthetic qualities of objects of domestic use. The DIA had started with the aim of fighting for industrially produced objects. For long, as Lord Crittall said in 1931,* there had been 'too much D and not enough I'. That battle is over now;   n.38 the objects one dismisses now are almost exclusively the outcome of D for I. In fact, the shortage is now one of truly contemporary craft, though such craft is essential for the designer and the public as a measure stick of personal initiative. But even there already in 1939 the DIA *News* had emphasised the importance of the modern-minded craftsman, not only in the Bauhaus sense as a laboratory-worker for mass-production, but as a vital factor in the economic and cultural life of the nation'.*   n.39

Similarly the DIA recognised early, indeed memorably early, that education must not confine itself to domestic products individually or even buildings individually, but must take a much wider view. 'The perambulating germ carrier', which is the DIA's term for the refuse collecting van in a pamphlet of about 1925, is as obnoxious forty years later as it was then, the damage of pylons across downs is, if anything, greater in 1964 than it was in 1929, when the DIA wrote against them,* and the need for cautionary guides is without any doubt greater than it was in the years in which Clough Williams-Ellis animated the DIA in its campaign against messy advertising, messy petrol pumps, shacks, bungalows and the rest.* Finally the committee on traffic signs on which Noel Carrington served in 1933 cannot have been much different from that on the same topic in 1963 on which he also served. So there are the old problems, forever new. But there are also new problems, though even they have at least been fore-told by perspicacious DIAers. One quotation then in conclusion. It comes from Hamilton Smith and the *Year Book of* 1951.

'The heathen no longer stone us out of their cities; they are more likely to offer us a cocktail. And this frightens me. Most certainly they are not all con-verted: can it be that we have grown less exacting?'* Today's answer is that most of us have, but that we needn't, and that the Council of Industrial Design also has, but as a prospering public body probably couldn't help it. So here is the only new answer I have to the question of the future of the DIA. In the present situation, when all along Tottenham Court Road and the suburban shopping centres so-called 'contemporary' furniture, light fittings, etc. crowd the win-dows, the battle is no longer as simple as it was when I—now in my sixties—was young. Then it was: Flat roof and no mouldings, you are right. Pitched roof and ornament, any ornament, and you are wrong. Now what is needed is a new kind of research, a new kind of critical tenacity and a new ruthlessness of action. The official bodies can help with the first but not with the second and emphatic-ally not with the third. But the new men of the DIA with their scorn of gentility are, I hope, tough and impassioned enough to expose gimmicks, to distinguish between functioning and the appearance of functioning and so to embark on the Great Sifting.

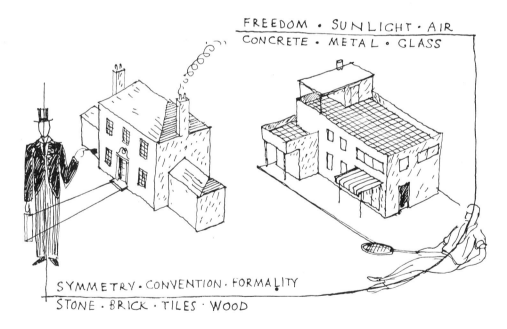

28 *Manifesto by Maxwell Fry ('Design for To-day', September 1933)*

1 *Aalto: House of Culture, Helsinki, 1958*

Journal of the Royal Institute of British Architects, 3rd Series, LXVIII, 1961

XIV
The Return of Historicism

THE relation between the architectural historian and the contemporary architect has changed fundamentally in the twentieth century. In the nine-teenth century, the architect, with a few notable exceptions,* was the architec-tural historian. As a historian, he would go and visit buildings of the past, draw them, measure them, describe them and date them, and would then go home, turn architect, and build more or less free imitations of what he had seen. But when, at the end of the nineteenth and the beginning of the twentieth century, there arose a generation of giants, who created a new style of architecture en-tirely independent of the past, one might have thought one had a right to assume that historicism was at an end. The historian now did his job and the architect did his, and while the personal relations between the two might remain warm, their relation was bound to be no longer the same.

n.1

The principal purpose of this paper is to draw attention to what I regard as an alarming recent phenomenon. It is what can only be called a return of His-toricism. This is, in my opinion, one aspect of a deeper change and, again, a change which represents to me one of the least attractive developments of recent architecture, although no doubt one which has been very highly attractive to others.

The change, generally speaking, is this. The principle of twentieth-century architecture up to this change had been that of form following function, in the sense that a building must first of all function well and should have nothing on its exterior to reduce its well-functioning, or, to put it the other way round, that the beauties of exteriors of buildings and, for that matter, of their interior spaces as well, must be developed subsequent to the assurance of their well-functioning. The new tendency is, if I am right, towards exteriors which are created not necessarily at the expense of function, although that is very often true too, but certainly at least with an expression which does not convey a sense of confidence in their well-functioning.

The return of historicism is one aspect of this change, and it is the one on which I want to concentrate.

Historicism is the belief in the power of history to such a degree as to choke original action and replace it by action which is inspired by period precedent. In that sense, in the nineteenth century, if you take philosophy as an example, the primary interest of the philosopher was the history of philosophy at the expense of new systems; if you take theology, the primary interest was the history of religion, again at the expense of new systems. That this kind of historicism was the almost universal trend in architecture I need not emphasize.

Then, what happened historically is known to everybody. There was, at the

2 Wejke and Ödeen: Guldheden shopping centre, Gothenburg, 1945

end of the nineteenth century, the episode of Art Nouveau, which represents the first phase in the creation of completely new forms—the first phase since the Rococo. There followed the earliest phase of the so-called Modern Movement. This was just as original in its forms as Art Nouveau, but it was, at the same time, propelled by an urgent quest for the fulfilment of function. Then, as a second episode, we had, for a few years, partly during and partly after the First World War, Expressionism, again fanatically novel in its forms, but not sharing with the early Modern Movement the regard for function. Finally, about 1925, we witnessed what we thought was the victory of the so-called Modern Movement, and we are now so used to it that we tend to forget the courage, the intellectual effort and the imaginative effort that were necessary to bring about not only its formal expression but even more its functional discipline.

Where was it going to lead? The so-called International Style of the thirties was an exacting style. It was not accommodating, and so a retreat from it began before it was universally accepted. It began before the Second World War, and it took, as I shall show, at once the form of a return to historicism, although quite an innocent one. Of course, even after the Second World War the nineteenth-century type of historicism was not entirely dead either. One need only think of such buildings designed by Georgian-Palladian diehards as those for the farmers and the financiers of the Farmers' Union and the *Financial Times*. That sort of thing can be left to die of old age. It is not what I am worrying about.

Instead, the phenomenon which interests me and which I mean by the return to historicism is the imitation of, or inspiration by, much more recent styles, styles which had never previously been revived. Of course, all reviving of styles of the past is a sign of weakness, because in revivals independent thinking and feeling matters less than the choice of patterns.

The patterns of the new historicists are these—to enumerate them before they are analysed. The earliest retreat was what one may call neo-Accommodating. Then there is neo-Liberty, the most talked about of these revivals. There is neo-Art Nouveau, which includes neo-Liberty and also includes neo-Gaudí. There is neo-de Stijl, there is neo-School of Amsterdam, there is neo-German Expressionism, and finally, to a certain extent, neo-Perret.

Neo-Accommodating first. Figure 2 is a shopping centre of 1945 in a suburb of Gothenburg in Sweden and shows very well this new attitude of just before and after the war towards something more friendly, something more relaxed, something less exacting. Figure 3 is a detail, actually of 1910 and representing Tessenow, who was one of the 'not-whole-hoggers' at the moment when the Modern Movement was created. This connection between a mild 1910 and a mild 1945 is worth noting even if there may be no historicism, i.e. no imitation

3 Tessenow: housing at Dresden-Hellerau, 1910–12

by the one of the other. On the other hand, Dr Banham kindly gave me figure 4. This bed is not from a catalogue of Heal's of about 1910 but from the Triennale of 1960. That I would call an extreme case and a very puzzling one.

Now neo-Liberty. Dr Banham, to whom I owe a great deal in the preparation of this paper, has drawn attention to neo-Liberty, by writing on it and broadcasting on it.* He also kindly showed me his photograph of this extraordinary lamp (figure 5), also exhibited at the Triennale in 1960.

Neo-Liberty, as I said, is only one aspect of neo-Art Nouveau. The historian can document this revival particularly well in terms of a series of exhibitions held and a series of publications brought out. The first exhibitions which took Art Nouveau seriously were the exhibition arranged in 1952 by the late Peter Floud at the Victoria and Albert Museum and called 'Victorian and Edwardian Decorative Arts', and in the same year, the exhibition at Zürich which was called 'Um 1900'. They were followed by exhibitions at Frankfurt, the Gaudí Exhibition at the Museum of Modern Art in New York in 1957–58, the Museum of Modern Art's special Art Nouveau Exhibition in 1960, and the great exhibition of the Council of Europe in Paris called 'Les Sources du Vingt-ième siècle' which included, in the field of architectural photographs and actual works of design and craft, a very full display of the period of Art Nouveau. That exhibition took place in 1960–61, and there have been plenty more Art Nouveau exhibitions since.*

n.2

n.3

5 Gae Aulenti: lamp, from the Triennale of 1960

4 Vittorio Gregotti: bed, from the Triennale of 1960

6 *Chédanne: 'Le Parisien', 1904*

7 *Belgiojoso, Peressutti & Rogers:
Torre Velasca, Milan, 1956–8*

8 *Hunziker: detail of villa at Gland,
1959–61*

Now a side step—a detail of the Torre Velasca in Milan (figure 7) by the Peressutti-Rogers Group, and side by side with it a photograph from *Casabella*, which was edited by Ernesto Rogers, and which shows the store in Paris called 'Le Parisien'. The store is by Chédanne and of 1904 (figure 6). Of course, the connection here may actually have worked the other way round. It may well be that the Peressutti-Rogers Group, seeing the accidental similitude thought it rather amusing and illustrated the building for no other reason.

Neo-Gaudí takes us a good deal further. Figure 9 is the Casa Milá, by now a very familiar sight. Figure 10, without comment, is the American Embassy in Dublin by John Johansen; and figure 11 a model by Howell and Killick for the new Science Building at Birmingham University. Figure 12 is a detail from a villa by Marcello d'Olivo, and figure 13 a detail from the Casa Milá. Here again, for the historian, the documentary evidence of the revival is very striking. Nothing could be more so than the fact that the first batch to come out in a recent American series of monographs on 'Masters of World Architecture' has Gropius out and Gaudí in. Also in this first set they were all live architects except

9 *Gaudí: Casa Milá, Barcelona, 1905–10*

12 *D'Olivo: Villa Spezzotti,*
Lignano Pineta, 1958

10 *Johansen: American Embassy, Dublin, 1959–64*

13 *Gaudí: Casa Milá, detail, 1905–10*

11 *Howell, Killick, Partridge & Amis: preliminary model for*
Birmingham University Science Building, 1960

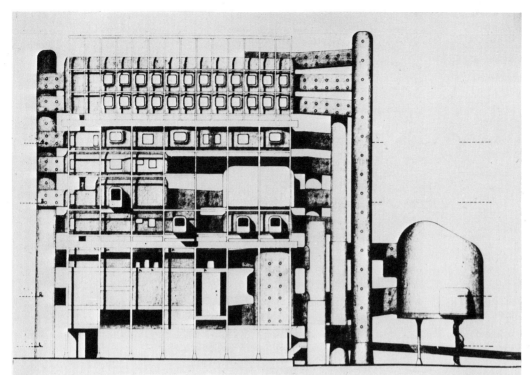

14 Regent Street Polytechnic: student's design for showrooms for the Furniture Manufacturers' Association, 1959

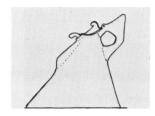

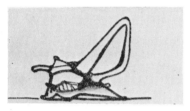

15 De Groot: teapots, labelled 'examples of the new zigzag style', 1924–5

for Gaudí. At Barcelona, if my counting is right, there have been seven books on Gaudí since 1955, and one of them has a foreword by Le Corbusier who, always eager to present himself in the best light, uses his foreword to state that already in 1928 he told us so, as it were. One of the most recent works on Gaudí is the excellent book by Sweeney and Sert, which is a fighting book. It need not have been; the fight was no longer necessary. (A splendid confirmation of this was in fact under construction at the very time when I gave my lecture: figure 8 is from a villa of 1959–61 by Christian Hunziker.*)   n.4

Students of the last few years have out-Gaudí-ed Gaudí quite easily as figure 14 demonstrates. And again it is baffling to read in the *Architectural Review** James Gowan commenting on this actual design and saying that this is 'a   n.5 particularly fine example of the work done recently at the Regent Street Polytechnic and their rather specialised preoccupation with structural techniques'. The building purports to be showrooms of the Furniture Manufacturers' Association. Now figure 15, some teapots, and figure 16, a design for an Arts Centre seem to represent the same kind of approach to a job. However, the teapots were published in 1924–5 and are by the Dutch designer Jan Hassel de Groot, and the Arts Centre is by the German architect Hermann Finsterlin, who appeared like a flash about 1919.* So we have here, after the extremism of 1960,   n.6 the extremism of 1920–25. In both cases of course such fantasies remained on paper.

Now there are also undeniable visual affinities between Finsterlin's Arts Centre and figure 17. But these affinities would of course be invalidated, if one can regard the set of sail or shell shapes of Jörn Utzon's design for the Sydney Opera House as a matter of structure. To decide that is outside my present concern, but I was interested to see that Nervi in *Casabella** called the Sydney   n.7 Opera House 'an eloquent example of the most straightforward anti-functionalism from the point of view of statics as well as construction'. So perhaps the Arts Centre and the Opera House do belong together, a little more than one might at first have assumed, though it is, I think, out of the question that Utzon knew of Finsterlin, and it is also at least arguable whether for so festive a building as an opera house, in so spectacular a position as the Sydney Opera House occupies, strictly functional forms would not have been too severe. To this we must revert later.

16 Finsterlin: design for an Arts Centre, c.1919

17 Utzon: Sydney Opera House, under construction in 1968

18 Rietveld: chair, 1917–18

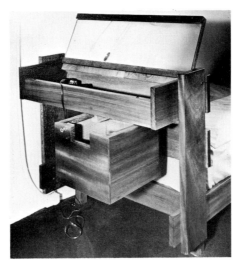

19 Howell: dressing table, 1960

20 D.L. Goble: dressing table, 1960

21 D'Olivo: Caffè Pascotto, Latisana, 1958

So now neo-de Stijl. Figure 18 is some of the celebrated furniture designed by Rietveld about 1917–18, and figures 19 and 20 are a recent dressing table by Howell, Killick and Partridge,* and another exhibited recently by the Central School of Art and Crafts and commented on in the DIA Year Book. In architecture, neo-de Stijl is just as striking. Figure 23 is a building at Harlem by the Dutch architect J. W. E. Buys illustrated in 1928, and figure 22 shows not another view of the same building, but the Marchiondi Institute in Milan by Vittoriano Viganò of 1957.* Figure 25, again by Buys, is the Volharding, a store at The Hague, also of 1928, and figure 21 a café of 1958 by Marcello d'Olivo.

n.8

n.9

Comparisons of today with the School of Amsterdam are a little less straightforward. But it can be pointed out that, in figures 24 and 26, the curious way in

22 Viganò: Marchiondi Institute, Milan, 1957

23 Buys: grammar school, Harlem

which odd bits, ledges and chunks of some kind, stick out of de Klerk's building in Zaan Straat has a good deal in common with Stirling and Gowan's flats at Ham Common. Figure 27 is a motif of the School of Amsterdam: the repeated rhythm of diagonals going across a smooth façade. As a comparison, figure 28 is Aalto's Dormitory at Cambridge. Mass., of 1948. Clearly influenced by the School of Amsterdam was a clinic in Brussels, illustrated in 1926 (figure 29) by a little-known architect, Pompe. As a comparison (figure 30) here is the recent Bottega d'Erasmo by Gabetti and Isola at Turin with its odd window shapes.

25 Buys: De Volharding, The Hague, 1928

24 De Klerk: Eigen Haard housing estate, Amsterdam, 1917

26 Stirling & Gowan: interior, Ham Common, 1958

27 De Klerk: housing, Amsterdam, 1920

29 Pompe: orthopaedic clinic, Brussels, 1926

30 Gabetti & d'Isola: Bottega d'Erasmo, Turin, 1953–6

28 Aalto: Senior Dormitory, M.I.T.,1948

31 De Haas: house at Rijswijk, 1923–4

32 Gregotti, Meneghetti & Stoppino: flats at Cameri, 1958

As a postscript to this, there is the puzzling historicist return of some Italian architects to the work of the tamer and weaker Dutch architects of the twenties, buildings like figure 31 which was illustrated in 1923 to 1924. Its details ought to be seen side by side with those of a block of flats by Gregotti, Meneghetti and Stoppino, in Piedmont (figure 32).

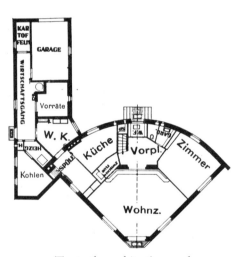

33, 34 Taut: the architect's own house near Berlin, 1926

35 Parent: house near Paris, 1959

Neo-German Expressionism is a much more important trend.* Figure 36,   n.10
the Chilehaus in Hamburg by Hoeger, shows one of the most familiar examples of this very sharp, angular, aggressive style which started in Germany at the end of the First World War, so different from the work of Behrens and early Gropius before the war. The same aggressive angularity appears in Bruno Taut's own house (figures 33, 34). Now this also is paralleled, although not very closely, today. Figure 39 shows a country villa near Ivrea by Albini, and figure 35 a French house by Claude Parent.

And there are also other aspects of German Expressionism which one can parallel. Compare, for example, the central hall in Peter Behrens' I. G. Farben Building at Hoechst (figure 37), which he did in the early twenties with the similarly reeded and similarly polygonal walls of the courtyard in Saarinen's American Embassy at Oslo (figure 38). In Germany itself you find a revival of the

36 *Hoeger: Chilehaus, Hamburg, 1922–3*

37 *Behrens: I.G. Farben Building, Hoechst, 1920–24*

38 *Saarinen: U.S. Embassy, Oslo, 1959*

39 *Albini: Villa Canavese, 1958*

41 *Ungers: house in Cologne-Müngers-dorf, 1960*

40 *Mies van der Rohe: Liebknecht and Rosa Luxemburg Monument, 1926*

familiar chunky style of the twenties—of, e.g., the Liebknecht and Rosa Luxemburg Monument by Mies van der Rohe (figure 40),* designed in his brief Expressionist phase—in a recent house in a suburb of Cologne, figure 41, by O. M. Ungers. Then there is Hugo Haering's farm at Garkau of 1920 to 1923 (figure 42), and its, of course, independent, counterpart in recent work by Aalto (figures 1 and 44). Nor were Haering's motif and the expression he wanted to create continued to him. Figure 43 is a house by Byvoet and Duiker of 1925.

n.11

Finally a postscript to Expressionism. Perhaps one ought to call a revival of German Expressionism also some of the very best stained glass that has been done in this country in the last few years, including that of Evie Hone and John Piper, or is that a belated direct inspiration?

43 *Bijvoet & Duiker: house at Aalsmeer, 1925*

42 *Haering: farm builders, Garkau, 1920–23*

44 *Aalto: Säynätsalo Town Hall, 1953*

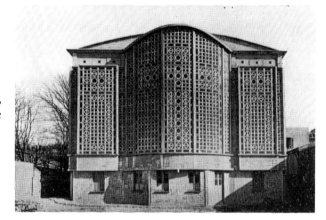

45 *Perret: Notre-Dame,*
Le Raincy, 1922–3

46 *Stone: the architect's own house,*
New York, 1956

Neo-Perret is only a postscript too. His favourite screens everyone is acquainted with. Take his church at Le Raincy (figure 45) and then any of a large number of decorative screens as they are with us now. Figure 46 is Ed Stone's house in New York. However here we must be careful, because for such screens there is, as everybody knows, a functional reason in countries with strong sunshine. But the reason does, of course, not apply to Paris at the time of Perret and I do not know whether Ed Stone would say that it applies to New York. Where there is a functional reason for a screen in front of a façade, why should the screen not be given a pattern? That would certainly be the answer in South America, and I am trying in this paper always to stop short, where shapes and forms of the kind I am concerned with have a functional justification.

That finishes my evidence. Now let us look at some problems that it raises.

The first thing is a piece of defence. Could you not say that the Return of Historicism is all our fault, and I mean myself in this case, personally, in two ways: as one of the editors of *The Architectural Review* and as a historian? The *Architectural Review* has got in its basement a Victorian pub, re-erected or rather re-assembled, and regarded by many as a blatant example of Victorian Revival. I do not agree, I would say that this pub is a 'folly' in the true sense of the word, and that the result of it, in the campaign of the *Architectural Review* for a new attitude towards the building of pubs, was certainly not an attitude towards the building of Victorian pubs, but towards modern pubs with as much as possible of the atmosphere of the Victorian pub recovered, in opposition to the cheerless and soulless neo-Georgian or otherwise denuded pub.

Another Victorian indictment of the *Review* concerns its typography. It is true that the *Review* was amongst the earliest to re-assess Victorian typography and revive Victorian display faces. There has been an article by Alan Fern of n.12   Chicago recently in *Typographica* dealing with this story.* He could trace back the renewed interest in bold and florid types to 1935, and personally, at least to a certain extent, to John Betjeman, who seems to have been interested in Victorian typography already when he was an undergraduate at Oxford, and published his memorable *Ghastly Good Taste,* with its famous title page, in 1933. But here again the position is slightly different from the Return to Historicism of this essay. *The Architectural Review* does not recommend cooking *à la Victorienne* but rather spicing with Victorian ingredients. It is, you might say, a question of display faces, not of Victorian *mise en page;* that is, Victorian materials are used in undeniably twentieth century layouts.

Now for the historian as such, and my own position in particular. I wrote my book on the Pioneers of the Modern Movement in 1935–36. The book came out in a relatively small edition, and it did not sell well at all. In 1949 the Museum of Modern Art took it over and sales improved, and finally it became a Pelican. So the book seems to have made its way and is now in the hands of several tens of thousands of people. Shouldn't I be very pleased? As a matter of fact I am not, because the book is certainly misunderstood by many as an encouragement to the new historicism, although, surely, its message is to show the creation and early development of the new style of the twentieth century, and, in any case, the message of the historian, with whatever style or phase of the past he deals, is not to present anything for imitation but to present it in its own right, to say: 'This is what happened in 1890 and 1910', leading up to the conclusion 'Here is a reason why 1930, 1940, 1950 should work in its own styles'. So, as far as Art Nouveau is concerned what really pleases me is that in Milan the façade of an Art Nouveau building has recently been re-erected as the centre of a modern block of offices (figure 47). The architects, Pasquali and Galimberti, must have felt that Cattaneo's Albergo Corso of 1907* was too good in its own right to be   n.13 demolished and deserved to be perpetuated as a monument framed by their own stylistically completely different frame.

Now at last I can turn to the question of why this return to historicism is taking place. What I would say, to put it very elementarily, is this. When the really original people in architecture start doing funny turns, then the less original people will imitate the funny turns on the one hand and, on the other, will turn to where they can find similar things in the past, provided this interest in the past is not likely to be branded as historicism in the sense in which they had learnt to regard historicism, that is as an imitation of Gothic or Georgian or neo-classical forms. The styles imitated now are never-before-imitated styles, and they harmonize with the particular aspect of the last years which I disrespectfully

47 Pasquali & Galimberti: modern incorporation of the Albergo Corso, Milan, 1959–60

48 Le Corbusier: Maisons Jaoul, Paris, 1954–6

49 A. Matthes: Atelier, 1957

called funny turns. The direct imitation of the funny turns themselves, that is of the highly original things done in the last few years, is, needless to say, a phenomenon which exists in all ages, and is bound to exist. Amongst between-the-war examples I want to remind you only of the random-rubble-racket. Then, after the war, you had and you have, for instance, the canopies which curl up, or do a Hitler salute, or snake to the left or right, and in fact do anything they can do to avoid a straightforward statement of what a canopy is actually built for. A second example is Le Corbusier's characteristic motif of a heavy chunk of concrete with a segmental arch on the underside, as it appeared prominently in the Maisons Jaoul (figure 48). That, as you probably know, has become a standard motif today (figure 49).

50 Niemeyer: Houses of Parliament, Brasilia, 1960

51 Manasseh: Rutherford School, London, 1960

Then there are the Ronchamp windows; I need not tell you what a hit they have recently made. They have produced a whole litter. I have noted seven
n.14 examples:* the beautiful church of the Madonna dei Poveri in Milan by Figini and Pollini, an extremely good church in Uruguay, two examples from Switzerland, two from France, and one from this country. All of them would never have been designed, if it had not been for Ronchamp. But only some of them are imitation, others are stimulus, and stimulus operates of course on a higher level than imitation. I take as an example of stimulus the group of the Houses of Parliament of Brasilia, with the office building in the middle and the Senate on the left, with its saucer dome, and the House of Representatives on the right with what might be called a 'dome saucer' (figure 50). The contrast of these two elementary geometrical shapes seems to me reflected in Leonard Manasseh's Rutherford School with the pyramid and the inverted pyramid on the roof

52 *Lutyens: Vincent Street flats,*
London, 1928

53, 54 *Scharoun: house for Breslau*
exhibition, 1929 (top), and maquette for
a school at Darmstadt, 1951

(figure 51).* And then there is all that goes on on the top of the Unité at Marseil- n.15
les and the tremendous progeny of these shapes on the tops of more recent buildings, and there is the chequerboard story which, curiously enough, starts with
Lutyens but is, I am sure, afterwards independent of him. Lutyens did the flats in
Vincent Street, Westminster, with their odd chequerboard pattern over the
whole façades in 1928 (figure 52). Then the motif was freshly taken up before the
war in the Rosebery Avenue flats by Lubetkin and Tecton and from there became an international fashion. It can be done by means of a pattern to conceal
regular fenestration, as for instance in the gilt-edged windows of the American
Embassy in Grosvenor Square, or by means of the fenestration itself being the
pattern.

But the fundamental matter for an explanation of the return of historicism
remains the fact that a change of architectural style took place from about 1938.
It appeared at first innocuous enough: the neo-Accommodating of Scandinavian
housing, and the Dutch Beton-Rococo in the work of Oud and others just before
the war. But it suddenly gathered tremendous vigour, when young Oscar
Niemeyer got going in Brazil in 1942–43.* His are the earliest buildings which   n.16
are emphatically no longer of the so-called International Style, and they are
buildings that have force and a great deal of originality. However, they are
emphatically anti-rational.

Why did this revolt happen? It is very easy to say: boredom; yet it is not
untrue. It is equally easy to quote Wordsworth's splendid remark about 'the degrading thirst after outrageous stimulation'; yet that would not be untrue either.
What is with us now has been called 'neo-sculptural', 'neo-plastic', 'neo-forma-
list', 'neo-expressionist'.* What all these terms have in common is, to repeat it,   n.17
that they express a revolt against rationalism.

The leaders are a strange, impressive, if disjointed group. To pick out a few,
there are first those who belong to the new post-modern anti-rationalism, because they belonged to anti-rationalism before, that is, those who lived long
enough to bridge, in their own work, that particular style which was created in
1900–10 and spread in the twenties and thirties. A very good example is Scharoun,
the German architect, who, in 1928, built things like figure 53, when most of his
friends had turned to the International Modern of the thirties, kept his Expressionism alive, and whose most recent work illustrated, e.g. a maquette for a
school in Darmstadt (figure 54) fits in perfectly with the neo-Expressionists. So
it is the old Expressionism which lasted.

The same is true of Frank Lloyd Wright. He belonged to the International
Moderns really in very few of his buildings, and the Expressionism of his design
for the Chapel of the University of Oklahoma, done in 1958 (figure 55) is certainly the direct continuation of such designs of his as the Tahoe Cabin of 1923.*   n.18

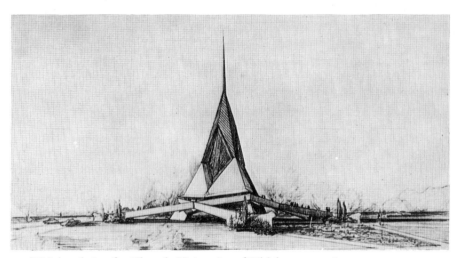

55 *Wright: design for Chapel, University of Oklahoma, 1958*

56 *Le Corbusier: detail of Secretariat, Chandigarh, completed in 1958*

57 *Candela: Church of the Wonder-working Virgin, Mexico City, 1954–5*

58 *Gaudí: Chapel of the Colonia Güell, Barcelona, c.1905*

59 *Bartning: Strahlenkirche (model), 1922*

That is one type of case. Le Corbusier's is the opposite, the complete *volte face*, not presumably in his character but in what we see in his buildings. His turn, as far as I can trace it, began with the Maisons Jaoul and culminated at Ronchamp on the one hand and Chandigarh on the other. Now to me this style is ideal for the emotions of a pilgrimage chapel, but when it comes to an administrative building, such as the Chandigarh Secretariat (figure 56), then I would speak of 'outrageous stimulation'.*

n.19

Finally, there is the problem of Nervi. Nervi, of course, is one of the great creators of new forms; forms initially probably stimulated by Maillart's bridges and perhaps by Max Berg's Jahrhunderthalle at Breslau. But Nervi's new forms are rationally controlled, not arbitrary. Now the question is whether my figure 57, Felix Candela's Church of the Wonder-working Virgin, belongs to Nervi or to neo-Gaudí and neo-Expressionism. As a historian I can answer only in this way: the similarity between Candela's church, the Chapel of the Colonia Güell by Gaudí, of about 1905 (figure 58), and the famous Strahlenkirche—i.e. 'radiating' or 'radiant' church—which Otto Bartning designed and made a model of in

n.20

1922 (figure 59)* is striking. Whether that implies a criticism of Candela is not my business, as it is altogether not my business to criticise the new anti-rationalism of the 1950s. If I am critical of it, the reason is that social and scientific conditions have not changed since the thirties, but a revolt was bound to come against the formal rigidity and the uniformity of the thirties. However, it is not odd and strange exterior effects which are the answer; the answer lies in planning, in siting, in landscaping, and so on. The individual building must remain rational. If you keep your buildings square, you are not therefore necessarily a square.

1   *Paul Rudolph: Yale School of Art and Architecture, 1963*

XV
Address given at the Opening of the Yale School of Art and Architecture 1963

THERE is a great fascination in standing in a new building. No rain has yet stained the concrete, no splinters have yet been broken out of the steps of the staircases, nobody has yet explained something by a rapid sketch on a wall. No human desires and disappointments have yet left their invisible but so unmistakable aura in the air. It is all still the dream of the architect miraculously come to life.

But there is a great fascination also in standing in old buildings, because they —to quote a great master of fantastic architecture, Sir John Vanbrugh, and quote him with special meaning in this particular building—'move lively and pleasant reflections on the persons who have inhabited them, and on the remarkable things which have been transacted in them.'

As a historian, moreover, I feel an intellectual fascination in the investigation of old buildings and in efforts to interpret them. You, Mr President, have been unwise to invite a historian to address this audience on this occasion. The historian is by definition a relativist. For such an occasion you need an absolutist. The historian is a relativist in so far as he operates in comparisons. He takes it for granted that the insignificant stays outside his field of observation—and you had better not ask him how he arrives at decisions as to what is significant and what is not—and then he compares the significant facts about 1250 with those of about 1300, those of 1500 with those of 1520. The result is the characteristics of Early English as against Decorated, of the High Renaissance as against Mannerism. In opening a new building, it should not be like that. The new building ought to be the one and all.

This chance, Mr President, you have missed. What you are going to get instead is a little history and a little of the historian's technique, inspired by the fact that this morning I went to look at the original building of this school, which is ninety-nine years old this year. Of course I cannot indulge in a comparison like that between High Renaissance and Mannerism, tempting as it would be. For 1864 and 1963 do not represent epochs following one after the other immediately. And yet there are certain features in Street Hall and in this building which set off the historian in me.

Take Street Hall first. I am fond of it, though in a funny indulgent way which has nothing to do with historical evaluation. If then I turn to history I would say this: In the middle of the nineteenth century opposition and even hatred against the Georgian century was virulent. There had been a universally valid style of smooth façades with a minimum of decorative stress round the doorway, a neutral style as it were. Windows were cut into the walls without any moulding. Roofs were hardly visible from below. In domestic architecture little was demanded of differentiation. Beauty or its opposite was the result of the finesses of proportion, the relation of wall and void. Now all this changed. Street Hall represents—*en miniature* of course—a hard individualism. It represents what the architects themselves at the time called *reality*, presumably in opposition to what they felt to be spectrally thin, timid and anaemic in the Georgian style. At all costs no symmetry. At all costs no window without some strange and unexpected emphasis. Crescendos from emphasis to over-emphasis, wherever possible. Projections are intensely stressed by square or polygonal shapes which pretend to be buttresses and turrets but were in fact introduced as geometry for geometry's sake. The same is true of the angular bay windows, the improbable openings in the form of diagonally placed squares.

This is what Peter D. Wight designed in 1864 when he was twenty-six years old. And this is what the historian sees and what I, as a historian—I hope correctly—have described in words which were intended at the same time to characterize. May the historian go one step further and add a value judgment? I would answer Yes, and so I will now add, without enough time to state my reasons, that Street Hall is thoroughly provincial. I hope you will take this judgment from one who comes from the country of such giants as Butterfield, Street and Bodley. Such an uninhibited judgment is in my opinion all the more important, because it also demonstrates a historical fact. In the history of architecture the United States in 1864—with a few exceptions—was still a backwater. One could write a history of Western architecture without mentioning it more than once or twice. But a few years after Street Hall all that was to change. Richardson's Brattle Square Church was begun in 1870, his Sherman House at Newport in 1874. And on we go to Sullivan, to Burnham & Root, to Holabird & Roche and finally to Frank Lloyd Wright, that means chapters of Western Architecture in which the Americans stand on the stage as important actors and here and there as the most important actors. From then there was no looking back, and what Paul Rudolph is designing now is heatedly debated at once from London north and Johannesburg south to Tokyo north and Auckland, New Zealand south, and to Toronto north and Buenos-Aires south.

Now what has he been doing here? The boundary between historian and critic is a real boundary; yet, if the historian tries to be a critic or appraiser, all he can do is to use his historian's tools of description and interpretation to the best of his abilities. The situation today appears to me like this. In the course of the thirties a style had gained international validity which, as you all know, had been created between 1890 and 1914 and which was the first style in architecture for nearly five hundred years to have invented its own vocabulary, grammar and syntax. It was an exacting style. Discipline and service counted more than individuality. It was a neutral style if you like. Façades were smooth, openings were cut in without any mouldings. Roofs were flat. Not much differentiation was granted the individual building. Beauty or otherwise depended primarily on the subtleties of proportion, of relation between glass and wall. I grew up with this style, and I would be dishonest if I concealed that this is my style, that it convinces me, and that in cases of fine grouping, composition and proportions it sends me, to use a term which is at the present moment perhaps just as out of date as I am.

But am I? May I at least be granted that as a historian I try. This then is what in my opinion has happened here: in the late forties and especially the fifties a decisive change took place. What I have just described appeared quite honestly to some of the older ones and the majority of the younger generation, to be dull and even sterile, of a false finality. So we experienced a return to individualism. You can no longer mistake one building for another, or one architect for another—at least not among the most important ones—and in the individual building not even one window for another. Violent stresses returned. In describing a design of Eero Saarinen's one can hardly use the same terminology as in describing designs by Kenzo Tange, Aalto or our Paul Rudolph. What do we see here? Massive piers of concrete rise. Projections are over-emphasized throughout. Heavy slabs are crossed by thin slabs. Spaces inside cross too and offer

2   *Peter D. Wight: Street Hall, Yale University, 1864*

sequences of most dramatic effects by unexpected vistas inside the building and even out of it.

It is all very exciting, a powerful stimulant for the students. May it not be too potent for them? Too personal as an ambiance? I would have thought so, if it had not been for the fact that I, about six months ago, sat on the same platform with Paul Rudolph. It was at the annual convention of the American Institute of Architects, and we both had to make speeches. What impressed me most about him and what made me hope that I would one day see his school in operation—a hope now realized—was what he proclaimed as his guiding principle, namely that a teacher of the young ought to have a very pronounced, perhaps even a provocative style, but that, for that very reason, he ought to help students to develop their own.

So my message to the students is simple and brief. You have the tremendous advantage of a controversial principal. Students will be students. You will worship him, you will tear him to pieces. Both will be equally salutary. But you must promise me one thing: don't imitate what you now have around you. Of course no young architect worth his salt imitates anyway. But the International Modern of the thirties could be imitated at least with impunity. The result was always something rational. serviceable, unaggressive. But woe to him who imitates Paul Rudolph, who imitates Saarinen, Philip Johnson (I mean Philip the Second), or Yamasaki. The result will be a catastrophe. The great individualist, the artist-architect, who is primarily concerned with self-expression, is inimitable.

But halt—for now I am really and provably wrong. Is this building primarily self-expression? In this question lies its pervading fascination for me. May I return to that meeting between Paul Rudolph and myself six months ago? My own address was commissioned to deal with a very vague subject. 'What makes for architectural quality?' I primarily spoke about the relation of architect to client. But since this new building also houses one of the most excellent departments of the history of art in America—and I may add my favourite of all such departments—I may offer you my basic tenet not in the words I used at Miami, but in the words of Antonio Filarete who in his treatise about the year 1460 wrote this:

'Lo edificio si rassomighlia all 'uomo. Adunque, se cosí è, è bisogno generare e poi partorire. Lo edificio per uno solo non può essere creato.'

'A building resembles a human being. If this is so, it must be conceived and then born. No building can be created by one man only'.

And then he continues:

'Colui che vuole edificare bisogna che abbia l'architetto e insieme con lui ingenerarlo e poi l'architetto partorirlo'.

'He who wishes to build, needs an architect: they will conceive it together, and then the architect will bring it to birth'.

Now I can go back to what I said six months ago. Architectural quality is of course aesthetic quality, but it is not aesthetic quality alone. The work of architecture is the product of function and art. If it fails in either, it fails in quality. The guardian of the aesthetics of architecture is the architect, the guardian of functional satisfaction is the client. His responsibility in briefing is as great as the architect's in designing. If, out of muddle-headedness, out of laziness, out of initial ignorance he fails, the building will be an annoyance, and the architect will, in my opinion wrongly, be reproached. And, this is how I continued, if the client gives inadequate information, because he is frightened of genius, he also deserves to be reproached; that is, if he does not say 'But if you put this window in this place in this room, I shall get a dark room'; or 'Your measurements of 26 by 6 ft. for a bedroom for two people will give me a room of unpractical, inconvenient proportions'. In much, this was my summing-up, of what I consider questionable in 1960 as against 1930, the fault must be attributed to the indulgence of the client or the lack of a working partnership between client and architect.

It is just this that strikes me as so pertinent here today. For here none of these problems can possibly have arisen. The doubts which so often torture me today, being an inveterate functionalist of the thirties, are here, must here be, absent. According to my definition a functionalist is an architect or a designer or a critic who regards it as the primary task of the architect and the designer to take care that his building or product functions and that no aesthetic feature is allowed access if it detracts from that task. Now here we have the rare case that—at least very largely—the client is the architect and the architect is the client. I know few such cases. One of them was Rudolf Steiner's Goetheanum, another the Bauhaus at Dessau. If you wander round this building, as no doubt you have done or will do, you must never forget that all you see and discuss is precisely in accordance with the programme. I find this a most stimulating and useful demonstration.

And now I have nothing more to add, except to thank you, Mr President, you, Mr Dean, and you, Paul, for having singled me out from far away to do me the honour of dedicating this new building. This I am doing herewith. May God bless it and the good work that is going on in it.

Postscript, 1968: And what has happened since? In 1965 Paul Rudolph left to concentrate on private practice, leaving his school, designed to fit him and him only, to another head. This demonstrates the necessity of neutral designs for neutral buildings, i.e. buildings which must function well under the command of a variety of men with a variety of ideas, and which must satisfy a variety of users.*

n.1

Appendix: Matthew Digby Wyatt

WRITINGS

(The following list of Wyatt's writings is from the catalogues of the British Museum, the Royal Institute of British Architects, the Victoria and Albert Museum, and from the obituary notice in *The British Architect*, VII.)

On the Art of the Mosaic, Ancient and Modern. *Trans. Soc. of Arts,* 1847.

Mosaics as Applied to Architectural Decoration. *Sess. Papers, R.I.B.A.,* 1847.

Specimens of the Geometrical Mosaic of the Middle Ages. London, 1848.

A Report on the Eleventh French Exposition of the Products of Industry. London, 1849.

Further Report made to H.R.H. Prince Albert . . . of Preliminary Enquiries into the Willingness of Manufacturers and Others to Support Periodical Exhibitions of the Works of Industry of all Nations. London, 1849.

Observations on Polychromatic Decoration in Italy. MS. R.I.B.A., 1850.

The Exhibition under its Commercial Aspects. *Journal of Design and Manufactures,* V, 1851.

On the construction of the Building for the Exhibition . . . in 1851. *Proc. Inst. Civ. Engineers,* X, 1851 (also in the *Official Catalogue* of the Exhibition, London, 1851).

The Industrial Arts of the Nineteenth Century, fol. London, 1851–3.

An attempt to Define the Principles which should determine Form in the Decorative Arts. *Lectures on the Results of the Great Exhibition.* London, 1852.

Specimens of Ornamental Art Workmanship in Gold, Silver, Iron, Brass and Bronze, fol. London, 1852.

Metalwork and its Artistic Design, fol. London, 1852.

A.A.P.C. Blanc, *The History of the Painters of all Nations,* ed. M. D. Wyatt. London, 1852.

Remarks on G. Abbati's Paper on Pompeian Decorations. *Sess. Papers, R.I.B.A.,* 1853.

The Byzantine and Romanesque Courts in the Crystal Palace (with J. B. Waring). London, 1854.

The Italian Court in the Crystal Palace (with J. B. Waring). London, 1854.

The Medieval Court in the Crystal Palace (with J. B. Waring). London, 1854.

The Renaissance Court in the Crystal Palace (with J. B. Waring). London, 1854.

Views of the Crystal Palace (1st ser.). London, 1854.

An Address delivered in the Crystal Palace at the opening of an Exhibition of Works of Art belonging to the Arundel Society. London, 1855.

Mosaics . . . of Sta Sophia at Constantinople. *Sess Papers, R.I.B.A.,* 1856.

Observations on Renaissance and Italian Ornament (in O. Jones, *The Grammar of Ornament),* fol. London, 1856.

Paris Universal Exhibition; Report on Furniture and Decorations. London, 1856.

Notices of Sculpture in Ivory (Arundel Society). London, 1856.

Notice of the late John Britton. *Sess. Papers, R.I.B.A.,* 1857.

The Sacred Grotto of St Benedict at Subiaco. *Sess Papers, R.I.B.A.,* 1857.

Specimens of Geometrical Mosaics manufactured by Maw and Co., fol. London, 1857.

On the Principles of Design applicable to Textile Art (in J. B. Waring, *The Art Treasures of the United Kingdom).* London, 1857–8.

Observations on Metallic Art (in J. B. Waring, *The Art Treasures of the United Kingdom).* London, 1857–8.

Influence Exercised on Ceramic Manufactures by the late Herbert Minton. London, 1858.

Early Habitations of the Irish, and especially the Cramoges of Lake Castles. *Sess. Papers, R.I.B.A.,* 1858.

On the Architectural Career of Sir Charles Barry. *Sess. Papers, R.I.B.A.,* 1859–60.

A Necrological Memoir of the late Sir Charles Barry, given at a meeting of the R.I.B.A. on 21 May 1860 and substantially reprinted as an obituary on Barry in *The Illustrated London News,* 2 June 1860, p. 515–516.

Illuminated Manuscripts as Illustrative of the Arts of Design. London, 1860.

The Art of Illuminating (with W. R. Tymms). London, 1860.

What Illuminating Was. London, 1861.

On the Present Aspect of the Fine and Decorative Arts in Italy. *Journal Soc. of Arts,* 1862.

The Loan Collection at South Kensington. *Fine Arts Quart. Rev.,* I and II, 1863.

On Pictorial Mosaic as an Architectural Embellishment. *Sess Papers, R.I.B.A.,* 1866.

A Report to Accompany the Designs for a National Gallery. London, 1866.

The Relations which should exist between Architecture and the Industrial Arts. *Architectural Association,* London, *c.* 1867.

On the Foreign Artists employed in England during the Sixteenth Century. *Sess. Papers, R.I.B.A.,* 1868.

The History of the Manufacture of Clocks. London, 1868.

Report on the Art of Decoration at the International Exhibition. Paris, 1867; London, 1868.

Introduction and Notes on Examples of Decorative Design, Selected from Drawings of Italian Masters in the Uffizi at Florence. London, 1869.

Fine Art; its History, Theory, Practice. (Slade Lectures at Cambridge.) London and New York, 1870.

Report on Miscellaneous Paintings, London International Exhibition, 1871. London, 1871.

An Architect's Notebook in Spain. London, 1872.

On the Most Characteristic Features of the Buildings of the Vienna Exhibition of 1873. London, 1874.

The Utrecht Psalter; Reports on the Age of the Manuscript. (By Sir M. D. Wyatt and others), fol. London, 1874.

ARCHITECTURAL AND OTHER WORKS

Adelphi Theatre, London, designs for redecoration executed by F. Sang. *Illustrated London News,* 7 October 1848, p. 224. (I owe this information to Miss Priscilla Metcalf.)

Pompeian, Byzantine, English Gothic, Italian, Renaissance Courts, etc., at the Crystal Palace, 1854. *The Builder,* XII.

Paddington Station, London (with Brunel as engineer), 1854–5. *The Builder,* XII.

Prize in Competition for Cavalry Barracks, Woolwich (with T. H. Wyatt), 1855.

Interior of Chancel, North Marston Church, Bucks (Memorial to J. Camden Neild, for Queen Victoria), 1855. *Illus. Lond. News,* Sept. 1855.

Royal Engineers' Crimean War Memorial, Chatham (Entrance to the School of Military Engineering, Brompton Barracks), 1861. *The Builder,* XIX.

Indian Govt. Store, Belvedere Road, Lambeth, London, 1861–4 (demolished).

Designs for the Albert Memorial. (Unexecuted. According to *The Builder,* XXI, p. 233, Wyatt sent in three designs, one for an open four-porticoed classical temple for the statue of the Prince, and other statues, one for a cross in the Italian Gothic style; and one more purely sculptural with the seated figure of the Prince crowned by Fame.)

Garrison Church, Woolwich (with T. H. Wyatt), 1862. *The Builder,* XXI and *Illus. Lond. News,* Jan. 1863.

Office Building, Grafton Street, Dublin, 1863. *The Builder,* XXI.

Saloon and Fernery, Ashridge, Herts., 1860 and 1864. Drawings for the Fernery at R.I.B.A.

(a) Works Illustrated in journals or Mentioned in Obituary Notices

Addenbrooke's Hospital, Cambridge, 1864–5 (extensions; new west front).

Rothschild Mausoleum, West Ham Cemetery, probably 1867.

India Office, London, Inner Courtyard, 1867. *The Builder*, XXV; *Building News*, XVI.

Castle Ashby, Northants, Garden Gates, 1868. *The Builder*, XXVI. (See also (*b*).)

Possingworth Manor, Sussex, 1868. For L. Huth. *The Builder*, XXVI; *The Architect*, I.

Clare College, Cambridge, 1870–2 (restoration of Hall and Combination Room).

R. Indian Civil Engineers' College, Coopers Hill, Surrey (now Training College), founded 1871.

Alford House, Kensington, London. Drawings shown at Royal Academy, 1872.

Offices for Lloyd's, Gracechurch Street, London, 1877. *The Builder*, XXXV.

(*b*) OTHER ARCHITECTURAL WORK

Azores: Mansion.

Burma: work at Rangoon.

Cambridge: Portico of the Pitt Club, *c.* 1865 and as purely classical as if it were Georgian.

Essex: Barracks, Chapel for the East India Company at Warley, 1857.

Glamorgan: The Ham.

Gloucestershire: Bristol, consultant on Temple Meads Station, 1865–78.

Hampshire: Brambridge House. (Reconstruction and redecoration for Sir Thomas Fairburn, illustrated in the sale catalogue of J. D. Wood and Co., 14 Sept. 1949.)

India: Post Office at Calcutta.

Lancashire: Aldingham Hall, between Barrow and Ulverston, 1846–50, for Dr John Stonard, the wealthy parson of Aldingham; Wyatt's earliest preserved building—Gothic in style, of white stone, symmetrical to the sea, but with an asymmetrically placed staircase tower at the back.

London: (i) Adelphi Theatre (with T. H. Wyatt); (ii) Burlington Fine Arts Club; (iii) East India Museum (perhaps adaptation of Elm Grove, now demolished); (iv) 12 Kensington Palace Gardens (reconstruction and redecoration of house for Alexander Collie, between 1865 and 1875); (v) Oxford Street, offices for Purdey and Cowlan; (vi) Piccadilly, Conservatory and Saloon, Northampton House; (vii) the decorative parts of the suspension bridge in St James's Park, recently replaced, 1857 (the bridge itself was by Rendell, the engineer); (viii) designs for the National Gallery competition, 1866.

Middlesex: Indian Lunatic Asylum at Ealing.

Northants: (i) Castle Ashby, Conservatory, Gloriette Gates (with much terracotta); (ii) Deene, extensive restoration of the parish church, 1868–9.

Prince Edward Island: varied work.

Surrey: (i) house at Caterham; (ii) Newells, Lower Beeding, near Horsham; (iii) The Mount at Norbury Hill, now Windermere House, Wistow Street. The house is called Norwood in the obituaries, and was enlarged by John Norton in 1873–6.

Sussex: (i) Newells, 1860, with additions of 1904, Elizabethan with mullioned windows and gables and a short, asymmetrically placed tower; (ii) Oldlands, Herrons Ghyll, 1869, symmetrical, in an indifferent Tudor; (iii) a house at Uckfield.

Wiltshire: (i) Rowde, front, 1850. Wyatt at the time owned Rowdeford House; (ii) the layout and architecture of Swindon New Town, the railway estate, is attributed by tradition to Wyatt. It was begun *c.* 1850.

(*c*) RESTORATIONS OF HOUSES

Baynards Park, Surrey.

Compton Wynyates, Warwickshire.

Isfield Park, Sussex.

(*d*) DESIGNS

Executed for Messrs Woollam (wallpapers), Maw (tiles, 1861), Templeton (carpets), Hurell James and Co., and others.

Notes

I DESIGN AND INDUSTRY THROUGH THE AGES
Pages 11–17

1 V. Gay: *Glossaire Archéologique du Moyen Age et de la Renaissance*, Paris, 1882-1928, vol. I., p. 580.
2 L. T. Belgrano: *Vita Privata dei Genovesi*, Genoa, 1875, p. 202.
3 R. Koechlin: *Les Ivoires Gothiques Français*, Paris, 1924, vol. I., p. 33, etc.
4 R. Papini, in *L'Arte*, XIII, 1910, and A. Bouillet in *Bulletin Monumental*, LXV, 1901.
5 W. H. St. John Hope in *The Archaeological Journal*, LXI., 1904, p. 234 and J. Evans: *Art in Mediaeval France*, Oxford, 1948, p. 281.
6 London, 1947, p. 281.
7 V. Goloubew: *Les Dessins de Jacopo Bellini*, Brussels, 1908.
8 A. B. Chamberlain: *Hans Holbein the Younger*, London, 1913, vol. II., p. 265, etc.
9 P. Jessen: *Der Ornamentstich*, Berlin, 1920.
10 M. Fenaille: *Histoire de la manufacture des Gobelins*, Paris, 1923; also E. Gerspach: *La Manufacture Nationale des Gobelins*, Paris, 1892.
11 H. Jouin, Paris, 1889; P. Marcel, Paris (1909); also L. de Laborde: *De l'union des arts et de l'industrie*, vol. I, Paris, 1856, pp. 121, etc.
12 Information kindly supplied by Messrs. Wedgwood.
13 F. Watson, in *The Connoisseur*, CIIL, October 1961, p. 166.
14 D. Ledoux-Lesard: *Les ébénistes parisiens, 1795-1870*, 1965, p. 251. I owe this and the previous reference to Francis Watson.
15 P. Lafond: *L'Art décoratif et le mobilier sous la République et l'Empire*, Paris, 1900.
16 F. Podreider: *Storia dei Tessuti d'Arte in Italia*, Bergamo, 1928, p. 267.
17 J. Godart, *L'ouvrier en soie*, 1899, p. 20-23. I owe this reference to Miss Natalie Rothstein.
18 H. Clouzot: *Histoire du Papier peint en France*, Paris, 1935, p. 47, etc.
19 *Sophie in London*, London, 1933. Mr. R. W. Symonds kindly drew my attention to this book.
20 H. Clouzot: *Historie de la manufacture de Jouy*, Paris, 1928; also E. Lewis: *The Romance of Textiles*, New York, 1937, which Mr. Alec Hunter told me about.
21 *Mechanization takes Command*, New York, 1948.
22 Sir H. T. Wood: *A History of the Royal Society of Arts*, London, 1913, p. 153.
23 Quoted from Harvard's *Dictionnaire*, vol. II, 1888, col. 84, etc.

24 *Philippe de la Salle; son oeuvre au Musée des Tissus de Lyon*, Paris, 1905.
25 Clouzot, *loc. cit.*
26 E. Lewis, *loc. cit.*
27 Clouzot, *loc. cit.*
28 H. Lefuel: *Georges Jacob*, Paris, 1923, pp. 142-43.
29 *Nouvelles Archives de l'Art Français*, 1877, p. 368, etc.; also Thieme-Becker's *Künstlerlexikon*.
30 M. Adams in *Journal of the Royal Institute of British Architects*, 1912, p. 646; also T. Perry in *The Architectural Review*, XXXIII, 1900, p. 119.
31 Mrs. Esdaile in *The Architect and Building News*, for January 19 and 26, 1940. See now the detailed account in R. Gunnis, *Dictionary of British Sculptors 1660-1851*, London, 1953.
32 A. Cox-Johnson: *John Bacon* (St. Marylebone Society Publications No. 4), 1961.
33 E. Metyard: *The Life of Josiah Wedgwood*, London, 1865, vol. II, p. 131.
34 Horace Walpole: Letter of Nov. 13, 1776.
35 Lafond, *loc. cit.*, p. 14.
36 N. Pevsner: *Academies of Art past and present*, Cambridge, 1940, p.159, etc.
37 Clouzot, *loc. cit.*
38 *Vorbilder für Fabrikanten und Handwerker*, 1821-37. On Schinkel see p. 164 ff of Vol. I of these essays.
39 Q. Bell: *The Schools of Design*, London, 1963.
40 For the following see in more detail the paper on High Victorian Design, p. 38 ff.
41 Thomas Hope in his *Household Furniture*, i.e. already in 1807, had written (p. 2) that handicraft was being debased 'by the entire substitution of machinery for manual labour'.
42 Wood, *loc. cit.*, p. 405.
43 Wood, *loc. cit.*, p. 154.
44 *The Collected Works of William Morris*, vol. XXII, London, 1914, p. 114-5.
45 See my *Academies of Arts Past and Present*.
46 A. V. Sugden and J. L. Edmondson: *A History of English Wallpaper*, London, ?1926, p. 159, etc.

III HIGH VICTORIAN DESIGN
Pages 38–95

1 *The Architectural Review*, LXXXI, 1937.
2 *The Great Exhibition*, London, 1951.
3 *Library Edition*, i.e. *The Works of John Ruskin*, edited by E. T. Cook and A. Wedderburn, London 1903-12, vol. III, p. 450.
4 'Ode sung at the Opening of the International Exhibition'.

5 *See* for all this Henry Cole's autobiography *Fifty Years of Public Work*, 1884.
6 *Journal of Design and Manufactures*, IV, 1850/51, p. 30.
7 T. Martin, *Life of the Prince Consort*, 1876, vol. 2, p. 365.
8 *The Principal Speeches and Addresses of H.R.H. the Prince Consort*, 1862, p. 110.
9 *Life and Letters of Macaulay*, 1876, vol. II, p. 210.
10 *Official Descriptive and Illustrated Catalogue*, vol. I, pp. 1 and 35.
11 Dr Giedion's *Mechanization takes Command*, New York, 1948, may be looked up with profit on the development of domestic and agricultural machinery in the early nineteenth century.
12 *See* for instance R. D. Best: *Brass Chandelier*, London, 1940, p. 128.
13 *Past and Present*.
14 *The Seven Lamps of Architecture*, Library Edn., vol. VIII, p. 218.
15 Library Edn., vol. VIII, p. 81.
16 G. Semper: *Wissenschaft, Industrie und Kunst*, Brunswick, 1852.
17 *Ibid.*, pp. 9-10.
18 R. N. Wornum in an essay to be referred to in more detail later (*Art Journal* Volume on the Exhibition, p. XIV★★★): 'These specimens of machine carvings . . . are quite equal to the general average of that executed wholly by hand; and when many examples of one design are required, as in church carving, the saving of labour and expense must be enormous'.
19 Library Edn., vol. VIII, p. 60.
20 According to information kindly supplied by Professor Walter Gropius he lived from 1821 to 1888 and was the son and assistant of Carl Wilhelm Gropius, a well-known diorama painter. Paul's title later was 'Dekorationsmaler für die Königlichen Bühnen'.
21 *The Builder* in 1851, p. 135, illustrated a Renaissance ceiling of papier maché put up in that year at Parnell & Smith's Army & Navy Club in London.
22 Other new materials never caught on, for instance Class 26 No. 125: 'Specimen of a material produced from the mixture of moss or peat, in certain proportions, with sawdust, etc. It is subjected to a pressure of 800 tons, to make it fit for use; it then becomes hard and durable, and capable of being polished and worked'. Also 'Plastic material made from moss and lime, which has been submitted to a heat of 160 degrees without showing any crack or flaw'.

23 Giedion: *Mechanization takes Command*, p. 326.

24 On railway furniture and indeed on all adjustable furniture Dr Giedion's book is again to be recommended.

25 *See* P. F. R. Donner in *The Architectural Review*, XCIII, 1943.

26 *See* for ample details Mrs. P. Stanton's yet unpublished monumental monograph on Pugin.

27 On Wornum see Ruskin: Library Edn., vol. XVI, p. 331.

28 Appendix to the *Art Journal*, Exhibition volume, pp. V★★ and VI★★★

29 How alien on the other hand the meaning of Ruskin's 'Lamp of Life' was to Wornum is crushingly proved by his remark (p. XV★★★) that the illumination of mediaeval manuscripts was 'an inordinate waste of labour over trifles'. His acceptance of machine carving quoted above (note 17) goes well with that.

30 See the next essay.

31 1851-53, plates 106 and 108.

32 *Suppl. Report on Design,* Reports of the Juries, 1852, pp. 725 and 717.

33 *The True Principles of Pointed or Christian Architecture*, 1841, p. 9.

34 Library Edn., vol. VIII, pp. 252-8.

35 Somerleyton, (illustrated in *The Builder*, IX, 1851, p. 363) and Preston Hall, Kent.

36 *See The Builder*, XIX, 1861.

37 E.g., R. Redgrave in his *Suppl. Report on Design, l.c.,* p. 726.

38 *See* K. R. Towndrow: *Alfred Stevens*, 1939.

39 But the *Art Journal* volume mentions about a dozen times staff-designers of firms by name, e.g. pp. 1 (Copeland), 138, 205.

40 *Art Journal*, Exhibition volume, p. 159; Catalogue p. 683.

41 *Art Journal*, Exhibition volume, pp. 69, 74, 109, 132, 149, 161, 165, 168, 191.

42 Illustrated *Journal of Design and Manufactures*, vol. I, 1849, p. 11, Grüner was also responsible for the publication of the garden pavilion. It was done through John Murray's, by Command of the Queen.

43 Pp. 39, 40, 321, 328.

44 On industrial designers from 1850 to 1950, *see* N. Pevsner in *Designers in Britain*, vol. III.

45 *An Apology for the Revival of Christian Architecture in England*, 1843, pp. 10–11.

46 Ruskin, *Seven Lamps*, Library Edn., vol. VIII, p. 28, added note of 1880.

47 Ruskin, *Seven Lamps*, Library Edn., vol. VIII, p. 67.

48 Pugin in an unpublished letter to Hardman kindly conveyed to me by Mrs Stanton speaks of the 'glass-monster', the 'glass-horror' and the 'crystal humbug'.

49 Pp. 109–110.

50 *See* too Note 47 to Matthew Digby Wyatt, below.

51 On him, *see* D. Harbron in *The Architectural Review*, XCII, 1942, and P. F. R. Donner in *The Architectural Review*, XCIII, 1943.

52 Though G. M. Young has found it used as early as 1851, *Victorian England*, p. 87.

53 Library Edn., vol. VIII, p. 252.

54 *Wissenschaft, Industrie und Kunst*, Brunswick 1852, p. 11.

55 *Towndrow, op. cit.,* p. 97.

56 Library Edn., vol. VIII, p. 101.

57 *L.c.* (Note 16 above), p. 11.

58 *The Builder* in 1865, p. 117 etc. has plates of modern naturalistic capitals.

59 Quoted from Y. ffrench, *l.c.,* p. 263.

60 *See* N. Pevsner in *The Architectural Review*, LXXXVI, 1939.

61 Quoted from J. Steegman: *Consort of Taste, 1830–70*, 1950, p. 201.

62 Quoted from A. T. Gardner: *Yankee Stonecutters*, 1945, p. 28.

63 Quoted from C. H. Gibbs-Smith: *The Great Exhibition*, London, 1950, p. 16.

64 *Journal of Design*, IV, p. 1.

65 I shall quote from this Journal in the *Matthew Digby Wyatt* essay to which I wish to refer also for the contents of the next few pages. *See* also S. Giedion: *Mechanization Takes Command*, pp. 347 etc. Professor Giedion however attributes too much of the Journal to Cole personally. The 'wry comment' on the Match Box in the shape of a Crusader's Tomb can, e.g., not be by Cole; for the Match Box was actually one of the Summerly Art Manufactures, *see* H. Cole: *Fifty Years of Public Work*, vol. 2, p. 186.

66 I, p. 3.

67 On the schools of design see now Q. Bell, *The Schools of Design*, London, 1963. Mr Steegman (*Consort of Taste*, p. 22) quotes Sir Francis Palgrave saying of the effects of the schools (*Quarterly Review*, 1840): 'A permanent glut of pseudo-art is created'. Palgrave was the first Deputy Keeper of the Records; Cole became Secretary to the Records Commission in 1833 and an Assistant Keeper in 1838.

68 Pp. 11, 1, 30, 23, 24, 23, 32, 40.

69 III, p. 88.

70 IV, p. 75.

71 I, pp. 87 and 110; III, p. 50.

72 The selling price in Parian was 3s. 6d., in ormolu 6 guineas. The beer-jug sold at 18s., the shaving-pot at 4s., 5s., or 6s. 6d., the Camellia Teapot at 16s., the bread knife at 20s.

73 I, p. 56.

74 IV, p. 15.

75 I, p. 80.

76 III, p. 175.

77 IV, p. 14, etc.

78 Ibid., p. 8.

79 Ibid., p. 11.

80 Ibid., p. 40.

81 Ibid., p. 41 (*The Times*, 1 July, 1851).

82 V. p. 158.

83 P. 708.

84 *See* F. M. Hueffer: *Ford Madox Brown*, London, 1896, p. 161.

85 J. W. Mackail, *The Life of William Morris*, World's Classics Edition, vol. I, p. 117.

IV MATTHEW DIGBY WYATT
Pages 96–107

1 Matthew Digby Wyatt was born at Rowde, near Devizes, in 1820, died in 1877, and was buried at Usk in Monmouthshire. His father was a barrister in Ireland. He was articled to his brother, Thomas Henry (1807–80), travelled in France, Germany and Italy in 1844-6, and became surveyor to the East India Company in 1855. Other dates and events are mentioned in the text of the lecture. Some of his travel sketches are in the R.I.B.A. They include Rome, Paris, Arles, Paestum, Aachen, Bamberg, Würzburg, Nuremberg, Augsburg. The R.I.B.A. also has patterns for floor-tiles and designs for metalwork.

2 Sir Henry Cole: *Fifty Years of Public Work*, London, 1884. See the preceding essay, also the Cole Papers at the Victoria and Albert Museum.

3 'The General Bearing of the Great Exhibition on the Progress of Art and Science' in *Lectures on the Results of the Great Exhibition of 1851*, London, 1852, p. 1.

4 Victoria and Albert Museum V. 1, and Box 85. They also contain Wyatt's watercolours for the German Medieval Vestibule, the English Medieval Vestibule, the English Medieval Court, the French and Italian Medieval Vestibule, the Renaissance, Elizabethan and Italian Courts and the Italian Vestibule. That these water-colours are by Wyatt's hand is borne out by a water-colour of S. Benedetto at Subiaco at the Royal Institute of British Architects which also owns a set of plans, elevations, sections and perspectives for the Fern-House at Ashridge, and a timid drawing of a Gothic window, dated 1848 (and probably by a lesser Wyatt). At the Victoria and Albert Museum in addition (C. 124) designs for roofing-tiles for Messrs Maw.

5 Among sources of the motif of the continuous, round-headed arcade on short piers with foliated capitals, which was so very popular for mid-nineteenth century town premises, is, for example, the Bargello courtyard in Florence.

6 Wyatt was a good friend to Scott. He advised and backed him in his fight to get the commission for the Government Offices which include the India Office.

7 Queen Victoria in her diary under 15 April 1851 calls him—not a great architect—but 'a very intelligent architect'.

8 IV, 1850–1, pp. 10, et seq. The article is not signed but Wyatt's authorship is proved by the text to his *Specimens of Ornamental Art Workmanship in Gold, Silver, Iron, Brass and Bronze*, London, 1852.

9 O. Jones, *The True and the False in the Decorative Arts*, London, 1863 (Lectures given at the School of Practical Art in 1852), p. 14. Cf. Morris, 'The Decorative Arts are in a state of anarchy and disorganisation' (*The Lesser Arts*, 1877; *Coll. Works*, vol. XXII, p. 9).

10 *Journal of Design*, II, 1849–50, p. 17. Morris: 'We, if no age else, have learnt the trick of masquerading in other men's cast-off clothes' (*Coll. Works*, vol. XXII, p. 315).

11 O. Jones, *loc. cit.,* p. 8. Morris on the Gothic Revivalists of the mid-nineteenth

century: 'They . . . thought it could be artificially replanted in a society totally different from that which gave birth to it' (*Coll. Works*, vol. XXII, p. 819).

12 O. Jones in *Journal of Design*, V, 1851, p. 90.

13 O. Jones, *The True and the False*, p. 39.

14 Ibid. p. 14. Cf. Morris: '. . . the necessary and essential beauty which arises out of the fitness of a piece of craftmanship for the use (for) which it is made'. (Quoted from May Morris, *W. M., Artist, Writer, Socialist*, Oxford, 1936, vol. I, p. 317. The quotation comes from a paper *The Ideal Book*, read in 1893. Stanley Morison drew my attention to it.)

15 W. Dyce in *Journal of Design*, I, 1849, p. 93.

16 *Journal of Design*, I, 1849, p. 80. Cf. Morris: 'As to paperhangings . . . the more mechanical the process, the less direct should be the imitation of natural forms' (*Coll. Works*, vol. XXII, p. 190).

17 W. Dyce in *Journal of Design*, I, 1849, pp. 91 et seq.

18 R. Redgrave in *Journal of Design*, IV, 1850–1, p. 15. Cf. Morris: 'As for a carpet design, it seems quite clear that it should be quite flat, that it should give no more . . . than the merest hint of one plane behind another' (*Coll. Works*, vol. XXII, p. 195).

19 Journal of Design, III, 1850, p. 175.

20 One of the *Lectures on the Results of the Great Exhibition* arranged by the Society of Arts (cf. p. 31). Wyatt's lecture was given on 21 April 1852.

21 Morris: 'Simplicity is the foundation of all worthy art' (*Coll. Works*, vol. XXII, p. 294).

22 *Seven Lamps*, Library Edn., vol. VIII, p. 60.

23 II, 1849–50, pp. 72 et seq. My attribution of the unsigned review is based on the identity of points of view with those in the later article referred to in note 34.

24 *Journal of Design*, VI, 1851–2, pp. 25 et seq.

25 Ruskin wrote (App. 12 to vol. I, Library Edn. vol. IX, pp. 436–9) that Pugin 'is not a great architect, but one of the smallest possible or conceivable architects' and links up that hysterical statement with equally hysterical ones against the 'miserable influence' of Romanism, the 'fatuity, self-inflicted and the stubborness in resistance to God's Word' which characterizes the Catholic. 'No imbecility', he goes on, is 'so absolute, no treachery so contemptible' as theirs. Later on, in 1856, he defended himself explicitly against ever having in the least been influenced by Pugin (Lib. Edit., vol. V, pp. 428 et seq.): 'I glanced at Pugin's Contrasts once, in the Oxford architectural reading room, during an idle forenoon. His Remarks on Articles in *The Rambler* (1850) were brought under my notice by some of the reviews. I never read a word of any other of his works, not feeling, from the style of his architecture, the smallest interest in his opinion.' One would be readier to believe Ruskin if it were not for such facts as the complete omission of

his married life from *Praeterita*.

26 *Contrasts*, 1836, p. 1.

27 *The True Principles of Pointed or Christian Architecture*, 1841, p. 1.

28 *The True Principles*, pp. 25 and 26. The position of Pugin in the history of architectural and art criticism is in fact much more complex than it must appear here. I have brought together some more passages of importance in a florilegium in *The Architectural Review*, XCIV, 1943. For an excellent summing up see Sir Kenneth Clark, *The Gothic Revival*, London, 1928. Briefly what happened was this. In Pugin, owing to his newly acquired Catholic zeal, the earlier aesthetic teachings of such romantic converts as Friedrich von Schlegel were revived and applied specifically to architecture and design. Schlegel (*Europa*, 1803, vol. II, pt. II, pp. 143–5) said: 'Vergeblich sucht ihr die Malerkunst wieder hervorzurufen, wenn nicht erst Religion oder philosophische Mystik wenigstens die Idee derselben wieder hervorgerufen hat.' Pugin said that churches of any, including architectural, value 'can only be produced . . . by . . . men who were thoroughly imbued with devotion for, and faith in, the religion for whose worship they were erected' (*Contrasts*, p. 2). This religious foundation gave a new twist to the *bienséance* and *convenance* of the classic French architectural theory of the seventeenth and eighteenth centuries. To consider utility now became not a matter of common sense but of truthfulness. Cole, Owen Jones and Wyatt took over the utilitarian theses without bothering about their philosophical premises, the Gothic Revival architects (notably Gilbert Scott, who in his *Remarks on Secular and Domestic Architecture*, London, 1858, p. 241, praised Pugin as 'the great reformer of architecture') took over the exclusive faith in Gothic form and the substructure of the system of which to Pugin it was the necessary expression, while Ruskin and then Morris took over the whole system but without its religious foundation. They agreed with Pugin (and the earlier Romantics—from Herder and young Goethe, and from Edward Young onwards) that art and architecture express the state of mind and feeling of a man and a society, but they did not draw the narrow conclusion that only a restoration of medieval Christianity could restore the arts. Still, their own vaguer medievalist sociology was perhaps no more real.

29 *Journal of Design*, IV, 1850–1, p. 75.

30 Cf. also *Fine Art*, London and New York, 1870, p. 75.

31 *Journal of Design*, II, 1849–50, p. 72.

32 'Ornamentation is the principal part of architecture', *Architecture and Painting*, 1853, Addenda to Lectures I and II, Library Edn., vol. XII, p. 83.

33 *Seven Lamps*, Library Edn., vol. VIII, p. 66.

34 Ibid. p. 67.

35 IV, pp. 10 et seq. and pp. 74 et seq. A passage from this article has already been quoted, see Note 6.

36 See my *Pioneers of Modern Design*, Harmondsworth, 1960, pp. 133 et seq.

37 In praise of iron and glass still a little earlier (and not mentioned either in Sigfried Giedion's *Space, Time and Architecture* or my *Pioneers of Modern Design*) is *Journal of Design*, II, 1849–50, p. 148, on Bunning's Coal Exchange (illustrated by Henry-Russell Hitchcock in *The Architectural Review*, CI, 1947 and later in this volume of the Pelican History of Art): 'We have a structure which manifests at once that the architect very properly made its purpose and destination the first and ruling thought. . . . Mr Bunning has successfully employed iron and glass abundantly, usefully and ornamentally.' Again an article on *The Prospect of Iron and Glass Edifices* came out in VI, 1851–2, pp. 16 et seq. Here we read: 'The novel union of building materials necessitates a new treatment, and we have our hopes will produce a new era in architecture'.

38 See for example, *Journal of Design*, III, 1850, p. 190.

39 Library Edn., vol. III, p. 456.

40 Library Edn., vol. XXXV, p. 47.

41 *Proc. Inst. Civ. Eng.*, X, 14 January, 1851, p. 133.

42 *Fine Art*, loc. cit., p. 243.

43 *Giotto and his Works* . . . (1853–60), Library Edn., vol. XXIV, p. 58.

44 *The Stones of Venice*, vol. II (1853), Library Edn., vol. X, p. 240.

45 Ibid., p. 268.

46 *Fine Art*, loc. cit., pp. 49–51.

47 Cf. the all-pervading emphasis placed on the lack of balance between thought and feeling during the nineteenth century in both Dr Giedion's monumental books *Space, Time and Architecture*, and *Mechanization takes Command*.

48 See, for example, in *The Lamp of Life*: 'So long as men work *as* men putting their heart into what they do . . . there will be that in the handling which is above all price, (Library Edn., vol. VIII, p. 214), and even more clearly: 'The right question to ask, respecting all ornament, is simply this: Was it done with enjoyment—was the carver happy, while he was about it?' (Lib. Edn., vol. VIII, p. 218). It is from this point of view also that Ruskin had to condemn the Crystal Palace and railway stations. There are indeed no happy craftsmen expected to be busy on them. But, and here appears a fundamental fallacy, while the criterion of the joy in making can be applied to craft—a hand-made vase possesses certain qualities due to the touch of the human hand which in the machine-turned vase must be absent—it cannot be applied to much that is best in architecture, unless one is ready to confine the aesthetic values of architecture to the values of decoration added to it, as indeed Ruskin did—see Note 31. But the strictly architectural values of architecture, i.e. values of siting, grouping, proportion, relations of solid and void, spatial rhythm, etc., have at all times been a matter of design largely independent of the executive hand. That is true of the Parthenon as of

the Pantheon, of Périgueux as of the Palazzo Pitti.

49 'The Exhibition under its Commercial Aspect', *Journal of Design*, V, 1851, pp. 153 et seq. Morris on competition can be read in several of his Lectures on Socialism (*Coll. Works*, vol. XXIII); for example: 'I hold that the condition of competition between man and man is bestial' (p. 172). Also, a little more in detail: 'so long as the system of competition in the production and the exchange of the means of life goes on, the degradation of the arts will go on', *Art and Democracy*, quoted from P. Henderson, *William Morris, His Life, Work and Friends*, London, 1967, p. 256.)

50 William Morris, *Collected Works*, vol. XXIII, pp. 150–51.

51 Loc. cit. (see Note 3), p. 18.

52 J. W. Mackail, *The Life of William Morris*, London, 1899, vol. II, p. 99.

53 *A Report on the Eleventh French Exposition of the Products of Industry*, London, 1849, p. 4.

54 *Making the Best of it* (lecture of c. 1878–9), *Collected Works*, vol. XXII, pp. 114–15.

V WILLIAM MORRIS AND ARCHITECTURE
Pages 108–117

1 The most recent are Paul Thompson's, London, 1967, and Philip Henderson's, London, 1967. Philip Henderson also edited the letters (London, 1950).

2 Stopford Brooke, 1867, *see* Mary Morris: *W. M. Artist, Writer, Socialist*, 1936, p. 79.

3 Mackail, *The Life of William Morris*, London, 1899, vol. I, p. 128.

4 J. B. Glazier: *W. M. and the early days of the Socialist Movement*. 1921, I, 22–3.

5 Mackail, *l.c.*, vol. I, p. 217.

6 Mackail, *l.c.*, vol. I, p. 215–16. The last-named story was told me personally, I think by Mackmurdo. I made a record at the time but lost it in the war, when I lost all my pre-war Morris records—and in fact nearly all my records on 19th-century architecture.

7 P. Henderson: *The Letters of W. M.*, 1950, 77 To an unknown addressee, 1876.

8 *Ib.*, p. 160; 1882.

9 *Ib.*, p. XIX.

10 Mackail, *l.c.*, vol. II, p. 99.

11 *Collected Works* (abbreviated as *C.W.*) vol. XXIII, p. 147.

12 *C.W.*, vol. XXII, p. 318.

13 *C.W.*, vol. XXII, p. 119.

14 *C.W.*, vol. XXII, p. 300.

15 Henderson, *l.c.*, p. 377.

16 *C.W.*, vol. XXII, p. 41.

17 *C.W.*, vol. XXII, p. 119.

18 *Ib*.

19 *C.W.*, vol. XXII, p. 73.

20 Henderson, *l.c.*, p. 11.

21 *Oxford and Cambridge Magazine*, I, p. 100.

22 Henderson, *l.c.*, p. 12.

23 *Seven Lamps*, Library Edn., vol. VIII, p. 244: 'Do not let us talk . . . of restoration. The thing is a Lie from beginning to end.'

24 *C.W.*, vol. XXII, p. 69.

25 *C.W.*, vol. XXII, p. 296.

26 Henderson, *l.c.*, p. 89.

27 Henderson, *l.c.*, p. 314.

28 Henderson, *l.c.*, p. 120 etc.

29 May Morris, *l.c.*, vol. I, p. 282.

30 Henderson, *l.c.*, p. 153.

31 Henderson, *l.c.*, p. 125.

32 May Morris, *l.c.*, vol. I, p. 266.

33 *Remarks on Secular and Domestic Architecture, present and future*, London, 1858, p. 171.

34 Mackail, *l.c.*, vol. II, p. 97.

35 Henderson, *l.c.*, p. 303.

36 W. R. Lethaby: *Philip Webb and his Works*, London 1935, p. 149.

37 *Ib.*, p. 120.

38 In the sense in which we speak of strains in the breeding of horses.

39 Lethaby: *Webb*, p. 140.

40 *Ib.*, p. 120.

41 *C.W.*, vol. XXII, p. 315.

42 May Morris, *l.c.*, vol. I, p. 285.

43 *C.W.*, vol. XXII, p. 318.

44 *Ib.*, p. 318.

45 *Ib.*, p. 326.

46 *Ib.*, p. 321.

47 *Ib.*, p. 325.

48 *Ib.*, p. 318.

49 *Ib.*, p. 315.

50 *C.W.*, vol. XXIII, p. 148.

51 *C.W.*, vol. XXII, p. 313.

52 *Ib.*, p. 149.

53 *Ib.*, p. 62–3.

54 *Ib.*, p. 128–9.

55 *Ib.*, p. 84.

56 *C.W.*, vol. XXIII, p. 14.

57 *C.W.*, vol. XXII, p. 183–5.

58 Paris, 1879, p. 113. Very pertinent in this connection and highly interesting is a remark of the Reverend J. L. Petit quoted recently by Professor Peter Collins (*The Architectural Review*, CXXIX, 1961, p. 374). According to *The Builder*, XIX, 1861, p. 351, he said that Queen Anne is simply vernacular and, added to it, ornamentation of a specially suitable kind—and he said that of Morris's Red House. So where are we?

59 London, 1940, p. 34. I don't agree with much that Blomfield wrote in this book and should therefore, in the present context, refer to a paper I wrote on Norman Shaw and which was reprinted in an amplified form in *Victorian Architecture* (ed. Peter Ferriday), London, 1963.

60 *St James's Gazette*, 17, 12, 1881.

61 It may be worth recording that the late D. S. McColl told me shortly before he died in 1948 how he had been as a very young man to a lecture or a political talk given by Morris somewhere in the East end and how, just before the entry of the speaker, in came 'Lady Burne-Jones and Oscar carrying a lily'. These were McColl's words.

62 *Decoration and Furniture of Town Houses*, London, 1881, p. 14–15.

63 *C.W.*, vol. XXII, p. 327.

64 Lethaby, *l.c.*, p. 132.

65 *C.W.*, vol. XXII, p. 85.

66 *Ib.*, p. 84.

67 *Ib.*, p. 327.

68 *Ib.*, p. 85.

69 *Ib.*, p. 329.

70 *Ib.*, p. 73.

71 Those who will not believe this assessment are referred to the letter of 1887 in which Morris calls Hans Place 'a very architectooraloolal region' (Henderson, *l.c.*, p. 265).

72 Lethaby, *l.c.*, p. 121.

73 *Ib.*, p. 111.

74 *Ib.*, p. 118.

75 *C.W.*, vol. XXII, p. 114–15. The passage is quoted in full in one of the preceding essays, p. 16–17.

76 This is the thesis of the first chapter of my *Pioneers of Modern Design*.

77 Henderson, *l.c.*, p. 13.

78 *Ib.*, p. 138.

79 *C.W.*, vol. XXII, p. 11.

80 *C.W.*, vol. XXIII, p. 170.

81 I am here dealing with architecture only. Otherwise there would be more to put down on the Victorian side: for instance, Morris's favourite colour-schemes (*see* especially *C.W.* vol. XXII, p. 101, etc.), his dislike of large windows, letting too much light into a room (*Ib.*, p. 92), and also his rabid hatred of the 18th-century monuments in Westminster Abbey.

82 *C.W.*, vol. XXII, p. 138.

83 *Ib.*, p. 72.

84 *Ib*.

85 *Ib.*, p. 138.

86 *Ib.*, p. 71.

87 *Ib.*, p. 72–3.

88 *Ib.*, p. 130.

89 *Ib.*, p. 93.

90 *Ib.*, p. 97.

91 May Morris, *l.c.*, vol. II. G. B. Shaw's description of Morris's own house.

92 *C.W.*, vol. XXII, p. 24.

93 *Ib.*, p. 76.

94 *Ib.*, p. 321.

95 Henderson, *l.c.*, p. 236.

96 *Ib.*, p. 64.

97 *C.W.*, vol. XXIII, p. 95–6.

98 *Ib.*, p. 152–3.

99 May Morris, *l.c.*, vol. I.

100 Henderson, *l.c.*, p. 242. So Morris could also appreciate 'the cosy snobbiness' of Dublin, *Ib.*, p. 253, and 'the ordinary little plain Non-Conformist chapels . . . of the Thames-side country', Mackail, vol. II, p. 20.

101 *C.W.*, vol. XXII, p. 120.

102 *Ib.*, p. 74.

103 *Ib.*, p. 63.

104 *Ib.*, p. 87.

105 *Ib.*, p. 114.

106 H. Nocq: *Tendances Nouvelles*, Paris, 1896, p. 46. Quoted from S. Tschudi Madsen: *Sources of Art Nouveau*, Oslo, 1956, p. 305.

VI ART FURNITURE OF THE 1870s
Pages 118–131

1 J. W. Mackail, *The Life of William Morris*, World's Classics Edition, vol. I, p. 113.

2 Mackail, vol. I, p. 143.

3 Mackail, vol. I, p. 150.

4 Mackail, vol. I, p. 154–155.

5 W. R. Lethaby, *Philip Webb and his Works*, London 1935, p. 37.

6 On Major Gillum see my article in *The Burlington Magazine, XCV, 1953.*

7 A. E. Street: *Memoir of G. E. Street, 1888,* p. 19; also p. 107.

8 More on Talbert will be found in the catalogues of the Victoria and Albert Museum exhibition of Victorian and Edwardian Decorative Arts, held in 1952. The exhibition was the work of the late Peter Floud and his devoted helpers and pupils. It remains the standard reference book on Victorian design and crafts. On Victorian furniture one should consult in addition the book by one of the Floud team, Elizabeth Aslin: *Nineteenth Century English Furniture,* London 1962. Also R. W. Symonds: *Victorian Furniture,* London 1962.

9 *Gothic Forms applied to Furniture . . . , 1867,* p. 1.

10 Fig. 4 was illustrated before the publication of the book in *Building News, 1866,* p. 136.

11 *Ib.,* p. 4.

12 Fig. 2 comes from *The Architect, 1869,* p. 42.

13 On Burges see Charles Handley Read in *Victorian Architecture* (ed. Peter Ferriday), London 1963.

14 Furniture in Burges's Castel Coch is illustrated and discussed in W. G. Howell's article in *The Architectural Review, CIX,* 1951, p. 39 etc.

15 Another architect who figured with Gothic furniture in exhibitions was S. J. Nicholl who designed for Cox & Sons (*see Building News,* May 31, 1871), a firm which also occasionally employed Talbert (*see* Talbert's *Examples of Ancient and Modern Furniture,* 1876, Plate 47).

16 *The Precious Stone,* 1949.

17 Another Orient enthusiast in London was Thomas Jekyll who designed the woodwork for Whistler's Peacock Room and metal grates for Barnard's of Norwich. On the Peacock Room see now P. Ferriday in *The Architectural Review, CXXVL,* 1959, p. 407 etc.

18 Edis, p. 214.

19 One man who should have been mentioned in this context is the designer Dr Christopher Dresser. He was, like Godwin, connected with the Art Furniture Company (for that is what Dr S. Tschudi Madsen: *Sources of Art Nouveau,* Oslo 1956, p. 150 must mean by Art Furnishers' Alliance) and visited Japan in 1877. I wrote an article on Dresser for *The Architectural Review, LXXXI,* 1937. Since then Mrs Shirley Bury has written in *Apollo,* December 1962, on his designs for silver, in the same number of *Apollo* in which Miss Elizabeth Aslin's paper 'E. W. Godwin and the Japanese Taste' came out.

20 'Very good for furniture' (*A plea for Art in the House,* p. 29).

21 On Mrs Haweis see now Bea Howe, *Arbiter of Elegance: Mary Eliza Haweis,* London 1967.

22 *The Revival of Architecture.*

23 *Collected Works,* vol. XXII, p. 329.

24 It is different with Mrs Haweis who goes out of her way to object to the 'aesthetic folks' (1881, p. 17) and to rooms 'all splinters and ashen tints,' presumably a mixed vision of Morris, Whistler and Godwin.

25 Incidentally they sold at 9s. 9d. for the armchair and 35s. for the long seat. This we are told on p. 27 of *Decoration and Furniture of Town Houses.*

26 And also such remarks as those on the desirable flatness of wall decoration (p. 8). There should, for instance, be no 'sprawling flowers' on carpets (p. 18). Mrs. Orrinsmith means the same, but she speaks of 'brilliant bunches of full-blown blossoms, convulsed scrolls and inexplicable twistings' (p. 60).

27 Especially p. 70.

28 Similarly Mrs. Haweis, who was anything but a social reformer, hastens to say that all art must be for the people (1881, p. 20).

29 Mrs. Haweis makes irritated remarks about those who sit among 'blue china and green paper. . . . There are other colours in the rainbow besides green and blue' (1881, p. 17).

30 An exception was apparently the exhibit of Messrs. Collinson & Lock at the Paris Exhibition of 1878 in which the colour-scheme according to Edis was of soft delicate yellow and yellowish pink walls, with pale blue woodwork, a fireplace glowing with red lustre De Morgan tiles, light pink and yellow muslin curtains and Indian matting on the floor—no doubt under Whistler-Godwin influence.

31 *Collected Works,* XXII, p. 92.

32 Edis mentions on p. 177 the prices of Morris wallpaper as 5s. to 12s. a piece, cottons as 2s. a yard 36 in. wide, woven hangings as 3s. to 12s. a square yard, and carpets as 6s. 6d. to 10s. 6d. a square yard.

33 *See my Pioneers of Modern Design,* Harmondsworth 1960 (but the book was first published in 1936), p. 91; and also the essay on Mackmurdo in the present volume.

VII Arthur H. Mackmurdo
Pages 132–139

1 The date is taken over from E. Pond: 'Mackmurdo Gleanings' in *The Architectural Review, CXXXVIII,* 1960. Other new literature referring to Mackmurdo is (in chronological order) S. Tschudi Madsen: *Sources of Art Nouveau,* Oslo 1956; H. Seling, ed.: *Jugendstil,* Heidelberg 1959; R. Schmutzler: *Art Nouveau,* London and New York 1962; J. Cassou, E. Langui and N. Pevsner: *The Sources of Modern Art,* London and New York 1962 (my part also separate as *The Sources of Modern Architecture and Design,* London and New York 1968); 'Mackmurdianum', a note by me in *The Architectural Review, CXXXII,* 1962; and S. Tschudi Madsen: *Art Nouveau,* London 1967.

2 It was introduced into literature by this page in its original form of 1938.

3 On the questions connected with the textiles of the late nineteenth century and of

design and craft altogether during the period here under discussion see the brilliant catalogue of Peter Floud's exhibition at the Victoria and Albert Museum, already referred to before (*Victorian and Edwardian Decorative Arts,* 1952). Two of these chairs, the first actual examples known, came into the possession of the William Morris Gallery at Walthamstow in 1966; but we are still no nearer to a date for them.

4 Recognized as much, by O. von Schleinitz in *Zeitschrift für Bücherfreunde* XI, part I, 1907–8, p. 49–50.

5 A. M. Hammacher, *Die Welt Henry van de Veldes,* Antwerp and Cologne 1967, p. 88.

VIII C. F. A. Voysey
Pages 140–151

1 On this matter and on Voysey altogether the most important contribution is John Brandon-Jones's paper in the *Architectural Association Journal,* May 1957. I have tried to place Devey in position in my paper on Norman Shaw (*Victorian Architecture,* edited by P. Ferriday, 1958) but a good deal more remains to be said about him.

2 The first published designs are in *The British Architect, XXV,* 1886, p. 522. On Voysey's wallpapers there is an excellent paper by the late Peter Floud, in *Penrose Annual, LII,* 1958. *The Journal of the Royal Institute of British Architects* more recently (August 1965) devoted a short colour feature to them.

3 Illustrated in *The Studio, I,* 1893, p. 225.

4 This is now confirmed by *Die Welt Henry van de Veldes,* Antwerp and Cologne, 1967, p. 102, quoting van de Velde's praise of Voysey in a review of 1897 in *L'Art Moderne.*

5 *The British Architect, XXXIII,* 1890, p. 296.

6 I, p. 234.

7 Page 88.

8 Mr Brandon-Jones ended his article with a chronological index of events and designs.

9 Article on Voysey in vol. I, 1898. See also H. Muthesius, *Das englische Haus,* Berlin 1904–5, *passim.*

10 *J. of Dec. Art,* XV, p. 82.

IX Charles Rennie Mackintosh
Pages 152–175

1 For help in connection with the present republication, the publishers and I are especially grateful to Mrs F. J. Bassett-Lowke, Mr H. Jefferson Barnes, and Professor Andrew McLaren Young.

2 See, for example, the designs of John Burnet, W. F. Salmon, N. Leiper, T. L. Watson and others reproduced in *Academy Architecture,* 1891, 1892, 1893.

3 XXXIV, p. 322; pp. 382, 402.

4 *Ib.* XXXVII.

5 Reproduced in *Academy Architecture,* 1894; *The British Architect,* XLIII, 1895.

6 Mrs Newbery said that another important source of influence was Carlos Schwabe

(1866–1926), who studied at Geneva and lived in Paris. He is known to have illustrated *Les Fleurs du Mal* and *Pelléas et Mélisande*; but I have never seen any of these paintings. However, *Pelléas et Mélisande* only came out in 1892, and Schwabe was only three years older than Mackintosh. Dr S. Tschudi Madsen in *Sources of Art Nouveau*, Oslo 1956, p. 180 shows a page from Schwabe's *L'Evangile de l'Enfance de notre Seigneur*, published in 1891. The main motif is a broad band of stylized irises.

7 *Cf.* for example Romilly Allen, *Magazine of Art*, 1888–9, and Margaret Stokes, *South Kensington Museum Handbook*, 1887. Dr Tschudi Madsen has more references to what he called the Celtic Revival.

8 Excellent illustrations are in a recent Mackintosh contribution: D. P. Bliss: *Charles Rennie Mackintosh and the Glasgow School of Art*, published by the school, 1961.

9 Professor Howarth has since drawn attention to the fact that McGibbon and Ross's classic work on ancient Scottish architecture was published in 1886.

10 Professor Dagobert Frey very kindly helped me to get this information. He received a letter from Dr Ankwicz-Kleehoven and one from Professor Josef Hoffmann. Dr Ankwicz-Kleehoven writes: 'Franz Wärndörfer . . . either ordered the furniture of his house in the Karl-Ludwig-Strasse [now Weimarer Strasse, at the corner of the Colloredo Gasse], or bought it at the exhibition. The house was later completely changed by Josef Hoffmann and was also furnished by him. But Mackintosh's pieces, and Margaret Macdonald-Mackintosh's magnificent relief panel have kept their place.' Josef Hoffmann writes: Wärndörfer lived for a long time in London and knew the whole movement. He asked Mackintosh for a plan, and in his house in the Hasenauergasse he made a dining-room completely in his style, the colour scheme of which was based on pale greys, pinks and violets.' Recently Professor E. Sekler has contributed some more evidence on the relationship between Wärndörfer and Mackintosh (*Essays in the History of Architecture presented to Rudolf Wittkower*, London 1967, pp. 239–40). Wärndörfer in a letter of April 29 1902 writes to Josef Hoffmann: 'Macsh has sent me the working drawings for the wooden fixtures', on 16 Sept. 1902 he sent Hoffmann a postcard from Glasgow, and in March 1903 he reported, again to Hoffmann, that he had received a letter from Mackintosh in connexion with the plans for the creation of the Wiener Werkstätte. Wärndörfer's Music Room is known in illustrations, see Howarth pl. 60. Another of Mackintosh's works on the Continent was pointed out to me by Sir Stanley Cursitor. He told me that in about 1914 he saw a house in Cologne that had been furnished by Mackintosh. I asked the late Professor A. E. Brinckmann if he knew about the house and if it was still there, and the answer to both questions was in the affirmative. The house is No. 7, Deutscher Ring. But Professor Brinckmann added:

'There is very little left of the interiors, and even a large part of the outside has been demolished.' The house was completely destroyed in the Second World War.

11 Berlin 1941.

12 It seems that some of the furniture from the Vienna exhibition was in Mackintosh's flat at 78 Southpark Avenue, Glasgow, whose furnishings are now in the collection of Glasgow University. Mrs Walton mentioned to me several pieces which were in Mackintosh's first flat in Glasgow (120 Mains Street) and some others from the Turin exhibition. It thus appears likely that Mackintosh took home with him the things he had made for the exhibitions and which were left unsold. The flat in Southpark Avenue was taken by the Mackintoshes only in 1906.

13 See *Dekorative Kunst*, March 1902.

14 Mackintosh was not as free as this in all his works of this period. A house at Killearn of 1906 (reproduced in Howarth, p. 110) is for example of a much more conventional 'Neo-Tudor' style.

15 Mackintosh also did the façade and the interior of his studio at 48a Glebe Place, as can still be seen.

16 These colours are also those of the Ingram Street tea-rooms.

X GEORGE WALTON
Pages 176–188

1 See P. Ferriday: 'The Peacock Room', in *The Architectural Review*, CXXVI, 1959, p. 407 etc.

2 Thanks to a large series of photographs taken by Mr J. Craig Annan, the distinguished photographer and friend of Walton, a record of this early work is preserved. For most of it is gone by now, superseded by more recent decoration. The following jobs can be mentioned. Photographed in 1891: The Glen, Paisley; Sir Frederick Gardiner's house in 5 Dundonald Road, Glasgow; Mr James Gardiner's house in Grosvenor Crescent; shop of Nelson, Shaw and Macgregor, Glasgow; Thornton Lodge, Helensburgh, for the painter Whitelaw Hamilton. Photographed in 1892: Park Head House; in 1894: House at Barrhead; in 1896: Alteration to house at Lenzie for Mr Craig Annan (Illustration in an article by W. J. Warren, *The Amateur Photographer*, 11 August 1899). James Guthrie's house in Woodside Terrace, a house for Mr J. Marshall (Illustrations in an article by Hermann Muthesius, *Dekorative Kunst*, V, 1900) and a house at Dunblane (Illustrations H. Muthesius: *Das englische Haus*, vol. 3, Berlin 1905) were also furnished by Walton.

3 I was kindly shown a cash price list of April 1897 illustrated by two pictures of the Walton interior, besides the splendid Beggarstaff poster for Rowntree's Cocoa.

4 Illustrations in *Academy Architecture*, XIII, 1898, also *Illustrated Building News*, 20 January 1899, and *Dekorative Kunst*, V, 1900.

5 Illustrated *Dekorative Kunst*, l.c.

6 Illustrations in *The Architectural Review*, LXXIV, 1933, p. 6 (J. Betjeman).

7 Illustrated *Dekorative Kunst*, XI, 1903 (article by Hermann Muthesius). Two of these also in H. Dan and E. C. Morgan Willmott's book (see Note 13).

8 Illustration *Dekorative Kunst*, VIII, 1901.

9 Illustrations *Deutsche Kunst und Dekoration*, XVI, 1905, *Berliner Architekturwelt*, VIII, 1905.

10 Illustrations *Studio Year Book of Decorative Art*, 1907. Views of The Leys are also in H. Muthesius: *Das englische Haus*, Berlin 1904.

11 Illustrations *Architectural Review*, LXXV, 1934 (J. Betjeman), also R. McGrath: *Twentieth-Century Houses*, London 1934, pp. 79–81 and fig. 6.

12 Illustrations *Studio Year Book of Decorative Art*, 1910 and 1913.

13 Illustration H. Dan and E. C. Morgan Willmott: *English Shopfronts Old and New*, London 1907

14 *Architects Journal*, LXXVIII.

15 LXXIV, 1933, p. 43.

Note: Photographs of most of the work mentioned in this article were presented to the Royal Institute of British Architects by Mrs Walton. From her and Edward Walton I received much help and information when I originally wrote this essay. I was also helped by the following: J. Craig Annan, John Dunlop, Mrs G. Ellis, Sir W. O. Hutchison, Sir James Morton, A. W. Paterson, Colin Rowntree, Douglas Rowntree, Messrs John Rowntree & Son, Messrs W. Rowntree & Son, Mrs P. Scott, A. Shepherd, R. Macaulay Stevenson, and J. B. B. Wellington.—N.P.

XI FRANK PICK
Pages 190–209

1 At the time of republishing this paper one would perhaps hesitate to make such a statement; at the time of writing it one could not.

2 And he got together the most admirable publicity department with exact photographic records of every notice, every poster, every piece of equipment, every architectural detail ever carried out. It would have been out of the question for me to compile this article without its help. I am especially grateful to Mr Carr, Mr Howells, Mr Patmore and Mr Burgess at 55 Broadway, and to Mr Graff Baker at Acton and Mr Blair at Chiswick who helped me at the time I wrote this paper, and to Mr Hope who corrected it for this revised reprinting.

3 I am following Nicolete Gray's *Nineteenth Century Ornamented Types and Title Pages*, London 1938.

4 I am greatly indebted to Noel Rooke, Gerard Meynell and Harold Curwen for information on the history of Johnston Sans given me, when I originally prepared this essay.

5 The importance of Charles Holden in the history of London Underground architecture makes it necessary to draw attention to

his very interesting beginnings, exemplified by such buildings as King Edward II's Sanatorium near Midhurst of 1905–6 and the Bristol Municipal Library of 1906, and analyzed in an article which I wrote for *The Architectural Review* in 1960 (vol. CXXVIII), and alas also to his deeply disappointing later years which could not be exemplified more depressingly than by such buildings as the Students' Union, the School of Oriental and African Studies and Birkbeck College, all three for the University of London, and the General Electric building in Aldwych which is the sad successor of the Gaiety Theatre.

6 I have recently summed up the development of English architecture from 1924–1934 in *Bauen und Wohnen*, December 1957.

XII GORDON RUSSELL
Pages 210–225

1 1914, p. 39.

2 *Ib.*, edition of 1929, p. 27.

3 See *Ernest Gimson, his life and work*, Stratford-on-Avon 1924.

4 See N. Pevsner: 'William Morris, C. R. Ashbee und das zwanzigste Jahrhundert', *Deutsche Vierteljahresschrift für Literaturwissenschaft und Geistesgeschichte*, XIV, 1934. English translation in the *Bulletin of the John Rylands Library*.

5 I am most grateful to the late Mrs Ashbee and the late Mr George Chettle for information on C. R. Ashbee, and to the late Mr Alec Miller for having put at my disposal his yet unpublished account of Ashbee and the Campden Guild. This is now in the Victoria and Albert Museum, as well as, thanks to Miss Felicity Ashbee, much Ashbee material.

6 Copy with the Misses Wells who kindly allowed me to see their relics of the life of their father.

7 Aug. 18, p. 313; Sept. 1, p. 450; Sept. 8, pp. 500 and 501; Sept. 15, pp. 545 and 549; Sept. 22, pp. 596 and 597; Sept. 29, p. 662; Dec. 15, p. 583; Dec. 29, p. 703.

8 He is not a relation of the Broadway Russells.

9 LXIII, Jan. 20 and 27.

10 Illustrated in *The Architectural Review*, LIX, 1926, p. 174.

11 Messrs. Heal's possess an enviably complete range of catalogues, and I had the privilege, thanks to the kindness of Mr Anthony Heal and Mr S. V. Bell, of using them for this essay.

12 *Studio Yearbook*, 1927, p. 95. He also still wavered in 1930 when he showed the design for the Olympia exhibition halls at the Royal Academy, with a façade heavy with Dutch memories.

13 For Schneck's work see for example *Die Form*, II, 1927, pp. 129, etc.

14 Marian Pepler was at the AA in 1924–9, Eden Minns in 1924–7, David Booth in 1925–31. (*See* the Class Lists at the AA.) J. M. Richards, who was also at the AA during the same years, confirmed to me this unrevolutionary atmosphere.

15 The only contract work recorded was for some simple oak tables and chairs for St Thomas's Hospital (1925–6).

16 Cf. again the sideboard C809, illustrated in Heal's catalogue of 1921.

17 So at least I was assured by the principal actors in the play. All the exhibition could do was to provide 'a huge confirmation.'

18 Mr W. H. Russell's first independent piece was the desk No. 943.

19 No traces at all would be just a slight exaggeration; for the desk No. 947, designed by Gordon Russell, has a concave, vertically fluted drawer front which was a modish touch, and the big tripartite wardrobe designed by R. D. Russell and illustrated in the catalogue of July, 1930 (*Catalogue of Furniture designed and made by Gordon Russell Ltd.*), on p. 37, has a top to its centre which is stepped up in what must again be called a modish fashion. The same motif appeared in the same year, or perhaps in 1929, in the fireplace at Mr Hartley's house Follifoot, near Harrogate, also by R. D. Russell, and illustrated in the same catalogue of 1930 (p. 40).

20 The earliest modern and well-designed Italian cabinet was, according to *Stile Industria*, No. 11, 1957, p. 6, that designed by Figini & Pollini and made by HMV Italiana in 1934. It was the result of a competition held by *Domus* in 1933. On well-designed radio cabinets in Germany I have not succeeded in getting reliable information. But all seems to point to a late start too. The only other English firm to approach cabinet design—at least for a time—with the same boldness was Ekco's. Their cabinets of 1933 and 1934 were designed by Chermayeff and by Wells Coates and made of bakelite.

21 *See* the Aalto catalogue of the Museum of Modern Art, New York, 1938.

22 They were designed in 1937, not in 1935, as stated in P. Blake, *Marcel Breuer,* Museum of Modern Art, New York, 1949, p. 56.

23 The Coxwell bedroom in oak of 1928 had sold at £30 16s. 6d. or £40 5s. (according to the dressing-table used) and the Dartington bedroom in oak of 1928 at £34 13s. 6d., but that was before the slump.

24 The same had been done by Gimson in a box illustrated in the Gimson monograph of 1924, pl. 39, No. 5.

25 The factory at Park Royal being available, similar contracts were made with Bush, Ekco, Ultra and RGD, all manufacturers of wireless cabinets. In 1939 simple but handsome stands were made for radio cabinets and sold by Murphy dealers. Their prices were remarkably low (22s. 6d., 27s. 6d., 30s.). Actually one radio table, X.802, had already been made in 1931. This was the first Gordon Russell furniture not to be handled in the Broadway and London showrooms of the company exclusively.

26 I have to thank for generous help in preparing and writing this paper, apart from Sir Gordon Russell himself, Professor R. D. Russell, Mr W. H. Russell, Mr E. T. Ould, Mr Anthony Heal and Mr A. V. Freeman. For those who want to know more about Sir

Gordon Russell's life, character and views, there is now his autobiography, *Designer's Trade*, London, 1968.

XIII THE DIA
Pages 226–241

1 According to Hamilton Temple Smith who was there and wrote about it in *Design for Today*, May 1935, and the *DIA Year Book,* 1951.

2 From 1905 to 1940.

3 *DIA Journal*, October 1918.

4 *Quarterly*, No. 5, p. 18.

5 Among members who by then had joined are the following. Manufacturers were specially strong in textiles (eg. the Calico Printers Association and Tootal's) and shoes (Clark's, Green's) and altogether in Leicester firms. In pottery Wedgwood's and Grimwade's had subscribed, and Siddeley (motors), Rhodes (bedding), Nairn (linoleum), the Birmingham Guild (metalwork), the Bath Cabinet Makers and Bassett-Lowke (model-making). Printers were plentiful (e.g. Bemrose, the Cambridge University Press, the Curwen Press, Maclehose, Gerard Meynell, the Oxford University Press, Percy Lund Humphries and George Pulman); so were merchants and retailers (Derry & Toms, Harrods, Horniman's tea, Oetzmann, Pettigrew & Stephens and Wylie & Lockhead of Glasgow, and Harry Trethowan of Heal's). Architects were strengthened by Greenslade, Keppie, Maufe, T. H. Mawson, L. G. Pearson, Baillie Scott, J. Simpson, Thackeray Turner and Wigglesworth, craftsmen by Muriel Barron, Dora Batty, Ann Macbeth, Douglas Strachan, Christopher Turnor and many others, designers by McKnight Kauffer and Reginald Silver, artists by Bayes, Greiffenhagen, Lavery, Rothenstein and Rutherston, Fred Taylor and Tonks, and authors and other amateurs by Collins Baker the art historian, R. B. Fishenden later editor of *Penrose Annual*, Holbrook Jackson, D. S. McCall, Seebohm Rowntree the sociologist, Michael Sadler, Sydney Schiff, Laurence Weaver and Perceval Yetts the sinologist. Some more art schools also joined (e.g. Reading and Sheffield).

6 *Werkbund-Jahrbuch* 1914, p. 87.

7 Among members who joined in 1918 and 1919 were T. D. (Sir Thomas) Barlow, Donald Bros., Major Longden, Francis Meynell of the Nonesuch Press; R. H. Tawney the great economist, Turnbull of Turnbull & Stockdale who were to follow Foxton's into modern designing for cheap cotton fabrics, and (Sir) Charles Tennyson.

8 *Journal*, July 1917.

9 *Journal*, January 1918.

10 At one London meeting Professor William Rothenstein of Sheffield University spoke and assured his audience that 'machinery has become a magnificent thing'—see *Journal*, January 1918. He did not think so any longer when he was principal of the Royal College of Art.

11 November 1916.

12 *Journal*, V, October 1917, and VI, January 1918.

13 *Journal*, XI, Summer 1919.

14 *Journal*, V, October 1917.

15 *Journal*, VI, January 1918.

16 *Journal*, VII, April 1918.

17 *Journal*, IV, July 1917.

18 *Journal*, VII, April 1918.

19 *Journal*, IV, July 1917.

20 *Journal*, X, March 1919.

21 *Journal*, VIII, July 1918.

22 *Journal*, XI.

23 On Omega see my paper in *The Architectural Review*, XC, 1941, p. 45, and the Victoria and Albert Museum exhibition 'The Omega Workshops 1913–1920' in 1963–4.

24 November 1921, January, February, March 1922. Among new members mentioned in those issues were D. R. Best of Birmingham, manufacturer of light fittings, and Herbert Simon of the Kynoch Press.

25 See the preceding paper.

26 After de Klerk's, Taut's and Poelzig's fantasies had been illustrated in 1922 and 1923 and Ostberg's Stockholm City Hall in 1924.

27 Even more completely neo-Georgian is the Laughton Post Office illustrated with approval in the *Journal*, IX, September 1929.

28 See the preceding paper.

29 *Journal*, XII.

30 *Journal*, VII.

31 *Journal*, VIII.

32 The British Institute, never a flourishing institution, finally closed down about 1930.

33 *Journal*, XI, April 1930.

34 Among new members of 1930 one notices with pleasure Anthony Heal and Roger Peach—two representatives of the second generation.

35 Miss Pheysey who had been secretary from 1926 onwards had resigned in 1935. She died in 1957.

36 Quoted in *Year Book*, 1959.

37 *News Sheet*, February 1922.

38 *Journal*, new series, No. 14, p. 19.

39 N. Pevsner, June 1939.

40 *Journal*, IX, September 1929.

41 It may be worth recording that in this campaign it comes out that Oldham had had a local amenities society since 1902 and Carlisle certainly had one in 1930—*see Journal* X and XI.

42 If you want to test the truth of this, have a look at the painfully genteel remarks of called-in experts on a piece of brutalist furniture made by a Central School student: *Year Book* 1960.

Postscript: All the printed matter to which reference has been made in this essay has been deposited by the DIA on permanent loan at the Royal Institute of British Architects.

XIV THE RETURN OF HISTORICISM
Pages 242–259

1 The most notable is of course Robert Willis, the greatest English historian of architecture. He was Jacksonian Professor of Natural and Experimental Philosophy in the University of Cambridge, and died in 1875.

2 *Architectural Review*, CXXV, 1959, pp. 231, etc. and CXXVI, 1959, pp. 341, etc.; *The Listener*, 18 August 1960.

3 It is the same with Art Nouveau literature. In the reprint of my *Pioneers of Modern Design* which Penguin Books issued in 1968, 15 new works were listed, all published in 1960–7. Neo-Art Nouveau in lettering, as everyone knows, has between my delivering this lecture and today become a plague.

4 On Hunziker *Werk*, December 1967, pp. 767–776; the bathroom should be compared with Gaudí's Güell Park, e.g. pl. 126 in Sweeney and Sert, *Gaudí*, London, 1960.

5 CXXVI, 1959, p. 320.

6 On Finsterlin *Frühlicht*, II, 1921–22, p. 36, and recently G. Lindahl in *Figura*, NS, I, pp. 226, etc. (Acta Universitatis Upsaliensis) and H. R. in *Werk und Zeit*, IX, November 1960, p. 2. Also, still more recently U. Conrads and H. G. Sperlich: *Phantastische Architektur*, 1960 and my article in *The Architectural Review*, CXXXII, 1962, pp. 353–7.

7 No. 226, July 1959.

8 Ill. *Architectural Review*, CXXVII, 1960, p. 195. I have in the meantime received a letter from Mr Howell saying that, although he confesses himself 'mad about de Stijl', he was guided more by his admiration for Japanese timber building and by his faith in the 'revelation of process' in general. Readers of this essay who might feel irritated by the historian's eagerness to discover sources, will be pleased with Mr Howell's last sentence: 'The Fylindales radar spheres look just like golf balls and because one can be sure that the designer had seen a golf ball can one maintain that the designer must have been influenced by that pre-knowledge?'

9 Ill. *Zodiac*, IV, 78.

10 It is telling that recently books on German Expressionism have begun to appear: Dennis Sharp: *Modern Architecture and Expressionism*, London, 1966, and F. Borsi and G. K. Konig. *Architettura dell' Espressionismo*, Genoa, 1967. I have not seen the latter.

11 Ill. Philip C. Johnson: *Mies van der Rohe*, New York, 1947, p. 37.

12 *Typographica*, XIV, 1959.

13 See *L'Architettura*, V, 1959–60, p. 364.

14 Madonna dei Poveri, ill. *L'Architettura*, III, 1957–58, p. 454; church at Atlantida by E. Dieste, ill. *Architectural Review*, CXXX, 1961, pp. 173–5; Agno Airport near Lugano by Otto Glaus, ill. *L'Architettura*, V, 1959–60, p. 461; design for St Thomas, Basle, by O. H. Senn, ill. *Architektur-Wettbewerbe*, XXVII, *Churches Today*, October 1959; new block for Marseilles University by J. Berthelet, ill. *Architects' Journal*, 12 January 1961, p. 70; Dominican Friary at Lille by P. Pinsard and Neil Hutchison, ill. *Architectural Design*, 1959, p. 408; St Mark Broomhall, near Sheffield, by G. G. Pace, ill. *Architectural Review*, CXXVII, 1960, p. 22, and more since.

15 Whether this particular stimulus can have worked, historically speaking, I do not know. Meanwhile Dr Banham has reminded me of the inverted pyramid of Niemeyer's new museum for Caracas which was designed in 1955 (ill. J. Joedicke: *A History of Modern Architecture*, London, 1959, p. 221). So there may be imitation after all.

16 And the Museum of Modern Art published its *Brazil Builds* (1943) for the world to see these new things.

17 Philip Johnson in a talk to the Architectural Association in December 1960 called it 'functional eclecticism', but also, the *Architects' Journal* (8 December 1960) reports a really nice juicy chaos'.

18 Ill. already in 1926, i.e. still in full Expressionism, in H. de Fries: *Frank Lloyd Wright*, Berlin, 1926, p. 44.

19 Niemeyer has not committed the same error of judgement. Senate and House of Representatives are neo-Expressionist, the buildings for the ministries are neutral. The President's Palace and the Law Courts have beautifully shaped and detailed neo-sculptural screens, the ministries have not.

20 Ill. e.g. G. A. Platz: *Die Baukunst der neuesten Zeit*, 2nd ed. 1930, p. 434. Also *Handbuch moderner Architektur*, 1957, p. 772.

XV OPENING OF THE YALE SCHOOL
Pages 260–265

1 For student, not teacher, reaction and the way students have converted the interior, see *The Architectural Forum*, CXXVII, July-August 1967, pp. 47–53.

List of Illustrations

Sources of photographs are given in italics

Index

Numbers in italics indicate pages on which illustrations appear